MW01164863

Ain't That a Miracle?

An Unlikely Journey into Music and Meditation

Book cover photoshoot with Gurudev Sri Sri Ravi Shankar outside
Ganga Kutir at the Bangalore Ashram, December 24, 2011

*"Jeremy has shared his music and sense of
humor with many people around the world."*
Gurudev Sri Sri Ravi Shankar

JEREMY OCCHIPINTI

Copyright © Jeremy Occhipinti 2022

All Rights Reserved

No part of this book may be used or reproduced by any means,
graphic, electronic, or mechanical, including photocopying,
recording, taping, or by any information storage retrieval system
without the written permission of the publisher, except in the
case of brief quotations embodied in critical articles and reviews.

Included photographs are from the author's personal archive.

This book is dedicated to Mom, Dad, Michele, and Jeff
for their continuous love and support on my unlikely journey.
Also to Gurudev Sri Sri Ravi Shankar
for his wisdom and guidance over the years.

FOREWORD

As someone who started off as a boy practicing martial arts in the Netherlands, looking for an authentic spiritual teacher who could initiate me into the mysteries of meditation, mantras, and the purpose of life and how to live it meaningfully, I can understand why Jeremy decided to write this book.

Meeting Gurudev Sri Sri Ravi Shankar during a public program in Amsterdam when I was sixteen years old changed my life, and not just for the better, but for the best. It led me to India following the completion of my university studies, where I eventually ended up dedicating my life to sharing the profound wisdom and powerful techniques that I learned from my Master.

I ended up traveling across continents, visiting many interior places, such as rural and tribal areas in Northeast India, Nepal, and Southern Africa to share what I had learned with the people there. More than once, I met people in these places who asked me if I knew Jeremy Occhipinti, as he had visited there once or multiple times already, many years before I had.

Some of you may have known Jeremy for many, many years, and some of you may have never met him—or have not *yet* met him. I guess I would put myself in the middle of this spectrum, having met him at various times in different parts of the world over the years, at different points in my journey, and in his. We shared a special bond from the first time we met, and we still do. We are both walking the paths shown to us by our spiritual Master—paths that have crossed more than once.

I still remember talking to Jeremy in 2010 at the Bangalore Art of Living International Center, where he told me about asking Gurudev about His plans for him. He had gone to meet Gurudev in the German Ashram a few months earlier, and his question to Gurudev had been something along the lines of, "What is Your plan for me? Will you get me married, or make me the first white swami?" This question shows the very personal and direct connection that Jeremy shares with his Master.

Laughing about the unusual question, Gurudev replied something along the lines of: "You are too late, Alex is already there! But maybe I can make you the first American swami."

This news came as a shock, as this was the first time I got a glimpse into my Master's plan to bless me as one of his swamis. Had it not been for Jeremy, I would have never known that my Master had already planned this so far in advance. And this is precisely what makes this book so precious and fascinating.

It is said that an enlightened master cannot be understood and that his ways and reasoning cannot be fathomed. However, we can see glimpses of his superhuman abilities and his divine nature through the eyes and experiences of faithful devotees.

Jeremy is one of such blessed souls. His commitment to service, his passion for music, and his love for people of all cultures and backgrounds have allowed him to travel and live in many countries and on several continents, making a difference in the lives of whomever he meets.

At the same time, he also has the ability to be very open and honest about his challenges, feelings, doubts, and experiences, taking readers along on this journey that is his life. He shares very intimate and personal details of his journey, struggles, challenges, and how he moved through and beyond them. By doing this, he not only allows us to relate his experiences to many of the challenges that we may face throughout our own lives, but he may also give us the insights or faith to move through our own challenges successfully.

Join me on a journey across the pages of this book and discover the unseen magic that is part of all our lives, but that only a select few have the eyes to behold. And if you are lucky, through Jeremy's eyes, you may even have a chance to discover some of the magic present in your own life!

Swami Purnachaitanya

Author of the bestselling book *Looking Inward: Meditating to Survive in a Changing World*; public speaker; and teacher of yoga, meditation, mantras, and Vedic wisdom.

ACKNOWLEDGMENTS

I would like to thank everyone on the Super Reading Team who provided valuable feedback and inspiration as early readers of this book: Nakul Dhawan, Kathleen Shaputis, Luckshmi Mirgh, Emma Seppala, Richaa Dawarr, Maria Collier, Priya Tindwani, Kiki Ciesielski, Tyna Pariani, Julia Tang, Dave Weisenfluh, Dibya Ray, Cathy Wasilinko, Mudita Chaturvedi, Jayne Archer, Shreya Gupta, Ken Matsko, Ashutosh Chawla, Sarika Ahuja, Simran Singh, and numerous others.

Thanks to Matthew Scharpnick for suggesting the book's title and supporting me through thick and thin.

Thanks to the entire Daily Satsang Family for inspiring me during the pandemic and beyond.

A special thanks to all my friends and family back home in Scranton, Pennsylvania, who always believed in me.

Thanks to Swami Purnachaitanya for writing the foreword.

Thanks to Rajeev Nambiar for capturing the cover photo.

And finally, an abundance of gratitude to my worldwide Art of Living family for all their love and encouragement for the past twenty-five years and counting.

Jai Guru Dev.

Don't be surprised if miracles happen.
Be surprised if they don't!
—Gurudev Sri Sri Ravi Shankar

INTRODUCTION

On a cool, mystical evening in Bali, I was onstage at a local temple's large outdoor amphitheater. I sat with my favorite guitar, "Kripa," nestled on my lap, and an SM-57 microphone two fists away.

As I had so many times by then, I was sharing the stage with some of my favorite people and absorbing the magnificent beauty surrounding me. Near us, a group of young Balinese temple singers chorused out their sparkling ancient wisdom with devotion. I turned up the volume of my guitar and played along.

I wondered how a kid from middle-class America had wound up here. A wild child of Italian descent, with a ready smile for most and an explosive temper for the rest, I barged through my early years blindly, without direction, full of anger and angst. My rowdy childhood had been further blighted with health issues, a drag on my ardent dream of becoming a rock star.

But here I sat, playing and gazing out on a sea of people dressed in beautiful Balinese colors.

In the middle of these waves of splendor and rivers of sound was the man they had all come to see. Not me, of course. They were there for Gurudev Sri Sri Ravi Shankar. In fact, I too was there to be with him.

Gurudev is one of the most respected humanitarians in the world and one of the world's most profound contemporary proponents of ancient spiritual knowledge. But it is the helpful wisdom, uplifting feeling, and the subtle inner transformation you go home with that is the real draw.

The main experience I have come away with in his presence is just simple joy. There is always happiness about him, and I feel elated, a similar experience to when I was a child. I also feel creative around him; my jokes flow easily, and music just flows from me. And there's always endless laughter being with Gurudev. He is also, by far, the sweetest, most innocent human I know. And I know a lot of sweet and innocent people, having made my living for many years teaching four- and five-year-olds.

After a few moments of silence, Gurudev gave me that familiar look to prompt me to start singing. I closed my eyes and strummed those familiar chords: G D Em C G D, *Narayana Hari Om,* a song I've sung with Gurudev across India, North America, and now Bali.

As I sent out those Sanskrit words, the atmosphere was instantly transformed into a sing-along merriment beyond description, the crowd singing each line back in unison, the energy and volume growing with every call and response. The temple was ablaze in oneness, and subtle bolts of lightning were shooting through my oversized body. The power of the music could not be denied. We four thousand humans sang so sweetly together, and it seemed all our minds were on the same wavelength. With eyes closed, I continued to steer the song in this musical miracle.

After the last line ended, everyone settled in silence, and Gurudev guided us deeper into meditation. That silence and meditation was unlike anything I'd felt, but it also felt so recognizable.

This special night with my guru was one of many prized and priceless moments I have experienced over the past twenty-five years. All like snowflakes, unique and beautiful.

An open but fickle heart, a knack for mischief and trouble, a growing desire to serve, and an unreasonably compassionate spiritual master, Gurudev. I invite you to step into my world.

CHAPTER ONE

〰 ◎ 〰

Born to Run (Wild)
in Taylor Town

Don't sit and daydream and only think about
miracles to happen. Miracles do happen, but
if you crave for miracles then they will take a
back seat. Nature wants you to be dynamic.
—Gurudev Sri Sri Ravi Shankar

Born to run. Truer words were never written for this baby boy, born less than a year after the celebrated Bruce Springsteen song first blasted through the airwaves coast to coast. But on June 24, 1976, at Mercy Hospital in Scranton, Pennsylvania, no one in the delivery room had an inkling of just how wildly I would run. There I lay, in the hospital's clear-plastic shoebox on wheels that someone had thought was a perfect fit for newborns.

Let me introduce you to the rest of my typical American household. Michele is my sister, seven-and-a-half years older and the first-born. Jeff, my big brother, is two years older than I. And Mom and Dad are the multitalented and ever-loving leaders. To my mother, I'll always be "the baby" of course, no matter how old I get or how many challenges I rise above.

I was born in downtown Scranton, a former coal-mining town, two hours' drive west of New York City, immortalized in the Emmy-winning show *The Office* as the perfect setting for the average American life. But home for me was Taylor, a borough on the southeast side of the big city. We lived in a nice-sized three-bedroom,

1

split-level white house, at 401 Lincoln Street, two blocks from the old ancestral house where Mom was raised.

Lincoln Street was a wide, fairly level street, perfect for bike riding and skateboarding, with only ten houses from corner to corner. There was a natural football field surrounded by pines in the backyard. In fact, Taylor, like Scranton, is a strip of city, only about 3.5 miles wide, with forests of state parks and 2,000-foot mountains on either side, full of trails and places to ski, snowboard, sled, and toboggan. I loved all snow activities.

My dad was born in Connecticut, and then moved to Paterson, New Jersey. He was the middle child in a family of three boys. Like many others in our region, his grandparents had sailed from Italy to America—the Land of Opportunity—in the early part of the century, coming through Ellis Island. My dad was a second-generation American in the Occhipinti family tree.

Mom grew up at 111 Lincoln Street in Taylor. The beautiful hometown girl, she was the middle child of five siblings: two sisters and two brothers.

My mother's younger sister, Aunt Joann, who was married to Uncle Ed, lived next door to us while I was growing up. They had the same style house, only yellow, and we shared a sidewalk. These were not tract homes, by any means, just identical in style.

Aunt Joann gave birth to three children, all around the same age as the Three Musketeers in our home. John was oldest, two years younger than Michele. The middle child was not only the same age as my brother Jeff, but his name was also Jeff. Joy was my youngest cousin and the one closest to me.

Having Aunt Joann and Uncle Ed next door was like having a second home only a few steps away from my own. Aunt Joann always fed me, talked with me, gave me opportunities to help her out in the yard, and scolded me when I needed it.

My mother's older sister, Aunt Alice, who was married to Uncle John, lived at the other end of Lincoln Street. Their house was another home for me, and I spent a lot of time there.

Mom and Dad were my heroes, and still are to this day. Mom and I would walk around the football field near our home and talk for hours about her childhood and other inspiring stories. She took me to the zoo at Nay Aug Park, fishing at McDade Park, and to my football games. Mom not only helped my friends, but she helped stray animals in our community too. Some of the sweetest moments I had with Mom were going for ice cream and sitting on the porch with her. Growing up, I was very close to my mother.

Dad played basketball with me on our makeshift court in our large backyard. He would show me his cool collection of yo-yos and demonstrate several tricks with them. His room downstairs (his man-cave) was fascinating, filled with music and recording equipment and his Ham Radio gear.

Dad was a hard worker and knew how to do almost everything around the house, including planting our garden. He would decorate the home and yard at Christmas with lights and decorations. Dad also built the deck on the side of our house by himself. Though I held the ladder steady as he climbed onto the roof, Dad did most of the work independently. He didn't have much patience, but he got things done. Naturally, our communication and interactions were lesser than with Mom, because of his work schedule and hobbies.

As far back as I can remember, I loved singing, dancing, and enjoying music; a natural-born performer at heart. My family recalls me running around the house at age four or five, singing the hit song "Elvira" by the Oakridge Boys. Whether it was the catchy rhythm, happy melody, or that bass voice on a chorus that let me belt out such words as "*Giddy up pa-oom poppa oom poppa mow mow*," I loved the entertaining 1981 song. It stuck in my head, making me flail and wail the tune over and over. I'd pay nicely for video footage of that little wildcat minstrel now.

Mom clearly remembers those energetic early years, saying that I always wanted to be outside, running out the front door and around the outside of the house to play in the backyard. She told me I was always singing, laughing, and being wild. "Every time you managed to unlock the front door and run outside, we would have to raise the lock on the door a little higher, so it would be out of your reach. But you always got a chair and found a way to unlock it."

My prowess at picking locks didn't stop at the front door of our house, either. Back then I went to Sesame Preschool at St. Paul's

Church. Mom says I went there because I was so smart. More likely, she needed a break from my zealous thrill of life at ninety miles an hour.

But no brick or mortar building could keep me in. I needed to be outside, to run in the wide-open spaces of nature. The preschool personnel had to change the locks so I couldn't run out. I wore the crown of being one of the most active children in Taylor; mere walls were not going to fence me in during daylight.

Come nightfall things didn't slow down much for this pre-schooler. I can feel the moms out there rolling their eyes. The wound-up child wouldn't automatically wind down when the sun sank behind those hundred trees. I did not like to sleep much, sur-prise, surprise. Too much to do, too many places to go. Many nights, Mom would hold me in the rocking chair, the soothing rhythm almost as good as wandering. Even in my dreams I spent a lot of time outside, playing in the backyard.

Yet there were times when I could fulfill my creative urges with a crayon or pencil instead of my vocal cords. Drawing pictures at the kitchen table or cross-legged at the coffee table in front of the televi-sion when I was six, seven, and probably even eight years old, I was convinced my art would be famous someday and bring me a fortune. I used to hide the sacred drawings in the ceramic cookie jars on the hutch. I wonder if Mom ever found them?

In first grade, I got a little crazy and cut my own hair the night before picture day. My hair looked bad enough on an ordinary day, since the local barber would put a cereal bowl on my head, using it as a guide to cut around the edges.

The morning after cutting my own hair, it flipped, flapped, corked, and stood way out of whack. I looked like a wounded chicken fresh off a henhouse fight with a cat. Boy, was Mom cross with my wonderful scissors and me. That new hairstyle was good for a few laughs.

Many of my earliest childhood memories of music are with or about my father. He wrote and played songs for hours on end in his music room downstairs. Did I mention my bedroom was right above his room? As a young boy I didn't realize how those rhythms, chord progressions, lyrics, melodies, and beats were streaming in subconsciously for hours on end. It's surprising how sound and rhythm soak through the flooring and heating vents of a home.

The thumping electronic drums were the most profound. They would beat and bounce right through my floor and throughout the house. At times it seemed the sound could break the glass windows. Other songs had a slower tempo, and Dad's keyboard sounds could be soothing.

A complete package of musical sounds came my way. Sometimes I hated them, sometimes I put my headphones on to escape, and sometimes I secretly tapped my foot along with the rhythm.

Finding Jesus when he was nineteen, Dad had cleansed his soul and left the "satanic" world of rock and roll for more Christian lyrics and songs. As an adult, Dad became a visiting assistant pastor, never having a home church of his own, but serving a large area, spreading his music and words.

When Dad played his accordion and preached in the various churches, we attended with him as a devoted family. Summer, winter, we traveled whenever he was needed to fill in. We'd pile into the car and drive to suburbs with old brick churches or to different downtown areas for services held in storefront basements or larger single-level sanctuaries. I know I would have liked to be somewhere else on more than a few of those Sunday mornings.

I will never forget how uneasy I was as a young, energetic boy, squirming on an unfamiliar varnished pew in the middle of a crowded, stuffy room with towering stained-glass windows, as Dad introduced us to the congregation of the day. We'd have to stand up in the middle of a few hundred church folk we'd never met before.

Jeff and I couldn't care less once he finished the introduction. We went back to drawing inside the songbooks we found in the wooden pews in front of us, or—if we managed to sneak past Mom's enormous reach—ran around the back of the church. I'm surprised I didn't bolt out of most of the sanctuaries, knowing my expertise and inclination for escaping to the great outdoors.

My finest memories of being the visiting pastor's son were at churches filled with mostly African Americans out in Paterson, New Jersey—Dad's hometown. Yes, his ministerial territory sometimes took us east. Inside those paint-chipped walls, amazing, big, Black ladies dressed in their finest threads would open their mouths and belt out songs to the good Lord with unbelievable passion and energy. I couldn't sit still when the music and singing hit its fevered pitch, especially this boy who embraced the positive chords of music and life.

Covering Sunday morning services wasn't the only pastoral task for my dad. Over the years we traveled to prisons, mental hospitals, and various weddings, where Dad played his music, soothing and celebrating the crowds through song.

Now and again Dad officiated at marriage ceremonies, and through the years I'd find myself at weddings of people I didn't know. At one of these weddings, a drunken lady came up during the reception and asked Dad, "Can you play 'There's a Tear in My Beer?'"

My dad, with his droll sense of humor, replied with a straight face, "No, but I can play 'There's No Beer in Heaven.'"

Looking back, Dad was probably my biggest musical influence, even though I only liked a few of his folk songs. I am grateful to him for the DNA; the ingrained musical aptitude; the exposure to Black churches; and the inspiration to be a traveling, enthusiastic, and creative musician, steeped in faith and spreading good news and cheer.

Growing up in a Christian home as the son of a preacher had a valuable spiritual influence on me. I prayed to Jesus every night religiously, without fail, wherever and however I was at the time. Even if sleeping at a friend's house after a hearty night of partying in my teens, I'd repeat, "Dear Jesus, there are four corners on my bed, there are four angels on each head: Matthew, Luke, Mark, and John. If I die before I wake, pray the Lord my soul to take. I pray for my mother, father, sister, brother, family, dogs, and the whole world. Amen."

In 1983, a few weeks before my seventh birthday, my world took a freakish somersault in both music and passion. I was curled up on the couch upstairs, watching the *Motown 25: Yesterday, Today, Forever* special on television. Michael Jackson was reunited with his brothers Jermaine, Marlon, Tito, and Jackie for the first time in eight years to sing some of their greatest hits. It's hard to believe that the Jackson Five were power players with number one hits before I was born.

When the older brothers left the stage, I saw Michael break into his "Billie Jean" moves and the first phenomenal performance of the now famous moonwalk.

From that dreamlike moment, that instant of televised entertainment, Michael Jackson became my childhood idol, and, as we all know, I was far from being alone with those feelings. Michael became larger than life and almost mystical. From his look with the black fedora pulled low on his forehead, waist-length sequined jacket, and sparkling glove, to the moonwalk routine in the song's bridge, his sound and persona produced something special in my budding life. His incomparable music and magnificent moves inspired me.

I listened to the album *Thriller* over and over, at any and all times. I sang along with him as I memorized each mind-blowing track, and I even dressed like him. Yes, I had *the* glove, (well, a copy of the original, like many Jackson fans around the world).

Out of my boyish hyperactivity, inherited musical inclination, and a willingness to make a fool of myself, I was dancing and imitating Michael's moves every chance I got. In the solitude of my bedroom I practiced the snap of the wrists, hip checks, thrusts, and did a perfect imitation of his breathy "hoo-hoo-hoo!"

I'd already been bitten by the entertainment bug with "Elvira," and my prodigious Michael Jackson performances did not stay in the privacy of my home. Picture, if you will, the typical middle-class summer pool party, the smell of baby oil on teen girls and of chlorine from guys doing cannonballs off the deep end. Around the sizzling neighborhood I'd be at someone's backyard soiree, where I'd break into dance, doing my best MJ dance moves around the cool water, whether I had an audience or not. This was the perfect outlet for me.

I was a hit with the older ladies, oh yeah. Once at a neighbor's high school graduation party up the street, at a house with an enviable in-ground swimming pool and diving board (and an often-ignored little sign about "No P in This Pool"), a sweet middle-aged woman asked me to perform my humble MJ dance routine.

Without a moment of hesitation, I broke into my gliding, well-rehearsed moves, and to my utter surprise, my audience of ladies—all well over forty or fifty, mind you—started placing money in an empty highball glass near me, a homemade tip jar. Shiny quarters clinked against the clear glass, and crisp dollar bills spilled over the top. Free candy money! At seven years old, I thought I was ready to turn pro as an MJ impersonator. Mom made me return all the money.

Yet recently, when remembering how I loved to sing and dance like Michael Jackson as a little boy, Mom told me she would pay me five dollars to dance in the living room and that she enjoyed the entertainment. She said that my youngest nephew, Nicky, is just like I was back then. "We actually call him Jeremy Jr. during his performances," she said.

The late seventies and early eighties were tough times economically. In 1981, the country fell into a recession the likes of which had not been seen since the Great Depression. My family was not protected from the fallout of inflation, with the accompanying high interest rates, lack of jobs, and skyrocketing prices. Reaganomics squeezed the financial blood out of the middle class with its trickle-down economic theories. More and more people applied for food stamps, and new government programs sprang up everywhere. Life for a father of three as a mechanic and visiting pastor was truly not easy during the stress and strain of double-digit inflation.

Children do not always understand the whys and hows of politics, or the harsh realities of running a household on a tight budget. Our wants and needs come down to the simple things in life. But tension cloaks everything during rough times. Everyone is affected in one way or another, and my family was no different.

I remember being in first grade when Dad was not working. Things were bad throughout the area, and I would hear about the tough times in the households of many of my classmates. We were learning to write, and one of the class projects my teacher assigned was to write a letter to our parents. The first line of my letter read, "Dear Dad, please get a job because I need new sneakers, Jeff needs new pants, and we all need food at home."

Our local fire station doubled as a food pantry, where they'd hand out government cheese, butter, and peanut butter in a program to help feed low-income families. However, kids can be cruel, and in the neighborhood, some would bust me, saying, "I was over Jeremy's house and saw government cheese in the fridge."

My family learned to do without the extras at certain times, which wasn't always easy for us, yet there was something blessed in growing up during the eighties. Saturday morning cartoons were a highlight, with a bowl of sugared cereal in hand and no worries. It's hard for people with 24-hour access to endless channels to imagine a time when you had to wait all week for your favorite shows. We had to wait patiently, Sunday through Friday, before stretching out in front of the TV and soaking up the animation, which just seemed to be the best ever.

As a family, we went through some of our hardest times in the early eighties but came out closer and stronger as a result. By the mid-eighties, Dad was back at work, now selling tires, and Mom was selling carpets at the Globe Store in downtown Scranton. Jeff and I were selling lemonade on Lincoln Street.

Dad disliked my music. As part of his religious interests, he was totally against rock and roll—though he openly told us he was into rock and roll as a teen before coming to Jesus.

I remember in fifth grade, the rap group Run-DMC was huge, and their new album in 1986 was *Raising Hell*. A masterpiece in its own right, it was also the first rap album to go multiplatinum. In music, once again, things were changing. This album brought powerful rhyme sequences, layered with drum machines kicking the beat. Great noise for a preteen.

Anyway, one day I left the *Raising Hell* cassette cover on our dining room "put everything on it" table. My mom woke me up with some breaking news the next morning: "You dummy! You left out your tape that said 'hell' on it. Your father threw it away."

I laughed and said, "Don't worry, Mom, it was only the case."

Every older generation complains about the younger generation's music. Teens in the fifties heard from their disgusted elders how Elvis was a degenerate, and kids in the sixties heard screams about what long-haired hippies the Beatles were.

I took my dad in stride. I can still hear Dad yelling and banging on our bedroom wall to turn down the music, shouting: "It feels like my ceiling is going to cave in!" But when Dad played music in his room below mine, damn, it was loud.

Let me finish describing the family tree with my Uncle Dennis. He took us for pizza, played basketball with us, helped us build our first igloo, and best of all let me drive his car when I was only eleven.

On one of those awesome childhood drives in his minivan, Uncle Dennis popped in a Keith Green tape and turned up the volume. We were rockin'. I was totally moved by Keith's awesome style, his progressive piano playing, and his open-hearted gospel songs. I immediately connected with this style of music. "Asleep in the Light" and "You Put This Love in My Heart" still get considerable plays on my iPhone.

Uncle Dennis suffered from asthma, as I did, but it often sounded like he had it twenty times worse than me. This life-threatening disease runs in my family, and Uncle Dennis helped me get through some rough patches of living with the disease. He helped me use my first inhaler—an asthmatic's survival tool—explaining it would help me sleep dead to the world, like a baby. He gave me invaluable tips, such as not to face the wall when I sleep, as I get less air that way. I believe Uncle Dennis favored me, perhaps because I was the youngest boy of his six nephews and nieces. But more likely because I also suffered from the same lung disease.

Music became healing for me as an asthmatic, a natural soothing aid that touched me deep inside and eased the pain of not being able to breathe easily. It made sleepless nights more endurable.

The pain and fear associated with not being able to breathe properly shackled me for many years. It crippled my sleep and erased any confidence of walking to school in the middle of a Pennsylvania winter. Eventually, during adolescence, this frustration and pain turned to anger and unspoken depression. On the several seventh-grade days I was suspended from school, I'd hide in the woods all day, too scared to go home, and I'd hum or sing the day away.

Later, in those same woods, as a teenager, I'd be drinking and partying wild with friends. Yes, it was challenging to breathe easily in the great outdoors, especially in the winter, but somehow, I always found a breath or two to keep me going.

Growing up, I had a love-hate relationship with elementary school, although maybe not with the concept of school. No, this had more to do with a child named Deno.

I was afraid of Deno as much as I loved him. A year-and-a-half older, he protected me like a fraternity brother, yet, when necessary, would kick my ass.

Deno and I were close. He found me funny; I found him a school-aged god. As a first-grader, this Taylor dynamo snapped pencils in between his fingers, crushed round-tin cookie containers over his forehead, and pierced his ears with a stapler, setting the stage as one fearless dude. Of course, he made me try this bizarre rite of strength too.

We used to switch shoes in the first grade (more often, one shoe), so we'd both have two different shoes on. We did this so Deno would be reminded to come over to my house on the weekend.

I remember the time when Deno came over in the middle of a frigid Pennsylvania winter with no hat, gloves, or coat. This was insanity. Mom, being the great humanitarian, made a big deal of him not having proper warm clothing, and gave him the needed winter attire to keep from freezing on his way home. Good ole Mom was always helping or taking care of my friends.

Deno was not the only wilder and older friend of mine. David was also a year-and-a-half older than I—tall, handsome, athletic, and cool. David's folks were divorced, and he lived with his father, a truck driver. Many times, David showed me how easy it was to take a few twenties and sometimes a fifty-dollar bill from his grandparents, who kept cash in their coat pockets. I don't know if they ever noticed the missing money.

Being David's friend didn't make me popular with the cool crowd. David was considered a bad boy, both by authority figures and young people, but I spent a lot of time with him in fourth grade. He'd come early on school days so he, Jeff, and I could walk to school together. David was in fifth grade and Jeff was in sixth.

One morning, we left the house around 7:00 a.m., even though the elementary and junior/senior high school did not start classes until 8:00 a.m. To get to school, as we did every day, we walked through "the woods"—a magnificent, tree-filled area surrounding our houses, and an excellent place for building forts and keeping healthy and active boys busy.

At the junior/senior high school, we had found some discarded fishing line. Seeing the school's two iron entrance gates open, David had an awesome, villainous idea. What if we tied the fishing line low, connecting the two gates so the first car that drove through would push against the line and get smashed by the closing gates? The boy practically rubbed his hands together in glee. I was nervous but went along with the plan because Jeff and David were older and cooler. Oh, the struggles of peer pressure.

No sooner had we finished tying the two gates when, our hearts pounding, we heard a car coming. We took off running and hid behind the nearby bushes.

BAM! SKID! SLAM!

Metal on metal blasted the silent morning, immediately followed by the screech of slamming brakes. A car had been smashed from our trap! We bolted from our hiding place and took off at full speed, making it to the elementary school on time.

I fell into my seat and breathed a sigh of relief. The morning classroom routine lulled me into a cocoon of normalcy, and I focused on my work. David and the fishing line faded from memory.

Then someone knocked briskly on the classroom door, and everyone leaned forward in his or her seat in nervous curiosity. Visitors hardly ever came to our classroom, and they rarely came with good news—certainly not visitors who knocked briskly. The low, rumbling murmur from the kids around me ceased when the policeman asked my teacher, Mrs. P., to step into the hall. This was not just any uniformed officer of the law, mind you, but my teacher's husband!

A few minutes later she came into the room staring at me with a look from hell. Picking up a piece of chalk she went back to the blackboard and continued her lesson. When the class was leaving for recess, she asked me to stay back. Scared and shaking, standing at her desk, I knew she could see my heart pounding against my chest.

She proceeded to tell me how I was spotted that morning with my brother and David, setting some sort of trap for a car at the high school.

But that wasn't the worst of her news. The smashed vehicle we'd heard crunch into the gates was *hers*. I felt my life drain from me like a puddle of ooze. Life as I knew it was over. This was it. There was no way I could possibly face that woman again. I would be a fourth-grade dropout.

The rest of the day dragged by in a fog of remorse and guilt. I'd helped smash my teacher's car.

Home from school, I avoided looking at Jeff, and went about my chores in a daze. That night, the same officer, still in uniform, came to the house and talked to my parents at length. This was not the last time a police officer would come to my house.

Thankfully, I did not drop out of fourth grade. I did my time, told the teacher I was sorry, and got through another year. The teacher was kind enough to forgive me and life went on. Luckily, her insurance covered the damage, or else Jeff and I would have had to sell a lot of lemonades on Lincoln Street.

You can't have a group of boys together for the long summer months without expecting them to deliver their share of mischief in the neighborhood. And we delivered a lot. Mom came home one day and found the plate glass window in our own upstairs dining room broken and a rock lying on the floor.

As I remember it best, my older brother chased me around the dining room table in some tirade or other. I usually managed to irritate him several times a day, or vice versa.

One day, I found myself standing behind the seat at the head of the table, where Dad always sat. Jeff got smart and went for the winning move. In a split second he grabbed the wooden table with both hands and shoved it hard, hoping to block me against the wall. Unfortunately, my dad's chair was not in front of a wall… it was in front of a large window. My rear-end shattered the glass and went right through the window, but I caught myself at the last possible instant and didn't take the second-story fall to serious injury.

Once the shock wore off, we both knew we were in deep trouble. We could almost hear how Dad would yell as he came home from work and saw this gaping, expensive mess.

Jeff was not done with his winning moves. He came up with the brilliant idea of getting a large rock from outside and placing it inside, right under the window, along with a few pieces of broken glass. Raise your hand if you think we got away with it.

Nope. Neither Mom nor Dad fell for this.

Growing up as younger brother to Jeff was often seriously hazardous to my health. I'm surprised I escaped into adulthood (mostly) intact. Some may remember that in the late eighties, something called "lawn darts" were banned in the U.S. after two kids were killed and thousands of others injured. But my brother threw *regular*, extremely sharp pool-hall darts at me one time when our parents weren't home. Did I look like a bullseye to him?

Another time, he began shooting at me with his BB gun, in the house no less, creating his own dangerous version of laser tag with real ammunition! I finally ran into Michele's room, breathing hard and leaning against the quickly slammed door. I thought I was safe, but BBs started coming under the door! Jeff managed to shoot through that narrow space, and I was hit in the foot.

Jeff picked on me a lot. (Brotherly love was overrated back then.) We fought like stray alley cats during waking hours and then had to share the same bedroom at night. This only lasted so many years. To the benefit of my health and my parents' sanity, Jeff's bedroom eventually moved to a spacious location downstairs, which later became a party place during my later high school and early college years.

My experiences in the early years boasted plenty of music, mischief, and growing pains. As these initial experiences suggest, there was much more to come.

I was a baby on Mom's lap, 1976

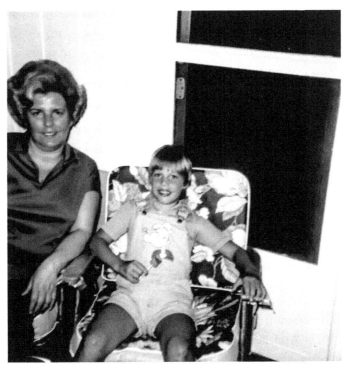

On Aunt Alice's porch in my Popeye outfit, 1982

CHAPTER TWO

Music (and Trouble) All Around

*Miracles happen naturally and spontaneously;
it cannot be forced. When everything falls in
place, miracles happen on their own.*
—Gurudev Sri Sri Ravi Shankar

I got a Hitachi boombox for Christmas when I was ten. The first
song I played was "Summer of '69," off Bryan Adams's 1984
album, *Reckless.* To me, boomboxes were like rock concerts in your
ear. It was really hip in the mid-1980s to walk around town, carrying
your boom box on your shoulder, looking cool, and blasting music.

The whole boombox trend grew out of the urban neighborhoods of New York, Philadelphia, L.A., and other big cities, along
with beatboxing and break dancing, two things that intrigued me.
I was okay at beatboxing (making realistic drum and percussion
sounds with your mouth), but break dancing was really hard, especially for a kid my size.

My sister had piano lessons at home, but my parents never pushed
me to learn an instrument. I believe my overactive nature was the
main reason. Though I never had any music lessons, my love for
music flourished in my adolescence. On Friday afternoons, we would
take a thirty-minute drive to a city called Eynon, where they had
this big, awesome place called Sugarman's Drug Store. This was our
weekly getaway. I could see the sign more than half a mile away.

Just about anything I wanted could be found at Sugarman's. That's where I bought my first pair of skis. Mom bought the latest Top 40 hits on 45-rpm records during these Friday afternoon runs: Kenny Loggins, Prince, Phil Collins, Madonna, and Michael Jackson (my personal favorite, of course). These albums were played when Dad was at work, outside working in the yard, or in his room. Musically, our home was interestingly divided; upstairs was the Oldies and Top 40 hits, while downstairs was Dad's gospel and original folk songs.

Yes, Mom was an old-school rocker. On Saturday nights you'd find her ironing clothes in our living room, playing *Saturday Night at the Oldies,* a weekly program on WKRZ-FM. I loved hanging out with Mom, listening to all the tunes we adored so much. Two songs stand out from those memorable times: "My Ding-a-Ling," by Chuck Berry, and "Suspicious Minds," by Elvis. And yet all the songs on that show seemed special.

I remember riding around with Mom in the car, going shopping or getting my braces tightened. We always listened to the radio, and I clearly remember some songs and lyrics much more than others. Bob Dylan's "Positively 4th Street" was one. The lyrics were nasty, hammering some girl in the meanest way, yet, at the same time, it was one of the most beautiful songs.

That mix of beauty and ugliness is one of the main reasons I love Dylan so much. No one can create a blend of good and evil better than he does. In terms of writing a song about something, I have not found an artist who can write so eloquently about a subject. That's one reason why I will always hold Bob Dylan as the greatest songwriter of our time.

Listening to the radio was and is the food of my soul. My mind holds a master list of tunes and what each means to me. Hearing them takes me back to the sights, sounds, and even the scents of a season, a moment in time. Movies, food, and novels have the same effect.

One song that hit me just below my neck and a foot above my belly button was "Pink Houses" by John Cougar Mellencamp. The striking chorus about America got me psyched up, ready to roll, and boosted a sense of indescribable pride in being an American. (The title of this book, *Ain't That a Miracle?* is, of course, a play on the main chorus lyric.) I would love to rock out with this tune at one of his live shows, especially if I could go back in time to any of the early Farm Aid concerts (the yearly benefit for farmers that Mellencamp first organized with Willie Nelson and Neil Young in 1985). Maybe I will see him live sometime soon.

My sister had the best albums and tapes. Her music collection, which I would beg, borrow, and steal as necessary, was my dream library and just one door down the hall. Suffice it to say, Michele was a huge influence in my life, and not only in music. She would protect me from my older cousin, and she once told off this big dude from our rival town, Old Forge, for kicking my behind with his big friends. He came to me later like a baby, asking me to talk to my sister and have her cool down. I just smiled.

Having an older sister was a delight in many ways. Michele was an outstanding student, often helped with my homework, and even wrote a research paper for me in ninth grade. She was very popular in school and a cheerleader for the football team. Many of her friends would often be over at our house, and it was nice getting a lot of attention from them, being her younger brother. Growing up, I looked up to Michele, and still do today; she's not only a loving sister but also a mentor as an educator.

Adolescence is a tough time for most kids, an unknown roadmap of blooming hormones, confusion, and frustrations. You were always too young for this but too old for that. Added to that for me was the double agony of asthma squeezing my lungs and braces pulling my teeth. The unspoken depression came and went like changing seasons. I was too active with my cousins and friends to allow it to grow wings.

Entering seventh grade with a puberty chip on my shoulder, I felt I had something to prove in my new school. It was a building that housed both junior and senior high students, grades seven through twelve. This large school was the big time, which blew the door open for more practical jokes and more escapades—meaning more chances to get into trouble.

On the very first day of school, I got sent to the principal for riding my skateboard in the hallway. Going to the principal's office was a nightmare, both emotionally and physically. First you had to walk through the senior-high hallway, which, for me, meant getting hassled by the tough older boys, who all knew me from being a water boy for the varsity football team that year.

Once I passed that first test of strength, I had to enter the principal's office. Mr. Kryzanowski, otherwise known by the students as "Crock," was best known for his "iron finger," which I had the pleasure of experiencing being poked into my chest that day. This daunting figure of a man, mainly because he was big, scary, the boss, and a strong disciplinarian, gave me a good scare and said, "I don't *ever* want to see you in my office again." My weak knees were still trembling after finding their way back to the junior high area.

But I did stay out of his office... for two more days. On the third day of seventh grade, I was in Mr. Bone's music class (yes, we had fun with his name, too). This man was fancy, dressed to impress, with full tailored suits, gold rings, a nice watch, and designer men's bracelets. And he drove a plush Cadillac. On this fateful Day Three of school, I wouldn't stop talking out of turn (I still have this problem, by the way), and after a few blunt warnings, he yelled, "Occhipinti, you're gone!"

I turned ice cold. This couldn't be happening. I tried to plead my case, but he wouldn't budge, and I left for the humbling walk of shame for the second time in only three days. I was a goner, walking back through the senior hall to the principal's office. I've blocked out the result, but I apparently survived the iron finger. Another incident where I failed to think about the consequences.

This hellish year included having Mr. K. for gym class—a big guy known for his subtle jokes. He was known among the students as a cool teacher. Once I was laughing, probably at something stupid, and Mr. K. said, "Hey, Chunk, what's so funny?" Chunk was a young character from the popular '80s movie, *The Goonies*, and that was all it took to stick me with a nickname that followed me for years.

Seventh grade was also when I started working at Grasso's Pizza with my cousin Jeff (the same cousin my sister would protect me from sometimes). When the restaurant first opened up, we went door-to-door with advertising flyers or stuck them under windshield wipers on cars. Tony Grasso, the owner and a local Italian American, took care of us with pizzas and hoagies (the local name for a submarine sandwich), and sometimes he threw us some cash.

As low men in the pizza hierarchy, we made hoagies, folded pizza boxes, washed dishes, and went on rides with the outrageous pizza delivery guys, who would sometimes ask us to get out of the car and check the tire and then take off, leaving us to walk home muttering words we were just learning.

My cousin Jeff and I were the token kids in the shop, and we got picked on. Me more than Jeff, as I was much more of a wiseass. I made up my own jokes, soon doing a stand-up comedy routine at Grasso's on Friday nights in front of the high school kids.

Often, they were the same tough kids who knew me as the water boy for the high school football team, so I'd be heckled mercilessly—and worse. Juniors, seniors, college-age kids, and older used to beat me up for fun. Punch me here, knock me over there, and put me in the large garbage can. But Tony never let it get too nuts, plus, Cousin Jeff, fearless and strong, protected me too.

Those minor setbacks did not stop me from breaking balls and making jokes about colorful locals. The audience would bust up laughing, and I got back more than I gave.

In seventh grade, I hung out with a kid who lived two blocks away, Paul Brennan. The oldest of three brothers, he grew up on the south side of Scranton before moving to Taylor. Paul was a half-year older and one grade above me, and we were like brothers. Paul and I were inseparable.

Taylor was full of jokesters, and during that time I was at the top of the list—both busting and getting busted. It paints a rather gruesome picture to note that I had numerous bloody occasions when I lost, easily due to my braces. My lips and gums bled easily when smashed against the metal braces.

I had no curfew back then. Hard to believe, I know.

Everyone I hung out with was a skateboarder. To get down to Grasso's for work, I used to sit on my skateboard—bum on the tail, feet on the nose—and zoom down the hill the three blocks to Main Street without a care about cars.

In my immortal little mind, when I got near Main Street's cars, it was time to slow down and stop. No problem, I'm twelve with no fear yet. But I soon wrecked on my board—this time I was standing up going downhill fast—by doing a Superman flight, landing on my belly and face.

This wasn't the worst of it. I was wearing my hot new Nike Air Jordan sneakers. Any guess how much they cost back then? $120. You don't want to know what Mom said after that dramatic event. It didn't help that I had already been in the habit of sticking my heels out to slow down before I hit Main Street. I quickly wore a hole in the rear soles of those shoes. I never got another pair of Air Jordans.

The transition from seventh to eighth grade gave way to another inevitable life change: puberty. During eighth grade, while hanging out with the not-so-in crowd, I was introduced to a new group of girls on the other side of town. We would hang out at their houses, celebrating life the best we could during that seminal time.

This was adolescent nirvana for a bunch of thirteen- and four-teen-year-old boys hanging out with cute and cool girls. Their houses were the perfect hideout spots when a few of us skipped school or snuck out of school early—two things I was a professional at.

Tobacco and rock and roll became the props and background for boy/girl games like Spin the Bottle and Truth or Dare. Many firsts happened that season: first kiss, first physical contact with a girl, and first sips of alcohol, to name a few. Those were splendid days, and when I told my other friends where I'd been hanging out, they could only react in awe.

Because of my lifestyle and the rogue band of bad boys I hung out with, I was considered a scumbag and a loser to some, maybe even a burnout. But, like a flotation device on a shaky sea, my devo-tion to the football team, my friendships with mainstream students, my older siblings at home, and perhaps my dedication to nightly prayer, all helped keep me above the chaos. Having faith in a higher power was something quite natural to me. This would prove to be most powerful later on in life as well.

From the age of eight, I was on the Taylor Lions football team, and I also played in the youth basketball league at the Community Center. Citing that the dirt would affect my breathing, Mom didn't let me play baseball, though football actually had worse conditions in the wide-ranging Pennsylvania autumn season. In eighth grade, I joined the freshman football team for the eighth and ninth graders. I loved football.

Memories of the summer after eighth grade are still vivid, especially one warm summer night in June. My rowdy crew and I were invited to a new girl's house in a neighboring town. Her parents were away, and she also mentioned booze and pretty friends. Cue the wild, dark music.

We red-blooded males couldn't ride our bikes fast enough—and it was a long ride to her house. We arrived before nightfall, and as promised, there were pretty girls and booze. We grabbed our drinks to look cool, but mostly we just sipped at the bitter spirits. It was all about impressing the young ladies.

And then, suddenly: "Party's over, kids!" The whole group was shocked to see uniformed cops barging into the backyard. We were scared. After some brief, curt questions, everyone was squeezed into the back of two police cars. Looking out the window into the darkness, I found myself heading to the Moosic Police Department on Main Street.

The charges? Trespassing! Which made no sense to me, as the girl who lived there had invited us. But being young and dumb, none of us spoke up. Parents trickled in, angry and embarrassed.

Remember when I said I didn't have a curfew? Things changed drastically after this night. Of course, the curfew didn't stop this boy with ants in his pants from going out late at night for other nocturnal adventures. How could I, the preschool escape artist extraordinaire, stay cooped inside walls when all suburban nature and teenage wild-life awaited me outside?

As soon as my parents went to bed, around eleven, I either jumped out my bedroom window or placed a cushion over the fence of the second-floor deck, leaping into the dark, where my friends would help break the fall. I'd quietly come back early in the morning or later the next day, as if I had dashed out early at daybreak to hang with my friends.

What a wild, rule-breaking summer. It felt more like a summer and a half. While most of the kids were home in bed, I roamed the night with the gang, looking for trouble and doing all kinds of typical teenage things. I would not trade any of the adventures for fortune or fame.

This became a wicked habit for the next few summers, staying out all night with Paul Brennan, Shaun and Eric Frederickson, and Eric Paroby. Being home asleep meant I might miss something, some action somewhere.

In the summer, when the girls were having sleepovers, I was there, hanging out. Seems I was everywhere, day and night, never missing a beat, a pop, or a step. Name a party, high school sports event, afterschool fight, car accident, hangout, or late-night restaurant, and I was probably there. Looking back, I can point to hyperactivity, a curious mind, and an inner search for something extraordinary in life, as to why I always needed to be everywhere. After high school, this would become perfectly clear to me.

I was an insomniac, for sure. And I'd probably be a world-record contender for the most all-nighters. I loved it and still flirt with the wee hours. By sixteen, I was partying two to three times a week during the school year. At this time, my brother Jeff was away at his first year of college. He was a big influence on me, having introduced me to the high school party scene a year before when he was captain of the football team and one of our school's biggest party animals.

A phenomenon happened in 1990 while listening to the two-tape *Europe '72* by the Grateful Dead. At the impressionable age of fourteen, my musical world changed once again. Listening to the Dead was a major turn in the road of my life—Deadman's Curve, the switchback to end all curves. A true Deadhead for many years, there's not been a band, sound or vibe that has shaped me more. Thank you, Jerry Garcia.

The average person takes breathing for granted; you don't think about taking the next breath, you just do. An asthmatic never takes breathing for granted, knowing that at any time an attack may come on, constricting the bronchial tubes and bringing suffocation.

While playing football at Riverside Junior/Senior High School, I often got angry with the coaches or other players, sometimes storming off the practice field for home, but the real foundation of my anger was not the coaches or players, but what you could call "breathing envy" and bone-chilling fear. This happened in junior high football, that freshman year, and, to an extent, on the varsity team, as I played football all five years.

Bump. Bump. Bump.

My lungs began to wage war on the rest of my body. My heart was beating faster and faster, and my chest felt like it was caving in. I was sitting in my ninth-grade science class when panic washed over me and I felt an unbearable pain I had never experienced before during an asthma attack. Quickly, I lifted the inhaler to my mouth and hoped for some relief, but it only worsened with each gasp of breath. Seconds felt like forever.

Too embarrassed to ask for help, I walked out of class, right out the back door, then up the hill to my home. The intense pressure and pain subsided at home, but I felt wiped out.

What I unknowingly thought was just an extreme asthma attack, I found out four years later were heart palpitations, where a sudden movement caused my heart to flip into spasm mode, beating a thousand miles a minute as if I'd run up Mount Everest in flip-flops.

The intense pain snatched my breath away, what little was left.

Vise-like chest pains, increasing shortness of breath, and extreme dizziness made these the scariest moments in my life. It's bad enough growing up with asthma, finding yourself suddenly clutching for air at random moments and experiencing frightening episodes of loss of breath, without adding insult to injury with vicious heart palpitations.

I remember telling myself in my senior year, during one of these horrible bouts where it felt like the end was only a split second away, "If this happens again, I am going to kill myself." Not once did I think I should stop partying every night, that maybe my body was trying to tell me something. If my body was going to screw up, then trash it completely, death would stop the insanity.

One other, teeny, tiny factor added to the mess: I kept these horrible episodes to myself. I didn't tell anyone—family or friends—when they hit or afterward. I felt desperately alone in this painful madness. The only thing I did when these insane bouts of triple-speed heartbeats and chest pains hit was use my inhaler. I thought my asthma kicked my heart into some wild, death-defying direction. Not content any more to rule and abuse my lungs, I thought the disease had spread to my heart.

Transitioning from my rebellious middle school years, I was one of the most popular kids in high school. The main reason? I was friends with everyone. If there's one human value that's blossomed more than others in my overgrown existence, then and now, it is friendliness.

One day, I was hanging out with a group of what some people would regard as "the armpit of the school." They chewed tobacco and smoked cigarettes as we stood outside the gym, where a football pep rally was about to start inside. Minutes later, I blasted through the gym doors into a sea of cheering friends and classmates, as they called my name and jersey number. It's interesting how opposites complement each other, vastly different students, both uniquely gratifying. I'm grateful for all these dynamic experiences in my life.

On the other end of the spectrum, with my wise guy attitude and big mouth running all the time, and by being everywhere there was action, I was always asking for it—and got it—in the form of being beaten up, mostly by older kids from neighboring towns. There was an insistent voice inside me, an inner dare, that constantly urged me to push the envelope, jump with both feet, gums flapping anytime, anywhere, against anyone.

I received a genuine beating by three of the toughest guys in rival town Old Forge when I was sixteen. I was chased by a car full of kids from the west side of Scranton. I had my eyes sprayed with mace on Main Street in Taylor. One thing was for certain, I could take a beating.

When you play sports in high school, the best defense against the other teams is spending countless hours in the weight room, getting stronger, building muscle, and feeling good about yourself.

The first years of high school, I took Weight Gainer 2000, a powder I mixed with milk into a shake. One glass had 2000 calories and tons of protein and minerals. It might have been hard to digest, or maybe it just combined poorly with other food, but either way, it gave me an ongoing case of class-clearing gas.

I ballooned from 210 pounds to 230, with the stretch marks to prove it. But with my long arms and a weak chest, I was not as strong as others my size. Asthma made bench pressing more difficult, but I found my groove with squats. I could squat a lot of weight, wrapping my knees to prevent blowout, and making the essential weightlifters' noises on my way up with the weight.

I stayed late in the weight room, especially during those long, cold Pennsylvania winters. It would just be Coach Armillay and I, listening to oldies radio, talking about everything while I got in extra lifts.

Coach was my seventh grade social studies teacher and was one of the bright spots from that hellish year. I began to learn about the world in his class. Geography helped me inquire into and think deeper about the various places, views, and feelings relating to locations. Coach's class opened me up to this worldly outlook.

Living just a block away, Coach was the mentor who I could go to with any problem. He always brought out the best in me as an athlete. He was a great leader: dedicated and funny. And did I mention crazy? Yes, he was wild, and I liked that about him; we were two of a kind.

In more ways than one, all that lifting paid off. But it could not save me from unseen dangers on the field.

The game underway, we were in scoring position, and there was a running play right behind me, probably a 43 Blast. I came off the ball to block my man, as Billy Posdon, our tailback, ran past me. One of the opposing defenders lunged to tackle him and missed—but he successfully took out my right knee.

Moments after the touchdown, I heard a gory snap in my knee, and I screamed at full volume. The referee warned me about my cursing as I was being taken off the field. It was a torn medial lateral ligament and I'd be out for the rest of the season.

Why me? I thought, as I lay in bed the next morning. All that hard work down the drain. My brother had blown out his knee a few years earlier, so I guess it ran in the family.

The hardest thing to swallow was, since a teammate had been sidelined for his on-field conduct, I would have been the starter by default. But I got a front-row seat on the sidelines in a knee brace instead. This tore me apart inside and I did not have the skills or maturity to handle it.

Without football practice, I took to partying and never looked back. At least until senior year, when I was able to play again.

I loved playing left guard. The best part was being able to "pull" from time to time, which meant that when the ball was snapped, instead of attacking the defender across from me, I took a step back, either going right or left, depending on the play, and leading the running back behind me. It was the greatest feeling when I got to trick the defender, the nature of the play. *BAM!* A blindside shot and the defender goes flying. I enjoyed being a big guy with enough speed to get out in front of the running back and knock someone around.

We had a good team that year, including two future Division One college players. The big game was against Lakeland on our home field, a Friday night under the lights in Taylor. They had a double-digit lead on us in the fourth quarter, when one of the greatest moments I have ever been involved in during a game began.

Touchdown, fumble recovery, late hit on Rich Conte, our quarterback, as he was running out of bounds—a welcome fifteen-yard gift for us on the winning drive. My team scored in the final minute of the game; we did it! The team, sidelines, and hometown crowd screamed insanely and cheered. I couldn't have felt any higher.

By December 1993, when football season was over, I was a senior without a clue to where I would be this time next year, and not the slightest bit of interest either. I clearly remember saying, "Now it's time to really party."

And that's pretty much what I did, surrounded by a new crew made up of Sean Gaidula, Joe Orr, and Mark Zielinski. Sean and Joe were the hyper ones, Mark the bull-throwing, nervous one, who used his inhaler more than I did. I was the glue, the funny guy, and the only one in the group without a driver's license or car. That was fine with me.

We'd skip school and party, get out of school and party, welcome the weekend and party, go back in the woods and party, go on long drives and party, show up at younger girls' houses whose parents had gone out... and party. *And* I hung out and partied with Dave Weisenfluh, Paul Brennan, and Stan Lewandowski, who were still my best friends. These three lived within blocks of me so we had a special childhood connection.

That winter, at a pizza shop, I ran into a girl who went to King's College with Jeff. "Your brother is a legend down there," she told me. "Everyone loves a party animal."

For sure, partying ran in the young males of the family. I was an animal in capital letters.

As ego-satisfying as continuous nightlife felt, it took a vicious toll on me. Within moments of returning home after a night of wildness, I'd sink into depression once again. Any interest I might have had in school began to vanish.

This downward spiral didn't go unnoticed. My teachers were concerned. I will never forget what my favorite teacher said to me: "Your head is in the clouds lately; do you even know what is going on? Get with it!" That was a wakeup call, but nothing sank in strong enough to last more than a day. I'd be back at it the next night.

Just before Easter, it all came to a head. After a wild, chaotic weekend of partying I woke up Monday having crashed and feeling as low as the scum on the ocean floor. I was on automatic pilot as I headed to school. I remember listening to Jimi Hendrix's "Manic Depression" on my headphones and thinking the DJ on Rock 107 played it just for me. A nasty, acidic brew of emotions, aches, and hangover left me with no patience for reality.

It was the period after lunch, in Mr. Hapstack's science class with a test I, of course, had not studied for. As he handed out the test paper, somehow, I got skipped. And the disastrous dialog went like this. Cue soundtrack:

"Occhipinti, where's your paper?"

"I don't have one!"

"Why not? I passed one out to everyone. Do you want to leave?"

A deep well of anger, frustration, past-life beatings, and pain came boiling out in a volcanic explosion. I stood, raised my voice, and shouted the f-word. Oh, boy.

"Get out of my class, now!" he thundered.

Well, that added an extra week of suspension to the already sweet Easter break. Mom and Dad were not happy, especially when they had to visit the principal's office with me. It only added fuel to the hot fire when I apologized to Mr. Hapstack without looking at him.

Winter was finally over. The endless carousing had added to its darkness, with each step leading me further into the dank numbness of tuning out. There is something about long nights of winter that can drag a soul down. The spring sun brought happier days, looking forward to the end of school, to summer, and to whatever waited on the other side. And what *was* waiting on the other side?

Sometime in February, someone asked what my plans were after graduating. What college was I going to attend, what was my major going to be? The typical questions for a senior. I shrugged my shoulders, but it wasn't long before that person and others asked again. "Um, I don't know" wasn't working.

A classmate told me he was applying to Keystone College, a junior college about twenty miles from Taylor. The light bulb turned on. I needed a school to attend in the fall. It would be something to do—and something to tell people. Mom helped me fill out the paperwork and I mailed it to the college on time. Turns out, they will take almost anyone. Since I didn't have a license or a car, I signed up to live in the dorms, another positive step.

February had also brought the announcement of a June 2 concert that hold the first inklings of two future currents in my life, one musical and one spiritual. Being a huge Pink Floyd fan, with a circle of friends almost as rabid for the band, I had gone enthusiastically soaring hearing about their upcoming release *The Division Bell* and their subsequent summer tour. Like millions of rocking youth around the world, I considered Pink Floyd the ultimate rock band, and I was not going to miss this mind-blowing opportunity to see them in concert.

Pink Floyd, like the Grateful Dead, Bob Dylan, and Michael Jackson, were a unique band, one that unlocked another section of my opening mind, while nourishing my soul. These bands represented spiritual music in my world.

The dreamed-about tickets would go on sale one wintry morning at the new Steamtown Mall where Aunt Alice worked, but as an employee she couldn't get us tickets. So I went the enthusiastic route. On the freezing night before they went on sale, my brother Jeff and I, along with hundreds of other young fans, stood outside in a ragged line, waiting for the doors of the mall to open at 9:00 a.m. Somehow, we managed to get ourselves pretty close to the front, and that wild, frigid night turned into a street party, with no cops, tons of loud, blaring music, and fun. We bought the maximum number of tickets allowed, which back then was probably fourteen. Not only did we hook our friends up, but we sold the rest of the tickets at a premium over face value.

The day of the concert came like a welcome gift from heaven. We all skipped school and drove in two cars down the Pennsylvania Turnpike to Veterans Stadium in Philadelphia.

It was my first concert parking lot scene, and it was the greatest party on earth, stretched out over acres of black asphalt. Uninhibited rock-related or drug-induced things you could only imagine assaulted your senses of smell, sight, and sound.

During the tailgate pandemonium, a Hare Krishna devotee approached my friend Mike and me. I'd never seen a man in what looked like a saffron, floor-length dress, his head completely shaved except for a tuft of hair on the back.

This calm young male handed me a book titled *Krsna, The Supreme Personality of Godhead*. I flipped through the pages and was blown away by the beautiful artwork. I did not read any of the words, but I knew I needed that book.

The dude in the dress agreed to our bargain price of eight dollars, which Mike and I split. I wound up taking the book home and the next day showed it to Mom and Dad with innocent enthusiasm, in the naïve hope of sharing something I'd learned about religion.

Total failure!

Suffice it to say, bringing home that book did not go over well with my Christian parents. Though we only attended church when Dad was a visiting pastor on occasion, we were a Christian household. Pictures of Jesus on the walls, Bibles in all rooms, and Dad's gospel tunes playing live downstairs.

Regarding the Hare Krishna book, Dad told me it was a cult and to, "Throw that book in the garbage!" Mom's response was, "We read the Bible in this house!"

I knew the ancient-spiritual artwork in the book held more significance than Mom and Dad were giving them credit for. Two years would pass before I learned what the Hare Krishna movement was all about. *Hari bol!*

Before I knew it, it was concert time, and hundreds of crazed kids ran like a pack of wild deer from savage hunters. The feral rush I felt running up the grass hill with this crowd was like no other. An hour later, the lights went down from our perfect seats in the thirty-second row and Pink Floyd opened with "Astronomy Domine," an ode to founding member Syd Barrett. Could there ever be another inner feeling comparable to this?

At the start of the second set, my sister came and hung out with Jeff and me, smiling and dancing. This was a happy and memorable moment—and the only time the three of us attended a concert together. We were close as siblings, but each had our own worlds, with Michele already having graduated college and Jeff away at college. This show was the catapult into plenty of life-defining live shows in the years to come.

I had only one more hurdle to clear before leaving school.

"Here's twenty dollars for your graduation gown, Jeremy. Make sure you don't lose it. And don't you dare spend it!" How do moms do that—hit the right balance of "love you but behave yourself"?

"Come on, Mom, do you really think that could happen? Spend my gown money? Don't worry, I got it." I was so sure of myself going out the front door.

But, as you probably guessed, that crisp twenty-dollar bill never made it to school. I did have another adventurous night out with the boys, sponsored by my high school graduation gown fund. The bad part was having to wear my brother's old graduation gown. Two shades lighter than everyone else, I stood out in the sea of graduates. But that was nothing new to my friends or teachers. It was just another Jeremy moment.

The summer after high school flew by in continuous days filled with music and parties. If there was one thing I learned in high school, it was how to party, and that led me to having a deeper appreciation of soul-stirring music.

The night before leaving for Keystone, I sat back for an enjoyable summer evening with one of my best friends, Sean Gaidula. "It won't be the same around here without you, Chunk," Sean said, calling me by my childhood nickname.

The kick in my heart surprised me. For sure, something was going to change.

Pretending to be a rock star, 1990

About to block number 5 as Billy ran for a touchdown, 1993

CHAPTER THREE

College Daze

*Don't underestimate your strength. I tell
you; you can make miracles. You can
turn things around 180 degrees.*
—Gurudev Sri Sri Ravi Shankar

Crash! Smash! Splatter!
Glass rained into the back of the car. Mom was in shock, my mouth dropped open, frozen, and Dad was yelling as the unthinkable happened. Dad, with his nervous-built nature, didn't wait long enough for the automatic garage door to open before hitting the gas, shattering the hatchback window of our white, three-door Chevy against the garage door. Glass poured in sharp, sparkling remains all over my bags which Mom had packed so neatly. Unbelievable. Another distinctive Dad moment indeed, and I left for a college with a bang.

A silent, thirty-minute ride ensued up to Keystone Junior College, a two-year liberal arts college, nestled deep in the mountains. Locals viewed Keystone as a "stoner school," or a school to get your grades up for a four-year college or university.

I found it a hidden secret up in the beautiful mountains. Keystone was the only place I had applied to and, happily, was accepted as a resident student. The thought of living in the dorms with a roommate and a whole bunch of new kids was as exciting as it was scary.

Walking into my dorm room, I was met by a long, lanky dude named Bill Mason, from New Hope, Pennsylvania. Bill was not your average first-year college student; at twenty-one, Bill was old enough to buy beer—ten points for my new roommate, right off the bat.

Bill had a peculiar strut and move about him, yet beyond that, he liked the same rock music I did. Bill and I got along well, as though he were my older brother figure.

Bill was a storyteller, a fiction writer of his own life, a tall-tale figure at six-and-a-half feet. In plain English, Bill was a bullshitter. I enjoyed his tales, though. I never called him on details and was his best audience.

Lots of guys were not happy with their assigned roommates, yet Bill and I were pretty chill together—especially when it came to partying. Like me, Bill was no novice to the party scene. Our basement floor was known as the best block party on campus, though staff called it the first floor of the South dormitory. We fondly renamed it The Dungeon.

A fantastic mix of jocks (mainly baseball players), cool kids, and trendy art majors stayed there. My buddy Joe Samsell, whom I graduated with, lived at the end of the hallway. My best friend in the dorm neighborhood was a hyperactive smarty-pants from New Jersey named Brian Battjer, who soon took the nickname Puck as he looked like the kid from the *Real World* show on MTV.

Overall, living at Keystone was a seamless transition from eighteen years with my parents to a dorm filled with a bunch of wild dudes who partied.

During those first weeks of college, I walked around with a picture of Jim Morrison around my neck, the flamboyant and outrageous lead singer for the '60s rock band The Doors. I got into the Doors thanks in part to the movie on the band that came out in 1991 with Val Kilmer. I remember thinking that, if given the most meager of opportunities, I could be just like the infamous Jim Morrison, a wild, charismatic, good-looking, funky front man for a rock band. I believed I had the creative energy and passion to be like him. I adored his music and stage presence.

Over the years, this was a dynamically huge teenage dream of mine. An asthmatic kid from Taylor: Imagine the ego. You could say that, over the years, I have been my own Jim Morrison, in more ways than one.

Deep down inside, I wanted to be like my dad who sang and played instruments (guitar, bass, accordion, tambourine, ukulele, and keyboard) in front of hundreds of people, writing songs and singing to himself in his room, just below mine, day and night.

I compensated my passion in high school by toting my yellow Sony Walkman, and music flooded endlessly from it. Many times the high school principal had to take my Walkman off me for listening and singing in the hallway. One rule of the ego was, "If I can't hear myself sing, then others can't either." I loved this rule.

Singing and playing in front of audiences was my dream, an intense personal dream I kept to myself. Seriously, how do you share a lifelong dream with the rest of the world? What if people scoffed in my face, or told me to get over it? I wrapped the musical desire securely, deep in my soul, letting the decorative color portrait of Jim Morrison around my neck tell it all.

Sadly, I had left my creative and carefree nature—and Michael Jackson moves—somewhere back in elementary school. Inside, I was waiting for that version of me to return.

My first semester came with a lot of new adventures, some familiar, like a rolling continuation of high school, and some remarkably brand new. One thing similar to Taylor was the fact that school was nestled in the woods and every spare moment a bunch of us were climbing, walking, chilling, or congregating among the trees. I was always up for a party.

Being away at college, naturally, meant things were changing for me. Not so much as it was for most freshmen suddenly being without a parental curfew, but for me it was more a sense of confidence.

Academics became another big change for me, can you believe it? My first research paper was on Pink Floyd. I called it "The Other Side of the Moon," a play on words from their landmark 1974 album, *The Dark Side of the Moon*. This is pretty much where my sour attitude toward education changed for the better. I found myself totally immersed in this paper, delving into my passion for a great rock band. Throughout the process, not only did I find it easy, fun, and creative, but I also found myself liking the academic side of school for the first time since probably kindergarten.

As the number one bad boy throughout my years of school (or at least a close second or third), my teachers always looked down on me, hardly ever supporting the merest spark of interest. If a teacher did try to reach me during my high school years, I was probably too blind from partying and late nights to recognize it. Coach Armillay did always keep me in check, but I was also great at hiding my darkest side from him.

In college, although waking up at 7:00 a.m. was still hard and miserable for me, I can say I actually liked reading books and doing homework. A blinding light of recognition clicked on: I enjoyed learning new things.

After writing two papers, the second one on dreams and nightmares, I'll go out on a limb and give credit to some of the professors for my new sudden interest in school. I had so much confidence in myself, I even offered to help write a paper for a procrastinating friend who, like me, postponed everything until the last minute. I still procrastinate today.

Reaching out to assist this student was a powerful moment of realization. I called my mom and said, "I think I want to help people in the world." She asked why, and I said, "When I do my own work, I only give about seventy-five percent effort, but when I help others, I give my all, a hundred percent." What an incredible insight into myself, a first for me, and Mom was happy to hear it.

Hanging out at Keystone with my new friends was like being on this little adventure together. Not the most happening place in the world, Keystone made up the whole little town of La Plume. It was a quick walk to the neighboring town, Factoryville, where a bunch of us went for raids on the food store. Midnight runs to the market included changing the letters on their lighted billboard to the funniest things we could come up with using the available letters. With Scranton a half hour away, we were pretty much stuck in the college woods for the week, and like any wild group of college kids, we did our best to make the most of it.

One night Brian (Puck), Doug Toth, and I got a little nuts from the stress of studying and ventured into this one-horse, redneck town. I made some jokes to this college kid who was bouncing a basketball and they didn't like that much, or the snickering from behind me.

When one of them tried to attack Brian, whom I considered my little brother, it brought out the best of Taylor in me. Rage and testosterone exploded. I threw a few vicious head-butts, a couple big Chunk swings, probably resulting in black eyes later, and we suddenly found ourselves chased by cars, each packed full of rednecks. The chase led to that food store in Factoryville, and we found the good old local boys' bark was far worse than their bite. They retreated into the night, defeated.

I am not proud of picking fights in my youth. Bullying and acting like a jerk would rank high on the list of things I would change about my past if I could.

Something that had gotten worse since high school was my heart palpitations. One day while hanging out at the mall with Brian (Puck) around Scranton, the palpitations happened not once, but twice. During the second episode, I brought my shaking hand up to my ashen face, took a deep breath with my inhaler, and broke down and told Brian what was happening.

He carefully put his hand over my heart and said, "These are heart palpitations." His face creased in concern. "Hey, don't use your inhaler, man; don't you know it's a stimulant? It just makes everything worse."

Puck's informational slap in the face forced me into research at the college library. Finally confessing to my family, I found out I was not the only family member who suffered from these horrific heart terrors: My cousin and mother both suffered from the same thing. It is called Wolff-Parkinson-White syndrome or WPW for short. I didn't live with *The Waltons* growing up, and at night I didn't stay in the house long enough to chit-chat with family. Who knew my own mother had experienced the same terrible heart episodes that had been plaguing me all these years?

A devastating sinking sensation, like riding a freefalling elevator from the top of the Chicago Tower, hit my stomach. My genes had again sabotaged my body. Not that I was doing a great job, riding a nonstop party circuit, but I felt cheated, angry. I wanted to be healthy, done with these intolerable breathing and heart problems. There must be a way, and I knew my chosen lifestyle was not helping.

At the end of my first semester at Keystone, my mother and sister could not believe my glowing report card of mostly Bs and an A. Just by completing my first semester, I was more successful than some of my other fellow graduates from Riverside who'd already dropped out. Partying without a curfew was a brand-new happening for them and they couldn't hack the new lifestyle on top of studies. They'd dived headfirst into partying, experiencing for the first time the freedom off the parental leashes with many yards of rope.

On the day I came home for semester break, Mom exclaimed, without joking, "Look at your stomach!"

I needed a diet. Call it the "freshman fifteen," call it what you will, it happens. Three buffets a day at the cafeteria, snack machines in the dorms, Ben & Jerry's ice cream, pizza in the student center at night, and an unhealthy amount of brewed barley and hops had caught up with me. I probably gained close to twenty pounds (nine kilograms). Growing up, I had always been chubby, and with a child-hood nickname like "Chunk," I was used to being bigger. But this newly added weight was something else.

On the first day of the year, I made a resolution to stop drinking beer. In weeks I lost a quick ten pounds. And that's when I met Erin Graham.

I met Erin on New Year's Day 1995 at the pool hall over in Moosic, the other borough that made up our school district, just across the Lackawanna River from Taylor. I spotted my friend Tara across the crowd.

Tara and her best friend, Cari, hung out with me and a few of my late-night boys during high school until late hours in the night, talking music and sex, telling jokes, and catching us up on the latest girl-gossip. Tara and Cari were two of the coolest girls and my best female friends from our rival town, Old Forge.

I asked Tara who the beautiful girl nearby was and found out she was Tara's cousin, Erin Graham.

The next weekend, I had a date with Erin, and then every weekend after that for the whole semester. Erin and I had a lot of fun together on the weekends in Scranton—nothing like the warmth of a girlfriend to ward off the dark, bitter chill of a Pennsylvania winter. I was in my first serious relationship, and Erin and I became closer every day.

Remember, I still had no car or license, making Erin the designated chauffer wherever we went during the early weeks of our relationship. She eventually taught me how to drive her five-speed, manual-transmission Honda and let me drive the car whenever I wanted. I love driving.

While I was at college during the week, we talked for hours on the phone or sent each other handwritten letters. This was 1995; it would take a few years before the buzzword *e-mail* hit the streets. Handwritten letters are more personal, a chance to slow down and think about what's in your heart while you fill the sheet of blank paper. Old fashioned? Sure, but letters can be read over and over again, savored, cherished.

Having a girlfriend also helped me keep my New Year's resolution to stop partying, and I mean I stopped cold turkey, no more anything. Love will do that. The flush of her female attention made it easier to corral my hyper energy into healthy habits. I went to the college gym a few times a week, started eating better, and lost quite a bit of weight.

Riding the momentum of my newfound friendliness for school and relative success from the previous semester, I was kicking ass in my classes… and, of course, still slacking when possible.

Erin had come to visit me at Keystone, and I took her to my PE class—she was my girl and I felt proud having her close by. Instead, the teacher got belligerent and angry, asking if I signed her in as a visitor at the office like I was back in grade school. I don't know what about her tone or words fired me up, but I yelled a few choice curse words and walked out of the gym, dragging Erin behind me. Who knows what flashed in my mind, but the rage bubbled out without warning and my bad boy attitude, ego, and words got me in trouble once again.

That thirty-second fiasco got me a C instead of an A on my next report card, keeping me from the coveted 3.5 GPA, which would have sent my mom into super-proud-parent heaven.

Overall, it was a high time: Grades were up from last semester and my waist size was down, but I still used my inhaler too much and endured wrestling matches with my heart palpitations at the darnedest of times.

During the last few days of that semester, I lost a bet with a cool dude nicknamed Big Bob. I don't know why the words came out of my mouth, but I said, "If you shave your head, I'll shave mine." He picked up the clippers and was bald in five minutes. I was bald in ten.

Astonishingly, Erin broke up with me shortly after. I am sure the incident with the PE teacher may have been more than she expected from me.

So my first relationship was a fine one, albeit short-lived. It took a few weeks of drowning in heartbreak songs on the radio to let go. I could now relate to the heart-wrenching lyrics. But I can attest that I enjoyed feeling and understanding the meaning of songs I used to enjoy only listening to. Chicago, Don Henley, plus the other thousand songs from the '80s that seemed to play on the radio just for me and the sharp ache inside. What a trip it was.

And speaking of trips, I went back to what I knew best, something I'd taken a five-month hiatus from, and was totally dissed by my friends for doing—partying with the big boys. There's nothing like it to numb a broken heart.

I started partying daily and, quite naturally, felt like hell and gained my weight back. All the self-destructive signs were back and with them the heart madness. We're not talking 78-rpm palpitations; on the contrary, my heart had declared war on me with battle lines drawn both physically and emotionally.

On the Fourth of July, at a friend's house party, I thought the end had come and I was going to die. Sweat trickling down my back, my hands shaking, I quickly locked myself in the bathroom—smart move, dummy—and sat on the edge of the bathtub. I watched my heart dance out of control like some tripped-out hippy from the '60s, going faster as the music outside grew louder, spiraling out of control.

41

Like past episodes of these angry heart circumstances, I prayed and prayed, promising Jesus the moon, how I would not party and abuse my body anymore. And, like always, once the pain stopped, I never followed up on my end of the deal. I took it for granted that he loved me and knew what kind of screw-up I was. I was not too religious, sans my usual nightly prayers, however when I felt helpless, I prayed as if my life depended on it.

I wasn't happy with myself that summer, but kept moving in the same old direction, as if I knew nothing else, racing headlong toward Deadman's Curve with the gas pedal pushed to the floor.

In June, a bunch of us got summer jobs at Specialty Records through a temporary agency. Specialty Records was a huge CD factory, manufacturing music from the Warner, Electric, and Atlantic mega-labels. I worked on various assembly lines, manufacturing music CDs, specifically boxed sets. The first one was a double live album, *A Live One,* from the band Phish, a band I had only heard a bit of at that point.

There are no coincidences, and a production warehouse was the last place I thought I would run into destiny. While working at Specialty Records, I met a mystical-looking girl named Scarlett, who, I found out, also attended Keystone. Her silent, radiant nature intrigued me. She'd pass me with an aura, a vision of wonder.

It wasn't long before I peppered her with questions every chance I got. She never gave me much attention and mostly just smiled when I approached her with my whacky questions and lack of awareness. At this point women other than good friends were still pretty much an unknown entity to me. I barged into her personal space like an over-friendly Saint Bernard.

One day she squared her shoulders and stood tall in front of me, taking in a slow, deep breath. I held mine while she said in a voice that will take lifetimes to forget, "You have to take Carolyn Elliott's Survey of World Religions class at Keystone… it will change your life." And she walked away back into the warehouse.

"What the hell?" I asked myself. "What was that all about?" I felt bowled over with a megaton weight of beauty, weirdness, and cool rain, like some magical monster had risen from the earth and shaken me. The piñata of my mind whirled as the pieces of candy rattled inside.

A class on world religion, cool, maybe like the Krsna book from the concert.

A zing went through me, invisibly weaving a glowing thread around my heart. I didn't understand the attraction, but I loved the feeling. Something happened to me in that moment, something I would not quite understand until the following spring semester.

An older dude at the warehouse who thought he was cooler than all, told stories of seeing the Grateful Dead in concert. When I told him I needed cash to go on a bus trip to see my first Dead show, he said, "Beg, borrow, or steal—you need to see them if you already love their music."

I borrowed a hundred and twenty bucks off of Dave Weisenfluh and he, my brother, and I got on that happy bus to the Meadowlands Stadium in East Rutherford, New Jersey, home of the New York Jets and the New York Giants, on Father's Day, June 18, 1995. Who knew as part of these three amigos I was heading into a life-changing experience?

The parking lot scene, though similar to the Pink Floyd show, was different in a million strange ways. Deadheads waved their freak flags in unique fashion, guys with long dreadlocks danced wildly in the parking lot, and vendors sold everything under the sun, sporting homemade clothing, matted hair underneath their armpits, and surrounded in toxic body odor. I enjoyed every minute of it.

Once again, I found myself on the field level, seventy rows back from the stage, great seats. When the lights went down, Jerry Garcia and the boys came out busting into "Feel Like a Stranger," and I knew I was inside something special, spiritual, awesome. Every bass note, every chord filled me like an empty, dusty vessel. I wanted to be on stage, bringing people to their feet with screams and cheers echoing in the metal catwalks over the stage. The unity and beauty of the music inspired me.

At a Grateful Dead show, Deadheads dance to the music in their own weird way. Some chill and groove, moving their feet a bit and nodding their heads, others go ballistic, shaking their heads in frenzy, bouncing like their feet are on fire. I wanted to make people dance. I wanted their feet to groove to my sound like I did at seven with Michael Jackson's music, and like the young and old did tonight for the Dead. They couldn't be still, couldn't resist the intoxicating rhythm.

My first Dead show, and I was hooked, addicted to the adrenaline and the sound of my idols, unknown mentors of rock. What self-respecting Deadhead wouldn't bust a gut to go again? I decided to go on June 24, six days later and my nineteenth birthday, the ultimate gift to kick off a new year and the last one of my teens. I didn't have a penny to my name, but I knew I was going.

Don Hart, my musical guru, came through once again, inviting me on a bus trip to RFK Stadium in Washington, DC, home of the Washington Redskins (now the Commanders). My first show had been cool, but a second in six days, plus on my birthday, was just awesome.

Getting off the bus, the parking lot scene was in full force. Known to the Deadheads as Shakedown Street, where hippy and wannabe hippy vendors sold everything from cold beer to stickers, is affectionately named after the title track of their November 1978 album. Music played, dogs ran around with barefoot little kids, and long-haired hippies danced. There were shirtless jocks with tattoos and hats on backward, older men in sandals, plus those well-hidden undercover police officers with clean weekend tennis shoes and suntan watch lines on their wrists, busting people for narcotics and more. The Grateful Dead parking lot scene was every bit as magnificent as it was havoc.

When the Grateful Dead came on, to my delight their good friend and old keyboard player, Bruce Hornsby, sat in with them for the show. Their "Jack Straw" opener got everyone psyched up. Fans began their unique hippie dances around me, and like a bolt of sonic energy, I felt it was okay for me to dance, too. Not totally free, but loose, smooth. What was I thinking? Oh, that's right, I wasn't.

By set break my heart was flying fast, in uncontrolled orbit while I was high. The frantic, pounding rhythm lasted for more than thirty terrifying minutes. The concert morphed between the peak of ecstasy and the depths of psycho heart hell for me.

Many things in my life were controlled by the fear of my heart going nuts. To put it crudely, it sucked. This underlying anxiety often made me feel helpless, weak, and worst of all, sad. But it did not stop me from living this wild lifestyle that only added fuel to an already blazing fire. My health issues gave way to a level of depression tucked away by my partying and never being alone long enough to deal with it.

Speaking of morph, those two summer shows catapulted me into Deadhead glory. I dove deeper into the music of the Grateful Dead with every bootleg tape, album, and song. My world grew brighter as I let my hair grow longer and proudly owned a psychedelic Dead tie-dye shirt from each show.

In July, after graduating from Old Forge High School (the next town over), my old barter buddy, Little Dave, moved to San Diego. He followed the road his cousin, Bobby Laurenzi, and Justin Fiore—who in my mind was the King of Old Forge—had taken the year before.

When Dave told me he was moving West to Southern California to live on the beach, I might have had a flicker of desire to go, but it fell away quickly. What was the draw for these guys? The beach, the sun? I wasn't a surfer dude, not this die-hard, East Coast testosterone guy.

Another all-star from Old Forge, Jimmy McCormick, had moved to San Diego the month before, in an attempt to live the Golden State dream. I clearly remember the day Jimmy returned, shirtless, shoeless, foolish, with the baggiest black pants I had ever seen. This look was beyond out there (and so was he for that matter) compared to the *normal* Pennsylvania style dressed in a nice tucked-in shirt with shoes on our feet. Just because I partied hard over the years doesn't mean I slacked off on looking good. I was smart style most of the way.

A house party that night brought me and Jimmy Mac together. Decked out in his new wild look, singing and partying hard, I found myself talking to him for a long time about his experiences in San Diego.

I felt a change deep inside. Was it the looseness I'd experienced from the Dead concerts that made his wild passion more acceptable? His stories flowed, cracking open a door of possibility for me. He painted a picture of the carefree Southern California beach lifestyle, of walking around shirtless and shoeless, soaking up the sunrays on the golden sand. Jimmy spoke of beach parties filled with beautiful women, cutting-edge music, alcohol, and drugs galore. San Diego sounded different from our short, sweet New Jersey shore vacations in high school.

From that night, all I wanted was to move to San Diego. Passion for sand and sun stole my heart and I began a yearlong dream of living on the beach in Southern California. Dream on and dream away.

Mom and I were relaxing at home, 1995

CHAPTER FOUR

California Dreaming in the Poconos

Miracles cannot happen without faith.
Faith takes you beyond limitations.
—Gurudev Sri Sri Ravi Shankar

*A*s far back as I remember, I've fallen asleep to music, be it the radio, a tape, or a CD. And the music would often play through the night. On August 9, 1995, somewhere in the morning hours, still falling in and out of slumber, I kept hearing radio-friendly Grateful Dead tunes, mixed with DJ talk about Jerry Garcia.

"Jeremy," said my mom as she opened my bedroom door. Her sharp voice forced me out of my tie-dyed colorama of sleep. "That man you like, that Jerry Garcia of the Grateful Dead, he died. It's all over the news."

"What? What are you talking about? Get out of my room!" I yelled. Seriously, I was barely awake, and I thought it was a terrible joke. A split second later, regret washed over me for yelling at her. She knew my passion for the Dead and had rushed in to let me know. I didn't have a habit of yelling at my family members, but I always regretted it when I did due to stress, tension, and misunderstanding.

I sat up like a sprung trap. Within minutes, the DJ on Rock107 was sadly announcing, "Jerry Garcia will be missed by Deadheads in America and around the world. His untimely death has touched the music world today."

I couldn't believe it from him either. I was in shock. It wasn't possible. Less than two months earlier, I'd been initiated into the uninhabited concert, rock-and-roll world Jerry Garcia had created thirty years ago. I had barely joined this distinctive musical family with its organic, homegrown audience, who, at their peak of devotion, followed the band all over America and to other parts of the world. I felt like a fledgling lost at sea.

A true rock icon of American music and of the hippy culture of late-1960s San Francisco, Jerry Garcia became much more than a band leader and guitarist. He was like a messenger from heaven, helping millions who had an ear for his soulful sound take an evolutionary step into being more kind and living free. Jerry Garcia's untimely death of a heart attack at fifty-three was the end of something unique in American music, but it further encouraged my ascendance into his legacy sound and the subculture he created for us grateful freaks of glory.

It was a somber day on Lincoln Street, too. A few friends came over and I played the unmistakable music of the Grateful Dead through my open bedroom window to our front yard and street. We sat outside with heavy hearts, talking, playing Hacky Sack (footbag), and celebrating the life of Jerry Garcia. During my makeshift memorial, not once did my dad yell to turn that racket off. Not one neighbor complained of the loud music. Respect was honored on Lincoln Street.

Returning to Keystone after an eventful, unforgettable summer, I could not wait to see old friends and meet the new freshmen. But I entered the campus acting and looking like a true Deadhead, wearing one of my tie-dyed tour shirts, throwing peace signs. As I walked on the overpass, looking down on a handful of friends on the green lawn below, they each called up some version of "Wow, you look so different."

In some ways, I felt that my experiences and Jerry Garcia's death had matured me, and a sad smile crossed my face. "Yes, I had an awesome summer of music and much more," I told them.

During my first days back, I told my friend Doug Toth about the stream of locals who had moved to Southern California. I shared my new dream of moving to San Diego once college was over. He picked up on my passionate speech about life with no more bitter Pennsylvania winters and pledged to join me.

I came back to school with my lungs rebelling from the summer of partying, and my asthma raging out of control. By October with the changing weather, I was sick. I called Mom, asking her to bring my breathing machine to the college.

This machine, known as a nebulizer, changes asthma medication from a liquid to a mist, so it can be absorbed by the lungs more easily. In all its glory, it sat next to me on the bed, growling a drone-like sound as I sat with a tube in my mouth for each twenty-minute treatment.

Not being able to sleep, plus having to endure that dreaded machine twice a day, kept me perpetually distressed. Sick and angry, school, once again, became the last thing on my to-do list. I was wrapping myself in a blanket of the old Jeremy, missing classes, doing little or no schoolwork, and, in general, not giving a damn about life. This symptom of depression continued to circle back into my life.

The fear that came with not being able to breathe washed all rational thought out with the miserable tide. Though partying would break the spell briefly, depression cloaked everything in a gray dullness.

One thin strain of excitement during this dark semester was learning about African cultures, which opened my mind to other worlds. The professor showed videos and pictures of Africans enthusiastically dancing in traditional celebration and other ways of life in their village. I wanted to quit college right then and travel to Africa. I felt the urge to bolt.

Another positive strain was that Doug and I were still both gung-ho on San Diego, dreaming of sunshine on a wintry day, of wearing suntan lotion and walking along the ocean. Our plan was to graduate, work all summer, and move out West in the early fall.

I found a gorgeous picture in a magazine of the University of San Diego and its spectacular view of the Pacific Ocean and Mission Bay. When no one was looking, I taped that picture on my own dorm room door. Under the title, "Slacker City, USA," I wrote, "Do you think you can hack it?" There was an ongoing finger-pointing drama as to who wrote that funny challenge.

Of course, our friends would bust us when we dreamed aloud about our plans, saying things like, "Yeah right, you can't move out there," "It's too far," and, "You won't be able to find a job, and you won't be able to afford it."

The human mind is a funny thing. It tends to focus mostly on the negative. People not only love to squash their own enthusiasm, but others' too.

That semester ended on a low note, with failing health, two dropped classes, and my stunning grade point average plunging back into the twos. The short, dreary days of November kicked me to the sidewalk and left me there. I had no will to fight back.

The battle with asthma during fall and winter was the worst I could remember. While spending the winter holidays at home, my season-long train ride with shortness of breath, fear, and pain went into hyper-drive and beyond.

Mom and Dad were so scared one day that they rushed me to the hospital. That was one of the longest, most grueling days ever. I endured three debilitating breathing treatments. Only those who have suffered through the worst of asthma know the discomfort and agony of the treatments. Picture this: Cramped in a confining hospital bed with an intravenous needle in my right hand, while an offensively uncomfortable breathing machine (think shoving a softball into the mouth of a mouse) was strapped securely around my head and neck with the rigid mouthpiece forced between my lips. Mom and Dad looked on, helpless and worried. I could see the pain in my mother's eyes; she couldn't fix this.

What has my life become? I asked myself in a mindless and silent voice. *If this is hell, I don't want to be in it. Please, Lord, get me out of this mess.*

After a long, soul-wrenching day in the hospital, I was allowed to go home.

The next day, Mom took me to another doctor. I bared my soul with rock-solid clarity and the sincerity of a young child. "Doc, I'm nineteen, I have my whole life in front of me. I have dreams. I'm moving to San Diego next fall. I can't go on living this hell of a life. There must be another way."

He encouraged me to look into alternative medicine in Southern California, and I was thinking that this was going in a positive direction. The doctor heard me. Then he gave me a Prednisone shot (steroids to help me breathe), near my right shoulder. But it seemed like he missed whatever he was aiming for and poked a bone or a ligament. Searing hot agony forced tears down my cheeks. My arm felt like a rampaging bull had stomped on it.

All night I stayed in my room and cried in pain and desolation. The extreme pain and the overall weight of the disease got the best of me. I caved and crawled into a black emotional sea. I was certain the next stop was the graveyard.

This nightmare overshadowed what turned out to be the last Occhipinti Christmas together for many years.

What I hoped would be my final semester at Keystone College started off with me being kicked out of the dorms for a week. I'm not sure if it was because I kept pulling fire alarms all night and watching in blissful fascination as angry and freezing students stood out in the cold, or if it was because I switched off the circuit breakers, killing everyone's digital alarm clocks and causing many students to sleep in and miss class.

I can't imagine why the students didn't appreciate my sense of humor. What a grouchy group. As an insomniac at a college in the woods, I had to be more creative than I was in high school. I couldn't jump out a window like I did in Taylor and find some easy action in town.

During that week, I lived with the college security guard, Clarence. I still had no car or license, but he took me to school when he got home from his third-shift job and drove me back to his home at night.

The worsening asthma continued, but for some reason, I started sensing a beautiful brightness around me, like some unseen presence was taking care of me. I didn't know why that was happening; it was not something I'd felt before. It was subtle but also concrete, and it made me feel that something good was coming.

Another highlight that year was Carolyn Elliott's Survey of World Religions class, the class that Scarlett, the mystical girl from my summer job, told me about. One look at the teacher and I knew she was special. I saw a quiet strength in her eyes, like the glasslike surface of a calm lake with an active volcano boiling below. Her voice was melodic. Its resonant tone soaked easily into my open mind, unencumbered and natural. I was receptive to most of my classes at college, especially Carolyn's Religions class.

And her teaching confirmed her initial impression. Carolyn explained that she held this class early in the morning so students could drift off through the lectures and absorb the knowledge better. She suggested we relax and close our eyes if we wanted to. She also explained that the class was only offered in the winter/spring semester, since she felt that in spring, our internal growth would be in tune with the energy of the sprouting plants, blossoming flowers, and the growth taking place in the rest of nature at that time. We meditated each day, and my mind began opening.

The first classes were an exploration of Western religions, but when Carolyn dove into Buddhism and Hinduism, the course really took off, as she guided us deep into the knowledge of these ancient traditions in a beautiful way. A Zen Buddhist herself, she had been studying under various spiritual masters and meditating for thirty years.

Her style of dress was more relaxed and colorful than other professors too; no uptight professional suits were necessary for this woman to earn respect.

The guided meditations were both subtle and wonderful. One thing that moved me was her eloquent story of Buddha and his path to enlightenment. Especially mind-blowing was the part of the story where Shiva (the silent, transformational aspect of nature) took the form of a dying man on the street, giving Prince Siddhartha—the future Buddha—one of three glimpses of suffering, and leading him to question the purpose and nature of life.

For the first time in my life, something was rising and ringing inside me while listening to someone speak, something beautifully powerful and remarkable. I learned new terminology, such as attachment, ignorance, enlightenment, meditation, *atma* (soul), *maya* (illusion), and *karma* (action and its effects). All were welcome in my opening mind.

Her introduction to Hinduism included two books I still have and hold dear. One was India's most beloved scripture, the *Bhagavad-Gita*, a conversation between Lord Krishna and an evolved warrior named Arjuna, taking place on a battlefield before the start of the Kurukshetra war. The other was excerpts from the *Upanishads,* the ancient texts that were cognized thousands of years ago by enlightened seers and considered by many to be the deepest expression of the ancient Vedic wisdom.

Both of these books inspired me, especially the *Bhagavad-Gita*. Each page I turned led me further on a familiar path, almost like I had read them before. I absorbed the verses and bathed in their truth and structure.

Doug and I would visit Carolyn at the library (she was also the head librarian that semester). We came with our questions, and talked with her about life, Jesus, meditation, yoga, and of course, our golden dream of San Diego. Carolyn was a powerful soul, and she knew something about life I just had to find out. She wasn't offering a path, it was more like a bridge to a path.

Growing up in a Christian family with a father who was a preacher, I sincerely wanted to know the truth about God. I had attended church with my family, mostly wherever Dad was a visiting preacher. I read the Bible in my own fashion, since reading wasn't my favorite pastime growing up. I didn't read it cover to cover. I'd skip a little, get serious, then skip some more. My favorite book was Jeremiah, because of my name.

A few golden passages from the Bible stood out for me, the most important being, "Truly I tell you, unless you change and become like little children, you will never enter the kingdom of heaven." (Matthew 18:3.) What an intense line. Yet, as I looked around any church growing up, I never saw adults with childlike innocence, openness, and enthusiasm. The only people who fit this bill were the youngsters running around the other parts of the church with me while my dad sang and preached.

I felt connected to Jesus, if only through my constant prayers and the picture of him in the hallway.

As a teenager, I developed spiritual concepts that helped me deal with life. This was my at-the-time philosophy on life: Firstly, everything happens for a reason. Secondly, every dog gets his day. Okay, not straight out of the Bible, but it got me through.

Nevertheless, I hadn't felt the peace in my heart or the connection to God from within that I'd heard about in so many Christian songs. I was Christian by birth and tried to learn about my religion. I had many questions but never asked Mom or Dad, mainly because I didn't want them to think there was something they knew that I didn't.

So it felt like progress—and a relief—that, with Carolyn, I was finally able to ask freely about spirituality and experience it with authentic interest.

Crunch time came in the fourth and final semester of my two-year college. I was gaining spiritual knowledge, but by spring break, I was failing both math and geology, and I needed to pass them to graduate. Adding to the pressure, Mom had already shopped for the perfect dress to wear to her baby boy's graduation—and graduation would be an accomplishment no one had ever dreamed of for me.

Luckily, my math professor was a young Pennsylvania woman. She enjoyed my frequent jokes within that rather stiff class of nerds.

On the other hand, my geology professor was nowhere near young, but old, set in his ways, and he didn't like me. However, I jumped through his hoops and survived his torture machine, settling with a D and graduating as a member of the first class of the newly named Keystone College (it was previously Keystone Junior College). I thought it was fantastic to drop the *Junior* from the name, as it looked much better on my resume and transcripts.

I graduated with an associate's degree in Liberal Arts, and with a better GPA than anyone could have imagined, including myself.

By graduation night, I was physically and emotionally running on fumes, but I kept it real and partied at a fellow graduate's house, later staying out all night, cruising with a friend up on Horseshoe Valley Road. I floated along that evening in a euphoric, yet slow-dying feeling. This happened a lot.

These killer forty-eight-hour marathons were common, tantalizing, and no one did them better than I did. From playing all-night Nintendo games as a twelve-year-old boy to jumping off the deck after my parents went to bed, it was a lifestyle cultivated from a toxic brew of sleepless, hard-to-breathe nights and childhood hyperactivity.

With fall coming quickly, it was financial crunch time. I needed an action plan for San Diego. It was August, and I had no job, no cash in my pockets, and not even a thought about savings in a bank account. Nothing. So I went back to the temp agency that had booked me at Specialty Records on and off over the past year.

There was only one problem. I wasn't welcome to work through them anymore because I'd quit my jobs too many times and, of course, for causing lots of trouble with my hometown boys at these jobs.

So I came up with another stellar idea. My brother, Jeff, was on good terms with them, and I had experience using his old, expired driver's license to… well, you know, buy *things*, since he was twenty-one. People always commented on how alike we looked. Maybe so, maybe not.

I showed up at the temp agency and pretended I was him. Did it work? I spent five weeks working twelve-hour shifts, four days on and four welcome days off, and managed to save six hundred dollars. My mother generously gave me another two hundred, and Doug booked us two one-way tickets to San Diego, flying out of Baltimore on the morning of October 5, 1996.

Wow, California dreaming was real, and it was happening. Wow! Did I say wow?!

Mom, Dad, Jeff, and I at Keystone College for my graduation, May 1996

CHAPTER FIVE

Across the Universe to San Diego

When energy is high, what you think is impossible
starts happening. Even from a scientist's point
of view, miracles are indeed possible.
—Gurudev Sri Sri Ravi Shankar

*E*very few weeks before leaving for San Diego, I'd call Dave. He was one of the people from Old Forge who had moved to San Diego the year before. I'd been telling him that I'd move out there in the fall of 1996. And here it was. His voice was like an anchor line to the golden land, always saying, "Right on, dude!"

Doug and I didn't have an actual plan until hours before hopping on our flight. In fact, we hadn't picked a date until Doug made the reservations. Nor did we consider normal concerns like housing and transportation.

I nervously called Dave one last time the day before our flight, beads of sweat trickling down my back. "Dave, it's Jeremy. What's up, man?"

"Nothing, dude. You here?" His voice flowed with a California calm.

"No, I'm coming tomorrow. We fly out at the crack of dawn, one-way tickets to paradise."

"Cool, man. Call me when you get here and be sure to come by and say hi."

"Come by and say hi" echoed through my brain. Come by? I thought we were staying with him. The cold sweat drenched my shirt with panic. *Quick, say something*, I thought.

"Um, Dave, we don't know where we're staying." Flashes of past conversations, many in the after-haze of intense partying, flew through my mind. Surely, I'd discussed being temporary roommates with him, hadn't I? I was flying three thousand miles with no place to stay?

"Get out, really? So what are you going to do?"

"Dave." Dead silence for a heartbeat. "I don't know. Can you help us, please?"

"Hey, man, call Justin, he might be able to help you." I felt his shoulders shrug through the phone.

"Okay, Dave, thanks a million." The drowning feeling eased somewhat. Dave had thrown a life preserver into an expansive, unknown ocean.

I used to see Justin Fiore at parties but had never talked to him for more than a few minutes at a time, and then he moved to San Diego. I stared at the numbers on the phone, lifted the receiver and called his home in the Mission Beach section of San Diego.

Bingo! His roommate, Bobby Laurenzi, another hometown local, was in Costa Rica for two weeks on a surfing trip, and Justin said that Doug and I could stay there for ten days, each paying ten bucks a night. Thank you, Jesus. Thank you, Lord! It was another miracle on Lincoln Street, and the whole town of Taylor was dancing in my soul.

All these months I had simply expected things to work out. I knew I needed to be in San Diego. Details? I did not have any details. I have not always been the best at planning ahead. My dream of moving to San Diego was so intense that it created an unshakable faith.

Justin was the King of Old Forge, the kingpin, the go-to-man, the tall Italian kid who had moved from the West Side of Scranton to Old Forge. I remember Justin most from his glory days, playing basketball at the Old Forge courts. He was a beast—in size and attitude.

Mom and Dad drove us the five(!) hours to Baltimore International Airport. I hadn't questioned Doug about the tickets. When you fly cheap, you go where you gotta go. Though sad to see me leave, my parents stood behind my dreams, as always. And I've always been grateful to them for that.

As we got out of the car, Dad handed me a Bible, probably a gesture of love in his eyes, as well as a parental "stay-close-to-the-heart and follow-the-straight-and-narrow" bit. I left it on the back seat of the car on purpose, rejecting the Bible. I'm sure Dad was hurt by that thoughtless action. I wasn't declining the Bible so much as I was snubbing Dad's generation and way of thinking as I set out on my new life adventure.

I swear that plane made a stopover in every major city across the country. Who knew we had taken the Greyhound of the skies? We sat in our seats and waited while people shuffled off and new ones hopped on. Over and over.

After our grueling day of hopscotch, we landed in San Diego, greeted by a glow of early evening painted against the western sky.

As I stretched my cramped leg muscles, I turned to Doug in my tie-dye shirt and long brown wannabe-hippy hair and said, "No matter what happens to us, I am going to keep smiling and stay positive."

Justin and Dave were there to meet us. Justin, tall and tan, his brown hair in a ponytail and his eyes glazed with wonder, said happily, "Welcome to San Diego!"

Little Dave, short like his name, with a similar light brown ponytail, exclaimed, "Hey, dude, you made it. Welcome to California!"

Justin picked us up in his traveling roommate Bobby's blue two-door BMW. Talk about a cool trip right off the bat. My first impressions of San Diego were a warm sea breeze outside the airport and a feeling of awe at the signature palm trees on our short ride to Mission Beach. Justin pulled a U-turn on Mission Blvd, putting us smack-dab in front of the boardwalk, looking at the magnificent Pacific Ocean just after sunset.

"Here it is, boys, the largest body of water in the world, and home to the most living things in the world—the Pacific Ocean!"

Doug and I looked at each other, and for that one timeless moment I felt I'd made my dream come true, or at least taken a monster-leap into tropical heaven.

Justin had a six-hundred-square-foot one-bedroom apartment, mere steps from the sand on San Diego's famous Mission Beach. Not blocks, not a quarter mile from the beach, but a dozen steps.

On the way into the apartment-size kitchen, Justin pointed to a wall calendar with a resplendent picture of a bearded, saintly looking man with flowing black hair, a timeless smile, and hands folded in prayer position. "And this is my guru," he said nonchalantly, continuing into the kitchen.

Wow, I want one of those, I thought to myself. Like hitting a perfect chord on a guitar, the thought felt big and right, and then disappeared as we continued to tour Justin's apartment. But seeing that calendar would become one of the most memorable moments of my life.

After a brief welcome party, Justin took us to Bahia Grill for burritos. Little Dave and Justin had become vegetarian since leaving Pennsylvania and ordered veggie burritos; I ordered a grilled chicken. Who knew I was eating one of the last non-vegetarian meals I would have?

After dinner, Doug and I ventured onto the beach and wearily sat down in the still-warm sand. The canopy of night sky twinkled over us as we gazed around at the nightlife and the mighty Pacific Ocean. I swear the stars looked more content here, hovering above the black expanse of salt water. The waves had a phosphorus glow as they broke on the wet sand, keeping a steady deep baritone rhythm; a maritime lullaby.

Doug looked at me and said, "Goddamn, we did it!"

The next morning we got busy finding jobs. Two Sunday *Union-Tribunes* were spread out on the table, as we highlighted possible leads, made calls, and kept notes. During this employment-search frenzy, Little Dave walked in and, observing the scene, yelled out, "Hell, yeah, this is how you make it happen in Southern California. Right on!"

Doug bought a cheap bike and I fired up my skateboard and we ventured out, going store to store, shop to shop, business to business, filling out applications wherever possible. As a transplant from Taylor, everything looked so colorful, clean, and friendly.

The employment road was not easy for me, and yet it was a wonderful adventure searching for jobs daily. Was there such a thing as being too tall? Too pale? What wasn't there to like about me?

Since finding a job was proving difficult, Justin invited me to help him with his day job, working for famous quadriplegic Ken

Cummings. Ken ranks in the top ten most unique guys I have ever known. He was a warrior with a big heart and a healthy ego. I was told he broke his neck in an accident involving a diving board in his friend's pool, leaving him paralyzed from the neck down. Some years later, to raise awareness and charity funding, Ken wheeled across the country in his electric wheelchair.

Justin, his roommate Bobby, and I all worked for Ken. Justin, being his main man, worked full-time from early morning. I'd skate-board three minutes north on the boardwalk to Ken's condo at the See the Sea resort, next door to the historic Crystal Pier, with its hotel cottages built right on the pier. The comic actor Pauley Shore's mother lived in the same complex, and Pauley would stop in from time to time.

After Ken buzzed me in, I would go up for my dose of Ken Cummings madness. I couldn't get enough of him. I laughed and listened during this wild time. My job included such duties as cleaning his condo, lifting him from his bed, massages, organizing his paperwork, driving his custom van around town (illegally, as I had no driver's license), and making calls. I was stoked to be working for him, and, of course, to be employed in general.

Remember, I came to paradise with my fortune of eight hundred dollars minus plane fare, which had to be managed with insane care. Not only was this the most money I'd ever had at one time, but it was all I had. My pockets were nearing empty, so working for Ken proved a welcome lifeline.

Doug and I moved to Little Dave's after those ten days, a smaller place shared with another dude, Steve Lombardo, who was raised in San Diego and later moved to—are you ready for this one?—Old Forge!

Where Justin's place seemed cool and comfortable, this was tight quarters, and it felt like the two of us were invading their small space. We'd been in San Diego for ten days, three hours, and a handful of minutes without finding an apartment. I prayed hard for something to open up that day.

A voice called out in my head. "Hey, Chunk, look at me, up here on the second floor. It's me, your dream house on the beach."

An awesome one-bedroom apartment at 718A Santa Rita Place, on the border of Mission and Pacific Beach, wore a "For Rent" sign in its window. The sign, in bright, shining neon colors, at least for me, exclaimed, "Pick me, pick me. Please. I'll keep you safe and cool and be the best beach house in California."

And that was how, two days later, on October 17, a mere twelve days after arriving, I signed a one-year lease, with my father co-signing via fax. I will always be grateful to Dad for his support.

Doug and I split the rent of $620 a month. I let Doug have the bedroom and I took the living room. Yes, I'm a nice guy, but the cool living room included a huge plate-glass window where sunlight poured in. A bar, which doubled as a kitchen table, separated the decent-sized kitchen from the living room. Doug's bedroom had a sneak-peak view of the ocean. Our apartment was on the second level, with five garages underneath for the landlord's other two beach houses. I found a used mattress, plopped it on the floor as my bed, and I was home.

"Hello," said a tall, beautiful, blue-eyed surfer girl, walking by our open front door. "You must be the new neighbor. My name is Janine. Welcome to the neighborhood!" She swept long strands of sun-kissed hair over her tan shoulders, and added, "I live next door with Fiona; you'll be seeing a lot of us."

In an astonished stutter, I said, "Thank you. My name is Jeremy... I'm from Pennsylvania." After some small talk, I watched her walk away.

Wow, my first apartment on the beach, exactly thirty-two steps from the sand, came with a drop-dead gorgeous girl and her roommate right next door. *Thank you, Jesus. I am in heaven!*

Mission Beach is an interesting section of San Diego. It is essentially a two-mile stretch of narrow land, bordered by the Pacific Ocean on one side and the manmade Mission Bay on the other. Boardwalks run along both the ocean and the Bay side and walking from the ocean to the clean sand of Mission Bay takes less than two minutes. An incredible geographic area. But, more incredible, it was the same exact piece of land that was in the picture I hung on my Keystone dorm room door, with the commanding title, "Slacker City, USA."

Now I could honestly say, "Yes, Jeremy, I *can* hack it!" This was truly my destiny.

My memories of Justin back in Taylor and Old Forge were mostly of playing basketball. He was one of the "Godfathers," playing with intensity, sweat to the bones, an East Coast brawler. Now he was inviting me to join him for a game in our new neighborhood. The basketball courts sat right on the bay, and I couldn't think of a more inspiring spot to play a game I loved.

One day, Justin and I got into a two-on-two with two visiting dudes. As the game came down to the wire, I was gasping for air, having a hard time breathing, and I stopped to use my inhaler. A second later the opponent drove by me for the winning layup. Justin was furious with me. I'm competitive in sports, but compared to Justin, who was devastated at losing to two goons on his home court, I was pretty laid back.

"I'm sorry, Justin, my lifetime battle with asthma got the best of me," I said with a sigh.

"Dude, you need to take the Art of Living course (Healing Breath Workshop). It could heal your asthma and much more," replied Justin in a convincing tone.

He continued, "I practice deep breathing and meditation daily. The course has changed my life in countless ways."

The conversation instilled hope that I might be able to be free from this dreadful lung disease someday. I began connecting the dots: the guru, the breathing, and meditation. My mind continued to open, and I wanted to learn more.

Walking back to the house with Justin one afternoon, I saw a tall, familiar-looking kid riding a BMX-style bike, sporting a shaved head and purple warm-up pants. Acting cool, with a "what's this kid from Taylor doing here?" kind of attitude, Bobby Laurenzi shook my hand and said, "Hi, welcome to the beach."

I owed this guy for leaving town and giving me a place to crash when we got there. Oddly enough, I never talked to Bobby growing up, though I was often down in Old Forge hanging out and pretty much knew everyone there. It turned out Bobby was a jock on the basketball team and hung out with kids I didn't associate with.

Justin punched my shoulder and asked, "Hey, Jer, wanna trip out?"

I saw a certain light in his eyes, a glow of energy. I could tell he wasn't talking about partying with drugs or alcohol, but I didn't know what he had in mind. I found myself walking with Justin, Bobby, and Little Dave five blocks to the Hare Krishna Temple in neighboring Pacific Beach. I kept an open mind.

I had memories of taking the *Krsna* book home from the Pink Floyd concert to my parents' dismay and ensuing rejection of the book. Also, how just five months ago, the *Bhagavad-Gita* had become my treasured textbook at Keystone, a book I carried with me to San Diego. I felt excited to enter the temple, like those events were steppingstones to this moment.

From outside, the temple was rather boxy and plain, until you came to the front door, which boasted Indian god and goddess figures I was familiar with from my Krsna book and religion class at Keystone. We took off our shoes outside before going in and, arriving late, we walked into a storm of ecstatic music—Sanskrit chanting, dancing, shakers, Indian drums, and men in white and orange robes with shaved heads, all looking like the dude I'd met in the parking lot at the Pink Floyd concert two years earlier.

This was their major weekly celebration, and the swaying and dancing participants were intense. Nothing could have prepared me for the beautiful craziness; the waxed marble floor, walls decorated with gorgeous pictures of Krishna, wild music increasing in intensity by the verse, Justin dancing like a fool, Dave doing the same, and Bobby just looking cool. I wanted to participate, yet my ego was a significant obstacle, as I felt unnatural in this ever-new and mind-blowing environment. It was also hard to breathe as I was not used to the smell of smoke from the Indian incense.

As the music stopped, everyone knelt and put their forehead on the ground. Out of respect, I did the same, without a clue why. Quickly, and in a graceful, orderly manner, everyone sat down in neat rows inside the temple. I followed suit but found it nearly impossible to fold my body and sit Indian style on the hard floor, mainly because of my size and bad knees from football. *Hey, I grew up in a chair.* But still, that first visit felt like an adventure.

The Hare Krishna Temple turned out to be a blessing for me. For starters, I was still struggling to get by on my meager earnings, and they let me take out the garbage on Sunday nights for free meals during the week. I loved their vegetarian food. The Gauranga potatoes, an Indian delicacy made with sour cream and rosemary, were simply out of this world.

I started attending their Bhagavad-Gita classes and talked to the various devotees about the ancient texts, Krishna, Sanskrit chanting, and more. I did not mention any of this to Mom during our phone conversations for fear of misunderstanding. I was not open about my spiritual experiences yet. However, I did call Carolyn Elliott at Keystone, excited to share my adventures at the Krishna Temple. She told me, "It's a nice path."

I completely agreed. They were drug and alcohol free, vegetarian, sang all day (even if there was mainly one song), danced, and studied the Gita.

One senior pundit (priest) was a joy to be around, and I often sat in his classes to learn more about Krishna consciousness, which made spiritual sense to me.

For years, the Krishna Temple became an awesome place for me to sing and dance, eat, and talk knowledge with the devotees.

I had known that George Harrison, one of my rock idols, was a devoted member of this movement, and had sung songs inspired by it, which enhanced my spiritual curiosity. John Lennon referred to it in two favorite songs of mine: "I Am the Walrus" (satirically), and "Give Peace a Chance." And here I was bathing in the same peaceful vibe. *Hari bol!* (Meaning "chant.")

While I was hanging out at Justin's on one of those early Mission Beach days, a strange man knocked once on our door and came in. "Hi, hi, I'm Richard, what's your name? Are you both from Pennsylvania, too?" He spoke in a way-out voice, but like he'd known us for years. Richard was friends with Justin and was Little Dave's neighbor.

Richard turned out to be a fifty-year-old native San Diegan, who seemed strange, but I liked him. Rather tall, he walked with a sway from side to side, always dressed in long pants, a long-sleeved shirt, and a sombrero to keep the sun off. He believed the unending sunshine was dangerous for the skin, and he always wore a backpack.

Richard knew a lot of things he'd learned from books and videos, but mainly from talking with people. More than I do, Richard *loves* talking with people. So, living in a mecca for worldwide tourists was heaven for Richard.

At Richard's house, with Doug, we would watch videos about Bali, Java, Africa, and—my favorite—India. Richard's passion for traveling fanned my desires to travel to India one day. He said the best time to visit was fall, and that set the stage for my intention: "I am going to visit India in the fall." I had no idea which fall that would be, but I held the dream close to my heart with both hands.

I lived on a dollar a day for food, going to Kono's Café for a boat-dish of potatoes, veggies, and cheese for a buck. That stretched into my breakfast and lunch, then I'd either go to the Krishna Temple for a free meal or over to Bobby's, where he was learning to cook Indian vegetarian dishes. This was a huge step for Bobby, opening his heart in service by cooking for us, and honing his skills as an eventually excellent chef.

I had two alternate options for food. A bag of day-old bagels from the bagel shop where Little Dave worked (I'd pop one in the microwave, then the toaster, for a mini meal to tide me over). Or a five-pound bag of spaghetti. With a little salt and olive oil, it was enough to keep me set for a while, though nowhere near Mom's Sunday best. I became humble—and skinnier—during those first few months.

I continued working for Ken, but the part-time hours weren't enough to maintain my apartment and eat. In late November, I applied for a job at Fresh Blend, a trendy new smoothie shop. Score! This was a terrific job in a clean place, working alongside beautiful girls, making and drinking smoothies at a decent wage.

Over the next several weeks, my life changed in many ways, including my diet. Turning vegetarian was a massive life transformation, though a smooth transition for me. I never missed meat or craved non-vegetarian food after Justin showed me a video of how animals are treated on factory farms. That was all I needed. Everyone around me in San Diego was a vegetarian. Eating vegetarian food, and now drinking healthy smoothies with several shots of wheat grass a day, my body was changing for the better.

As I watched Bobby and Justin practice their breathing yoga and meditation daily, my curiosity to learn more about Indian spirituality with an authentic Indian guru grew. I asked Justin all sorts of questions, just like I'd asked Carolyn Elliott. Justin was fantastic at conveying knowledge. I was secretly envious of his verbal skills and wanted the ability to share things just like he did.

Justin loaned me three mind-blowing self-knowledge books. One was Paramahansa Yogananda's *Autobiography of a Yogi*. Yogananda was a spiritual master from India who came to America in 1920. He was one of the first gurus from India to live and teach in the West for an extended period. The book's inspiring pages held tales of his childhood, spirituality, and his guru. I surprised myself by reading the book in a few short days.

The beautiful ashram where Yogananda wrote *Autobiography of a Yogi* is still nestled in Encinitas, in northern San Diego County. I've enjoyed visiting there sometimes, meditating on the hill, and gazing out at the ocean and sky.

The second book Justin loaned me was *Be Here Now*, by Baba Ram Dass, birth name Richard Alpert, the famous PhD from Harvard, who, along with fellow professor Dr. Timothy Leary, was an early advocate of the psychedelic drug LSD. In 1967, he traveled to India, found his guru, Neem Karoli Baba, had life-changing experiences, and wrote this trippy, knowledgeable book about his improbable journey, finding the spiritual path, and self-knowledge.

Get this, I read this book in one sitting, a first for me. This is a book for those with an inquisitive mind.

The most powerful book was *Sri Sri Ravi Shankar: The Way of Grace* by David Lucas Burge and Gary Boucherle, not to be confused with famous late sitar player associated with George Harrison of the Beatles and father to pop star Norah Jones. Gurudev was Justin and Bobby's guru and founder of the Art of Living Foundation. Based in Bangalore, India, Gurudev travels the world, inspiring millions of people with his ancient wisdom, authentic humor, and boundless compassion.

In Sanskrit, which is the oldest language used in the world today (some say more than ten thousand years old), the word *guru* means one who dispels the darkness. In this book (which can be read online for free at www.srisri.com), I read about the Healing Breath Workshop, various healing experiences from course participants, information about this growing organization, helpful wisdom, and remarkable miracles that happened around this spiritual master from South India.

With each page and every line, I found myself more intrigued, as a strange sense of connection with Gurudev filled my soul. Somehow, I knew this man, this organization. In my heart, I felt a certainty that this new world would take care of my chronic lung disease and give me the spiritual knowledge I had been seeking.

My typical autumn night followed like this: After basketball with Justin, he'd go and do his breathing yoga practice on a big mound of sand on the beach. Bobby came home from work and body boarding to make us a vegetarian dinner, usually from the *Krishna Cookbook* he was currently enjoying.

After dinner, the three of us sat in the living room, listened to R&B and old-school East Coast hip-hop. We talked about our hometowns and how we'd escaped our old lives and small-town culture for new opportunities in picturesque surroundings.

Around nine o'clock, we'd watch one of Gurudev Sri Sri Ravi Shankar's videos and I'd trip out in a whole new fashion, not from alcohol or drugs, but from a new energy of wonderment. Gurudev's look, the way he talked to his audience, and his phenomenal stillness—at times I thought the video was frozen, that's how still and silent he was in between his lines—captivated me.

This was quite a change from the wild partying back home, but I welcomed it. This is what I was really looking for. His talks covered a variety of subjects—love, peace, happiness, ego, awareness, yoga, breathing techniques, meditation, the mind, emotions, selfless service, and more. Each talk interwove this deep knowledge with his simplicity and fine humor.

I loved to contemplate and recite some of his early quotes: "Love is not an emotion, it is your very existence." *Hey, I am* love. *George Harrison was right!*

"The only true security that can be found in world is in the process of giving love." *Okay, I am love and all I have to do is give it away to others to find security and happiness. Cool!*

And there was an exceptional one just for me: "If you follow fun, misery follows; if you follow knowledge, fun follows." *Um, Mr. Gurudev, where were you four years ago when I badly needed this knowledge?*

And finally, one that hit me: "Religion is the banana peel, spirituality is the banana." Gurudev goes on to say that often in this world, people hold so tight to the peel, they can't enjoy the banana.

With his depth and humor, he had summed up the root of so many problems on this wild home we call Earth. I knew during these nightly videos I had stumbled on something very special. How special? I couldn't know—that was the beauty of it all.

On the first Wednesday of every month, an introductory session of the Art of Living course was held at Bill and Lucinda Robertson's beautiful Pacific Beach home. Justin had spoken fondly about this couple and their lovely home. I waited a month to attend this session, and I welcomed it like a cool plunge into the Pacific Ocean.

The ranch-style house was pure Southern California décor, with a splash of India here and there in each room. The sweet pervading smell of incense grabbed my nose, the peaceful beauty of Buddha statues and other gods soothed my eyes, and the serene atmosphere stilled my mind.

Bill and Lucinda had helped start the Art of Living programs in California in the late 1980s and were now the teachers in San Diego. Bill had already been meditating for years, initially teaching Transcendental Meditation (TM), a silent mantra meditation, under Maharishi Mahesh Yogi. TM became popular in the West in the 1960s and '70s. Like many old "TMers" in the late 1980s and early '90s, Bill made the fairly seamless transition to Gurudev and the Art of Living. I later became good friends with a lot of the old TMers.

A native Southern California surfer, Bill was similar to Carolyn Elliott from Keystone, in that they both had that "I'm detached from the harshness of the real world, like the calm surface of a deep pool" look. He spoke distinctly and said "yeah" often.

Lucinda was a graceful angel; light, happy, and compassionate. This beautiful woman sang like a finely tuned harp. Tears filled my eyes and elation rose from deep inside when she sang, that feeling I'd experienced in the Black churches in Paterson, New Jersey.

Bill talked about the nature of the mind, about stress, and about the little-known value of our own breath. His words flowed around me and through me, and I liked that he talked from experience. Most of all, it made complete sense, like pieces of a complex puzzle falling neatly into place. He led us through a guided meditation, which took me deeper than I went in Carolyn's religion class.

Interestingly, while I was experiencing all this with Bill, I heard the regular Art of Living group, which included Bobby and Justin, in another room doing their breathing practices. Strange, unique sounds flowed from that room, and I found them most curious. I also found that I would be able to learn the "healing breath" techniques they were practicing in a class being offered the next month.

After my session, I watched the regular group of dudes and dudettes stroll out of the back room looking refreshed, bright, and happy. Ah, this was the peace and harmony I wanted. This was what I had been searching for.

In the meantime, I basked in my life on the beach more each day, making smoothies for the local health-conscious and trendy crowd, and blasting shots of wheat grass instead of Jäger.

I woke up on Christmas morning with a remarkable feeling. It was my first holiday three thousand miles from home, and the emotion elevator was going up and down, stopping at every floor, from ecstasy to calm reverie. I hit the beach, where the crashing waves were my carols. I walked in awe, enjoying seventy-five-degree sunshine in a pair of shorts. This was my dream.

The phenomenal year of 1996 ended, and I couldn't wait for the new year, especially my upcoming Art of Living course with Bill and Lucinda.

As I lay in bed that night, I looked back over my momentous year. Graduation from Keystone, my year-long dream of moving to San Diego, and three unfathomable months on one of Southern California's most popular and awesome beaches. I closed my eyes in gratitude, prayed to Jesus, and dreamed away.

My first month living on Mission Beach, San Diego, October 1996

CHAPTER SIX

Childhood's End… Then It Began Again

We must take the advice of doctors, but at
the same time, what I am telling you is,
give a chance for miracles to happen.
—Gurudev Sri Sri Ravi Shankar

"Yo, Occhipinti, what are ya, lost?" Bobby called out, as I looked for his cousin, Dave, behind Bobby's apartment. It was Friday, January 3, 1997, the Art of Living course was starting at seven, and I'd planned on walking there with Dave. But Bobby said Dave was already there. Bobby saved me and drove me to the house just in time.

Though only my second time at Bill and Lucinda's house, I felt like I was home. Have you ever walked into a place and known you were in a safe, comfortable place of peace? It had that kind of vibe.

Of the twenty diverse people there, Dave and I were the youngest at nineteen and twenty, respectively.

I found my boundaries from the first time melted away and a sense of belonging began to rise. My uneasiness settled, and my energy increased.

I was in for the ride of my life. First and foremost, I wanted to relieve myself of the decades-old, disastrous breathing hell. I wanted to learn how to breathe again. I also sincerely wanted to learn as much as I could about spirituality and the nature of our existence. I wanted to dive into Gurudev Sri Sri Ravi Shankar's knowledge, and I wanted to evolve. These were the things I had longed for since childhood, though I did not know how to express them in words or thought, or where or when to find them—I just prayed each night, smiled in the daytime, and knew I was being taken care of.

This day I reached an electric rainbow of knowledge I wanted to slide down with my mind fully open, arms stretched, and smile wide. This was my time to shine.

For the next two-and-a-half hours, Bill and Lucinda talked about the secret of the breath and the nature of our minds, and then they taught us a few simple, yet powerful breathing techniques. The first, called *Ujjayi* Breath (or Victory Breath), was one Justin had demonstrated to me back in October. Justin's inhalation lasted so long, coupled with strange Darth Vader–like sounds coming from his throat, it blew me away.

Deep breathing, as you can well imagine, was difficult work for me. My body fought against stretching the old, stiff lung and diaphragm muscles. But I got the basic techniques down. I knew it would take time to get my breathing stronger. These techniques were both physical and spiritual, breathing through the nostrils in various rhythms with the eyes closed. The night ended with a guided meditation and, as with the intro session, I managed to go deep and felt a wonderful presence of peacefulness inside me.

Dave and I headed to Bill and Lucinda's for day two of the four-day course. I was super stoked because this was the day I would learn the much-hyped *Sudarshan Kriya* I'd heard so much about from Justin and Bobby. In Sanskrit, *su* means proper, *darshan* means vision, and *kriya* in this sense is a purifying action.

Bill said, "During this process, you will get a proper vision of your true self."

How cool, I thought.

I welcomed this new adventure like a warm and sunny morning after a long, frigid Pennsylvania winter. We started with yoga and then light but profound knowledge discussions, and finally practiced the *pranayama* breathing techniques from the night before. I nearly bounced where I sat as I anticipated the instruction of Sudarshan Kriya.

This simple, powerful breathing technique was recognized/ created in 1982 by Gurudev Sri Sri Ravi Shankar during ten days of silence in Shimoga, India. For years prior, Gurudev had traveled around the world, giving spiritual talks and teaching yoga and meditation. He found people everywhere voiced the same complaint, "My mind won't allow me to relax and meditate."

In the spirit of helping humans calm their wild minds, increase energy and release unwanted toxins from the body, Gurudev emerged from his period of silence with this unique technique. Millions of diverse folks worldwide, including me, are grateful he did.

Sudarshan Kriya uses the natural rhythms of our breath, harmonizing the body and emotions, releasing strong-rooted stress and tension on a deep, cellular level.

Well, it sounded wild, and that is what it was during my first experience. Who could imagine that a process meant to lead one into peace and tranquility would lead me into a physical train wreck?

As I practiced the breathing, following along with the tape of Gurudev's distinctive voice, my body started to shake, and my chest tightened with an intensity of iron bands crushing my ribs. A knife-sharp pain struck, and tears welled up from deep inside. My old nemesis, asthma, clutched at my throat, constricting the weakened airways deep in my chest. Excruciating pain attacked, like someone poking me with red-hot pitchforks, stabbing over and over in time with my heartbeat. I wanted to scream. Beads of trickling sweat ran down my back.

Is this how Houdini felt locked onstage in a tank full of water, unable to breathe?

When I thought I would pass out from the intense pain, Lucinda, like the angel she is, whispered in my ear, "Relax, be with the sensations, keep breathing."

Her comforting voice felt like the bridge to what happened next. What seemed like dire hours of horrendous, debilitating pain was probably but a few minutes before relief came. Suddenly, I felt this explosion like a wrecking ball blasting through a desolate building back home in Scranton. Like a brick of dynamite exploding through the side of a mountain, making way for a new highway—there was sudden destruction in my chest.

After the explosion, it felt as though ten thousand pounds of bricks lifted off my chest, minimized, humbled into millions of tiny granules of sand and, with my rhythmic breathing, blew away like dust in the wind. In that instance, like the first blinding ray of sunshine breaking through black thunderheads of a heavy storm, like or seeing beloved family members after a long deployment—my tears from pain transformed into tears of joy, relief dampening the neckline of my shirt. Sudarshan Kriya had broken through my asthma.

After the process, I shared my experience with the group. My breathing flowed smoothly as precious air ebbed and flowed in my lungs and I talked in a continuous string of words. As it turned out, other healings and out-of-this-world experiences had taken place and were shared by other participants.

In Gurudev's words, "When the energy is high and when there is love, healing happens automatically."

One more thing happened during my first Sudarshan Kriya, as if this whole experience could get any more astounding. I have never shared with anyone what I'm about to tell you. The thought of writing it now for the world is invigorating.

After the course ended for the day, I was holding my chest, mostly in relief and perhaps in disbelief of all that had happened over the past hour. In one frozen moment under my warm, broad hand, I felt a lump. A medium-sized lump on my left breast, next to the nipple.

Feeling the bulge, I went into shock, a chilling stillness as the word *lump* reverberated in my mind. My immediate and only thought was of my mother—if in fact this was a cancerous tumor, how was I going to tell her?

From childhood until maybe the eighth or ninth grade, Amity Landfill was a mere three blocks away from my home on Lincoln Street. Hundreds of trucks from New Jersey and New York dropped mounds of garbage and waste there.

The Amity Landfill reeked of nauseous fumes constantly, the border streets filthy from the trucks and spillage. The convoy of trucks created an eyesore as they drove up and down Union Street. Empire Landfill opened on the hill nearby after Amity closed. The political powers-that-be took a beautiful local mountain and filled it with garbage.

I remember one humid night being abruptly awakened, gasping for air with a searing, raspy cough in a heart-stopping scare. Chemical and waste fumes floated through my window and the paralyzing gas took no prisoners. I will never forget how frightened and alone I felt. The next morning, I told Mom and the same thing had happened to her. We lived only a couple unprotected blocks away from poisonous Trashtown.

An astounding number of cancer cases sprung up in our neighborhood, more specifically on my block, and unfortunately, in my family. There were three cancer cases on Lincoln Street alone, including my second mother, Aunt Alice.

Aunt Alice was a rock of a lady, filled with humor and sweetness, yet she developed breast cancer and endured radiation treatments. Ultimately, she had an operation on December 6, 2000. I had the good fortune to visit Taylor three weeks after her surgery and stayed with Aunt Alice for a week. Before her passing on May 23, 2017, she would fight cancer again and again.

I thought more about the lump I'd felt and the shock that ensued. But for some reason, I had a peaceful feeling about myself and thoughts of a cancerous lump in my chest were not shredding my sanity. It was as if I were observing the scene from a distance. Before, I would have run to the nearest phone, searching for validation from my mom that cancer, such a vicious disease, couldn't strike another unsuspecting member of our family. Yet inside my soul I knew whatever this was, it was part of this awesome healing experience. I knew I must ride the breaking waves of this massive yet subtle transformation, and I welcomed the experience with open arms and an open mind.

The night passed and on Sunday morning Dave and I walked to the course. Despite my intense experience from the day before, I was excited to learn the second part of Sudarshan Kriya today. No hesitation, I welcomed the balance.

The session flowed much easier. It was enjoyable and full of life. I bounced with joy, along with Gurudev's voice, bubbling with energy, and felt myself breathing and smiling like a child on the first lazy summer morning after school let out. I felt high, yet grounded, happily unbounded, limitless, and content.

On completion of the breathing session, before I opened my eyes, I immediately took my right hand and placed it on my left chest, feeling for the lump. To my complete astonishment, the lump was gone. I moved my fingers. Nothing. Where had it gone? Where had it come from? How had it appeared during one session of Sudarshan Kriya and disappeared after the second?

Did I need answers to any of these questions? No. I remembered what Lucinda said at the beginning of the course: "Turn all your questions into wonder, just like a child—this is enlightenment."

So I wondered away the doubts and eased my mind. I do believe that Sudarshan Kriya brought out the cancerous tumor from inside me from living in Taylor all those years close to highly toxic landfills and washed it away. I have held this belief within me all these years, thinking about it from time to time and being flooded with gratitude.

Along with my healing experiences came the best part, a sense of belonging that grew among the course participants in less than twenty hours. The spirit of this group was special, something I hadn't experienced before. I felt a deep, authentic connection with each and every person on the course. This type of community is what I was looking for.

Strolling on the beach that night, something beautiful happened; actually, it was just a few simple thoughts and a grateful feeling. With a deep smile, I realized two things: Firstly, I knew an aura had returned in me, a naturalness I'd missed since childhood. Secondly, I knew it was going to grow and become better.

I found myself singing a random song as I had as a boy. The little buckaroo crooning "Elvira" and the talented seven-year-old belting out "Billie Jean" followed me along the darkened, magical beach, glad to be back. And I was happy.

My days began with a shower, light yoga, and sitting cross-legged, the best I could, on my old and ripped couch practicing pranayama and Sudarshan Kriya, as the brilliant California sun through my big living room window warmed me.

My experiences during those initial days were deep and genuine. During Sudarshan Kriya, my spirit rose, my body radiated, and my mind stilled. Sweet oxygen saturated my system as the moment stopped. Shackles around my chest weakened and shattered increasingly with each day's practice. I didn't have to *think* about breathing, rather I gulped in deep breaths of the cool, clean air off the Pacific Ocean.

Full of life in my comfortable position, I found myself bouncing lightly like a happy child—and a happy child was exactly what I felt like after the Art of Living course. After a few minutes of this extraordinary breathing, I sat with my eyes closed and a mounting feeling of gratitude. Not only for Gurudev Sri Sri Ravi Shankar and his breathing technique, but also for my teachers, Bill and Lucinda, and of course Justin, but also for my parents who had brought me into this world, where I am able to actually experience that love "… is not an emotion, it's your very existence."

For my mother, whom I've always been close to, I felt a wealth of gratitude for all she has done for me, our family, and my friends over the past twenty years. She is a super-mom.

One thing I realized after practicing Sudarshan Kriya for a week was that I did not know how to express my gratitude for everything this woman had done over the years. I needed to learn how to express my feelings to her. I started writing open-heart letters and mailing them to her, and she realized there was a change in me. I can't imagine what she thought after receiving those first letters. I poured out my childish awe at her support, her love, and what it meant to me in page after page of writing.

Trying to sort and deal with my feelings about Dad was more complex. One day, maybe a week after the course, my roommate Doug was playing his punk music at full volume on my two-speaker Sony system. I didn't prefer the alternative punk style of music, though I didn't hate it. On this day, I yelled at Doug to turn the music down. He did without argument, proceeded into his room, and closed the door. The next thing I did was pop in one of my

Grateful Dead tapes—music Doug didn't like one little bit—and cranked the volume up to ten.

What happened next was revolutionary. I was crushed by a blast of knowledge, a realization, a truth so bold, it not only blew me away, but I found myself soaked in tears with a heavy heart.

I suddenly remembered, back in my religions class at Keystone, when Carolyn had said, "What you hate is what you become."

What you HATE, is what you BECOME. Oh my God. Without knowing, I had become my father. Without knowing, I had taken on the very things I hated about him in my crazy, ignorant youth. How many times growing up would Dad run up the stairs, bang on my bedroom wall, yelling at top pitch, for me to "Lower that noise!" Then he'd turn up his own music on a Peavey PA System, and our midsized white house at 401 Lincoln Street would shake, rattle, and roll.

Now, here I was, just three months removed from that household, pouring this acquired torture on my poor roommate, Doug. I immediately turned off the music, ran over to Justin's, and told him what had happened.

"Oh," he said with a huge smile on his face. "You *are* digging deep and about to get into the hardest and most essential spiritual work on the path of self-knowledge, healing the relationship with your parents."

Justin knew about this crust-breaking process and had been working hard at moving many of his own adolescent mountains. He told me about these often never-ending cycles: Without knowing, a son takes on his father's negative habits, patterns, and shortcomings by hating these things. He then passes these on to his children through the same vicious cycle. It's astonishing how this happens in families and other relationships, too. Hate and fear are strong emotions.

Gurudev says, "Hate and fear are just love standing upside down." He also adds, "What you love is what you become." And, "Where you put your attention is what grows in life."

The next day I called my mom, who I have always been closest with, and tried to tell her of my realization. How do you explain the angst and anger of adolescence that suddenly pops out in a blinding spotlight, taking the darkness away and letting it melt in the sunshine of understanding?

Typical Mom reaction: Out of unswerving love for me, she cared more about me worrying over this situation and told me not to think too much about it.

Thanks, Mom, I love your compassion, but that is not going to help me evolve, I thought to myself. Knowing she couldn't understand me fully on this one, I didn't talk any more about it.

I wanted to share the wonderful healing experiences I felt from the Art of Living course, like millions of others throughout one hundred and fifty-six countries worldwide. People, quite naturally, want to share great news. In brilliant twenty/twenty hindsight, I could have come across with my enthusiasm and excitement more gracefully, with more skill—not! I was twenty, what did I know of expressing something mind-blowing to me in softer, more conservative laymen's terms?

I went to the two women I love most in my life, my mom and sister, like a tsunami of joy. I wanted them to come with me on this new-found spiritual journey. I thought they could benefit from the course and its offerings. How could they not?

Back then, the Art of Living published these nice one-page talks by Gurudev, with his picture at the top. One was called "Are You Tired?" So, like a good boy, I sent both Mom and my sister a copy of the talk plus another one (if one is good, more is better) accompanied with a detailed letter going on and on about my experiences in the course.

"Mayday, mayday—family member overboard!" sounded the pleading family SOS to anyone who would listen and the universe beyond. "Jeremy has fallen into a sea of cult madness led by a peculiar-looking man with a black beard, talking about senseless things. We need our son back ASAP—please help!"

In mere days I received a de-cult letter from dear old Dad. He told me in his straitlaced fashion how, years ago, this idiot Jim Jones convinced hundreds of people from his cult to die in a mass suicide. The paragraphs went on about how I needed to get out of the cult now, before they brainwashed me, and the family lost me forever.

Doug was home when the letter came, and we fell over laughing reading it. This was my beloved whacky family, this is how they were. I couldn't blame them; they didn't know any better. They didn't understand. I smiled in compassion, which I was getting very good at doing those days.

Mom also wrote and called, telling me to, "Get out of the Art of Living and back into reality." I kept smiling, gritting my teeth sometimes, clenching my jaw other times, but smiling.

A few months later, a cult in San Diego (of all places in the *entire* United States, what are the odds?) called Heaven's Gate made headlines. The members decided to take their own lives when some comet or other passed by or something, I didn't watch the news. I innocently came home late from Justin's, and as I walked in the door, Doug was hyperventilating from laugher. "Dude, your family keeps calling. They think you're dead!"

Not one of his words made any sense. I heard the phone's shrill ring. It had to be after 3:00 a.m. on the East Coast. Before I could finish the word "Hello?" into the receiver, my Aunt Alice breathlessly said in complete panic, "Jeremy, are you alive?"

I took a deep breath, smiled, and sang the chorus from the Pearl Jam song, "Alive." She, along with my family, had been glued to the news for hours about this suicidal cult in San Diego.

I understood their concern, realizing they must have had hallucinations of tainted Kool-Aid flashing through their minds, but I felt a bit disrespected. Didn't they know me better than that? In full acceptance of their ignorance, I assured Aunt Alice I was fine and promised to call her and Mom the next day.

I called each of them in the morning, listening to their ranting and raving, then explained again how I was fine, adding, "Never in a million years would I do something so foolish to hurt myself and my family."

In hindsight, I may not have been as loving as I could have been. Again, I was only twenty. I hadn't been sitting and listening to depressing news hour after hour, working myself into a frenzied lather.

It was an interesting event, to say the least. I could see how far I had come on my spiritual path in those several months by witnessing how I handled this wild cult situation and how I might have handled it a year prior. I didn't miss the wild emotions that had ruled my world for nineteen years. I was happy being in charge of them for once. This is the magic of the breath, in concert with self-knowledge. Both working together, letting the wild mind know who is boss, and living from a space of peace and joy, which is our real nature, living free, with appreciation for life.

A few more days after hitting my head against the proverbial brick wall trying to tell Mom and my sister, Michele, of the joy I'd found in the Art of Living course, I heard an impressive and poignant line by Gurudev. He simply said, "You can't change anyone, you can only change yourself, and then be an inspiration for others." A wave of relief washed over me.

With this consciousness came the realization of recognizing other things I didn't like within me, such as judging people and caring what others thought about me. Like peeling away layers of an onion, different attributes came to the surface.

During this time of finding out more about myself, I saw a glimpse of my future. While practicing Sudarshan Kriya one fine day in January, an image became clear. I knew, I felt what I wanted to do in life: I would be a schoolteacher like my sister, but the classroom was filled with younger children, perhaps kindergarteners. I also felt a deep understanding, an urge to dedicate my life to helping others. I didn't have a clue how to do either of these things yet, but I knew, as sure as the eternal tide ebbed and flowed outside, the path would present itself.

The following few weeks after taking the Art of Living course were a roller coaster of healing. Revelations screamed through corkscrews and deep, soul cleansing dives. The clarity that was slowly lighting up what I was meant to do was spiced with family drama.

I was thrilled to find out there were weekly Sudarshan Kriya follow-up sessions at Bill and Lucinda's home. After finishing our breathing, we had something called *satsang*, which means "The company of the truth." People would just come together and sing uplifting songs and talk spiritual knowledge. And it rocked.

Outstanding musicians joined us, from reggae pop to guitars and drums. Quino McWhinney, the lead singer of the popular band

Big Mountain would show up from time to time. I'd been searching my whole life for spiritual sounds, and this is what drove my interest in the various bands I loved. The satsangs with the house rocking, people singing and dancing, swaying in an ocean of oneness and bliss were perfect for me.

To inspire people to sing the response part of each song, Lucinda encouraged us by saying, "When you sing in the chorus, pretend you are leading the song." I took this to heart and started to develop my voice. I had sung as a child and with my headphones on as a teen, but this was different. My favorite was "*Jaya Jaya Shiva Shambho*," a traditional song in Sanskrit. I continued to sing these songs at the weekly satsang, as well as after my morning practice of Sudarshan Kriya; I was in such a sweet space then as a beginner, and it continued to grow in beauty.

And then there was a bump in the road. When a new manager came on board, I lost my job at Fresh Blend, and we got into a couple of heated arguments regarding my work. My childhood upbringing came back to haunt me. In some ways, I was growing personally; in other ways, I remained stuck in old patterns.

Suddenly I was back to square one, without a steady job, needing to eat and pay rent. I fell back into helping Ken and doing odd jobs where I could find them, like handing out flyers for restaurants around the beach.

At the end of January, Bobby and Justin were driving up to Los Angeles for an advanced meditation course in the presence of Gurudev, or Punditji, as we called him back then. *Pundit* means scholar and *ji* is added to names in India to give respect. The same goes for *Sri* at the beginning of the name. Since the man is so cool, I guess they gave him double respect in front of his given name, Ravi Shankar.

Without any cash in hand or a job in sight, I knew there was no chance in hell I could attend. I was excited, however, when I heard Gurudev was giving a public talk just an hour north in Irvine. Dave and I asked our older friend, Patrick, if he would drive us, and he agreed.

On a Saturday night in late January 1997 while the three of us drove up to Irvine, thoughts flitted through my mind like a dozen butterflies. I'd seen his photo, listened to his tapes, and watched the videos. Was I finally going to see this wondrous man in person?

I asked Patrick, who was on his own spiritual path, "How do you know if someone is your guru?"

Without turning his head, he replied, "You'll know by the unmistakable feeling inside."

As I entered the hall at the Marriott Hotel, people shuffled in around me while musicians sang and played cool Sanskrit songs on stage. "*Om Namah Shivaya*" was an ancient Sanskrit phrase I knew from our weekly satsangs at Bill and Lucinda's home. We took our seats near the front, and I observed this remarkable woman strumming an acoustic guitar and belting out powerful verses that others in the crowd would repeat.

I later learned her name was Divya Prabha from Nova Scotia, Canada, one of the first Art of Living teachers in North America. Divya is well known for powerful and beautiful Sanskrit chanting, songs she wrote herself, which are known as *bhajans*, which means "sharing." This label made perfect sense given the simple call and response nature of these songs. And boy, were they powerful.

After two or three songs, the energy in the room shifted like a welcome sea breeze on a hot, humid evening, like the room had turned 180 degrees toward the coolness. The music, like a dramatic soundtrack of good news, kicked into high gear as the audience, filling around a thousand seats in the ballroom, stood to welcome Gurudev walking in from the back of the hall.

I unfolded myself to full height to catch a glimpse of the man, the person whose breathing technique had awakened the sleeping child in me and kicked out demons of pain and anger. In walked the world-renowned humanitarian and spiritual leader, Gurudev Sri Sri Ravi Shankar.

Awestruck barely describes my feelings and emotions when I first saw him, dressed in traditional white Indian clothes, with a black beard, flowing hair, and a smile as resplendent as the sun shining on everyone. What I found most fascinating was the way he floated into the room. Seriously, this is what I saw while being stone-cold sober—Gurudev looked as though he floated across the crowded room. His every movement was graceful and touching to my soul.

As he floated closer, his electric eyes connected with mine and something deep inside rang like the glorious bells of Notre Dame. His stare shook and bounced through me like a host of lightning bolts smashing steel poles in a midsummer Scranton storm. My mind was swept away in his glory; my heart felt full, and my soul sang in those few fleeting seconds.

Gurudev took his seat upon the stage, closed his eyes, and went into what looked like deep meditation. The music continued, and after a song or two, he opened his eyes, smiled at the roomful of people and said, "Hmm... what should I talk about today?"

The audience, one by one, called out various topics such as: love, stress, ego, family, yoga and meditation, fate, business, and religion. He heard the requested topics and for the next hour spoke remarkably on each one. The topics of love, yoga, meditation, and religion resonated with me the most.

His accented words melted over me like gentle warm waves, nudging against me as the topics broke into my spirit. His voice, like I'd heard on the various videos and tapes, came across deep, powerful, and at the same time, funny, light, and easily understood by my chaotic mind. I laughed with the crowd, our responses rolling across the room, when he joked in his unique fashion. This intelligent, intuitive man was funny.

At the end of the talk, Gurudev asked if anyone else had questions. I had no questions about the breathing techniques at this point, but there was one intriguing thing that had been on my mind since October. A couple dudes at the Krishna Temple nagged me often to "Get the beads," that are used for counting the rounds, 108 exactly, while chanting their Hare Krishna mantra. It was much the same idea found in various other religions, such as Catholicism's use of a rosary for prayer.

These past remarkable weeks made me enthusiastic to tell everyone at the temple of my healing experiences and joy after taking the Art of Living course. Everyone remarked, "Jeremy, you're doing good things, now you have to take the final step, get the beads and start chanting Hare Krishna." I only smiled at them and their insistence about these beads.

Gurudev, himself, was wearing a string of traditional beads around his neck. Against the white cloth of his Indian garments, the beads stood out, easily visible from my spot in the room.

So, I went for it and raised my hand high in the air. Gurudev looked at me like I was the only person in the room and asked, "Yes?"

In all innocence I asked, "Do you chant rounds with your beads?"

Picking up the dark strand in his hands he bounced them up and down, smiling in a mischievous silence for maybe five time-stopping seconds. Seriously, it felt like five long forevers before he replied in his signature childlike fashion. "No… I just play with them."

The entire place exploded into laughter while I began to burn—and I mean burn up inside, something hot as all heck and hell. I stood there with my twenty-year-old ego in my hands, an ego which had been built up and, of course, battered, blown up, and brutalized over the years. My eyes glazed over with egotistical pain as everyone, including Gurudev Sri Sri Ravi Shankar, laughed at me! Big old Jeremy the Great, Super Funny Joking Boy—but this time it felt like they were laughing at me, at my expense… and it hurt.

An instant fire seared hot throughout my body. My face felt scorched, hands damp and sweaty as they hung next to my body. I felt like a fool. Anger abounded with a sinister growing frown—I was in a frying pan and Gurudev was the cook. After all the busting and beatings I had taken while being the biggest wiseass in Pennsylvania, this one moment was the lowest I'd ever felt in my life.

During this burning hell, which seemed to last an hour but was mere seconds, the music started. Gurudev stood and placed himself at the front of the stage to meet everyone. The crowd moved and swirled around me, lining up to take his blessings.

Thoughts ping-ponged in my pounding head. "This man is just mean. I am *not* going to practice his breathing technique anymore!" Now, I was punishing myself.

Dave suddenly hit me on the shoulder and said, "Come on, dude, let's go meet him."

In my fury, I spat out, "No way!"

Dave pushed me, edging us into the surging crowd as if he hadn't heard me, and I gave into the mass mentality. The positive energy from these hundreds of smiling people packed in line enveloped me. Then in bad-boy fashion, I snuck right up near the front of the line, yet still had to wait around five minutes as several people were ahead of me.

As my turn approached, I handed my camera to Dave to take pictures. The positive vibrations shattered the anger inside me like direct radiation blasting a cancerous tumor. I found myself waiting, watching, as Gurudev greeted each person with a smile and a hug. Standing there on deck, things seemed surreal, yet beautiful. Shreds of burning anger licked the back of my mind, yet at the same time I wondered about this man I was about to meet and hug.

My turn came and similar to the way I saw Gurudev enter the hall, I simply floated to him like someone had a remote control guiding me, and I fell into his open arms.

What I felt in his arms was like nothing imaginable, like hugging a soft cloud of tremendous love. The feelings of love and comfort were so intense, I burst into tears of joy with an enormous splash of gratitude thrown in. I'd never felt a fraction of this kind of pure, positive emotion before. I was blown away. A lesson beyond all final exams occurred as I stepped out of my fears, my anger, and let myself just be in his presence.

As the embrace ended, he asked me in such a beautifully innocent voice, "Are you happy?"

Was he kidding? I was the new poster boy for overflowing bliss, my face transformed into a glowing never-ending smile. I nodded and whispered, "Yes, I am."

In the middle of this grandiose experience, he gently took me by the arm, turned me around toward the edge of the stage and kindly said, "Sit here."

I don't remember moving to the edge of the stage. I sat there in awe and bliss as he met the next person in line. He'd hug a few people and turn toward me with a wink and a smile, giving me a lot of attention. The love he gave me in those intimate moments felt spectacular and continuous. All I could do was absorb it while Dave took photos.

Sitting on the flat stage, thoughts struck how mere minutes ago Gurudev Sri Sri Ravi Shankar had made me feel as low as I'd ever been with his joking answer to my sincere question. And now I sat right behind him, by his quiet request, perched on the stage, soaring higher than I've ever felt, like king of the world. Without exaggerating, I can say that I felt fantastically happy, sailing on tangible waves of love and joy from this guru from India, this master of yoga, this man beyond description.

How and why was this happening to me? As I watched him hugging multitudes of people facing me, I smiled, closed my eyes, took a deep breath and silently said, "This is my guru."

Now, I am reminded of Buddha's quote: "When the student is ready the teacher will appear."

When Dave, Patrick, and I finally crawled into the car to head home, Patrick asked me, "Well, Jeremy, did you get your answer?"

My face lit up with a Cheshire cat smile in the dark car. I said, "Yes, without a doubt." I leaned back, relaxed, breathing in the warm Southern California air. "After that experience, he is my guru."

*During our first meeting, Gurudev asked me to sit
on the stage in Irvine, CA, January 1997*

Gurudev rejoiced in the music, and I had the biggest smile.

CHAPTER SEVEN

≈◎ ◎≈

Within You, Without You

*Your needs are fully taken care of. You are being
loved very dearly. This reminder softens you; brings
about miracles around you and changes your life!*
—Gurudev Sri Sri Ravi Shankar

Bereft of a full-time job, I was fetching Ken a sundae at Dairy
Queen. This fast-food haven of soft-freeze delights was right
next to his condo. In the glaring sun, I spotted the "help wanted"
sign in the window ten paces away. I asked for the manager and filled
out the application immediately. I was hired quickly and remained
grateful to be working again.

My hours were 10:00 a.m. to 4:00 p.m., six days a week, leaving
me plenty of time for practicing yoga and Sudarshan Kriya in the
morning. A bonus was the fun three-minute skateboard ride up the
boardwalk from my apartment. The perks of the job included, but
were not limited to, serving ice cream to happy beachgoers who came
to the drive-through or the walk-up window, and, of course, all the
ice cream, milkshakes, and banana splits I could eat.

I felt totally blessed to have this job and most grateful to make
$600 a month. When I told my sister, Michele, she asked, "You mean
$600 every two weeks, right?" No, a month. This worked out to three
hundred for rent, a hundred for bills and around seven dollars a day for
food. What more does a young dude on the loose in San Diego need?

Dan, the manager who hired me and son-in-law of the own-
ers, worked with me during the day. His father-in-law, Bill, a retired
Navy guy, came in around one in the afternoon and closed the place

at 10:00 p.m. The only downside was covering Bill's day off every Wednesday, leaving me in charge of closing the shop. This meant I couldn't attend the satsangs at Bill and Lucinda's, and that did punch a bruise in my gratitude.

Dan was the same age as my sister and loved the same great music as me: Grateful Dead, Led Zeppelin, the Rolling Stones. While getting the store ready for customers, we listened to the radio and, sometimes, my Grateful Dead tapes. This Dairy Queen franchise was in an old Wienerschnitzel building (Wienerschnitzel is a popular Southern California fast food chain), shaped like a thin A-frame house with a bright-red roof and a drive-through in the middle. The front side opened for walk-up customers on Mission Beach Drive.

When it was busy, it was kicking. Dan and Bill loved me and quickly made me the assistant manager. I had keys to the building and responsibility. I'd open the store on most days and close it on Wednesday nights. Their praise for my outstanding customer service led to the honor of training new hires, mainly younger cats from Mission Bay High School. My talent for communicating and instructing made me the big man of soft serve.

After a half-hour of yoga and Sudarshan Kriya in the morning, I went to work and unloaded my joy and enthusiasm onto the diverse Dairy Queen ice cream lovers. My euphoric feelings of new energy and sparkling spirit couldn't be blamed on the ingested processed sugar; I knew my morning routines took me to another level in life. I worked at Dairy Queen for a year-and-a-half and loved every day of it.

During my early days at DQ, I read a book written by Maharishi Mahesh Yogi, the enlightened spiritual master Gurudev had studied with in his teens, called *The Bhagavad-Gita Chapters 1–6*. This man brought meditation to the West with his transcendental meditation technique and was the same guru the Beatles studied with in Rishikesh, India, for a month in 1968.

I read passages and listened to discourses at the Krishna Temple on the Hare Krishna version, translated by Srila Prabhupada, the founder of the Krishna Consciousness movement, called *The Bhagavad-Gita As It Is*. The Penguin Classics version, translated by Juan Mascaro, was also one of my textbooks at Keystone College.

The fourth chapter is on karma yoga, or service, and Krishna says, "Offer all your works to me…" Long explanation short, I made an otherwise rudimentary job of making Blizzards and ice cream cones into serving God with each one I made. I thought of God with each frozen confection, bringing my mind totally into the present moment with devotion and dedication. This was an enlightening experience.

I continued a step further by looking into each customer's eyes, working against my negative concepts and fenced-off boundaries to see the common divinity in front of me. Making brief eye contact, validating the customer, and embracing the Art of Living instruction of service was a humbling and intense practice. I dug deep within, getting past that junk piled up in my soul about people from different backgrounds and cultures, people who might look, act, talk, or walk differently from myself.

Day after day, I reversed and erased years of hellish mind-mess which led to judging, hating, and even fighting others who I saw as different from me. It's probable my past aggression stemmed from a football mindset to seek and destroy. I saw differences in the way most men see disgusting rats, beating them back as if stomping and squishing tiny black ants. The tide for me was turning with a new wind of change—rolling on, turning away. I was melting and growing at the same time.

Me, Jeremy—who am I? What am I? Why did I judge others? How would I feel if others judged me by the way I look, talk, or act?

The childhood scab of pain and hurt was coming loose, and questions emerged from somewhere deep inside that couldn't wait to come out. As I handed strangers their chocolate-dipped, soft-serve ice cream cones, I did it with awareness, looking into their eyes briefly, but long enough to learn about myself. I continue this practice, traveling the ongoing road of wisdom, the path of self-knowledge, the path of yoga.

I was a beach bachelor, so decorating the apartment was not a top priority. I did quite well with my simplistic lifestyle. However, nothing brightened up my beach pad like an altar showcasing Gurudev's picture in the center, some photos from our first meeting on either side, a soft glowing candle, and a special gift from Richard—a Sanskrit "Om" symbol. This collage of goodness created an aura of gentle happiness.

I added a picture of Gurudev to the wall by my bed. The first night I hung it up I had a sweet dream where I was protected by an enormous shield of light and beauty, assurance that nothing could ever harm me. The first thing I saw when I woke up was my guru's picture, and I did what he was doing, held my hands against my chest in prayer position and smiled. This photo of him was the same one I saw at Justin's when I first arrived in San Diego. To me, it's the most beautiful picture of him and the most meaningful.

Gurudev recorded several fantastic knowledge series in the early '90s, the *Ashtavakra Gita*, *Patanjali's Yoga Sutras* and the *Bhakti Sutras*. Gurudev called the *Ashtavakra Gita*, "The most beautiful conversation to have ever taken place on Earth." The series included thirty-three videos to be watched in a group, facilitated by an Art of Living teacher. I've enjoyed them several times in a group and transcribed them word for word years later.

The Bhakti Sutras was in audio format on cassette tapes and available for library-style checkout at Bill and Lucinda's house. I took two or three tapes per week and popped them into my yellow Sony Walkman while walking or riding my bike around Mission Bay. Each tape brought me closer to Gurudev and his philosophies. I loved how he conveyed ancient and complex knowledge with simplicity and humor. I adore Gurudev's humor; he jokes and talks with the innocence of a young child.

This study of self-knowledge was the perfect complement to the yoga, deep breathing, and singing I had been practicing since taking the Art of Living course.

Of the new and different experiences in my health and lifestyle, sleeping during regular nighttime dreaming hours was delightful. I slept like a contented baby. Insomnia was gone. It had bolted south for the winter and decided the tropics were too nice to make the dreaded trek back to the healthy and ever-new me. On one level, I recognized this pleasant change, but on another level, I never knew how messed up I had been with a spastic, erratic heart and diseased lungs. I'd been Prince of Sleeplessness, but now the tide was turning. My body was healing progressively.

Gurudev says, "It's the pain, trouble, and hard times which give us our strength and depth in life." He adds, "You can't know and appreciate health unless you have been sick."

Opposites, though they may seem totally unrelated, are, in truth, complementary. This panoramic view of my new, healthier life was made possible by the massive difference from the hell I'd been through. I can now welcome any challenge, as I know by going through it, I will become stronger. The old saying "What doesn't kill you makes you stronger" holds a deeper understanding for me now.

Along with this sense of change I noticed my heart had not gone ballistic or manic for months, the longest I could remember since those nasty, paralyzing spurts began back in ninth grade.

Out of nowhere one day the palpitations revved up like a 1976 Ford Mustang Cobra II at high rpm. Wild Heart was back with a vengeance. Being at work, I was thrown off by the sudden attack but headed to the backroom. I sat down and made peace with my heart. I closed my eyes, took a long, deep breath like the Pacific Ocean's sea breeze rolling over the sand, held my breath for a moment, and as I let it out, I put Wild Heart to bed. He just needed to be cuddled and conquered. This is what two months of deep yogic breathing had taught me. The manic heart strain exists as a genetic weakness in me, but I now have the tools to work through it any time I need the magic of healing.

I wanted to dance like a child again because of this healing, I wanted to freak out, but growing up as a tough guy had stymied that inner freedom without asking. The same old story for billions of people around the world is about ego. "What will others think about me? They will think I am a fool, and I don't want to look like a fool." This insanity had to stop. If I were to follow Jesus's words of becoming a child before I could enter heaven, I knew I had better do something quick. It was high time to dance again.

I absolutely love the Grateful Dead. Maybe I was a roadie for them in a past lifetime, back in the sixties. Having the apartment to myself while Doug was at work, I locked the door, closed the blinds, and popped in my *Live Dead* CD. I cranked my little double-speaker Sony stereo up to ten and danced like a lopsided donkey, drunk on cola. I started to open up after Sudarshan Kriya, melting away layers of thoughts and hesitations.

I danced around the room like a freaked-out madman. I started making weird sounds, opening my mouth for those remaining ego demons to fly out. Those noises must have been heard by my neighbors and could have scared the horns off a bull or the paint off the walls. I wailed, and feelings blazed and bubbled throughout my body with pure ecstasy. These dancing sessions were so exhilarating that when finished, I'd lie down in the corpse yoga pose and just let it all go, witnessing my body vibrating and glowing.

Music would never be the same. I no longer heard the music, I felt it. And it didn't stop with dancing; I started understanding songs with greater perception than I had heard from a young age. Take an old familiar Beatles song, for example. While working at Dairy Queen, I heard one I'd listened to hundreds of times, "Across the Universe." I always thought the first line of the chorus John Lennon was singing went, "A cruel day, oh…" But that day I heard what he was really singing "*Jai Guru Deva Om…*" Holy smokes! I was shocked, stunned, and blown right away.

I listen to the second and third verses attentively, and those words spoke to me as though Gurudev himself spoke to me personally. The Sanskrit words *Jai Guru Dev* is the main slogan in the Art of Living, which Gurudev defines as "Victory to the Big Mind."

He adds, "So many times your small mind wins over the Big Mind. Anger, jealousy, fear, hate, and other emotions take control over us. When we say, '*Jai Guru Dev!*' this means the Big Mind wins."

Since taking the Art of Living course, I'd wanted to learn how to meditate to complement my daily practice of Sudarshan Kriya. I kept asking Bill and Lucinda when the next Sahaj Samadhi meditation course was. *Sahaj Samadhi* is the Art of Living's mantra-based meditation technique. Using a Sanskrit mantra or sacred word, this practice leads you to deep-space centeredness.

One day in early May 1997 after I again asked Lucinda about the course, she looked at me with love and said, "You really want to learn how to meditate, don't you?"

I grinned from ear to ear.

A few days later she arranged a course with another Art of Living teacher from San Diego named Tom Johnson. Tom was another TMer and told a story of being in an advanced meditation course on a beach in France in the late '60s with Maharishi Mahesh Yogi. I loved Tom from the moment I met him. He was cool, light, funny, and always smiling.

On a perfect Pacific Beach day in May, I walked up to Bill and Lucinda's, ecstatic about learning to meditate. Loud, annoying construction across the street from their house caused doubts as to how I could meditate with shrill, noisy machinery polluting the atmosphere. But as Tom guided me into my first meditation, lightly instructing and giving me a personal Sanskrit mantra, something magical happened. Moment by moment, breath by breath, I dove deep inside the heart region of my body. The deeper I went, the lower and softer the construction noise became. Within minutes, the noise transformed into something reminiscent of classical flute music as I drifted away to a sweet space.

After twenty minutes of utter silent bliss, Tom brought me back to planet Earth and its most beautiful surroundings. I told him about my experience, and he said, "Welcome to the world of meditation. Enjoy."

I used the technique as suggested, right after Sudarshan Kriya in the morning and after work in the late afternoon/early evening, twenty minutes each time. Inside I was becoming quieter and more centered, but this didn't equate to near-perfect harmony outside.

Back at the home front, exchanges between Doug and me fizzled down to a few mere words a day. I felt bad about the situation but had zero communication skills to fix it—or was too lazy, it's hard to tell. I wanted to tell Doug how I felt and suggest we part ways as roommates, i.e., a nice way of asking if he would move out so Dave could move in. The fallout was a lowlight of my life at the time.

I left a note for Doug, trying to explain as best I could. After reading it he kicked my ass with one of his one-line masterpieces in answer, "Your vision of heaven put me through hell."

Ouch, that hurt. I felt it was mostly my fault things had become so strained. When I'd let go of partying, Doug had found his own set of party friends. I accumulated a set of friends who understood how greedy I was for a spiritual home. If Dave moved in, we'd be on the same path. Doug and I talked after the letter, and he agreed it was best if he found a new place. Dave moved in that June.

Living in California enabled me to see Gurudev twice a year. That summer, a bunch of us took a road trip up to L.A. to see him again, my second time in seven months. The event was held in a nondenominational church, a spiritual place created for a wide variety of different beliefs. I felt a noticeable aura in this church, different from many of the ones I grew up attending. Being in a holy place of worship where people practiced meditation and chanting, I felt the place had a natural buzz, unlike the crowded banquet room where I first met Gurudev.

The Art of Living musicians, led by the incomparable Divya Prabha, were in full vibrant force. Having more background and experience with Sanskrit songs, I rocked away with the beat.

Listening to Gurudev in person was refreshing, mesmerizing, especially now that my life felt saturated from listening to his tapes and practicing the breathing techniques daily for seven months. When my turn came to meet him, I was enveloped in a wave of gratitude, like a boy lost on a dark, frozen street suddenly bestowed with many wonderful gifts and love. All that anger I felt moments before the first time meeting Gurudev was long in the past. In my Grateful Dead tour shirt with my hair tied up in a ponytail, I hugged Gurudev in one of the sweetest moments of my life.

I didn't spend that summer entirely in San Diego. I could not have been more excited when Josh Bigelsen invited me on a road trip to Shoreline Amphitheatre in Mountain View, California, in the heart of Silicon Valley, to see the band Phish on July 31st. Shoreline was *the* Grateful Dead's outside-home venue. Five of us packed in one of the family's BMWs and headed toward the San Francisco Bay Area.

Close to the venue, I spotted the street sign that read "Jerry Garcia Blvd." The late Garcia's birthday would have been the next day, so Trey Anastasio, singer and guitarist for the band, played the familiar Happy Birthday riff in the middle of their last jam in the second set. I believe this was the first time I cried at a concert, but definitely not the last. He saluted Jerry and the crowd, thanking us for keeping Jerry's spirit alive. Was it only two years ago Mom woke me up out of a deep sleep with the shocking news of his death? And here I was celebrating his legacy with thousands of other music fans.

After Labor Day, the unofficial end of summer in America, the beach returned to a normal pace. The chaotic crowds of summer tourists faded into a distant memory. The weekends stayed busy year round, but weekdays were more peaceful, roomier and enjoyable.

One Saturday at the beginning of September, as I walked along the ocean, I noticed a beautiful blonde, like a spectacular mermaid, rolling around in the shallow water. Wearing a one-piece swimsuit, she had a smile as gigantic as the sun, and her innocence came across the sand in waves.

With a smile I asked, "The water's warm today, isn't it?"

"Yes, it is," replied what was surely not a mermaid, but a most beautiful, blue-eyed princess holding court on the sand, bewitching my mind and soul.

"My name is Jeremy; I live right over there." I pointed behind us to my building. "What's your name?"

"Pam," sounded the one-word note, as if from heaven, like an ocean of its own, throwing waves on my mind and raining hailstones on my soul. "I'm from Flagstaff, Arizona."

I jumped in the water like any decent young male, splashing around with her, talking about life, living on the beach, and of course, music. Her innocence struck me like a mountain avalanche force. It felt like we were made for each other, and all I had to do in life was make her smile.

Our first date was a boat ride with her sister, a professional snowboarder, and some of their trendy friends. Afterward, we walked around Mission Bay under the San Diego stars and a California moon. We talked about yoga and meditation, and she knew of the self-knowledge I shared without having a guru to impart it. She shared my views and we talked openly about various topics. Service in life? Check. Compassion for all? Check. Yoga, deep breathing, and meditation? She was open to it. Singing yoga? You betcha!

I developed an awesome crush on her, and we hung out most days.

Late one night, I paced in my room, contemplating a way to profess my feelings for Pam. How did I say she was remarkably splendid, and I liked her more than as a friend? I fell into bed, exhausted, without an answer.

During my morning Sudarshan Kriya, something hit like an orca whale breeching out of Northwest waters, like a storm of goodness pelting drops of glory on my mind—it was a poem for Pam, my very first one. Looking back, it was a simple poem, I'll admit, cheesy with rhyming lines like, "Flower in full bloom, take away the world's gloom."

My next problem was how to give this sonnet to her. Painstakingly, in my best handwriting, which took a ton of sweat-breaking effort as I have always been challenged in penmanship, I wrote it down. Putting it in an envelope, I slid her favorite lollipop inside, too.

Before I could lose my love-blind confidence, I walked a block over to where Pam worked as a waitress in a seafood restaurant and handed her the envelope. My hands were shaking like a lamb against the ropes in a lion's den. I told her to open it later and said goodbye. Smooth, romantic mission accomplished.

I don't remember walking home. The rest of the night was spent on pins and needles driving myself nuts on the inevitable seesaw, asking myself, *Should I have given it to her? Will she like it? Will she think I am a weirdo, or fall in love with me and let me be her prince?*

Pam didn't call after her shift, leading to more mind chaos during the endless, dark night.

As I left for work in the morning, I found an envelope with my name on it underneath the door. Pam had written a two-sided letter thanking me for the beautiful poem and letting me know she had just come out of a hard relationship. She asked if we could remain friends. Overjoyed that she liked the poem *and* was okay with being friends, my work shift flew by.

For anyone who knows my "Go Big" style, they'd tell you that was not my last poem for Pam. I kept hanging out with her and writing poems about this incredible transplant from Flagstaff. I learned how she needed help and support at this time in her life, and my poems evolved. I used the self-knowledge from Gurudev and applied those thoughts and emotions into wonderful prose, raising Pam's spirits and cultivating a newfound creativity and expression outlet.

Two months later, the phone rang late at night. It was Pam, wondering how I felt about her. Was she kidding? I told her to reread the first poem. She hesitantly told me she really liked me, and I told her to hang up and come over before she changed her mind.

Ah, the joy of an all-nighter between a lovely woman and love-struck boy can be summed up with two lines from the chorus of Sir Elton John's "I Guess That's Why They Call It the Blues." What a song—what a night.

Our romance sparkled and flowed like daybreak on the beach of a perfect summer day. But all too soon Pam broke the news she was going back to Arizona to be with her family. I accepted this—I'm a cavalier kind of guy—and bid her goodbye. I knew how sweet life could be with a spectacular girl, and I felt confident she and I would rise in love again sometime soon.

Pam did make it back to San Diego for one night, months later, jumping out from behind the door in my apartment in a surprise moment set up by Pam and my brother. Trust me, I don't think I've ever been that surprised in my life. We talked that night and assessed how we'd changed since we first met. With an extended hug, we said our goodbyes. After the visit, I knew Pam and I were not meant to be. I am most grateful for the gift of poetry she inspired, a talent I'd later take around the world.

Toward the end of the year a thought hit me on the back of the head like a ton of bricks. I hadn't been sick in the past year, not once since taking the Art of Living course. Beyond the successful ability to breathe again, my heart dancing in perfect rhythm, plus sleeping like a baby—like I did when, you know, I was a baby—I had no sniffles, cough, colds, sore throats, headaches, flu, nothing. Common ailments that had plagued my life for years didn't exist as each day I felt healthier and happier. I could get used to this easy breathing, meditative, and vegetarian lifestyle.

After enjoying a festive Thanksgiving feast at the Krishna Temple, my sister, Michele, called and wished me a happy holiday. She dove right into an invitation to visit Atlanta for Christmas—a two-week stay at her new house with round-trip airfare included. Awesome. However, in the next breath she revealed Mom and Dad were driving to Atlanta for the celebration.

My brain almost exploded with mixed emotions about this trip. G-force pressed against my damp forehead. On the high side of the extreme roller coaster, I wanted to show my family how much I'd grown, more specifically how the Art of Living had totally changed me. On the straight-down elevator drop, I was nervous about seeing my parents.

Would I be able to open my heart to them, declare how I felt, how much I loved them, and my gratitude for having them as my parents? Or would I completely freeze up in fear and let old patterns of avoidance prevail?

The days passed in an extreme teeter-totter effect. *I can do this. What am I thinking? It's too soon! No, I can do this.* Turbo thoughts kept the back and forth going as I packed, then boarded the plane, my second flight ever.

Being my new self around Michele was easy. She watched me practice my breathing and meditation every day with zero problems cooking vegetarian food for me. I shared stories and information plus an article from the *Yoga Journal* on love and gratitude.

As Mom and Dad pulled into Michele's driveway, we went out to greet them. Mom, with tears in her eyes, hugged and kissed me, her over-eager youngest and formerly prodigal son wanting to share volumes of self-knowledge.

Dad, acting a little unnatural with a strained cheerfulness, said, "Look, Jeremy, this is my new car." My expectations and stomach smacked the ground hard, forcing me to drag myself into the house. It was going to be incredibly daunting to express all I'd realized to Dad.

The rest of my vacation continued in plastic-coated fakeness around my parents. Discussing sports and the weather aren't bad things, but it was not the heart level I wanted of promoting emotional growth. At no time day or night was I close to telling Dad how I felt, how I wanted to heal the relationship between us, and that I loved him.

But there was one memorable moment during the visit, and it actually came from him. My brother, Jeff, after hearing stories about my life in California, asked if he could move West in January and live with me.

While around the kitchen table, eating our last meal together, Dad mustered up every ounce of love and guts he had, looked me straight in the eye, and said, "Jeremy, you look great—I am very proud of you. Please help Jeff when he moves out there; help him stop drinking and smoking." Those brief words echoed Dad's sincere and courageous acknowledgment about my personal growth, however he saw it in me.

A few hours later I flew back to San Diego, my comfort zone. Maybe I'd do better next time.

Jeff and our good friend, Don Hart, drove cross-country to San Diego a few weeks later. Don was over for a week, enjoying the frantic and festive Super Bowl activities around San Diego. Oh, yes, the biggest game of the football season was happening only fifteen minutes away from my apartment.

I'd stopped watching TV and used mine as a nice piece of furniture to hold my Sony stereo system. Television is a huge pacifier, dulling your senses from dealing with your mind. When I walked down the boardwalk, looking into gorgeous beach homes, I couldn't believe how many homeowners were perched on the couch, glued to the tube, with the most beautiful panoramic view of the Pacific Ocean outside their windows.

These two fresh souls from Taylor were ready to crank up the volume that Super Bowl Sunday. I'd lost my obsessive interest in professional sports, another major shift in my life. After a long day at work where I hadn't had time for my breathing yoga practice, I chose to go into the bedroom to do my breathing instead of watching one of the finest finishes in Super Bowl history with them in the living room. I'll never forget the scandalized look on Donny's face.

The two guys wanted to drive up to Los Angeles, L.A., or "Hell-A" as the local San Diegans called it. They had never been there and were stoked for the road trip to the home of Hollywood, Hanks, Madonna, Michael, Malibu, and more. The serendipity of the moment: Gurudev Sri Sri Ravi Shankar was giving a public talk at a Los Angeles hotel, similar to last year's event in Irvine. Dave was on board for the L.A. trip, too.

Excitement was an understatement to describe my emotions about a road trip to L.A. with my brother, two best friends, *and* for seeing Gurudev for the third time in one year.

While the four of us walked along Hollywood Boulevard in the afternoon, we were handed tickets for a famous television show, *Politically Incorrect* with Bill Maher. What a trip, guys from Taylor sitting in a studio audience with camera crews and celebrities in front of us. Bill Maher was genuinely funny, and his jokes made us all laugh. I am still a big fan of his comedy and current television show, *Real Time with Bill Maher*.

Night came, and as expected, Jeff and Don dropped Dave and me off at Gurudev's talk and continued cruising around Tinsel Town.

I walked into the packed ballroom like Dorothy stepping out of black-and-white Kansas into the brilliant colors and songs of Oz. Music was blaring and Divya Prabha was singing her heart out, the masses singing along. The place buzzed. I felt positively high.

As the music kicked into a higher gear, the crowd rose like a gigantic wave from their seats. Gurudev, decked out in his signature whites, bright smile shining upon us, floated into the room like his feet didn't touch the ground, again. I was overwhelmed with the feeling of spiritual déjà vu.

Gurudev took his seat, closed his eyes, and slipped into deep meditation. The music continued, and I was singing, swaying, clapping in musical heaven. The moment he opened his eyes, it was like the room filled with neon colors and the energy transformed to a peaceful calm. Then it was time for questions.

The best question of the night came from a little girl, probably four or five years old, dressed up in fluffy finery in the front row. "Sri Sri," she called out with sweet innocence. "Is there such a thing as too much love?"

Giggles trickled around the audience like spring rain for this touching question. "Yes, that's you!" replied Gurudev, with the same smile I remembered when he'd answered my question a year ago. The place exploded in applause and laughter.

The night dissolved in a blur of positive energy and unbreakable calm. Soon it was time to meet Gurudev. This process is called *darshan* in Sanskrit, and it means "vision." Standing in line with Dave to meet and hug this vast ball of love, I couldn't help but remember the love and attention he gave me during our first two meetings.

As the person in front of me hugged him and walked away in tears, I took a deep breath, and as I hugged him, it was like melting into infinity, like I was growing humongous and at the same time shrinking into nothingness. I had left reality, happy, blessed, and blissed out. I had received the divine darshan of my guru once again.

Gurudev says, "In the presence of a *satguru*, knowledge flourishes; sorrow diminishes; without any reason, joy wells up; lack diminishes; abundance dawns; all talents manifest. To the degree you feel connected to your guru, these qualities manifest in your life." There was no doubt my connection was strong, and there was no mistaking my immense joy. During each of these three satsangs with Gurudev, my soul was lifted to unexplainable heights and glory.

There was no tangible reason to be this happy, no one gave me a million bucks, and no virgin princess was coming to sweep me away—I was simply happy. When Dave and I walked by our teacher Lucinda, sitting in the front row, she commented on how we looked and acted, saying, "Look at you two, you're all blissed out." In a seamless fashion, just as Gurudev had entered the room, I floated out of the hotel to where Jeff and Donny waited.

While sitting in the back seat of my brother's car, I thought to myself, *If this blockbuster, animated feeling is any indication of how beautifully incredible my life is going to be with an enlightened spiritual master, then I couldn't ask for anything more.*

As happy as a puppy playing with an old sock,
Pacific Beach, CA, October 1997

In line to hug Gurudev for the second time in six months in Los Angeles, CA, July 1997

The warm embrace of endless love.

106

CHAPTER EIGHT

The Tide Is Turning

*If we get into the habit of relaxing and meditating
just for a few minutes in the morning as well as in the
evening with this feeling, then we find that miracles
begin to happen, and keep happening. This is what
I wanted to tell you. This is what I call faith.*
—Gurudev Sri Sri Ravi Shankar

During the winter of 1998, new neighbors moved into the building next door, girls from the UC San Diego. Initially I said hello now and then, but nothing more. In April, however, I started hanging out there, getting to know an international student from Cyprus named Maria.

Maria was a beauty, an ocean of love with big dark eyes, another super sweet girl in my world. She spoke softly and laughed at my jokes. In the first week, I opened my heart, telling about my past relationship with Pam.

"Why don't you talk about Pam anymore, Jeremy?" asked Maria, about a week later.

"I'm letting it go, I guess." Well, that was a load of bull said with a straight face. In reality, I found myself falling for Maria with stanzas of poems galore in my crazy mind for those electric eyes and her sweet-soft smile. I began this major crush on her with a fresh batch of awesome poems flowing effortlessly from me.

We were total opposites: I, loud, outgoing, and a big guy, and her, quiet, shy, and more than half my size. We hung out every day at her place, on the beach, or sometimes on top of the seawall watching beautiful California sunsets.

One Sunday in May, Maria and I sat in the sand, our backs against the sun-warmed seawall while she bent her head over her studies, and I wrote two brilliant poems. The first was for Maria called "One Time Once Upon," and the first lines flowed:

> *I spend the days and catch some rays,*
> *with her out on the sand;*
> *she reads her text and says, "What's next,*
> *I found the Holy Land…"*

A most magical poem that would later find a grand place of honor in my ever-evolving creative world.

The second was inspired by my mother and her devotional love for me and those around her. Mother's Day was quickly approaching. I wanted to express my love and gratitude to my mother. Last year I'd cracked the shell around my heart, pouring my feelings out in letters. This felt different, though, more spiritual. With emotions bubbling inside like a fountain of joyful kids, I took my favorite blue ballpoint pen to the off-white paper of my jubilant poem book and wrote a *five page* poem for my mother. The words, the meter, flowed unbidden. I called it "My First Love."

I felt continually surprised at how creativity, happiness, and gratitude overflowed from me in various ways. It had been almost a year-and-a-half since the Art of Living course. I was young on the spiritual path, a walk-on rookie, a white belt in karate. Though I had learned a lot in a short time and saw noticeable progress, I kept half a glance toward the future, where I knew more was waiting.

Signed, sealed, and mailed, I gave four working days for the old Pony Express service to get my poem back home to Taylor. Two days after mailing the letter, I made a routine call to Mom.

"Jeremy…" Mom said, obviously crying.

Immediately my heart pounded from zero to sixty and I went on familial alert. "What's the matter? Is Aunt Alice okay?"

"Jeremy," she said, still crying. Her tears were breaking my heart. What had happened to make her cry? "I don't know what you are doing out there on the beach, but whatever it is, it's beautiful."

What the hell is she talking about? I thought to myself. I almost missed her next words.

"Jeremy, I got your poem, and I just finished reading the first page. It is the most beautiful thing I have ever read in my life. Thank you so much for this gift I will never forget."

I froze with the phone against my ear. "Uh, okay, uh, please continue reading it," I stuttered. "I'll call you on Mother's Day." I abruptly ended the call, my mind on hold.

How did my poem get across the country in less than two days? Who knows? Hearing her tears probably shocked me as much as the poem astonished her. I called back two days later on Mother's Day, and we shared a nice long heart-to-heart talk, another landmark on this spiritual path for me.

As the calendar turned its page to June, I was riding a bus up Garnet Avenue with my poetry book in tow when a thought arose: *Well, I wrote a poem for Mom for Mother's Day, what about a poem for Dad for Father's Day?*

And that was all my muse needed. Lines set in rhythm like a Bob Dylan song soared through me in record time, and my pen scribbled across the paper. I put down in words which I could not express in person or on the phone. Words describing how I felt about my father, mistakes I'd made in the past, and most importantly, how much I loved him.

The poem flowed naturally—this was the most powerfully beautiful poem I'd written.

When I finished, though, the hardest thing in the world was sending it. With a burst of courage and the relieved realization that I was three thousand miles away from home, I folded and packed it in an envelope, licked the thirty-three-cent stamp, and sent it off.

On Father's Day, I stared at the phone for an endless moment. My heart pounded as I reached to pick up the receiver. I dialed the familiar numbers, my mind a blank slate, not knowing what would happen next. My heart was beating faster, but not in chaotic, crazy rhythm, just a solid beat as I reached across the universe.

Hearing my mother's voice gave me great relief. I didn't know what I would have said if Dad had answered. My voice trembled slightly as I said, "Hello, Mom."

"Jeremy, I'm telling you, I can't believe it."

"What?" The word came out in three syllables as a billion thoughts bombarded my mind.

"I knew what was in that envelope the minute I saw it. I knew you wrote another beautiful poem. And let me tell you, I have been married to that man for thirty-seven years and I have never seen him shed one tear. But you won't believe this, when he read your poem, he started crying. Jeremy, I don't know what you're doing out there, but it is wonderful. Here he comes now. John, Jeremy is on the phone."

The world stopped as I tried to soak in my mother's words, the tone of her voice, and her explanation of how touched he'd been with my poem. Tears! My written words had created tears in my father's eyes.

There was a moment of silence as she passed the phone. "Jeremy, how are you?"

"Good. Happy Father's Day, Dad." I felt dazed, stunned.

"Jeremy, thank you for the beautiful poem, it was very nice."

"Oh, yeah, that was nothing, really, my pleasure." *Why am I playing it off like it meant little to me?* I wanted to smack my forehead with the receiver.

The brief conversation in Dad's rushed fashion was perfect to break our discomfort. "Okay, Jeremy, thanks again, talk to you soon. I love you. Here's your mother."

I let go a long breath. What a moment. I'd begun to heal the relationship with my father. Relief filled my soul, though I knew tougher work lay ahead, hard emotional work of talking face to face with the man and letting years of junk, frustration, and anger roll away like morning dew.

Just Like You

It's in my voice, but not by choice, I hear it all the time
And it's in my face and how I keep my place
and most definitely in my eagerness to rhyme
For years I was wrong, in the way I sang my song
And the fact, I never knew
How similar we really are, and in life,
the apple doesn't fall too far, and
that I'm actually, just like you
When I was young, I lived my life too fast
And the time flew past, and I really never grew
So now I've slowed it down, and
I've finally come around,
to see I'm just like you
These days the knowledge flows, and
in quick form, the ignorance goes,
away, as I find a clue
And here I sit and listen to the sound, in
my heart, for I know I've found...
that I've always been just like you

Earlier, I'd found out my sister was getting married in Atlanta on July 11, 1998. Now that's my sister, making her wedding date easy to remember, seven/eleven. Is that good luck, Las Vegas style?

I planned on going back to Taylor for a short visit, then driving to Atlanta with my mother, father, and Aunt Alice. What better chance to get in a lot of talking time with Dad than on a family road trip?

During the spring months I started seriously getting in shape in anticipation of going home for the first time in almost two years. I would be toned, tanned, and legal to drive.

That's right; I finally went down to the Department of Motor Vehicles and got my driver's license.

I felt as nervous as I was excited, anxious going back to my childhood hometown, yet knowing it probably hadn't changed in the time I had gone through the remarkable, perpetual transformation chamber of yoga and Gurudev. I couldn't wait to show everyone, *See, I did it. I made my dream happen. Here I am with a brand-new perspective on life.*

A few days after my twenty-second birthday I boarded a jet, a crystal-blue sky overhead, flying back to Taylor, jumpy, but calm. Being home on Lincoln Street was a trip: hanging out with old friends, eating great food, and walking around with my shirt off, flaunting my tan and toned beach body.

Mom couldn't wait for me to come home, and I surprised her by arriving a day early. She loved how the phone rang off the hook like it did while I was growing up. Home is where the fridge is always full of food and the living room filled with friends. How totally awesome was practicing yoga, Sudarshan Kriya, and meditation in the bedroom where I grew up?

Driving down to Atlanta with my parents and Aunt Alice, I sat in the front for one leg of the trip, less than two feet from Dad while he drove. I found myself taking cleansing breaths. The miles stretched out before us, and I prayed the time would present itself to talk to him. The endless minutes clicked by and the pavement passed in a gray asphalt blur as I waited with pins and needles for him to bring up the poem. Finally, he did.

"Jeremy, I loved the poem you wrote for me. I even made it into a song."

My brain exploded in a kaleidoscope of color. He'd made my poem into a song? He'd read the lines over and over, hearing notes and chords from *my* words?

"I have to admit after reading it, I even cried."

A wave of warmth calmed my fears. We talked, and I felt a heavy burden lift off my chest. It wasn't as bad as I thought it would be, this ride and conversation, starting the uphill climb in the relationship with my father.

We continued to talk about what it was like living on the beach in San Diego, and now, being roommates with my brother after several years. I also shared what it was like having the Super Bowl in my city and how I attended a San Diego Padres baseball game. Dad told me about his job, music, and his hobby talking on the Ham Radio. Though I didn't share anything about my spiritual experiences, it was healing to be able to communicate with Dad in a relaxed and fulfilling way.

When I returned to San Diego later that summer, Dad sent me a tape of the song he wrote from my poem, his voice reverberating back my words in sharps and flats. Could my life get any more miraculous, fun, and fantastic?

It was then that I recalled one of Gurudev's talks: "Yes, love is also a gift, so when it comes, feel grateful, and when it is not there, feel the longing for it. That is when prayer will arise out of you; poems will arise out of it. Poems come not only when there is love, but when longing is there, poems come, prayers will happen, and many miracles can also happen, so enjoy them."

In mid-July, my old roommate Doug stopped by the Dairy Queen, and we walked for a long stretch on the beach. It seemed like old times. We got along well. He told me of his spiritual path, and I shared mine. We joked and laughed while walking, and I felt at peace, happy with the situation. He still lived in Pacific Beach, and we bumped into each other from time to time. It was great to reconnect and mend our relationship. I apologized for my inappropriate behavior that might have hurt him.

July 1998 never seemed to end. Jeff and I took our long-awaited road trip up the coast of California to the San Francisco Bay Area. The plan included attending two concerts of The Other Ones, the latest incarnation of the Grateful Dead. Not one, but two, for the Occhipinti brothers, twice the exposure and phenomenal joy. The venue was at Shoreline Amphitheatre where I'd seen Phish the year before.

As you've probably figured out, for me rock concerts are life-changing; they are hours of incredibly intense sensations, surrounded by thousands of people in the moment. During one of their most famous songs, "Scarlet Begonias," in the first set of the first show, something mystical happened.

Steve Kimock, one of the lead guitarists, soared a solo over the jam for long-elastic minutes, when all of a sudden, I lifted from the ground, or it felt like it, easily two full feet above the grass. Not just floating as I'd felt in Gurudev's presence, but lifted, soaring. My mind was blown away like a skydiver taking his first jump above planet Earth.

After the solo, my out-of-this world experience brought me back to earth. I looked over at my brother, and we both said, "Holy shit!" Our words tumbled into one another; we couldn't get our next words out fast enough. Jeff had experienced the same indescribable, airborne, lifting experience; we'd both felt zero-gravity happening. I had no explanation for this, nor did I want one. It was beautiful and real. Life was incredibly awesome.

CHAPTER NINE

Playing in the Band—Yes, I Am

You can't take anything for granted. Every moment
there is a miracle happening; every moment,
there is grace; and there is something new.
—Gurudev Sri Sri Ravi Shankar

During the summer of 1998, my personal muse arrived and laughed her way into my heart forever. I believed it to be a product of practicing Sudarshan Kriya and meditation daily. I continued writing poems, inspired by life's boundless beauty.

It was a typical summer sunset on the crowded, narrow boardwalk in Mission Beach. I was weaving in and out, skateboarding through locals and tourists—and you *could* tell them apart—when I heard my first full-blown song in my head. Seriously, both music and lyrics for the first verse and chorus came to me while I balanced on my board, like catching a thread of gold in the wind. My own song!

Not one of the nameless faces I passed knew what had just happened. I kept my cool on the boardwalk, gazing at the spectacular paradise of sun and sea around me.

The first verse burst into my mind like this:

Sometimes they're different or that's just how it seems
Sometimes they hang around, just hangin' on their dreams
By now I see my light, I see it shinin' everyday,
by now you see it bright oh, won't ya come my way...
won't ya come my way

I called the song "Walk the Line." I needed a hotshot guitar player to help me write songs and fulfill my lifelong dream of being a music man. I did not play an instrument yet, though I knew deep inside me that my first song could be the start of something wonderful.

During this fantastic year of traveling and personal growth, I worked with a lady named Mary at Dairy Queen. Every day, I shared my poems with her, which I kept in a book. Once creativity came calling, it never backed off. I read her stanzas and lines, a trusted listener of what came from my heart.

She'd constantly say, "Jeremy, you need to meet my husband, Chris. He plays guitar really well and writes songs but has no lyrics."

Time and again she'd nudge me about meeting her husband after one of my readings, but weeks flew by, and I didn't take her offers seriously—though I don't know why. My summer was booked. I was traveling to the East Coast for my sister's wedding and had more traveling adventures lined up with my brother as well.

One Sunday at the end of August, I'd finished Sudarshan Kriya and meditation when the strongest urge grabbed hold of me with both hands, telling me to call Mary. You know the kind where you're encouraged, almost commanded, to listen to your gut feeling? This instinct was yelling for my attention. It wasn't an invisible memo to call Mary, but to talk with her husband, Chris, and how we needed to meet right now, this minute. I couldn't wait any longer to make music with someone. It was like a spigot of desire had turned on at full force.

I grabbed my phone book and was flipping through the tightly filled pages looking for her number when the phone rang. I stared at it for a split second, holding my breath, before picking it up.

An unfamiliar male voice asked, "Jeremy? This might seem strange, but my name is Chris, Mary's husband. Are you busy? I wanted to see if you were free today to play some music."

I couldn't believe it. This wasn't a Hollywood movie; this was real life. I stared at the base of the phone.

"Chris, I was just looking for Mary's number. I had this tremendous force come over me after meditation that we had to meet today! Please come over right now. I live on the beach at the end of Santa Rita Place in Mission Beach." I felt lightheaded, like an overdose of

116

oxygen had come through the receiver still in my hand. The room looked brighter, more detailed than thirty seconds ago.

"We'll be there in ten minutes!"

With a tear in my eye, inside my melted mind I heard Gurudev's glorious words: "Your life is perfect. It is a perfect plan, and it is a spontaneous miracle. It is both every moment."

When your muse's lightning bolt of creative energy strikes, do not ignore it, do not procrastinate; do it. Chris and Mary showed up at my door less than ten minutes later. I sang "Walk the Line" to Chris while he played his twelve-string Yamaha guitar, turning my entire world upside-down.

G–F–C. These three chords changed my life. Within seconds, my first song had come alive, and I sang it like a bird, probably out of tune back then. Chris added an Em–G change, and I sang new words that poured easily from the universe somewhere. My first song was complete! What came to me on an ordinary day on the boardwalk now had musical wings.

We left the apartment for a break, though I don't remember opening the door or my first steps outside. Walking out to the beach speckled with people sunbathing and splashing in the waves, Chris strummed a bluesy progression on his guitar as our feet dug into the hot, baked sand.

"Is that one of your songs?" I asked.

"Yes," was the simple reply.

Without hesitation, I started singing along with the chords, words magically appearing in my head. As they worked with the notes, I wrote them down in my book. Chris brought his guitar, and I had my poetry book out there in the sun. The song became "Tail End Blues," a fiction-blues song with fantastic lyrics.

Bam, one hour, two songs! I was walking on air.

Heading back inside my apartment, Chris asked, "What else do you have?"

I pulled out my first poem book and flipped the scribbled pages to "One Time Once Upon." The memories against the sun-warmed seawall with Maria flooded back into my mind—my main muse who was studying at the University of California, San Diego, and living next door.

As I read those first lines, Chris blasted with a monster progression off the D chord, and basically just ran it up and down the fret board. He followed with a dynamic key change, and I sang along, scoring additional new, cool lyrics from thin air.

Only ninety minutes had passed between the two of us, and three songs! It was like a far-out dream for me, strange yet so right at the same time. Time stopped as my senses reverberated with the creative flow. This combination of Chris's sounds and my words felt like an ultimate union, a blended taste of salt and sweet, unknown until now.

The couple left for lunch and insisted they'd be back in an hour. Too jazzed to eat, I rambled on to a favorite getaway, the Best Western Blue Sea Lodge's bubbling hot Jacuzzi in the next building. I snuck through the fenced door daily into this cozy, warm paradise for soothing relaxation and fun opportunities to meet new friends from around the world, two of my favorite things.

Fairly empty today, I hadn't been relaxing in the Jacuzzi for more than a half hour when a beautiful song surged through my mind from somewhere special. I sang the words aloud, "Help me get to where I'm going, light my soul and keep it growin', help me get to where I'm from, sing your song with guitar strummin'…" I let my breath go on the last syllable.

Numb, with jets bubbling a rhythm around me, I slowly shook my head. Where were these emotional lyrics coming from, and who was the person in the song? Could they be describing Chris or my old roommate, Dave, who had hitchhiked back home to Pennsylvania in May? Maybe. I didn't have a clue.

Relaxation disappeared as the next verse popped up and I sang along, enmeshed in this creative roller coaster ride. I jumped out, drenched in chlorinated water, and ran toward home in flip-flops and passion. I wanted to sing Chris my new song.

As I dashed around the corner from the alley to my building, I nearly ran into Chris, who was peacefully standing outside my apartment with his twelve-string in hand. He knew by the look on my face I had something special ready to explode. All he said was, "Sing it."

Our fourth song in three hours was born… on the spot.

How do you sleep after you've been to the moon? Saying good-bye to Chris and Mary wasn't the end, only a pause in a corkscrew amusement ride that had merely left the building. I had no idea what was ahead. I just knew I'd stepped into a rock and roll fantasy that I never wanted to end.

Later that week, we wrote three more songs, mainly from my poems. The rocking muse wouldn't stop. We also covered "Thank You," by the mighty Led Zeppelin, and "Wish You Were Here" by Pink Floyd. In my mind, we were ready for Pacific Beach stardom.

A mere nine days later, after inviting my good friend Brian Chase into our band on rhythm guitar, we played for an hour at Javanican Coffee House in Pacific Beach, minutes away from my apartment. Why might the coffee house sound familiar? It's one of the venues where the famous Jewel got her start years before, while living in her VW Bus, exactly one block away from my place on Pacific Beach Drive.

We packed the intimate venue with around thirty of our friends. I sang each song with my eyes closed as Chris and Brian played their guitars behind me. This felt like the most exciting, nail-bitingly nervous event of my life, though I had nothing this indescribable to compare it to. I was no longer seven years old, singing around a swimming pool. This was real; I was the lead singer in my band.

Maria eased into the crowded room late, yet right on time to watch me play rock star for the first time in my life. I had enlisted my landlord's seven-year-old to give her a piece of paper with my newest song, "Fallin," on, written for her only the day before. Stage fright had nothing on me for the tsunami of nerves crushing my chest as I sang the first two lines:

> *Four months ago, I fell for you,*
> *like a ton of bricks off a ten-story building...*
> *right through your eyes I saw your heart*
> *and now you got this little boy singin'...*

Talk about an adrenaline rush. There is nothing like the applause from an audience.

If you ever have the chance to do what I did—or to live out any other phenomenal dream—go for it. For what it's worth, I had never even held Maria's hand. I thank Maria for her inspiration that helped lift me into the music world.

Management at the coffee house liked what they heard. We signed up for two gigs a week, filling the audience with friends and locals.

I was in a rock band, belting out songs I'd help create! If this was a hot fudge sundae, the topping came during a special concert a few weeks later with my mother, brother, and Aunt Alice down front. Two of the most wonderful women in my life flew out to celebrate my first professional break in showbiz. While I was wrapped up in the incubation period of the band, my parents had sold their home in Taylor and moved to Atlanta, near my sister.

One phenomenal month, that's how long the euphoria and gigs lasted. In heartbreaking reality, Chris ended up in jail for domestic violence against the same sweet Mary who believed in her heart it was my fate to meet her husband. And with that, Brian bugged out during the turmoil for Colorado to snowboard.

My world crumbled into a gray, silent heap. The band was ripped apart, stopping the music abruptly. What would I do now? The lyrics of "The End" by the Doors played like a broken record in my heavy heart, a perfect dirge for my dark mood. Having the entertainment rug yanked out from under me, a devastating breakup of a hot and exciting relationship on stage, I landed at a crossroads, a decisive time for me.

Did I let this abrupt halt leave a bad taste in my mouth about music, and dash any hopes of a national tour? To not move forward from this initial plunge or not propel skyward into sharing music with countless others that would change my life?

No way—life said it was high time to shine, sing, and rhyme.

Once you have a guru, you are taken care of every step of the way. An event in Los Angeles brought Gurudev to California and my brother, Jeff, offered to drive. His offer was perfectly timed to ease my loss. Like the previous summer, I got to the church early, excited to see the same musicians setting up. Layers of the outside world peeled away as I took a deep breath and stepped into the room. Instantly, warmth surrounded me like a heavy cloak on a wind-chilled night.

Soon I rocked in my seat, bouncing up and down, side to side, deep in the *Divya Prabha* experience; her music was moving, rockin', and divine.

During satsangs at Bill and Lucinda's, I felt part of a huge positive wave created by everyone in the room. Tonight, I felt alone, strong and independent, in the packed, colorful crowd, rocking solo with Gurudev a mere twenty feet in front of me.

Gurudev shared, "Being in a crowd when you are alone is ignorance. A feeling of oneness in a crowd is a sign of wisdom. Being alone in a crowd is enlightenment." Each of his words streamed through my soul as if specifically for me, like splashes of cool, rejuvenating water in a barren desert.

Two years ago, back in Pennsylvania, I had partied all night and struggled for a decent breath. Now, in Los Angeles, I was singing Sanskrit songs with hundreds of people I did not know in a church. I was having an extraordinary spiritual experience with my enlightened Spiritual Master a snowball's throw away from me. The transformation was still in infancy, yet I had traveled light years from the past.

After the talk I stood in line, eager to embrace him, my fourth time meeting my guru. I walked right up to Gurudev and felt spiritually driven as I hugged him. A powerful energy soared through my heart as a soft pressure filled my arms. He asked, "How are you? Are you happy?"

With the joy of a thousand gift-laden children on Christmas, I smiled wide and replied, "Yes, I am very happy and grateful for all you have given me."

He smiled like a beacon shining across miles of dark ocean and patted me lightly on the shoulder, saying, "Good, good, good."

In the next instant, a question came out of my mouth, with no idea where from or why it came, but I didn't resist once the words appeared. "Gurudev, I want to learn piano and guitar. Can you please bless me with a little bit of musical talent? I promise I will do the most with it."

His smile never wavered and with a slight nod of his head, he blinked both of his bright eyes, infusing me with what I believe to this day to be my granted musical blessings.

The musical door was halfway open from the wonderful genetics from my music-making dad, and Gurudev, with his world of strength in love, kicked me right through it. The door was now wide open and singing tunes out into the world.

Wrapped in a world of contentment, joy and gratitude, I exited the church to find my dependable, adventurous brother waiting for me in his car. He asked how it went this time and all I said was, "Beyond description," and smiled.

Jeff never pressed for details about these events, never uttered a negative or joking word. I know he respected my spiritual path and gave me time and space to do my breathing and meditation each day. It was a cool, unspoken respect, and I have always been grateful to Jeff for that.

One day Jeff came home with a fresh roll of developed film. He opened the envelope and handed me one of the photos, saying, "Check this out." His eyes sparkled, a wide smile on his face, like he was the proudest person in the world.

I can't tell you how meaningful his look and demeanor was in that moment or how much I wanted to break down and cry when I saw this surprising picture of me, on the couch, with the rays of morning sun shining on me, cross-legged, shirt off, long, light-brown beach hair on my shoulders, deep in peaceful meditation. I never knew he took the picture. It was a rare, precious gift that tugged at my heart. The photo captured the peace I felt and allowed me to see a glimpse of my own happiness, a gift of perspective. It meant a lot to me and still does.

And life kept getting better. I landed a new job as a produce clerk at Henry's Market, an awesome job in a popular natural food market. The owner's pride and joy was his produce, and did we ever sell a lot of it. The locals there were a health conscious lot. The new specials came out on Wednesdays and the place looked like a busy weekend farmers market—tons of fruit and veggies all around.

In this job I could observe how much the yoga, deep breathing, and meditation had done for me. For example, when hordes of people tore the produce section apart, setting fire to the aisles from their million footsteps back and forth, my surroundings were chaotic. I would take in one deep breath (as I'd done many times each morning for the past year and a half) and center myself to shoot straight down the firing line and be a hundred percent with the customers.

The same service-oriented mindset I'd implemented at Dairy Queen applied here and I connected with each customer—even the bitter old ladies who yelled obscenities because they wanted greener spinach, riper avocados, and organic everything.

The job at Henry's was fulfilling in many ways. I worked at the coolest market in Pacific Beach, with access to snack on fresh fruit and veggies all day, and continuous opportunities to connect with customers on a genuine level. Plus, I was getting paid while learning a useful trade. Not to mention some of the most beautiful women in San Diego shopped there. Ah, the innocent joys of being twenty-two.

The musical blessing I received from Gurudev swirled daily in my mind and heart. Reruns of his smile and the blink of his eyes played over and over.

I bought myself a used electronic keyboard for $50, stuck a Grateful Dead sticker on it, and started teaching myself to play. Have you seen a baby take its first step and, despite falling on its padded rear dozens of times, continues to work at the marvel of walking? I felt that same determination with my hands perched over the keys. The baby doesn't read a manual to walk; he just keeps trying with encouragement. Within a day, I wrote my first song on the keyboard.

Determined to learn the guitar next, a big helpful push came from my old band mate Brian's friend John, with whom I shared my guitar goal. After hearing my cry for musical ability, he said, "Here, take my guitar; you can learn this, no problem."

It was an unexpected, positive blast of energy in the face, a shock I did not take lightly. In honor of his statement and belief in me, I grabbed his dark-brown acoustic Epiphone guitar and started fooling around.

John showed me some basics, including how to play a few of my own songs—I was playing music by ear. This was December 1998. I took every opportunity to go over to his house and borrow the guitar for a minute or two, oftentimes more.

"Can the guitar come out and play?" I would ask. I tried not to be a pest, yet I craved the feeling of the smooth-wood neck in my hand and my fingers ached for the steel strings.

During one visit I wrote another simple song, this one with lyrics. As the last note faded, I sat in stunned silence. I had written a complete song, lyrics and music by Jeremy Occhipinti. Super stoked, I knew I would be moving forward into the musical world with my guitar playing soon.

The Art of Living Silence course was the next step after the Art of Living course, and I had wanted to attend the course for a long time. I found, as with the instruments, that I had a deep passion for learning. I had a natural desire to absorb more. I almost flipped my lid, spinning cartwheels in my mind, when I learned there would be one in Apple Valley, about three hours away from San Diego, during New Year's.

Back then, it was a three to five day residential course, usually held at someone's home or a rented space, as there were no formal centers. For most of the course, the participants would be in silence, enjoying yoga, deep breathing, and guided meditations. The course aimed to give one deep rest and rejuvenation, a welcome break from their busy lives. There were a handful of trained teachers for the course in 1998, but I didn't know them as I was still relatively new.

The last days of December flew by in a crush of work, friends, and meditation. At the end of my shift, I hitched a ride with a friend, and headed for my first Art of Living Silence course. I paid my dues by waiting patiently, saving my pennies. Now was my time to experience a course I'd heard so much about.

New Year's Eve 1998 found me in Apple Valley with Michael Fischman, the teacher, at Anu Reddy's spectacular house in the desert. A humorous Jewish man from New York, Michael's jokes were subtle, but very funny. The way he conducted the course was simply perfect. I remember Mikey giggling, while leading the morning yoga, at my lack of flexibility in some postures. Bending my big and tall frame into yoga positions is rather comical, I admit. My heart and passion are agile and limber, my body, not so much.

Michael encouraged me to take more yoga classes. The Silence course was a fantastic blend of yoga, deep breathing (*pranayama*), mind-blowing guided meditations by Gurudev on tape, knowledge, stories, service (*seva*), silence, and, of course, my favorite portion, the evening satsang, or company, of the truth/like-minded people.

Before I left San Diego, I explained to my coworkers how I was taking this course, and on it, there would be a period of silence that I'd have to complete.

Rightfully so, they burst into laughter and said, "No way—not you!"

For someone who was either talking, laughing, singing, or snoring every minute of every day, they were perfectly justified with their comments of hilarious disbelief. I didn't know what to expect with this vow of silence, but like everything else I had encountered over the past three years, I blazed into the concept with an open mind and bright spirit.

To my surprise, the silence—and I mean super-silence, as I gave it my all—was astonishing. After the first day jitters of not being able to talk and communicate all the wild thoughts and jokes playing ping pong in my mind, a most remarkable feeling dawned deep inside. For the first time in my life, I felt free, released from the burden of feeling obligated to talk to people, to entertain them. Years of nonstop chatter a burden? Who knew?

It's hard to explain how light I felt unfettered from speech. I could just be me, do the practices, and enjoy nature walks in Apple Valley, while watching my wild-child mind settle down to a calm and collected time.

One huge bonus, I considered a large payoff for keeping perfectly silent all day was singing our hearts out in satsang each night. Those musical escapades were grand. Being on my first Silence course, the depth of release, of satisfaction in song, was unreal, plus celebrating on New Year's Eve! Being a part of the spiritual silence released to the glory of songs was intoxicating, and I glowed.

When all was said and done, I flew out of that house, all the way back to Mission Beach, on the wings of fulfillment.

I knew life would continue taking its many twisting turns. I couldn't wait to see what lay ahead in 1999 with my music, my spiritual practice, and the ever-vibrant and resplendent spiritual path with Gurudev Sri Sri Ravi Shankar and the Art of Living.

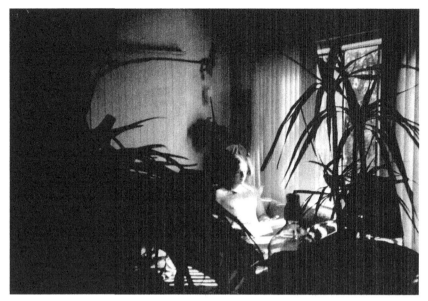

My brother took the photo while I was meditating, February 1998

*My first concert at Javanican Coffee Shop and my brother
Jeff was in the front row, September 1998*

Mom, Jeff, and me on Crystal Pier in Pacific Beach, CA, October 1998

CHAPTER TEN

The Music in My Hands

Miracles happen. Do not go after miracles.
Miracles happen to bring that trust in you
that the Divine takes care of you.
—Gurudev Sri Sri Ravi Shankar

A New Year's resolution to myself for 1999 was to buy my first acoustic guitar. After spending a couple hundred dollars on the Silence course, plus missing a few days from work, I was in no position to buy even guitar strings. But when had a lack of money ever stopped me from dreaming?

While working at Henry's, I had met and become good friends with an older lady named Denise, a single mom who smiled and laughed like me, and a kindred spirit of positive energy.

One day I asked if she'd take me to the guitar store to look at acoustic guitars. I still didn't have a car or a driver's license. Drool may have been involved from the sheer thought of the wood and steel machines. With a hundred dollars to my name by then, I was in no way, shape, or form expecting to buy one. As we walked into the local shop, the owner greeted us and over his shoulder I spotted this beautiful Sigma acoustic guitar on the wall.

I nervously asked if I could play it, knowing only four chords and scattered bits and pieces of a few songs. The man reached up, carefully lifted it down and handed me the instrument. It was so cool, sweet in sound, strong to the touch, and I knew I had to have it. The price was $400, and I sighed, "Well, I can't afford that right now."

The owner's next words perked my ears up like my dog, Coal, back home, when he heard the words *cookie* or *walk*. He said I could put it on layaway. I dug down in the pocket of my shorts, grabbed the five twenty-dollar bills—my life savings—and without rhyme, reason, or an ounce of hesitation, handed them over. Minutes later I walked out of the store, dazed and confused about how I would come up with the other three hundred to bring my dream guitar home.

I had the next day off from work and began the morning with yoga, Kriya, and was just finishing meditation when the phone rang.

"Jeremy, Brad here over at Henry's. I know it's your day off, but we need help today, can you come in and work?"

I didn't waste a breath. "Yes! I'll be right there."

"We'll pay you time and a half for your work today, and you can work as long as you want."

There it was, an omen of the blessings to come as my dream would rise into fruition. I jumped off the couch, got dressed, tucked my long hair under my hat, and hustled down to the store. As it turned out, they needed tons of help. I was allowed to work twelve-hour days, earning time and a half for every hour over eight each day, plus everything over forty hours for the week—score! Time was my new best friend as each sweet minute on the clock brought me closer to my dream guitar.

I received a large paycheck the following week and called up Denise for another ride. She was thrilled for me as I walked into the guitar store and paid cash for my first guitar! *Jai Guru Dev*! I am blessed having a guru, one who seemed like a nonstop miracle-maker in my life. In Gurudev's words of wisdom, "If you establish a connection with the divine in your heart, you will see how miracles begin to unfold in your life."

I'd had the guitar for less than half a day when I enthusiastically walked over to Javanican Coffee House and played a three-song set. Imagine the bravado, me stepping up on a public stage, my old stomping grounds, as a solo artist. I'd asked Gurudev for musical talent, and my new guitar helped kick open the door even wider.

Sitting on a wooden stool, I explained to the crowd how I only knew four chords. I barely knew one person in the entire audience.

With nerves tightly wound and a trickle of sweat running down my back, I felt stoked to be playing songs I had written and with my own guitar in front of people. Another cherished dream came true right in front of my eyes that night. The music probably sounded very funny, but nonetheless, I went for it anyway.

At the apartment, I played every day, strumming so loud it could irritate a saint, yet it was music to my ears and rhythm to my soul. With Jeff staying at the group home where he worked half the week, I had tons of time and space to jam.

The first song I wrote on my guitar was for Maria, titled "Painted Hazel Eyes." Hours later, I called a family friend, telling him of my first solo song. His next words about rocked my world. "Yes, Jeremy, that's what your last name means in Italian—painted eyes." I nearly fell off the couch at the revelation, a fact I'd known before but had forgotten. Now it had shown up as the main theme of my first song written on my first guitar. It felt like a sign.

At the end of January, I realized I could use a little professional guidance and enrolled in a singing class at Mesa Community College. Learning warm-ups was fun. With the opportunity to sing in front of dedicated music majors, this class helped me get my vocal cords in tune.

After my first day of class, while standing at the bus stop, I met an interesting-looking hippie named Matt. One glance at the brown nappy ponytail, baggy pants, beat-up shirt, and a look of wonder in his eyes, and I knew Matt was a Deadhead. In fact, my first words to him were, "Hi, you like the Grateful Dead?"

"Yeah, how'd you know?"

Less than ten seconds later we ditched the bus stop idea and hitchhiked back to the beach. Drawn like magnets to the energy flow, we walked and talked about anything and everything. I brought my used keyboard and brand new guitar over to Matt's and we hit it off like John and Paul of the Beatles. I swear Matt and I played two awesome chords, A to D, for thirty minutes, with me switching from keyboard to guitar and back again. We jammed and created a musical bonding that would last for two solid years.

Matt played with an intriguing guy named Todd. A scientist by trade, Todd approached music and the guitar in a similar way to his science: deep in his head. Todd and Matt called themselves the Cosmic Riders. A few nights a week, I was their keyboardist at Todd's house—teaching myself to play on the spot. I believe I broke all world records for missed notes and chords, though Matt and Todd had been playing music for a few years and were pretty good at their craft. Despite my skill level, it was out-of-this-world fun and continued into spring.

During our jam sessions I played my acoustic guitar for songs I wrote like "Help Me," "Tail End Blues," and "Walk the Line" from my first band, as well as new songs I was writing, including the biggest one yet, a song I wrote on March 23, 1999, called "Dream Away." This all-out, three-chord rocker screamed of my personality, told the tale, and was one song I could call my own and sing with strength, knowing I could now write my own hits. At least, they were hits to me in my little own rocker world.

Weeks later at Easter time, the youthful newlyweds, my sister Michele and her husband, Dave, came out to the beach and stayed with Jeff and me for a week. Matt and I played every Tuesday at Javanican Coffee Shop, so when I heard my old roommate Dave and his family were coming for the Easter holiday as well, I set up a show with Matt, Todd, and myself, billed as the Cosmic Riders. Including me, nine people from the Taylor/Old Forge neighborhoods of Northeastern Pennsylvania were packed into this intimate corner coffee shop amidst a crowd of music lovers.

I introduced the band. "We're the Cosmic Riders, and so are you."

We blasted into "Dream Away" for the second song, with Todd doing some masterful leads over Matt's rhythm and my own. Besides my first performance a mere six months earlier, this was the most exhilarating show of my then short and sweet music life.

Dave's family sent a photo of me playing at Javanican and a short writeup to the hometown newspaper *The Triboro Banner*, which meant pretty much everyone I grew up with saw the article. Oddly enough, I had written a retirement poem to my old football coach, Steve Armillay, and sent it to the same newspaper only a few weeks before. My poem was published the Thursday before Easter. Old teammates told me my words brought tears to their eyes. Again, the serendipity of things is awe-inspiring if you're open to seeing.

A few weeks later, we found ourselves playing at a weekend festival with other local San Diego bands on the beach in Baja, Mexico. My first outdoor venue, a rock jam with amateur roadies, was filled with a colorful wave of groupies in board shorts and bikinis. There was probably more sound checking than playing live, but it was a blast.

During the summer the group went through some personnel changes when myself, Matt, and my old friend Jeff from Pacific Beach, who played bass, started jamming and getting tight on some well-known covers. Todd had other things keeping himself busy, and there were no hard feelings. We three remained friends.

In addition to the covers, we also started playing songs written by Matt and me. It was the best of all possible musical worlds for me. I played my new Yamaha keyboard when Matt sang his songs, strumming an acoustic guitar. Yes, I had bought another keyboard by this time. Does Jay Leno own only one roadster? A musician needs his tools.

Indulge me a moment with one brief story on how dispassionate I had become from this avid and super-fun spiritual life. I got called into the boss's office one day at work. He asked me, with the most serious look on his face, clearing his voice a few times, if I was selling drugs.

My typical grin lit up my face. I said, "No, why do you ask?"

He said in all his years in the grocery business, no one had ever left a paycheck in the office for more than a single day, but "You have three of them sitting here!"

Without batting an eye or dropping my smile, I shrugged.

On my way home I made two stops, one at the bank to cash the checks, the other at the music store to buy the new keyboard. The life of a performing artist living his dreams on the beach.

We started playing regularly at Javanican as a three-piece acoustic rock band, with Matt and Jeff plugged into amps. Matt used a microphone, but I never needed a mic or amplification for my loud guitar and big mouth.

In the middle of autumn, a hippie dude named Scott started showing up at our gigs. He played sitar and percussion instruments. He liked our vibe, as we did his, and we invited him to join in our set. He knew our songs. On his first night, his drumming was out-standing. He added a sweet element to our music.

When my childhood friend, Stan, came out to visit, he gave our nameless band the handle "Halfadummy." We loved the one-word name and it stuck.

Shortly afterward, a good friend and neighbor on Mission Beach, Adam Bigelsen, offered to record Halfadummy in his ocean view apartment. Studio recording is more restrictive than the loose style of playing live, but I loved it. The three of us readily agreed and bartered for the costs. I thought of the greats and how they must have started out in their first studio gig.

At the same time as my musical passion was soaring, I wrote my first children's poems. The creativity came from the beach's local children, by whom I was surrounded.

I had a dream to make these poems into a book, and that April, I followed my dream into publishing. I have seven poems ranging from cute to powerful in the collection. On a sun-drenched San Diego afternoon, I bought matching cartoon paper from Kinko's for text stock and bound twenty books together.

You cannot believe how proudly I mailed out packets of my first book, titled *Children's Fountain of Poetry* with a copy of my band's first demo CD. I'll autograph this antique collector's edition if you have it.

At the end of 1999, I left Henry's for a new job at the group home where Jeff worked. How else would you celebrate in the New Year 2000 but with new employment, of course. While Jeff worked with the younger children, I worked with the teens. My big brother helped me get the job.

Being a live-in counselor for six teenage boys was different from my typical resume listing, and it opened new doors of responsibility. One was waking them up for high school at 6:00 a.m. I, the original early morning groaner not all that long ago, was now in charge of wake-up calls. I can't make this stuff up. Pots, pans, water, my guitar—you name it, I pulled out all the tricks on those boys, whatever it took to make them rise, if not shine.

A Silence course was coming up in San Diego sometime in April. I couldn't wait. Once again, it was taught by Michael Fischman (Mikey). Michael's personal story on this path is highlighted in his memoir, *Stumbling into Infinity*. His challenges and transformation, written in a unique storytelling style, inspired me while I was writing this book.

Over a year had passed since my first course, and this nature retreat was well needed. The group home demanded exhausting hours with malcontent teenagers. It was a continuous outreach to the teens day after day. Even positive attitudes need a tune-up, an attitude adjustment of love and serenity at times.

Imagine trees, paths for nature walks, and sweet birds singing wake-up calls in the morning at my paradise of salvation. I found myself soaking much deeper into the entire experience: the silence, meditation, singing, and, to my surprise, the service (or *seva*) commitments. Somehow, cleaning bathrooms, washing dishes, cutting veggies, and other various housekeeping duties felt joyful, liberating. There's an uplifting spirituality in serving others.

One afternoon I decided to take a nature walk. Carved into the acres were paths carrying spiritual, Biblical names like Salvation Walk and His Glory Path. But the sign that jumped off the painted wood, flew round my head, and smacked me a good one in the face was the trail called Service Road. Just seeing the words, visions of Jesus helping others in his time filled my mind and poetry emanated from my creative heart.

I sat down, pulled out my trusty pen and pad, and wrote a beautiful, powerful poem about how I wanted to make service my path during this lifetime, citing Gurudev's famous quote, "The only true security that could be found in this world is in the process of giving love."

The walk, the simple sign, the vision, the ever-inspiring messages of Gurudev, and the service I had taken part in during this course all gave rise to this monumental moment for me.

From the message and meaning in the poem, I felt inspired to finally attend the yearly summer celebration during the full moon in July called Guru Purnima.

Work and money usually ran interference against me. Including travel to Lake Tahoe, the Art of Living Silence course, plus room and board, would have been around $1000.

On the last day of the Silence course, I walked up to Mikey with the wide-eyed look of a five year old wanting desperately to meet Santa Claus. I asked, "Mikey, I really want to go to Guru Purnima this year, but I don't think I can afford it. Is there another way for me to go there and do seva?"

Michael smiled. "Call Bill Herman, he's the head of the kitchen team. Maybe you can take out the garbage or something like that."

And that was all I needed to hear. Michael's words changed my life forever. Never be afraid to ask. You won't get an answer if you don't ask.

As soon as I got home, I grabbed the phone and called Bill. His first question was whether I had any experience. Experience? I told him of the various restaurants I'd worked in since I was twelve, plus told him I was a fast learner and a hard worker. All those jobs had led me here, to this moment. He invited me to join his team.

As I hung up the phone, I realized I was on my way to Lake Tahoe to join my first Guru Purnima with Gurudev Sri Sri Ravi Shankar and over a thousand devotees on this path of service and celebration.

Good news travels fast. Cyndie Pendleton, our local Art of Living teacher in Pacific Beach, was also going to Tahoe. She asked if I could drive her car. I immediately accepted the sweet offer, which answered the question of how I'd get up there.

The route from San Diego to Lake Tahoe is a scenic wonderland, driving through Bishop, Mammoth, and the historic and beautiful Sierra Mountains. Driving past the turnoff for Yosemite, in Mariposa County, with rolling hills of wild wheat grass dotted with California scrub oak beckoning as the gateway to the majestic park was difficult to ignore. It was hard not to take the turnoff.

Finally, we arrived in Lake Tahoe with its magnificent views of pine-tree-covered mountains and crystal-clear skies. The clean scent of the pines was glorious. The event was held at Alpine Meadows, an awesome ski resort down the road from the famous Squaw Valley, USA.

Bill introduced himself, and while getting settled in the house where the kitchen team stayed, I innocently asked him, "How many people are we going to cook for?"

"Five hundred daily, and around Guru Purnima it builds to maybe fifteen hundred people."

With a scared smile, I said, "How do we do that?"

Bill just smiled like a Cheshire cat. Neither of us will ever forget that moment.

Getting my feet wet in the kitchen was fun. I was good at following orders, fetching things, and arranging the fruits and veggies in the cooler. And it only took a few takes to get comfortable throwing down oil, spices, and veggies onto the big stove.

The fantastic team around me included an Indian American dude named Jessie, a Sikh with a turban and a sense of humor that could tip a ship. We connected immediately. Larry and Geo, an awesome couple from Los Angeles, helped me in many ways, too.

Bill was captain and called or yelled the shots. He kicked my butt when needed, but overall, he was a really cool, old school, kick-ass guy. A retired high school art teacher from Chicago, which explained where his bark came from, and another Old TMer, Bill had a photography business at Alpine Meadows.

One of the most beautiful aspects of being on the team was the daily morning *Guru Puja*. *Puja*, meaning born out of fullness, is an ancient gratitude ceremony. Hearing Bill sing this with such devotion was truly moving, a perfect start to our crazy days in the kitchen. It also kindled my desire to learn how to perform the Guru Puja, a new passion I tucked away in my pocket.

Another delightful aspect of being on the team was welcoming Gurudev into the kitchen once or more daily. The smiles, hugs, high-fives, laughs, and chit-chats were unforgettable. He even helped us cook, carry the hot trays to the serving area, and, of course, helped to serve the food, too. This was all a pleasant surprise to me.

I was blown away at his fine attention to detail when he would come in to visit us. He was always asking about what we were making, inquiring about spice levels and even asking what we were planning for the next meal. Every moment in his presence was a learning experience with the main lesson always to be a hundred percent in all we do. He taught us this by example, time and time again. A keenness of awareness was dawning inside me.

On the second day of cooking side-by-side with Jessie, he turned to me and said, "Jeremy, you cook all day in here, you burn off all the bad karma and you walk out an angel."

And at the end of the day, sitting in satsang with over five hundred like-minded people singing Sanskrit tunes in oneness, indeed, I felt like an angel—and I saw angels all around me.

Gurudev always says, *"Responsibility is taken, not given."* And during this two-week gig in the kitchen, that was what it was all about. When a huge order of produce came in for the week and being only seven months removed from my produce-clerk job, I jumped in and took care of it.

During my last six months at Henry's, I had volunteered for the dreaded job of "Cooler Man." After the initial setup each morning, a truck with twenty-five-plus pallets of produce rolled in. It had to be put away, skillfully, in an orderly fashion. I rocked that job with my headphones on, not only getting stronger, but crafting a skill that would be super useful… right about now in Lake Tahoe. Bill was surprised when he came into the cooler an hour after the shipment arrived and saw how I had cleaned, ordered, and stocked the fridge.

"Wow, I've never seen a cooler look that good. Awesome job, Jeremy!"

And there it was, as I sat on a box of carrots in my newly decorated produce cooler, I was blasted with the thought of a lifetime. The work I'd been doing in the kitchen these last few days—guiding course participants who were in silence and telling them what veggies needed to be cut, cooking in front of a grill, taking orders in the middle of rush-hour cooking madness multiple times a day, washing dishes, cleaning the kitchen, and of course, making the produce cooler look like a million bucks—were in direct correlation to those odd, crazy jobs I'd had since I was twelve. I realized that pizza joints, factories, fruit smoothies, Dairy Queen, Henry's, were nothing but essential training for these two weeks at Guru Purnima. I now saw every dish washed, floor scrubbed, ice cream made and served, pro-

duce stocked and sold, person served with a smile (and the ranting
bosses) as training for this.

What an astonishing revelation, which guided me the rest of
the two weeks. Bill watched me grow from a mouse to a lion, from
a nervous yet excited boy to a gallant disciple. I was growing by the
moment, changing in ways I could not fathom.

During the second week, Bill graciously let me experience the
never-ending joy of being around the Art Excel youngsters for half
the day. Art Excel is the Art of Living's dynamic and fun program for
children ages eight to thirteen. Mona Joshi, a teacher from Atlanta,
Georgia, whom I would later become very close to, was the teacher
of the course. Rafting on the Truckee River, ice skating, taking
art classes with Bill, and much more, filled that second week with
unimaginable childlike fun and joy. I was a little kid once again.

Speaking of kids, I got to meet an overgrown one just like me,
"Dvorahji" Dvorah Adler, the self-proclaimed "Shut Up Guru."
Dvorah was as colorful as they come with her big personality, bigger
voice, dyed hairdo, cool California clothes, and an extreme way about
her. Dvorah, another Old TMer, was a mother of two teenagers and a
loving, wildly crazy devotee of Gurudev. The woman wore a variety of
hats to the satsangs, and she put many more on Gurudev's head, too.

Over the years, having Dvorah in a satsang meant comedy and
good cheer. But being around her didn't start that way for me. (*Do
you hear a deep bass playing the notes of dread coming? Something huge?*)

Dvorah was the head of the children's kitchen; I'm sure Billy
allowed this to push people's buttons. Well, she sure pushed mine.
On my first day doing seva, there were two things that made me pull
out what was left inside from my old Taylor days. First, this woman
used bottled sauce for the pasta! Coming from my homemade Italian
pasta and pizza sauce household, this was downright sacrilegious.
Plus, Bill had taught me in the adult kitchen how to make homemade pasta sauce, so all she had to do was ask me to make some for
the young ones. Yes, I was quite extreme back then.

Second, I spotted a large bottle of Kraft mayonnaise on the shelf!
Hello, this was obviously a vegetarian kitchen, and yes, that means the
eggs in the mayo were no-nos. In general, that stuff is disgusting, and

she could have—should have—asked Bill to buy the healthy kind. Again, I was over-the-top obsessive about these things at the time.

I lost it and opened fire on her, yelling in her face what I thought was wrong with the sauce and mayo. Well, Dvorah didn't back down— actually the polar opposite—she yelled right back threatening me! It was quite the sight to see in a kitchen at a meditation retreat.

Aren't crazy moments such fun to look back and smile on? Bill jumped in and cooled us down. As for me, I walked away with her front row center in my mind. She stayed there all through satsang and even twisted my thoughts while I slept. Negative thoughts played like a record skipping over and over, a broken shutter slamming against a house in a storm. Of all the people in their different worlds of colors and craziness, Dvorah was the only one I couldn't accept.

That night Gurudev shared, "Have compassion at other's mistakes or else you are bound to get angry at them. Have you noticed that when you are angry at somebody, that person occupies your total mind? Anger subsides and goes into the background, but the thought of that person persists… your whole mind gets clouded. Make your smile cheaper and your anger expensive."

His words came like a soothing ointment on a vicious blister. The next day I purposefully used the knowledge points from the Art of Living course to accept her and have loved her ever since.

My heart goes out to the millions of people in this world allowing people like Dvorah, or myself, for that matter, to creep into their minds as hate and anger that controls their emotions. Once again, I was grateful to Gurudev for his knowledge and its aftereffect—my peace of mind.

During my time in Tahoe I saw how raw I was still, finding hidden pockets of boiling aggression. And of course, there was me just being me with twenty years of growing up in Taylor. *Sadhana*, or spiritual practices, had centered and calmed me, waking the sleeping child inside me, but percentages of my hometown still existed in me. I was wild by action, outspoken, sometimes unaware in my joking, and always loud in the volume that defined me.

One sun-filled afternoon in the kitchen, I stood at my usual helm in front of the big stove, cooking up veggies for a meal to feed hundreds. In a split second, the safflower oil overflowed down the side of the pan, and a burst of flame rose inches away from me and three feet above my head.

The blinding licks of fire were wicked cool. I was scared and stoked at the same time. I looked up and synced my eyes with the top of the wall of flame, as I sounded my personalized air horn. "Holy cow!" I yelled, not only to signal my astonishment but to warn the hundred or so course participants cutting vegetables around me.

However, the wrong—or right—person was also in the kitchen at that time. Enter Meenakshi Srinivasan, a devotee from San Jose, California, originally from South India. Meenakshi felt like Dvorah's evil Indian double to me, as she tore out my heart, yelling at the top of her lungs at me, for using the expression, "Holy cow." Little did I know someone like her took these words as offensive, coming from India where the cow is sacred and revered.

Stunned, I just stared at her. She wasn't yelling about the fire, which could have destroyed the kitchen or put people in harm's way. No, she was screaming about two innocent American words that really had nothing to do with a cow—or did they?

Meenakshi remembers me as being a loud, wild-mouthed kid in the kitchen back in those days. Her personal, inspirational testimony about my growth over the years, which she has recounted to hundreds of people over time, has been one of the most remarkable things I have heard.

During this magical time in Lake Tahoe, I had so many diverse experiences; it was like living in a dreamland. And what would this two-week adventure in the mountains of Northern California be without a crush on a beautiful girl? I'd met this American-born Indian girl at a satsang in San Diego a few weeks before Guru Purnima. All I remembered thinking was, *Who is this sweet, beautiful girl?* Petite, with dark skin and large eyes, when she spoke it felt like feathers tickling my ears. I was in love and speechless when Savitha told me she'd be attending her first Silence course at Lake Tahoe.

I talked to her every chance I got during those two weeks. I walked her back to her house each night, sometimes hand in hand. I wrote her a poem that I had one of the young students hand her.

Do you see a pattern with my heart? On one level, I didn't want
to interfere with her first advanced meditation course and her silence.
On the other, I wanted to run away with her to the top of Alpine
Meadows and do what any young, wild, poetic novice romantic
would do. We both held back our raw emotions because of where we
were and what we were doing there. I truly had no problem with that.

After my first week of getting used to the routine in the kitchen,
hundreds of devotees started piling into Alpine Meadows Lodge to
celebrate Guru Purnima and the full moon. Although it was crush of
humanity from all around the country, the crowd oozed positive energy.

Guru Purnima is the "Day of the Master," but Gurudev says it is
actually the day of the student, a day where one could look back and
see how far they have progressed on the spiritual path. Like a spiritual
new year. At the end of the day, the kitchen staff and I had cooked
breakfast, lunch, and dinner for 1,500 people!

The volunteers decorated the hall beautifully. I came decked
out in my first *kurta* pajama, the traditional Indian shirt and pants.
The place vibrated. I looked forward to the gallant satsang that night.

Cyndie, Savitha and I sat close to the stage where Gurudev was
about to perform the Guru Puja. The energy kept rising, growing
like a tsunami of power.

During the ceremony, my soul soared into outer space, another
galaxy, and never fully came back down to boring old normal earth.
Despite being a poet and songwriter, it's challenging to describe the
thunder and lightning, the dazzling fireworks going off simultane-
ously in my body and soul. Heat, euphoria, and ecstasy blended
together as I felt sweet tears of joy and gratitude for the million and
one blessings in my life trickling down my cheeks. A dictionary of
words couldn't paint you a picture of this twenty-four-year-old bad
boy turned yogi… and how much love I felt inside and around me.

As my emotions hit their peak and the tears rocked my face, both
Savitha and I looked at each other like little children on Christmas
morning. The pure joy was profound.

This extraordinary moment, which seemed to last a lifetime,
was the most mind-blowing feeling. While Gurudev's younger sister,
who we affectionately call Bhanu Didi, sang "*Jaya Guru Deva Guru,*

Om Namo Narayana," my heart flew beyond the stars and bounced off Pluto and Saturn like an astronomical ping pong ball.

Gurudev stood on the edge of the stage while all 1,500 devotees lined up to receive his darshan on the most auspicious day of the year to be with one's guru. After the mesmerizing hugs and smiles, he placed a silver crown on everyone's heads. When my turn came, his twinkling look, smile, and hug melted my soul and tears trickled down for no reason other than happiness. As Gurudev placed that crown upon my head, electric lightning bolts blasted down my spine, with a level of *shakti* (energy) that soared me super high. Never had I felt that elevated before. It was simply divine, and I would never be the same again. I was blessed beyond belief and stoked beyond compare. *Jai Guru Dev.*

Spending two weeks with Gurudev was just what I needed and more than I could have ever dreamed of. Each day seemed real yet dreamlike, as if stepping out of reality and into Disneyland with Walt Disney himself.

"Hi, Gurudev, are you coming rafting with us today?" "Come into the kitchen later, Gurudev, we're making some nice dishes for tonight." Or, "What's up, Gurudev?" How actually super cool, walking and talking with him during the retreat, being in the kitchen with him, watching as he served food to hundreds of people with a smile. Priceless.

Then there was Divya Prabha, what a Shakti Blaster-Master she was and still is, the Satsang-Bhajan-Queen. Divya's bhajans were larger than life, especially for young dudes coming up in the Art of Living. So beautiful, powerful, everyone sang and danced, clapped and cried—and came alive. I'll never forget the day I got up the nerve to ask her, "Divya, what are the chords for *"Om Namo Bhagavate"*?

She said, in her firm, loving voice, "You figure it out!"

Those four words inspired me and set my own satsang path in motion.

Watching Gurudev leave in the car was an emotional moment, to say the least. As I stood at the end of the line (my favorite spot to wait for him over the years) he waved goodbye to me and said, *"Jai Guru Dev"* in his loving voice. Those multicolored, spirit-strong inner feelings collectively consumed me whole. Fire-like heat mixed with the chill of a blizzard rushed through my body, as tears of joy and gratitude danced on my face. I was growing.

Those two weeks nestled in the mountains changed everything. For three-and-a-half years I had practiced yoga and meditation. I never missed a day of Sudarshan Kriya. I attended as many weekly follow-ups as I could and sang with an open heart in satsang. Giving myself fully into the service of others, cooking for hundreds of people each day, however, set a fire inside my heart—the fire of *seva* (service) would be impossible to extinguish.

Back home in Mission Beach where I had lived out my fantasies: playing guitar and keyboard, singing in a beach band, as well as writing my own pop / rock songs for the past two years, I felt restless. Dreams I'd harbored most of my life had come true, but it was as if the party was over, and the sunrise of reality had dawned. Not that the sun was any less brilliant or the glint off the crashing waves any less sparkling, but I took out my notebook with the words of three songs and took Divya's advice to figure out the chords myself... and can you imagine, *nothing* happened. I could not figure the tunes out for the life of me.

Frustrated between being home and away from the love and grace I had just experienced at Tahoe and not being able to figure out the tunes on my guitar, I closed my eyes and prayed to Gurudev to help me.

When I opened my eyes, I felt a strong difference in the room. I picked up "Shakti," my old (and first) guitar, and all three tunes rolled effortlessly from the strings under my fingers—"*Om Namo Bhagavate*," "*Jaya Guru Deva Guru*," and "Woke Up This Morning with My Mind / This Love That I Feel / This Little Light of Mine." It felt like I was on my way to satsang heaven.

Nine people from Scranton, PA at my concert at
Javanican Coffee Shop, April 1999

CHAPTER ELEVEN

Oh, Atlanta—I'm Coming Home

It is a miracle how the same consciousness is
present in every being in this creation! There
is no other miracle greater than this.
—Gurudev Sri Sri Ravi Shankar

Off and on I'd tried to fire up the engine of education again. If I was going to be a schoolteacher, following in my big sister's footsteps, I needed more college under my belt. During those years in the glorious sunshine of San Diego, twice I attempted to enroll in an education program, but I was not ready. I lived moment to moment in my bohemian lifestyle, yet with an underlying burning desire to teach young children.

While working those two weeks in the Tahoe kitchen, I was my usual openhearted self and shared my dreams and desires with my fellow chefs Larry and Geo, sincerely expressing my passions and dreams for the future each day while we worked. At one point I flat-out asked Geo if she thought I could be a teacher.

She replied, "Jeremy, you will be successful at anything you do in this lifetime."

That single line of words, given with grace, love, and power boosted me into a life-level I needed to be during that point in my life. In a grateful moment, I hugged Geo and set out to play Superman around this world.

Home from Tahoe, I knew I had to knuckle down and make some moves and changes to get to where I wanted to be. I felt confident from my two weeks of sadhana, seva, and satsang galore.

I believe you create your own destiny and working at the group home was not pointing me in the right direction, so I gave my notice. I got another produce clerk job, this time at Jimbo's Naturally, a super-cool health food store featuring all organic produce and vegan snacks. I enjoyed the opportunity of eating the organic goodies plus greeting and serving the local health-crazed community. Among those special folks we called customers was the popular musician Jewel, who frequented the store.

After a few weeks of working at Jimbo's, I also took a second job as caretaker for a seven-year-old boy. Okay, I give in, I confess… you can say I was a nanny. That's right, a nanny! Or *manny*, as is the more popular terminology for the male variety.

Whatever you want to call me, it was an awesome job that opened many doors for me. Abraham was a smart, shy little boy with a keen interest in the world and a wide, luminescent smile. We got along well, and he blossomed in confidence and enthusiasm in my care.

It was the ultimate job. I arrived at his house early in the mornings and did my sadhana before waking him up to get ready for school. Going with him to the local elementary school, Abraham introduced me to his former first-grade teacher, Ms. White. She needed volunteers, and I couldn't raise my hand fast enough to sign up. Nothing like gaining classroom experience while earning a paycheck as a manny, eh? After school, Abraham and I played, sang, and laughed until his parents (both doctors) got home.

Abraham's parents owned a beautiful grand piano tucked in the corner of their living room. One of the perks of my job was being allowed to play, and I did all the time. The bhajans I was learning sounded nice on this quality piano.

Here's what Gurudev says about this form of music: "*Bhajan* means sharing—sharing from the deepest level of our existence. The body is made up of millions of atoms and every particle has the capacity to absorb energy and radiate energy. And when you chant and sing, that particular energy is radiated into the body.

"Our consciousness is so old, older than the trees; mind is nothing but energy and intelligence. When you sing bhajans, chant, the deepest layers in our consciousness vibrate with the oldest sounds; the whole system resonates—it is very powerful."

Often, I called Cyndie Pendleton and sang a few bhajans with the piano accompaniment onto her answering machine. At one of our Sudarshan Kriya follow-up sessions, Cyndie told me, "You should play some of those songs you leave on my answering machine in satsang."

That was all the encouragement I needed; the next week I played Divya's "*Om Namo Bhagavate Vasudeva*" on my guitar. I started out being nervous, the same pre-performance jitters I'd felt on stage, but the energy soon took off and we sang my first bhajan, which is still one of my favorite songs to play at satsang. Thank you, Cyndie, for inspiring me to share.

"Jeremy, take your super reading group to the back table and read *The Cat in the Hat.*"

Ms. White's trust in me, plus her enthusiasm and guidance, helped me form a solid foundation as an aspiring teacher. Volunteering in her classroom accomplished two important things for me: First, it afforded real-time experience working with first grade students (a grade level that would mean the world to me five years later) on my resume. Secondly, it increased my desire to become a teacher and the dream of having my own classroom.

Often, I sat back looking around the decorated four walls and thought, *I can totally do this.* My fingers itched to have my own class-room to help mold young minds with positive energy. I had clear visions of teaching, encouraging students while reading my poems or singing songs with the class. I'd be in the middle of a jam and know in my heart I could see myself doing this on a large scale for years to come and for generations of souls. This was my calling, my destiny, and I needed to make it happen.

The first hurdle: going back to college. By November 2000 I had set in motion the plans of leaving my dream life on the San Diego beach for Atlanta, Georgia, to pursue my goals of becoming an early childhood educator.

"Jeremy, when are you going to see your baby nephew, David?" And *that* was the draw to get me to Atlanta. There was a new little guy in the family, and Uncle Jeremy was missing some great moments.

My next move was to visit the local library, where I looked up colleges and universities near my parents' home, boiled it down to which ones had early childhood education programs, and I applied to the best possible choice, Kennesaw State University, a thirty-minute drive from their house. Within two weeks I was accepted for the Winter/Spring 2001 semester.

In addition to the familial and professional pulls for change, after Tahoe I found myself feeling a strong oppression of over-comfort. I freaked out accordingly. I mean, life was too perfect: living on a strip of land steps from the sands of Mission Bay and Mission Beach, holding two cool jobs, playing in a band with my best friends who fully supported my music with enthusiastic spirit, knowing the locals and being on a first name basis with cooks in my favorite restaurants. Of course, also being a part of a great Art of Living group for four years. This is what life fantasies are made of; the life I'd created with intention, attention (hard work), and manifestation. Now it was the life I wanted to leave behind.

Gurudev says, "Whatever you put attention on will start manifesting in your life. Intention, attention, manifestation; that is how the universe works."

Complacency is numbing. Yes, I had paradise, but my life is not about just me or my own joy. I'd made a commitment to serve others, and I needed to head out on the quest.

"Dude! You're crazy for leaving Mission Beach for Georgia, what's wrong with you?" screeched my neighbor at the beach.

I understand his confusion, and I hope he understands the rewards were greater than that moment in paradise.

So I saddled up my 1994 black Nissan Sentra, bid everyone a strong goodbye, and headed to Atlanta at the beginning of December 2000. My first cross-country trip gave me hours of peaceful, memorable time to myself. I stopped in towns and cities that had inspired me from childhood on. Toward the end of the trip, I cruised into

New Orleans, a city as cool as the cats who made and continue to make that place sing.

I made it home for the holidays. There is such heart and warmth to those words no matter who you are or how far away from family you may be.

After the presents were opened and one set of festivities came to a close, I had the pleasure of driving to my childhood home in Taylor with my sister and her family for New Year's. This was my second time being back since leaving there over four years ago, but the shining star of this group coming into town was my baby nephew, David.

I stayed with Aunt Alice, who had just undergone surgery from her bout with cancer. It was special to be by her side. I'll always remember her as a second mother to me, so full of love and faith.

I rocked in the new year with a wild, fun party with friends I'd graduated from high school with. The loud, festive night was a chance to cherish the old and familiar before stepping into a new realm at Kennesaw State University.

Though returning home was a mostly happy event for me, I was saddened at how messed up some of my childhood friends had gotten from using hardcore drugs. I partied as a teen, but these highly addictive drugs were another story. For the first time in my life, I saw how opioids ruined the lives of people close to me. The region saw many overdoses, and I lost several friends to this severe epidemic.

My first day of class started at nine o'clock on a chilly January morning, sitting in my Introduction to Pre-School course, with approximately thirty women. College girls, single moms, mid-forties career changers, nonstop talkers, complainers, silent and pretty, loud and large, pants-wearers of their family, and every other category there could possibly be filled the desks around me. I was the only male in a college classroom filled with women!

Now my hometown boys might very well say, "What's the matter with that?" Yes, who could complain, right? I got along well with women. I made them laugh, I was a great listener, should be a piece of cake, right?

But then, the instructor passed out large chart paper where we had to write things down about ourselves. When the paper came to my desk, a wash of sheer panic enveloped me. I stared at the sheet of white paper, unable to breathe. Each box now held words in well-painted, perfect penmanship from female hands that rolled effortlessly across the paper. I sat frozen in my chair, locked out, without the ability to lift a pinky.

Before I applied to this program of childhood education, two huge doubts or fears were chopping at my self-esteem: my wild, never-developed little boy handwriting, and my shortcomings in spelling. (*Now I depend on my computer's spell-check feature and use it on everything—though I'm aware it has probably made me a worse speller.*) I'd have been a shoo-in as a doctor if bad handwriting were the key to a diploma. The only things I'd written in years were my poems and lyrics. No one saw the scribbled pages of verses I'd scratched into various notebooks. Being in this classroom filled with women, writing in fluid perfect cursive, and talking, and—well, you get the point—sent me into depression.

After class I shuffled my way through the crowds of students out to my car to eat my veggie and cheese sandwich Mom had made for me. I stared out the front windshield, lost, wanting nothing more than to crawl, run, or swim back to my comfort world in San Diego.

God, can you hear me? Please, please, please, take me home—I want out of here! I'd never felt so out of place in my life. A coldness seeped down my back as the winter chill, devoid of warm sunshine, frosted the inside of my car. *What the hell am I doing here?*

We all have moments of doubt; we're human. It's what we choose to do when the moment strikes that makes all the difference. I realized I had to get out of my own way. I picked up the pieces of my fractured ego and made it to my next class, keeping in mind I was going to do whatever it took to excel in this challenging early childhood education program. There is no word *quit* with Gurudev. Why would I give my fears the power to stop me, to stop my dreams from reality?

Gurudev often says, "We only doubt the positive things in our life—so doubt the doubts!" Wise words indeed.

During that semester and all that followed, I was pretty much the only male in my classes. One of my favorite, funniest professors would say at the start of class, "Good morning, ladies and Jeremy!"

As it turned out, I was favored by most of my professors, maybe for being a breath of testosterone in a sea of estrogen. But I also believe it was for my undying enthusiasm, commitment, and of course, my pride and joy—humor. I made a lot of tongue-in-cheek jokes in my classes.

Two months into my first semester, I had the opportunity to student-teach in a first-grade classroom in my sister's school, as well as substituting for pay on Fridays. A boost to my resume. I wrote papers, collaborated with fellow students on different projects, all with excellent grades, while flashing my signature smile.

The only downside of that semester was no long Sudarshan Kriya follow-ups in a group, as I was extremely busy. (Though I didn't stop the daily routine by any means; I practiced Sudarshan Kriya every day without fail.) And the extra twenty-five pounds I packed on from living at home with my "cook for her baby son" mother. Man, could I go for some of Mom's homemade pasta right about now.

"Jeremy, I think your tax return is here. Hurry up, come see!" Mom was possibly as excited for my $1,500 check from Uncle Sam as I was.

For me, this sweet and welcomed bonus was going to buy my first Taylor acoustic guitar—510 CE. I probably played twenty different models in guitar shops around both San Diego and Atlanta, yet I bought this one over the phone, flying high on blind faith, and the choice was perfect. This gift to myself made the adventure back home with my parents all that much more enjoyable. And Mom knew what to say when I got on her delicate nerves: "Jeremy, go in your room and play your guitar!" If that was punishment, then please, lock me up with that instrument. I loved playing that sweet guitar and continued writing original songs about life, love, and fantasy.

Toward the end of my first semester, spring arrived. Atlanta was covered in trees blossoming in vibrant colors. The air squeaked of freshness, awakening things deep inside me, stirring my soul. I had an intense desire to get back to Art of Living, even though I'd never really left. I called Bill Herman, one of my biggest inspirations on this path, and asked if I could be on his cooking team in Lake Tahoe for Guru Purnima once again. He gladly accepted my offer.

Two weeks before I left for Lake Tahoe, I read on the online *eSatsang Daily Digest* an announcement for the first-ever International Youth Leadership Training Program (YLTP) sponsored by the Art of Living Foundation at its international center (*ashram*) in Bangalore, India, during the fall semester 2001. Without a dollar in my pocket, I yelled out to no one in particular and the universe in general, "I'm going!" You gotta love passionate, intuitive faith.

When the semester ended at Kennesaw in May 2001, I quit yet another produce job, cashed in over a hundred dollars in coins I'd saved in my top dresser drawer, and drove back to San Diego. My brother, Jeff, happened to be in Atlanta on one of his many cross-country trips at the time, so we drove together but in separate cars. We separated somewhere in Arizona, and I continued west. This was before we had cell phones, so communications with Jeff were primitive for pit stops and layovers.

Leaving my car in San Diego, I took the train to Tahoe, a beautifully scenic adventure through California. The relaxing train ride allowed me to meet a lot of wonderful people, which began a noteworthy trend for me on all my future travel adventures. Most often, I sit by someone who is very open to my sharing the ancient and universal self-knowledge that I have learned from Gurudev. It has been wonderful over the years, sharing, learning, and relearning through some brilliant conversations.

Arriving in Lake Tahoe for my second celebration, I was met with many surprises, adventures, and opportunities to take responsibility. Beyond all this, Gurudev was there for the whole two weeks again.

Bill Herman was once again the chief of daily morning Guru Puja, the recipes and the now familiar yelling at people. I can't say enough about Bill and his unique style of running the show with vibrant energy, making things happen and teaching me every step of the way.

On a drive to pick up groceries, Bill turned his head, barely taking his eyes from the winding road, and told me he was going to attend the first-ever international Youth Leadership Training Program (YLTP). My breath caught in my throat before I excitedly told him I was going too. The man didn't blink once at my blind faith, as I didn't have an extra penny to my name.

Over the next two weeks, a million and three things happened. The most memorable was the first time Gurudev came into the hectic and happening kitchen to check things out. I remember the moment as if it were last night. I was at the stove cooking up some veggies. Aromas of seasoning penetrated the air and here comes my guru, shining like the sun and moon in tandem, sparkling like ten thousand stars during the midnight sun.

He said, "Ah, Jerome (a name he called me in those days), how are you?"

I said, "Really well, Gurudev. I just finished my first semester back at college, and I am going to attend the YLTP in India this fall. May I please have your blessings?"

He lovingly grabbed me by the shoulder and said, "You're going!"

Whoever got those veggies I cooked must have tasted a mouth-watering meal, as I was stoked. I felt three feet off the ground after that meeting. I didn't drop a single vegetable and finished my work by rote. I could barely breathe, but I didn't need oxygen. I couldn't stop smiling; I had Gurudev's blessing for my long-dreamed-of first trip to India!

As soon as Gurudev left the kitchen, I looked over at Geo and Larry, two of my close friends, as well as fellow cooks from the year before. I said, "I have no money."

They didn't shrug their shoulders or blink twice before stating, "Don't worry, we'll do a fundraiser here."

I was stunned at their unconditional willingness to help me with their "Yes Mind" attitude. I felt humble yet excited as an opposite composition played tag in my soul. I had Gurudev's blessings, I had

Geo and Larry agreeing to help. India. How often the dream of visiting had sparkled ahead of me from the videos and studies of the past.

The following night for dinner, Geo and Larry, along with Ron Sharp, another very kind devotee, helped me initiate a fundraiser. *Jai Guru Dev.*

I couldn't wait to call Mom and share my insanely terrific news. "Sure, Jeremy, you got the blessings, but where are you going to get the money from?" was the response.

A day later I called her with $2,000 cash in my hands (a total of $4,000 was raised). I was flying high on optimism and enthusiasm, and sometimes they can prevail over realism.

The most miraculous thing for me in hindsight wasn't the initial funds raised the first night, but rather how every single penny was taken care of, whether in preparation for the trip or during the adventure itself, down to the twenty dollars that Tara (an older devotee from America who lived at the Bangalore Ashram) gave me as I was leaving the ashram. It turned out I needed that twenty for food during a twenty-hour delay at JFK Airport in New York City when I arrived back in the United States—the only cash I had... down to the penny.

But it could've been easier. One Indian family at Tahoe asked me to marry their youngest daughter for visa purposes and in return they promised to take care of my entire trip to India. Did I think about it? Maybe for a second or two. I turned their offer down for several reasons.

When I told Bill about this wild offer he said, "Don't. You have a tremendous opportunity in front of you to serve, and also to give many other kind people the opportunity to do seva by helping you out." I stared at him without making a sound. Bill explained the concept through a fascinating story.

"When Gurudev was first starting out and the ashram was only bare land, one very rich devotee said to him, 'I'd like to fund the development of this whole ashram.' But Gurudev kindly said, 'No thank you, this would take away the wonderful opportunity that many devotees from around the world are going to have in helping to build this place up, stone by stone.'"

The story was an important eye-opener, helping me realize how special this fundraiser truly was and how fortunate I was to be on the receiving end of it. I can't describe in words, nor in song or poetry, how remarkable it was, hour by hour in the natural beauty of the Sierra Mountains, seeing the box fill up and people coming up to me with smiles of support. It was like a showering of Divine blessings raining on my head. I stood there with arms raised high, eyes to the sky, in gratitude and oneness—something miraculous was happening. Another miracle. I was halfway to India.

Just then, Gurudev's words filled my mind: "The most important is the faith in the being, the highest self—the faith that I'm going to get whatever I need and whenever I need. Then you give miracles a chance!"

At least five people came up to me with the same request. "Please let me know if you need any more help; just give me a call."

From financial support in dollar bills to the strange marriage proposal, perhaps one of the most sincere donations was not of money, but a business card. On the back was written, "Jeremy, get in touch with me, I have some important information to share with you about India—*Jai Guru Dev*, Daren."

I turned the business card over in my fingers, feeling the simple stiff cardboard. Daren Black was another former TMer and had been with Gurudev since the early days in the late '80s. Daren's seva in the organization encompassed making the Sudarshan Kriya audiotapes, plus all the responsibilities that came along with the process.

Daren gave me useful tips about traveling in India, from closing my mouth in the shower to wiping off silverware when out to eat. His most appreciated contributions came by way of his ayurvedic medicine he produced in Los Angeles. These little colored pills helped me many times on various trips around the world.

Ayurveda is a "natural" and holistic physical and mental health approach. As one of the world's oldest medical systems, Ayurveda is one of India's traditional health care systems.

The fundraising magic and its glory comprised only a thin slice of the magnificent time I had in Tahoe. As a returning cook from last year, I walked into the familiar kitchen without hesitation and started making things happen. Once again, the cooler was my domain, and I loved being in front of the stove, cooking up all the meals.

Probably due to karmic debt and "everything for a reason," Bill got sick. Gurudev personally told him not to be in the kitchen. When Bill told the group, it was like he and Gurudev were telling me straight to my face to kick it up a few gears and take over. Try not to resist when the universe has other plans for you, go with it. I scooped up more responsibility and it felt awesome.

Gurudev's famous words rang inside me, "Responsibility is not given, it is taken," and, "The more responsibility you take in life, the more powerful you become—wake up and find out the whole world belongs to you and take responsibility for the whole world."

At that moment, I stepped out of my comfort zone, doing more than I thought I was capable of, helping the kitchen and staff run smoothly in feeding hundreds of people. In the bigger picture, Gurudev teaches us that we are not the "doers," we are all just puppets on strings, controlled by the Divine—we, as devotees, have the great opportunity to be involved in *seva* (service), and at the same time, be dispassionate and not concerned about the results or what we might think we are "doing." Dispassion is liberating, freeing a person from the chaos of thinking feverishly and stressing out.

Gurudev says, be a hundred percent in all you do, then there is no confusion, doubts or regrets. He adds, "If your hands are one hundred percent busy, heart one hundred percent full and mind one hundred percent empty, then you'll be giving yourself to the moment and will get the best results—and even then, you have to drop the results and just be."

In the time Bill was out of the kitchen, my whole world grew, flipped around, and exploded in bliss, because I took more responsibility in his absence. My heart filled with joy and grew twice its size at the same time. These days were sweet in service, and the best part was delegating seva to the several hundred course participants who were in silence. I'd become much better at this since last year, when I was loud and a lot less aware.

Guru Purnima 2001 saw around 1,500 spiritual seekers and devotees of Gurudev Sri Sri Ravi Shankar gather in celebration of

July's full moon, plus all the knowledge, grace, love, and blessings they received from their guru, on this most auspicious day.

Moving slowly in the long queue to get Gurudev's direct blessing in the form of a hug, smile, his twinkling eyes, and a few words, was the greatest wait in the world. These phenomenal moments, and I have had many over these past twenty-five years, can only be experienced, not explained. I can only paint a miniature portrait on these white pages. This type of magic is just unfathomable and incomprehensible to the human mind, yet at the same time simple, subtle, and real. Come hang out with me at our ashram in Bangalore, India, or on Guru Purnima in America any summer, and experience the miracles and madness, grace, love, bliss, and magic that surround my guru wherever he goes.

My free time from the kitchen was spent with the children again this year. Later that week, on an ice skating trip at Squaw Valley, Gurudev, being his normal, youthful self, tried to ice skate for the first time. I had the immense pleasure of holding him up, being the big guy with prior skills on ice. The afternoon with Gurudev showed me how simple, childlike, and enthusiastic he really was. I mean, trying his best to ice skate with youngsters is such an atypical thing for an Indian spiritual master to do, or at least you'd think so.

CHAPTER TWELVE

※◎ ◎※

Thank You, India—I Think I Found My Second Home

Always keep room for possibilities. Logically you might think that something is impossible, but many times it becomes possible. So give miracles a chance.
—Gurudev Sri Sri Ravi Shankar

I must admit, I thought of myself as well-cultured, having lived in California and Atlanta among lots of international friends of various nationalities. Arriving at the international terminal of JFK airport in New York City on September 9, 2001, though, was overwhelming. Ahead of me was an eleven-hour flight to Kuwait and I was definitely the only white boy—or white anything—boarding the plane. Well, there were those white traditional Arab outfits (thobes) on many a man.

Was I nervous? Yes. I'd only been on nine flights so far, and flying was still pretty much a new experience. On each flight I had walked through the first-class section and thought to myself, as other people probably do, *Wow, I wonder what it would be like to sit in first class?* The moment would pass, and I'd fold my big and tall body into a seat somewhere in coach.

Flying international for the first time, I stepped through the hatch to see this huge first-class section. Nerves aside, first class looked remarkably luxurious, and I had ample thoughts and desires of enjoying the entire flight right there in the lap of luxury. I moved on down the aisle with a silent sigh.

158

The next sequence of events are an excellent example of how miracles manifest on this spiritual path with Gurudev.

I'd been assigned a window seat, the worst possible choice not only for my less than petite size, but also my old football knee injuries. I get phantom aches just thinking about it. The seat seemed to shrink second by second and I had eleven hours of flight time ahead of me. More uncomfortable by the moment, I prayed to Gurudev to make this flight more relaxed and to make it happen fast.

An Arab man, dressed in his traditional attire, as a host of passengers were, sat down next to me. I momentarily shoved all my mental junk and stress aside, conjuring up my holly-jolly self, and extended my hand saying, "Hi, my name is Jeremy, what's your name?"

Not only did the man not accept my handshake, but he also didn't look at me, respond, or even blink.

Great, I get to fly with miserable physical contortions and aches plus be emotionally ignored, too, for the next umpteen hours. Could the torture get any worse?

My narrow-minded, small-town upbringing was about to kick in hard. I'd reached my last straw, the last nerve, my breaking point. I visualized the handful of flight attendants having to lock me in the closet for wild, out-of-control outbursts. My prayers intensified a thousand-fold. I closed my eyes and slowly took in a deep breath as my calls for understanding screamed in my mind.

Within a minute, a male flight attendant appeared and asked for my boarding pass. *How strange is this?* I stared at him blankly as he quietly said, "Please get your carry-on luggage and come with me."

My prayers were answered—Hallelujah! I truly believed they were kicking me off the flight, realized this was all a horrible mistake, and I'd be free from this whole mess. I foolishly thought that I would be able to catch another flight. As I moved into the aisle to follow the uniformed attendant toward the hatch opening, a smile crossed my face. Being thrown off the plane meant goodbye window seat and the man of stone.

Wrong!

The attendant walked me to the front of the plane and to my surprise, stopped next to the first row in the first-class section. I almost barged into him as he said with a huge smile on his face, "Please sit here, Jeremy."

I looked at the man as if he had grown two heads in the short walk down the aisle, then down at the smooth, wide seating and ample legroom. *Sit here?* A single question popped in my mind. I stuttered, "What about my bags?" as I stared at the man's glowing face of happiness.

His remark was no stranger than anything else that had happened in that last minute. "No one is sitting here [the seat next to me]. You can put them underneath the seat." *Jai Guru Dev*! All I could think was, *Walk (and sometimes fly) like a king and be a perfect servant.*

The long eleven-hour flight was nothing less than grand. I felt like a hologram of Gurudev. They treated me with that kind of love and respect, the type he gets everywhere he goes. The list of amenities was luxurious: of the entire flight, I was served food first, unlimited exotic smoothies were available, and I had two personal video screens and two flight attendants taking care of me the whole time while I stretched out in extreme comfort. Who knew first-class service was this complete?

At the end of this unbelievable flight, the attendants continued their generous care by giving me four bottles of water, toilet paper, and snacks to make my journey in India more comfortable. Astounding. I didn't ask why I was upgraded, nor did they tell me. I flew with a deep sense of gratitude.

Still euphoric, as if that wasn't enough, on the next flight to Mumbai (where I would connect to Bangalore), I met an Indian man who was so kind, he changed his seat to sit next to me. I'm sure I looked lost and perplexed by my far-out travel experience. This wonderful man even took care of me at the Mumbai international and domestic airports, which would have been intense for me alone. Foreign signs, scents, and scenery dotted the space around me as a crowded symphony of voices I couldn't understand played a strange tune.

It was absolutely apparent Gurudev was taking care of me every step of the way, which I believe he always has been, always is, and always will be. In his brilliant words of wisdom: "When you feel the obstacle is too much to handle, deep prayer can work miracles." *Jai Guru Dev.*

Having watched videos of India since 1996 and had my head inside a variety of book pages, my eyes were glued to the words and bright pictures of this historic place. I often requested many of my Indian friends to tell me about their homeland in detail. But no book, video, story, or dream of mine could have remotely prepared me for the sonic blast of all five senses that is India. This country I had dreamed of visiting for years—nothing and nobody could have done it justice. I had to dive into this sea of madness and ocean of beauty, swimming for my life, swallowing saltwater, with the hopes of one fine day being able to tell or sing my tale. Oh, India—I had arrived.

The extremely nice Indian man and I walked outside the Mumbai International Airport at 6:00 a.m. in transit to the domestic airport, and intensity awaited me like someone had ordered ahead for breakfast in bed with an astonishing dessert of smashing cake in your face.

First of all, the smell in the airport was not only foreign to me, but hard to digest. Fortunately, my asthma had been cured since joining the Art of Living and the graces of Gurudev. I kept my breaths shallow as we walked.

One step outside the terminal into the early-morning Mumbai humidity fogged up my glasses, blinding me. Then a second later, I was almost mobbed by a bunch of Indian street beggars. Luckily, being tall kept me from being swallowed up in their pressure. My glasses were so fogged I had to take them off and endure a sixty-percent decrease in visibility in perhaps the most extreme moment of my life.

The super kind gentleman from India guided me onto the domestic flight to Bangalore. I swore I could feel the ashram from the sky.

Bent and folded into the cramped back seat of an indescribable vehicle with four tires, I leaned forward and kindly asked the taxi driver, "Hello, could you please take me to Gurudev Sri Sri Ravi Shankar's Art of Living Ashram?"

"Yes, yes, Ravi Shankar Ashram, yes, I can take you."

"Cool." That was easy enough.

What I wasn't prepared for was the high-grade, teeth-gripping, hair-raising, seat-of-my-pants amusement park thrill ride when he stepped on the gas. If you saw the movie *Eat Pray Love*, Julia Robert's taxi ride to her ashram depicted a fraction of the one I endured. This guy flew fast, barely missing moms with kids in tow, huge cows with bells around their necks, other miniature cars, wooden fruit carts, and pedestrians by mere inches, maybe millimeters.

Cows? That's right, you heard me, I saw cows everywhere! Hindu sacred cows were content grazing in garbage piles on the side of the street, crossing the road at leisure, stepping in front of traffic, and flaunting better karma for not getting hit by my lunatic driver.

I swear, for most of the first hair-raising moments in that taxi, my eyes were squeezed shut and sweat poured down my back as my body went rigid in fear. Thoughts of death crossed my mind every other half-minute.

To ease the off-the-Richter-scale insanity, I reached for what I do best. I started composing a song and singing the words back to myself. Singing is a great way to regulate your breathing and calm strained nerves. The title was "Inches Are Golden on the Streets of Bangalore." God, that was an awesome song, also because it was created during a life-threatening ride.

Toward the end of the forty-five-minute ride, I let go and almost enjoyed myself, repeating with conviction, "This is normal, and I am not going to die." And I didn't. We arrived at the ashram in one piece.

Entering the gates of the Art of Living International Center on Kanakapura Road, I felt not only relieved at surviving the travel, but an intense feeling of being home, at peace, and very grateful to be there.

The first thing I noticed was a serene energy that enveloped everything, a pulsing entity. Beautiful trees and flowers surrounded the area, and I saw a statue of Ganesh, the elephant-headed god and son of Lord Shiva. Ganesh is the remover of obstacles. In India, people pray to Ganesh when they are starting something new and/or to overcome obstacles in life. Seeing the statue as I walked through the Ashram gates felt symbolic and reassuring.

The taxi stopped at the reception building. At the top of the twenty-odd steps leading up to it, a young, good-looking Indian boy named Sanjay greeted me. There were many like Sanjay who volunteer their time to help the ashram. He took me to my room, Shiva 4. I was the first to arrive.

I took a quick shower, letting the tepid water wash away the stench of travel. I stretched my aching body with yoga, practiced Sudarshan Kriya, meditated, and went out for a refreshing walk. Only a few people milled around, and the first ones I met were two girls also in the program: Jamie and Charlotte.

The three of us walked to the meditation hall, peeked inside, and immediately felt the subtle energy. We journeyed up a flight of stairs and reached the magnificent and resplendent Sumeru Mantap.

Back in 1981 while searching for potential ashram land, Gurudev asked the driver of the car to stop at a barren, rocky hillside in the middle of nowhere. The people in the car with him, including Pitaji, his father, could not believe he wanted to stop at this desolate location. The story goes, as only the late Pitaji can tell it, Gurudev walked to the top of the rocky hill, meditated, and came back down to say, "This is it; this is where we will make our ashram." The spot where he meditated is where Sumeru Mantap stands today.

No blade of grass, green or burnt-brown, existed back then. There were no trees or water supply, no nothing; just five hills filled with rocks and something special that Gurudev sensed. I felt the serene, blissful energy generating from this marble structure at the ashram. To this day it is my favorite place to visit, sit, meditate, look out into the distance, and play music.

During lunchtime in the old kitchen, my small group assembled outside on the patio to eat our meal, and I first saw Matt. I know it's strange, but this is a different Matt than my San Diego dude. One look was all it took, taking in his rocking blond, dirty dreadlocks, scrubby facial hair, and eyes that could pierce through the skin of a rock. I blurted out, "Hi, Matt. I'm just trying to figure out what lifetime I remember you from."

That was it; we were on-the-path brothers again. Musically, Matt and I grew up on the same classic rock and jam band scene, namely the Grateful Dead and Phish.

Speaking of Phish, Matt looked like he'd jumped off the Phish tour bus from the summer of 2001 and landed at the Art of Living Ashram. This is what I loved most about him at first impression. Matt and I are so alike that before coming here, we'd bought the same pair of shoes.

My first night at the ashram, Matt and I rocked off jet lag and the astonishment of being there by listening to all my Dead tapes and talking for hours into the middle of the night. And then we moved into Shiva 5 with guess who? Bill, yes, the head chef at Tahoe—Bill Herman right here in India, as he promised.

The purpose of the Youth Leadership Training Program as designed by Gurudev is to make the most of the high natural energy of the rural youth in India. The program encourages and empowers them as strong, inspired leaders so they go back to their villages and make a difference. And what an enormous difference they have made in India, and other parts of the world, over the past two decades!

Youth from villages all around India were invited to the ashram in Bangalore to undergo this training. These young people had megawatts of useful energy yet were not doing anything constructive, and many times were destructive to their bodies and community. I recognized my own young exuberance in their stories; youth is universal. Deep inside, they naturally wanted to do more and ultimately give back to their communities.

During these two-week programs, though sometimes longer, youth experienced vigorous training, first learning yoga, Sudarshan Kriya, and meditation for an essential foundation. Team building activities followed, with physical fitness training and learning how to teach health and hygiene awareness courses called Breath Water Sound.

Our college team of six, led by Bill, was grouped with thirty wildly enthusiastic youth from Maharashtra (a state in West India— home to Mumbai and Pune). We nestled together into this special hall called Narayana, the meditation hall at the ashram where Gurudev recorded the first Sudarshan Kriya audiotape back in the early '80s. The hall was only twenty or so steps from Shakti Kutir—a modest round building where Gurudev lived.

The first day, the course saw the crowd in the expansive room divided with the Americans in rows on the right and the Indians on the left, with our teacher, Ajey Vij, sitting in the front of the room. After that first morning session, no boundaries or barriers existed. The warm sense of belonging spread like wildfire among everyone— as it does in every Art of Living course. This new awareness in friendship, laughter, cooperation, and acceptance was as big for us as it was for them. As I wrote in my first group email back home, "All the Indians in our course are so cool. It took them a half hour to get used to me—then they locked me in the bathroom!"

The fifteen-day intensive course began early in the morning with Anil Bahl, a tall and wonderful devotee, leading us in yoga. We then broke for breakfast and seva, which usually included cutting veggies, cleaning toilets, picking up trash around the ashram, and a host of other things.

Ajey was a confident, intelligent, slightly balding man with a significant smile. He was as hard on us as he was patient and kind, a yin-yang of emotion. His expectations of respect and responsibility were fearsome. For example, one day a bunch of us were late for morning yoga by a few minutes. He made us run all the way up the steep hill to Sumeru Mantap, grab one rock, and bring it back to the hall, within three minutes. Talk about boot camp. His intensity for structure, punctuality, focus, and dedication became well known.

Joking and fooling around one morning after breakfast when none of us were really engaged in service, Matt and I saw two ashram workers from the neighboring village struggling to carry several big garbage cans held up with two metal poles. Without thinking or discussing, Matt and I grabbed an end of each pole and helped the guys out. They were happy and appreciative, but we worried we were going to be late for the next session at 10:00 a.m. With a deep breath and a shrug of our shoulders, we continued helping the workers anyway.

"Hi, Matt. Hi, Jeremy," piped a briskly-walking Ajey as he passed us.

Our faces paled; you know, that sinking feeling as sweat dripped down the side of my face and I thought, *Oh, we're in trouble now. He's going to beat us to the hall, and we'll be late.*

Matt and I finished the job, emptying the big cans into the compost pile recycling area and rushed to class. We were dead meat and couldn't imagine the consequences waiting for us.

165

Ajey, however, went off on an interesting tangent, blasting the whole group for not doing seva after breakfast. He ranted how this group was not a hundred percent committed and—get this—that, "Jeremy and Matt are the only ones I see doing seva! You should see these two American boys carrying heavy garbage cans in the hot sun, risking being late to class."

Matt and I looked at each other and tried like hell not to burst out laughing. We were as guilty as the others, slacking off that morning moments before, only to jump into some quick seva at the end, be seen by our teacher, *and* get praised for it. Matt and I still joke about it. Thanks, Ajey!

We were five most fortunate college students: Matt, Erin, Jamie, Charlotte, and I, along with our fearless leader, Bill. We all had taken off a semester of college to attend this fine program, and what we received in return was what I refer to as true education: hands-on experience and immersion in service learning you cannot get from lectures or books.

Matt and I got word that Gurudev would come home around midnight. Being young and wild college students at the time, we ventured out of Shiva 5 and joined around twenty ashramites (people who lived at the ashram) waiting for his arrival.

Forgetting all about the incredible flight I'd experienced the week before, I was mindless in front of Gurudev, again. He looked at Matt and me, asked how we were, and asked me, "How was your flight?" And, with that distinctive twinkle in his eyes and beam, "Did they take good care of you?"

I had no words to speak, nor did I need any. I held my hands in prayer position against my chest and smiled wide, feeling intense sensations of love rising inside my body. I could have instantly melted right there into a soggy puddle, but I stayed strong until I looked at Matt, who knew the story, and then the tears rolled down. I floated back to Shiva 5 for a couple hours of sleep before our next day of YLTP boot camp with Ajey and Anil.

By leaving the United States on September 9, I was across the Atlantic, thousands of miles away, when the attacks of 9/11 struck.

There is an innocence being out of the mainstream media, the shock and screams were not replayed over and over for me. Without television and radio, I was isolated from the sheer terror and dom-ino-effect of emotions during this time. Instead, I was focused on learning to serve the world and its children with an indelible passion.

My heart and blessings go to all who were affected.

"Bill, could you please turn the fan back on?" Matt's voice hissed in the darkness.

"I would like to sleep now. I prefer it off," Bill replied.

For the second time in two minutes, Matt got up and turned the fan back on, with me grinning, holding back laughter from this mini-drama.

The next moment, Bill gets up once again and turns the fan off.

"If you turn the fan off one more time, I am going to kick your ass, Bill." Matt flicked the fan's switch.

I was, by now, biting my tongue, trying to keep from falling off the narrow bed in laughter. Bill, who taught high school art in Chicago for twenty-five years, was not going to let some hippie-punk twenty-year-old get the best of him. He sprang up for the last time and shut the fan off, which was at the foot of my bed in this humid, cramped three-bed-filled room.

The next moment was reminiscent of my high school days, where fights broke out in the hallways at the drop of a backpack. As soon as Bill flicked the off switch, Matt's tall, lanky body appeared and gave him a solid shove. Bill shoved him right back. After a few rounds of immature Indian wrestle mania, Bill stormed out of the room in anger around eleven o'clock. I'm sure he heard Matt and me laughing our tails off on his way out.

I'm also sure, like many other times that season, our laughter added unnecessary fuel to an already overbearing fire. Knowing Bill, he probably headed straight to Sumeru to meditate and ask the heavens, "What am I going to do with these two cracked-up kids in my room?"

If putting up with me in the kitchen for those memorable weeks in Tahoe was not enough, now Bill had a Tasmanian Devil–like American kid with not only his crazy characteristics but who could light my fuse and send me shooting in any direction, anytime. Matt and I were a sight to see together—and still are. The combined laughter alone is enough to push some humans to their breaking point. If button pushing was an Olympic team sport, hand Matt and myself the gold.

We felt Bill, at times, was like a five-year-old trapped in a fifty-year-old body. I love him dearly, the best sub-guru on my spiritual path. Bill will flow through stories again and again on this journey.

Things ultimately got better in our room. One reason was we got a new roommate because of the large number of people who were arriving for the magnificent *Navaratri* celebrations at the ashram. Cimi was a former TMer, around the same age as Bill and had been living at the ashram for some time. He was the kind soul who drove me to my first Silence course in Apple Valley back in December '98.

Now the floor was even—two older American meditators and two young American meditators/button pushers. Shiva 5 was much more serene and humane. That does not mean we didn't bust Cimi and his unique and humorous habits on frequent occasions.

Everything was new and exciting, including learning to eat with my hands. This Indian custom was fun and challenging at the same time. My friend Pranav Desai would bust me for taking the vegetables and rolling them up in the chapatti, as if I were making a burrito. The locals take lentils, mixed vegetables, and rice and mix them all up on the plate with their right hand. (Even lefties are trained from a young age to eat with their right hand.) They scoop it up and eat happily. I tried it, failed miserably at it, but then eventually succeeded, all in good fun.

Getting used to the Indian squat toilets—shaped porcelain holes on the ground with the same design for both male and females—was not easy. There's a space to put your feet, but being a big guy, my feet were always further away than the suggested footprints on the edge of the toilet.

Besides having to squat down, there was no toilet paper, just a waterspout and a big and small bucket.

I worked out a system: take all my clothes off, hang them on the door, squat down, use the water to wash, and then put my clothes back on. This is still how I do it in India, so I won't get my clothes dirty or wet. Sound fun? Go on, give it a try someday.

The water was another beast. Like warnings I used to get in Mexico, we were not to drink the tap water in India. Daren Black took further extremes to tell me not to brush my teeth with it, to use bottled water instead. Also, the rule in the shower was always close your mouth! These concepts took some time and awareness to get used to. And were unavoidable at times, like a little tap water in the food, or on the plates and utensils in the kitchen. I was lucky to be hit with what is known as "Delhi belly" only twice that season, each for one night.

Being able to live and exist in this culture daily was enough education to last the next five years. It was like a bachelor's degree in Indian culture, with a lot of field work. I am sure that season there were thousands of foreigners in India, but sometimes I felt like the only one.

On the first night of our program, I told Matt how I'd love to sing in satsang, and he said, "Go for it!"

Only a year before, I'd led my first bhajan, and I could probably count the times I led a song in satsang on both hands, and maybe a few toes. I was raw, nervous, and gung-ho about throwing myself into this.

There wasn't a guitar for me to use, so I sat myself in front of the keyboard owned by the resident musician, Prasoon. He hadn't arrived yet, so I jumped in and began the satsang with over one hundred people sitting around and behind me. I started with my favorite bhajan at that time, "Om Namah Shivaya Gurave Sachidananda."

I was confident enough on the keyboard to lead the song, and after the first few notes, something mystical happened. Since Gurudev was not in the ashram at the time, his picture sat on his swinging chair on the stage. I locked my eyes onto his picture and sang with all my heart. I felt like he danced on my hands, enabling me to not miss a single note—I didn't lay a wrong hand or finger down.

As I basked in this spiritual experience, with the serenity of many Indians singing with me, I looked down at my hands, with the thought, *Wow, look at me playing.*

That was it, I hit two wrong chords, and realized it was not *me* playing at all; that I am always on the strong strings from the Divine. I quickly re-fixed my gaze on Gurudev's picture and completed the song flawlessly.

Even now in satsang, one will notice I mostly have my eyes closed; it is such an inner experience. And like that first song on the keyboard at the ashram, whenever I open my eyes and think I am the doer or try to get fancy on the guitar or keyboard, I always mess up.

The beauty of this music is that it is always for other people. Gurudev says, "All of our talents are for others. If you don't make use out of them, they will be taken away from you." As if I needed another reason to keep singing like a bird.

As satsang singers, we have a huge responsibility to drive the train, making sure the people on board are taken care of, feel safe and comfortable, and have the space to express themselves. If this was the only blessing Gurudev Sri Sri Ravi Shankar had given me on this path, I would be ever so grateful. It is one of many and all are equally magnificent. I'm grateful.

Ajey gave our team one day off, and Bill led us into the city. It had been over a week since my first taxi ride scared the pants off me. I jumped in and sat in the front. *Yeehaw, look, Mom, no hands!* I treated this ride like a G-force adventure ride at Six Flags. I embraced every near-miss accident, every sight, sound, thrill, and joy driving forty minutes to inner-city Bangalore.

We headed straight for pizza, then ice cream. After eating only the food at the ashram for over a week, I think we were all dreaming of pizza. And this would not be the last time, at least for me.

I didn't bring my guitar with me on this trip to India because I had no idea what it was going to be like, but I quickly found I needed one. I bargained for one in a local shop, and then managed to strum every penny of use out of the sweet thing.

In satsang that night, I sat up front in the meditation hall, determined to lead a song or two. I plugged in my new and shiny acoustic guitar and put myself out there for the first of many times with a guitar at the ashram.

I had been secretly practicing a Divya Prabha song behind closed doors that summer, "*Shiva Raja*." I did my best to sing the words like she did on her latest album—in a peppy style. But, and that's a big but, at the ashram and in India in general, they sing her songs and others differently than we do in America. This took me time to learn.

Anyway, I blasted, and I mean rock and roll blasted, into that tune, with my mispronunciations, foreign style, and accent. I had my eyes wide open and was surprised at all the people walking up to the front to look at who was singing that (to them, funny) song. Like there was a clown in the hall, with balls of fire circling my head, in full makeup and the like.

Besides my different style of singing, one of the local devotees told me I was also mispronouncing one key word. Instead of saying, "*Shiva Raja, Mahesh Wara,*" I was saying, "*Shiva Raja, Mahesh Wada.*" Wada being a tasty Indian savory! Ha ha, joke was on me, again. I didn't mind, it was all good fun.

After that wild song, everyone clapped. What a trip.

I played one more, this time a more complicated traditional one with the same reactions and results. I was creating my own bhajan sound that season, and all things considered, I was learning from various angles and corners, even from Indian savories.

The fifteen days of YLTP were ending. I was unexplainably happy being at this most remarkable spiritual center in India, letting go of past impressions and self-centeredness, and growing stronger in knowledge, teamwork, and love.

On one of the last days, I shared with the group my experience in one sentence. "I feel I have gotten five years younger over the past two weeks, from sadhana (yoga, Sudarshan Kriya and meditation), new friendships, and laughter."

It was really that great. Waking up early in the morning for group sadhana and seva, followed by interactive and fun sessions where we were learning how to teach the Breath Water Sound course for underprivileged and wonderful humans, eating healthy and yummy Indian food, and celebrating each night with rocking satsangs.

Ajey told us that while traveling around India, he encountered intense obstacles when setting up and conducting Art of Living courses for corporate professionals. He noted that just when he could not handle the pressures anymore, he prayed to Gurudev in a helpless plea. Miracles showered down on him, and even the most difficult of situations were taken care of. These stories reminded me of my flight to India and how the miracle arrived when I felt most helpless. Ajey's accounts reassured me that I was never alone on this path.

I sat cross-legged against the back wall, with one cushion under my bum and another behind my back, bawling my eyes out, frozen, a feeling of oneness with everything, and immense gratitude for Gurudev for everything he had brought to my storybook life. I could have sat there for a year, maybe more, basking in stillness and absorbing the bountiful love.

The day arrived when we'd find out which of us would become teachers of the program by receiving a course manual. The ones who did not receive a manual were no less than the ones who did—everyone was involved with the organization and its many aspects of the course.

I felt confident I would become a teacher, based on my indelible faith in Gurudev, passion for this knowledge, never missing a single day of Sudarshan Kriya in four-and-a-half years, my communication skills, and after this tremendous course, some much-needed leadership skills, too. But who knows how the whole selection works?

Enter Swami Brahmatej. Swamiji was a very peaceful-looking man, somewhere in his forties, dressed all in white, with short hair and a clean-shaven face. His smile was as simple as it was powerful, his soul as bright as it was angelic. Both advertised the contentment this man had achieved in his life.

Today, Swamiji was to present the Breath Water Sound manuals to the new teachers from our group. Ajey had told us much about him, how kind, sweet, and devoted to Gurudev he was. He said that Swamiji communicated to Gurudev in silence. I said to myself, *Wow, I want to experience that.*

We sat and listened to Swamiji talk for some time on the importance of being an instrument of Gurudev and becoming one of his
teachers in the Art of Living. And then Ajey announced the names.
One by one, each excited new teacher went up to the front to receive
their manuals and blessings from Swamiji—and I was one of them.
Billy (already an Art of Living teacher), Erin (who had recently completed the teacher training course in Canada), and I became teachers
from our group. I felt bad for Matt, as he seemed a bit down because
he did not become a teacher at that time.

The night before, Bill had given us a talk about this process,
what it meant, and that some would and others would not become
teachers the next day. Bill explains things in a strong, direct manner.
He did this again for Matt after the new teacher ceremony. Matt got
over it quickly and we moved on in seva and celebration.

Our first service journey found us in one of the slum areas of Bangalore,
helping by cleaning the streets, taking part in a free medical camp organized by local Art of Living doctors, and serving food to all the community members. This adventure was very humbling, being in one of
the poorest sections of the city, where income is minimal, food is insuf-
ficient, poor health and hygiene conditions exist, and education is rare.

Looking around, I saw cows lying on the sidewalks and streets,
grazing on rubbish, with hundreds of flies swarming around them.
It was not difficult to spot a street dog, usually sick-looking, skinny,
eating the garbage that runs rampant on the sides of the roads. The
bitter, acidic smells in the slum area are something unique, and
most people I know would not be able to stomach them. Brightness
around those parts is almost nonexistent aside from the young children giggling and smiling.

One thing is for sure, there is no lack of people there. Bangalore
is a large city, and in the slums, there seems to be a higher percentage
of people per square inch than on the city streets.

All in all, the uncleanliness of the areas cannot cover the innocence, love, and kindness of the people who live there. They make

up in human values what they lack in monetary goods. They are the people Gurudev speaks of when he says, "People in India will borrow off a neighbor just to feed a stranger." I would never be the same after spending time in these slum districts. I was grateful to Gurudev for sending me there.

Engulfed in the street cleaning, I didn't have much time to think about myself and how fortunate I was growing up in an American middle-class family, as hundreds of little Indian kids came out to join us. Different shapes and sizes, the children showered me with smiles and giggles. Their clothes were worn yet brought splashes of color to the streets, like a garden of blooming wildflowers.

After the street cleaning, we served food to the people in the village. The children were ecstatic, lined up with excitement, eager for their portion, with minimal shoving as they danced from one foot to the other as they waited. And they kept coming back for more, holding their bowls between their hands.

Finally, we went over to see how the free medical camp was going. The doctors were local Art of Living volunteers, giving check-ups and medicine to people.

I could not help noticing a bowl of candy on the table at the front and one skinny little tricky boy who kept sneaking back in, again and again, to get some. They asked me, being the big guy I was, to man the entrance and make sure the kids did not keep coming back in. This kid would sneak under my legs to get back in, until I decided to use my own tricks. I picked him up and hoisted him on my shoulder, and he loved it. So did I.

The next day, Bill showed me a picture of this boy on my shoulder, and I swear it was the greatest photo I have ever seen. This picture-perfect glimpse of joy in service went on to be the cover of flyers for the following year's Youth Leadership Training Program in America.

My first four and a half years in the Art of Living were mainly sadhana and satsang; practicing yoga, pranayama breathing techniques, Sudarshan Kriya and meditation, plus singing Sanskrit songs in satsang whenever I got the chance. This is where I was at when I first arrived in India.

This season was the transition into seva. From self-centeredness to selflessness, from asking what more I could get to asking how I could give, from being the loud stereotypical American in India to being a more reserved and quieter boy. Okay, maybe not reserved and quiet, but something inside me was becoming more silent by the day, by the meditation and with each hand I put out in service, and of course, with each joyful scream in celebration each night during satsang. Life was changing dramatically for me, as it was back home in America, going through post-9/11.

Our second seva trip was into another slum district in Bangalore. The same medical team set up a free camp, and we brought lots of homemade food to share with the community.

I got a bunch of kids together, and although they did not speak any English, I proceeded to communicate with them. I asked them, using my skills in body language, if they had a ball. The consensus was a resounding no. Once again, I inquired through hand gestures where we could buy one. The kids, easily over thirty strong, led me down the street to a local shop that sold balls. I bought a few with what rupees I had in my pocket, and we skipped back to their neighborhood. We played volleyball without a net and a great game of dodge ball, filled with enthusiasm and no formal language communication.

I called the folks in Atlanta with the news about having the greatest day of my life with these children. I called home once a week during my time in India.

The net of my life was being cast wider in the sea of possibilities. I thrived in the adventures and new corners ahead. I experienced more, saturated in the Indian culture and aura, including a crush or two.

Though my heart was cracking open like a broken dam pressed by a thousand tons of barreling water, I still had the kid from Taylor inside of me. As Matt and I headed back to our bus, the children followed us. I noticed a young Indian dude, maybe around twenty, though he looked older with his signature south Indian mustache. He was smoking. Being the teacher to be that I was, and, of course, a straightforward American male, I asked him not to smoke around the children.

As you could imagine, he didn't like that. He started yelling at me in English, along the lines of "Who do you think you are to tell me not to smoke?" and, "Go home. This is my Bangalore, I'll do whatever I want!" And, straight from the lines of a Snoop Dog or gangster rap album, "I'll break you off something!"

So, keeping myself and Matt amused, I cracked a solid joke on him, something wordy, turned around, and almost fell over laughing with Matt. Call this dynamic, call it rude—this is how I was, and I was doing better than before and more good than bad. Matt and I were having a ball in India, on all levels. Either way, Gurudev accepted me as I was.

Of all the fun and laughter I had in India, the phone calls with Mom brought a smile. Rightfully so at this time, Mom was terrified for me being far away from home during the height of post-9/11. I assured her I was safe many times, adding, "This is the safest place on earth," copying a quote from Bill on the same subject.

I'll never forget when I called her from the ashram, and she was not worried for the first time. Mom said in all seriousness, "So what is it like there—do they have roads?"

Between the time of that phone conversation and our next one, Mom caught a documentary on TV about India. And she made sure to tell me everything she knew about India now, including the cows on the street. Mom is lovely, always was, and always will be. She wins the Best Mom Award coupled with Funniest Mom Award, too! I look forward to the day I can take her to the ashram.

Our team had considerable street cleaning experience by now, walking around another slum district in Bangalore, doing our best to inspire others to join us in the cleanliness campaign. By no means did we ever feel indifferent about the living conditions around these parts, but it was what it was, and we knew why we were there. My country engaged in dirty politics and business, used dirty words, and created dirty movies and songs—this slum district just had dirty streets. We were there to help and inspire the locals who had what most humans in developed world areas lack: *human values.*

This was the essence of the Art of Living's Youth Leadership Training Program: to help spread health and hygiene awareness, to teach simple and powerful breathing techniques and meditation, to promote good health and peace of mind, and to aid in the blossoming of human values, which they already have an abundance of.

What the people in these communities were lacking was not friendliness, or a sense of belonging (they lived mere feet from each other), or a willingness to help each other—but the tools to better health, the tools to become strong leaders in the community, especially the youth. With all their great energy, they don't know how to use it in positive ways.

Of the many milestones I have seen Gurudev effortlessly achieve over the years in this large organization, the effect these Breath Water Sound courses and the Youth Leadership Training Program have had on villages around India and elsewhere is beyond comprehension.

A showcase of Art of Living's work around the world in partnership with International Association for Human Values is encouraging:

8,447,300 benefitted through hygiene and medical camps
5,915,000 benefitted through free trauma-relief workshops
80,000 children benefitted from 702 free schools in India
40,212 villages reached with the 5H Program
2,200,000 farmers trained in natural farming worldwide
81,000,000 trees planted worldwide
800,000 inmates transformed worldwide

"*Govinda na na na na—Gopala wooo wooo!*" So sounded the celebration horn from the loudmouth of the big kid from Taylor once again. This time followed by a hundred smiles, a hundred pounds of enthusiasm, and a hundred seeds of love from a hundred little boys and girls from a slum district near a famous Shiva temple in Bangalore, India. Walking with my team and trusty guitar, rounding up locals to come out and join us in street sweeping and cleaning, the little children began to swarm. The kids were always the first ones on the scene, with their lovable smiles, chirping laughter, and impeccable innocence.

I was playing some song, but it was not working. The kids weren't joining in. As it has been with music and me (and still is), I made things up on the spot, faked it 'til I could make it. This time, with the glisten of a fairytale in the air, these hundred young souls ready to rock at the drop of a hat, or the sound of my guitar, I rolled with the moment and responded to the need. I knew we needed an easy, rockin' song as we had all these kids walking down the street with us, in what would soon be an even more extended moment of bliss.

I busted out one of the seven or so traditional songs I knew, a bhajan, "*Govinda Jaya Jaya, Gopala Jaya Jaya.*" Putting my own twists and turns on the song, the kids were singing along, but they weren't getting the more complicated second part. I tapped into creativity's glory chest one more time and came out with something catchy, "*Govinda na na na na—Gopala whoo!*"

I can't tell you how exciting that moment felt, from the time those words sprang to the next moment when those little heroes of enthusiasm sang it back to me, louder than I was putting it out. Walking down the street, with all the kids following, singing my new song creation, I felt like Michael Jackson—or at least how I thought he might have felt on many occasions.

I'll admit, a little went to my head, but more went right to my heart and emerged as creativity in service. I felt the essence of my guru's grace and love flowing through me, as I was an instrument of his to bring smiles to this world—a world that desperately needed all the smiles it could get. That catchy, captivating line took souls high, made my mind happy like sunshine, and was to stay around for another two years strong in North and Central America. I played the songs as I heard them, without thinking too much about chords and words.

These village children had less to eat than what I might waste in half a day. They were exceptional humans—so inspiring. They brought me back to a humble space, one I had been internally longing to rediscover. These were some of the best days of my life. That season in India was about growing something magnificent, and it would only get better, or shall I say, *deeper.*

A white and red ambulance drove slowly up Kanakapura Road, pushing along at 5:00 a.m., on its way for another day of service.

"Hey, y'all, here comes a truck. Let's hitch a ride."

So our team of four flagged down the ambulance, jumped inside, and was greeted by several bright, innocent smiles.

"Jayanagar, please?"

Today was a big day. We were going to one of the slum districts to teach our first Breath Water Sound course. We wanted to start the course at 7:00 a.m., so we got an early start doing yoga, Sudarshan Kriya, and meditation in Narayana Hall at the ashram.

On the way, Matt asked me to learn a new song. We settled on Divya Prabha's "*Narayana Hari Om.*" I had never played it before, but I was more confident now as a musician, as well as with bhajans. "I bet ya I can figure it out in one minute, Matt," I'd said, and that was it, G D Em C G D, and we had a beautiful song to greet the welcoming locals with at 6:00 a.m.

As we arrived in the slum, there were a few aunties doing the morning chores, but everyone else was asleep.

Picture this: Shoeboxes of concrete-made homes, stacked pretty much on top of one another, doorways around two feet apart, one step in both directions and you are practically in someone's living room. We walked up and down the narrow lanes, playing guitar and singing, as people woke up, popped their heads out their doors in authentic curiosity, and young children joined us.

We started organizing the three-day course at 6:00 a.m. It took a solid two Indian-hours to get the course underway. Even then, it was a master challenge of patience and wit to keep everyone seated and the children outside. The course ran two hours a day for three straight days.

There was another dynamic we had to tackle: how to get the same group back to the course the next day. If there was a button-pushing session bigger than organizing and teaching these courses, I'd like to see it.

Overall, our first course was sweet. Erin Smith and I taught it, with a local Art of Living teacher translating into Kannada. This was my first course. I vividly recall the serene moment after the first meditation. I was looking at Erin, with an expression which said, "Should I bring them out of meditation?"

She whispered, "Let them meditate." Erin waited a few minutes and then, with her beautiful voice, started singing "*Om Namah Shivaya*," as soft as a songbird on the banks of the Ganges River, celebrating the rising of the summer sun. Oneness abounded.

"Gurudev is calling your team from America to his kutir right now." Here comes extra happiness! Gurudev's humble home at the ashram was called Shakti Kutir. It was a small, round hut with a gatekeeper standing guard at the bottom of the stairs letting only senior teachers or anyone with an appointment in. Fair enough. So, to be called to his kutir was an overwhelming joy. Suffice it to say, our feet were on fire, shuffling to get there as quickly as we could.

"I wonder what he is going to say to us," I thought.

As we entered, there were only one or two others sitting on the floor. We plopped ourselves down, sitting cross-legged, and eager to talk with Gurudev.

"Hmm... how are you all doing? Are you comfortable and happy here?" he said in his innocent voice and gentle manner.

A resounding, "Yes, yes!" came from us all.

And with that, our hilarious master read a list of jokes someone had emailed him. The topic: Course names at the Terrorist University. I remember "Rock Throwing 101," "Advanced Slogan Chanting," "Crash Course Flight Training," and "A Million Things to Hate about George W. Bush." (Now wait a minute, I thought that was a course at the UC Berkeley!)

Out of the darkest depths of recent events back home in America, came the healing of laughter. We were rolling in laughter, smiling like carefree children, Matt and I hitting each other on the arm.

But wait—wasn't this an enlightened spiritual master, world renowned humanitarian and saint, sitting five feet in front of us, in his own living room? Aren't gurus supposed to be holy, serious, and saintly? Well, for the hundredth time, I witnessed, as well as enjoyed, Gurudev Sri Sri Ravi Shankar's childlike humor, joy, and jokes—and this is one titanic reason why I have been his devotee for so long, why I take every opportunity to be around him, why I am so super, super happy when I am in his presence. He is better than a five-ring circus mixed with Disney World and Six Flags Amusement Parks, all in one. He is a master of rare flavor and skill, he is a master who is only love and shines on all to see, feel, and share with others.

To be around Gurudev is to be in utter joy, happiness, celebration, and laughter. And then, of course, we all go out into the world and share our joy with others. This is the Art of Living. Having such a fine appreciation for life in its totality, having a guru work on you, washing away the junk the world loves to pile on us, and bringing out the best in human values and smiles in us. This is a true master-mix of lovable innocence and understandable, unfathomable intelligence. *Jai Guru Dev*!

The boy on my shoulder during a medical camp
in Bangalore, September 2001

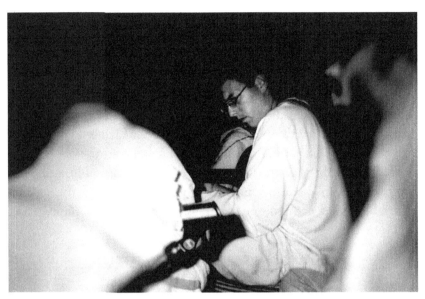

Satsang in the Old Meditation Hall at the Bangalore Ashram, October 2001

Bangalore Ashram village road, which is now all built up, October 2001

CHAPTER THIRTEEN

Navratri

Let this place be a chance for miracles in the lives
of millions of people—where tears turn into
smiles, desperation turns into hope, dullness turns
into creativity and hatred turns into love.
—Gurudev Sri Sri Ravi Shankar

The ashram was abuzz, more than just something in the air. There was an electric current of anticipation, almost tangible, as if the universe had imploded to this area. In a few days, thousands of people from around the world would arrive to celebrate Navratri. Navratri means "nine nights" and honors the nine aspects of the Mother Divine.

Our YTLP group knew little about it—a lot of things were new to us—but Bill had celebrated it here several times. He told us how it is a very auspicious nine days when there are specific and powerful *pujas* and *yagyas* (ancient Vedic ceremonies of Sanskrit chanting and offering), performed to purify the environment and send positive vibrations out into the world.

With all the people coming to join us there was lots of seva to do. Our team started by cleaning the various rooms around the ashram. Luckily, I was very good at cleaning, thanks to years of kitchen jobs, produce coolers, and my own apartments in California. It was hard work, but we did it with joy. I never thought scrubbing toilets could be fun. With Matt and me in a room, jail could be fun.

Traditionally on Navratri, Gurudev goes into silence for a few days—for one of the busiest men in the world with flights, meetings, text messages, phone calls, emails, satsangs, courses, and worldly dealings, this is a much-needed break. I believe there is a much deeper meaning and happening with his silence. The only devotee around him was Swami Sadyojathah, an ex-communist turned spiritual man who hailed from the royal family of Kerala in southern India. Essentially, he renounced his throne as the Prince of Kerala to be a full-time volunteer teacher with the Art of Living. He's also a good friend of mine.

The energy at the ashram during this time was super high, yet subtle.

It was said we could also take a period of silence while Gurudev did, if we chose. Being the big mouth American in heaven, with all these wonderful people around, the last thing on my agenda was keeping my mouth closed.

Bill, along with Matt, opted to take this special period of silence. I respected them the best I could, being their roommate. I was a bit jealous, seeing how serene they were becoming each day. I felt bad as I blabbed all day while they enjoyed the stillness and silence of their own inner faculties. I valued my periods of silence in the Art of Living Silence courses, but this significant festival was different for me then.

During the afternoon of one silence day, I was in the outside amphitheater where the nightly satsangs took place, and I heard one of the teachers announcing from the stage: "Gurudev has sent a message that the participants who are in silence are too somber. The total energy here has gone down. If you want to come out of silence, you can. If you remain in silence, please be joyful."

I thought, *How could one not be joyful at this ashram?*

The teacher's words clicked a switch. I folded back into a self-centered pattern from my childhood. I told both Matt and Bill, "Gurudev told everyone to come out of silence, stating people have become too serious."

I've done many stupid things in my short life, and hurting people's feelings, I'm sorry to say, has been high on the list.

They broke their silence, asking someone if it was true, and got a negative reply. Bill found me soon after and yelled a tirade from his heart. I felt like chump change—this was one of the low points of that season. Luckily, both Bill and Matt forgave me, choosing to go back into silence for another day and all was well. It was another mark on the chalkboard against me in Bill's mind.

For as long as I've played guitar, people have asked if I would teach them, though I've never taken formal guitar lessons. I've taught several people, mainly children who had an eagerness to learn. I've found great joy in teaching music, as with anything else I've taught.

After a few sincere requests, I started teaching solo and then group guitar lessons up the hill at Sumeru Mantap—a spectacular place to do anything, including an afternoon meditation. From there, others wanted singing lessons, so I taught what I knew and each day we sang songs and played guitars in the afternoons of Navratri. There was a group of about ten to fifteen of us, plus a revolving door of mostly young adults.

One student stood out in my heart. I honored the request to give basic guitar lessons to a sixty-year-old Indian woman. She told me about her dream of learning to play the six-string wood and steel music machine.

With each lesson I taught, I found myself becoming a better musician. Detailing how-to tips to others made my own fingers more sensitive to the sounds. It is like an expansive confidence, moving brighter with each success. I found the same was true when teaching the Breath Water Sound courses in the slums and villages.

People arrived from all over the world for Navratri: South Africa, America, Dubai, Russia, Taiwan, Singapore, Germany, and a beautiful girl from Dehra Dun, India, named Aparna.

"Wow, where did you come from?" I asked myself in joyous wonder. Add to the uncommonly innocent, strikingly beautiful female pattern I was experiencing in India, Aparna was the bright star on my childhood Christmas tree. She was a typical looking north Indian princess (*Maha Rani*) in my wildly creative mind, with big, dark, bright eyes; fair skin; a gleaming smile; long, flowing, black hair; and a style of her own.

She was as sweet for me as I was for her. We got to know each other during walks around the ashram. She hung out in the background at Sumeru during my music lessons, her eyes twinkling under thick, dark lashes. At night, during the traditional Garba dancing, we danced together, smiling and singing. Call it an illusion, call it the angels of the ashram playing their cupid games, call it Gurudev playing his—it was a sweet time for both of us.

One day, we planned a walk to the lake on the backside of the ashram. As we walked together down the dusty path, we got stares from onlookers. A blip of concern cropped up on my radar; I was having second thoughts about this walk. Just then, a midsized cobra crossed our path, paused, looked at us, and moved on. I said to myself, *Okay, this must be a sign.*

Rationale said one thing and a beauty next to me enjoying my company said something else. Being the daring kid I am, I let the supposed sign slide (or slither) away, and we kept going. It was a nice walk, being with nature, sharing our youthful joy. Keep in mind, this was as new an experience for me as it was for her.

On the way back, we crossed paths with one of the senior members at the ashram. I will never forget the look he gave me, the whites of his eyes showing wide, like "Oh my God" when he saw the two of us together.

I was innocent as a schoolboy in this new relationship without intentions or wants. I was happy merely being with Aparna. I had no idea of the blasphemy, the bad talk that would surface around the ashram of our being together. At the end of Navratri, Aparna told me the bad news of how her family had seen her with me and they didn't want her to talk with me anymore.

My own Indian drama series—my first creation, though not my last. Saddened by the news, I handed Aparna a note in passing that afternoon, knowing she was boarding the train back home late in the evening. It simply said, "Meet me in the palm tree field at 3:00 p.m., directly across the street from the ashram, behind the little shops."

We sat there, amidst the natural and pristine south Indian landscape, talking, laughing, and even planning our next meeting for some time soon, hopeful for further communication. We gave each other a hug and bid each other a sweet goodbye.

Little old me—I had songs in my head I wanted to sing to her, poems on sheets of random paper written about her. I was inspired, creative, and rockin'. My first Indian crush, as sweet as an alphonso mango.

Now some of you, especially my mom, might have stopped to ask herself while reading the above, "Cobras?!" Yes, cobras. India is where they live, or at least one place. Thailand, for sure, is another.

After I saw my first one, which was sitting on a large rock outside my room one fine morning, I stopped dead in my tracks, astonished by its beauty, and also surprised that it did not spit on me. One of the ashramites (people who lived at the ashram), was passing by at the same time and saw it, too. He was less surprised, as he had grown up in India where exotic snakes live, breed, and grow. He told me in the early days of the ashram, Gurudev performed a special puja, one that would never allow any of the animals—poisonous-killer snakes included—to harm anyone who came here. I was overjoyed to hear this.

Recently, an ashramite named Datta rescued around two-thousand snakes over four years, many of which were cobras. He rescued other animals as well.

A few weeks later, while walking in a small group with Gurudev to his kutir, he gracefully stopped, held out his arm, pointing, and told us to look to our right side. To our delight was one of the most beautiful phenomena I have ever witnessed. Two baby cobras danced, and I mean, graceful, swaying, swooping, wonderfully in tune, like two figure skaters dancing to music only they heard. It was if they were celebrating Gurudev's arrival, his mere presence on the brick-laid path. We watched for a while, then the two lovebirds, I mean snakes, danced away. I looked at Gurudev with a silent, "Was that real—did you make that happen for us?"

He just smiled and said, "Hmm... Wasn't that beautiful?" and continued walking.

I have often looked for those two snakes, just in case I ever get married. I want them to dance at the wedding. Perhaps by that time, it would be their great-grandsnakes. Of course, my mom hopes it won't be *that* long. You know, the maternal hope lives on.

In less than one day, an army of thin Indian men erected a tent as a roof for the outside amphitheater. Bangalore was still enduring the rainy season and we needed to stay dry. At full capacity, around 5,000 participants could squeeze in there. How did I know? Stand on a busy road and gape at the physics of a full family on one motorcycle, or the way ten slim Indian boys squeeze themselves into a compact car, or glimpse the overflowing buses at rush hour, and that gives you the idea more could fit in there.

The night before the celebrations kicked off, we had a nice satsang inside the tent with Gurudev. At the end, he kindly called up the international participants, and gave the women a shawl and the men a brand new *dhoti*, a traditional men's garment in India. It is a rectangular piece of unstitched white cloth, around seven yards long, wrapped around the waist and the legs and knotted at the waist.

My fashion sense went on alert. *I have to wear a dress?* Flashing thoughts filled my mind. *How will I wear it? What if it falls down? How about going to the bathroom?* Think Mahatma Gandhi, no buttons, no zippers, no instructions, which no male would read anyway.

The next morning, Matt and I took the offered help of a local male as we tied up our new white dhotis and headed out for the first morning puja of Navratri. The sleight of hand in folds and tucks is remarkable.

The old meditation hall was all decked out with sounds, scents, and an energy as sweet as I have ever encountered, and I knew there would be much more.

My favorite part of the pujas was the band. Like an Indian version of wild Celtic music, around four or five guys chill in the corner, blowing horns, cracking drums, and making other appropriate sounds for the ceremony. They were prompted by the Vedic priests who performed the pujas.

At seven each morning, Gurudev performed my favorite one called *Rudra Puja.* It is also held every Monday morning in the ashram—even when Gurudev is traveling the world. All the young students from the Vedic school sit on the stage and chant the Sanskrit *shlokas,* as Gurudev offers up fruits, flowers, water, and fire, back to the Divine. A lot of these Vedic schoolboys have gone on to be head priests in temples all over India.

It is fascinating to watch and be a part of the ceremony. What I like better is closing my eyes and basking in the expansive energy from the puja. I always drop so deep into meditation during these pujas that my head falls, my chin to my chest, like it's one hundred pounds of rocks. No jokes now. There's no pain, no neck strain, and I only realize what's happened when I come back to my body, the room, and environment a few times during the hour. Like many things I am writing about in this book, it must be experienced.

"Quick, do short Kriya, everyone do short Kriya now; Gurudev has sent a message."

The announcement spread quickly. Our group of young adults, just chit-chatting in the amphitheater while Gurudev was doing puja above us in the meditation hall, started our ten-minute Sudarshan Kriya. We followed the resounding Sanskrit sound, "*Om*," chanting it three times before we started our revered breathing yoga practice. The entire area transformed from waves of talking voices to cool sounds of rhythmic breath.

Within moments, my body felt elevated, and I went with the flow. After a few minutes of inhale/exhale bliss, my whole body lit up from my toes to my nose, traveling to the top of my head. And without any knocking, special, or elegant entrance, Gurudev was inside my body. My eyes were closed yet I saw and felt with every cell of my physical body, Gurudev sitting with his eyes closed in deep meditation, right inside me, perfectly aligned with my body. My big mind was alive with experience, silence and shakti, there was little room to analyze, judge or blink—my guru was in me.

The one simple thought I had, outside of pure gratitude was, *Is this happening to everybody?* I later shared my experience with Matt. He was blown away but didn't report a similar experience. I have never told anyone else. During the first day of Navratri, I experienced something I will never forget. *Jai Guru Dev.*

The next day, I woke up an hour after Bill woke, around 4:00 a.m. I did some light yoga and practiced Sudarshan Kriya and meditation, ready for the second day of Navratri. That morning, I rambled peacefully to the meditation hall early, probably an hour before Gurudev would start the Rudra Puja. Sitting and meditating alone in there was incredible enough to call it a wondrous day... but the day's spiritual goodies had not even begun.

I often look back at my first visit to the Hare Krishna Temple in Pacific Beach, California. I remember with a smile how freakishly hard it was for me to sit cross-legged (or an attempted position of it) on the hard marble floor to eat dinner. Worn football knees and oversized thighs weren't built for low gravity contortions. In the four years since, I had become more flexible and could sit comfortably in that position for a solid forty minutes with back support—the time it took to practice Sudarshan Kriya and meditation. I was surprised, then, to find I'd sat for over an hour during the Rudra Puja, basking in morning stillness, way beyond any depth I had experienced up until that point on the spiritual path.

After the puja ended, I quickly grabbed a cushion and found my spot, around fifteen feet away from where the day's pujas would take place, and about the same distance behind the chair where Gurudev would sit, as he came and went throughout the day's rituals. From 8:30 a.m., I sat in a comfortable cross-legged position, enjoying the enormous amount of love, energy, and subtle nuances of this most spectacular Indian/Vedic tradition. The musicians played tunes and the priests chanted as around two hundred blessed souls shared the hall with me. Gurudev joined us on three separate occasions.

When all was done for that part of the day's activities, I asked someone what time it was. The response? 1:30 p.m. I was blown away by the fact that I had sat, super still, without any of the typical cross-legged pain that had always ailed me, in that same exact spot for several hours. No back rest, only a thin cushion under me, yet I felt relaxed. Another minor miracle, a flavor of *samadhi*, fantastic, and for sure Gurudev continually blessing the others and me on that day.

I was thoroughly enjoying the Navratri celebrations. That day I did not go up to Sumeru to teach music. I didn't think the students would be too disappointed. I had a light lunch and took an inspiring nature walk around the ashram, letting the peace and gratitude flow through my heart with the rhythms of my life.

That night, the satsang rocked. I heard a familiar tune we sang in San Diego, but it was on fire this time. The notes had a life of their own, a quality of crystal heat. I could not see who was singing, but I felt his soul and the pure joy he sang with. As I crept forward,

I saw this handsome Indian man, sitting in the front row, holding the microphone with two hands, his long, flowing, black hair flying around with the cool breeze. I instantly knew this guy was a serious singer and, more than that, a serious devotee of Gurudev. His name was Rishi Nityapragya, a veteran teacher from Gujarat, who taught Art of Living programs worldwide, and was well known for his satsangs.

I enjoyed his music for years. In late December 2021, Rishi Nityapragya left his body and merged with the divine. Upon learning of his untimely passing, millions of people worldwide were shocked and saddened, including me. His music touched the hearts of many, his soft-spoken loving voice pierced through the most rigid hearts, and the love he shared with so many was inspiring.

As soon as Gurudev left, the music took another path, this one like a twisting, turning, uphill road, filled with divinity all along. *Garba* had started, a traditional folk dance that originated from Gujarat and is traditionally performed during Navratri.

A few days later, there was an afternoon culture show in the amphitheater. I didn't think about attending, as I planned to teach music up at Sumeru and hang out. I had left my guitar in the back of the amphitheater, so I went there to get it. As I entered, classical Indian female dancers were performing on stage. I grabbed my guitar and walked through the crowd of around a thousand people. As I neared the middle, the announcer, one of the Indian teachers, Deepak, called me up to play some "American rock songs." I readily agreed; I've never passed up a request to perform. I sent someone to Sumeru to invite the students to the show.

Matt was sitting up front with a bunch of youths we'd been hanging out with. As I passed by, Matt said, "Hey, could I come up with you and do my Jesus on the Cross?"

I had to think quickly because by the name of it, I didn't think it was appropriate for this Indian and diverse audience. I asked him what it was.

He replied, "You'll see." His eyes crinkled with a wicked smile.

I told him to let me get on stage and feel out the audience, then I'd call him up if it was cool.

I kicked off with the Stephen Stills hit, "Love the One You're With," a song I loved to play and sing. Now I was wearing my traditional dhoti, sitting delicately on a small milk crate, crossed-legged in front of the better side of a thousand folks, hoping my underwear wouldn't suddenly show. I was super self-conscious. It'd only been a couple of days, and I wasn't confident I had this new dress wear understood.

As the first song ended, I called up on stage all the youth sitting up front, who were our friends, including Matt. As I busted into "This Little Light of Mine," I once, or maybe three times, ducked my head down like I was grooving to the beat, but checked my legs. As the whole crowd sang, and my friends sang and danced on stage, I was in my element, performing.

Suddenly, I felt this wave of laughter erupting from the crowd, and I immediately looked down to see if my legs were still crossed—thank goodness, no sign of my white underwear. Not having a clue of what they were laughing at, I turned around and saw Matt, projected on one of the two large video screens—in all his glory—acting out "Jesus on the Cross."

Picture this: Matt, a tall, white-skinned, hippie boy, with dreadlocks hanging down from his head, a scruffy beard upon his ancient-looking face, eyes closed, arms stretched out, head hanging to one side, body perched as if he were, indeed, nailed to a cross.

And if all that was not bizarre enough, in all the madness of performing the act, Matt's (probably loosely tied) dhoti had fallen to his ankles! He was blissed out with the energy of a thousand people's laughter flowing toward him, so he didn't even feel the light, thin piece of cloth falling, completely unaware that he was standing there in theatre pose, in his tighty-whitey underwear. To top it off, one of our Indian friends tried to pick the dhoti back up but failed. This might have been the funniest, craziest, out-of-this-world humorous happening I have ever been a part of.

As Matt awoke from his frozen statue pose, he picked up the dhoti and tied it back on with a look of bewilderment, mixed with a slightly crooked smile. I finished the song, and we all left the amphitheater laughing hysterically at Matt's wardrobe failure. I have told this story on several occasions, each time casting copious laughter and good cheer among the listeners. God bless Matt—God bless the Indian dhoti.

An interesting aspect about being at the ashram, is if one must go through something to burn off karma, it will happen here. Most people think of an ashram for meditating and service, yet if one has buttons ready to be pushed, they will get pushed here. Ashram means place of rest, but it can also be a place of growth—substantial growth for the right person.

During Navratri, people were getting sick, falling down the slippery hills hurting themselves, and experiencing numerous other ailments. I'd lose my voice, but it would come back when I needed it most. When asked about these occurrences at satsang, Gurudev said, "If someone suffers something inside the gates of this ashram, they will not have to go through that same thing again outside these gates."

I was stunned at the thoughts his words provided and embraced them with my arms open wide: "Okay, here I am, bring it on."

One of my youthful friends was a beautiful, innocent girl from Rishikesh named Monika. Did I mention beautiful? I was awestruck the moment I saw those deep-dark Indian eyes, and when she spoke, the softness in her voice knocked me over. One night after satsang, a bunch of us stood outside, and there was Monika, limping around on crutches. It turns out she also had some karma to burn off at that time, as she slipped and fell down a muddy hill, injuring her ankle. I couldn't help but notice her crying, so I went to her and offered my shoulder.

"What's the matter?"

"I went to the kitchen today and they would not let me do seva because I was injured."

My eyes watered, my heart hurt, my body froze in stillness so moved by her innocence and willingness to do seva. I have never seen anything like this in American girls; they were just different from these semi-traditional Indian girls. Raised differently, taught differently, even lived differently. Moved by her words, I asked a friend to hand me my guitar lying in the grass, and with this angel leaning on my shoulder, in tears like heaven's rain, I wrote her this song.

> *Monika, some times are tough, but it don't get any better than this*
> *Guruji says, "If you suffer here, you won't suffer anywhere else."*
> *Monika, lay your head down in a pillow of grace*
> *The sun will shine, to call your name, so lay your troubles down to rest.*

If that isn't inspiration, I don't know what is. Back in my room, I etched out two more verses, and wrote them down in my best kindergarten handwriting. I've been given a gift in my music and when the muse strikes, I follow.

The next day, I helped Monika to a quiet spot, sat her down, gave her the lyrics on a piece of paper to follow as I sang my heart out. Tears rolled down her face, inviting mine to do the same while I sang. What a great joy to touch someone's heart with a few stanzas of words and the strum of my guitar. That was one of the sweetest and most poignant musical moments of my life.

Navratri continued and finished with more of the same: beautiful, powerful and life-changing pujas during the day, and gallant singing and dancing celebrations at night. Although I thought I had experienced everything imaginable during the first eight days, nothing prepared me for the sheer ecstatic shakti that was in store on the final day.

I had heard interesting and various accounts of how Gurudev leads a man who walks behind him with a pot of the blessed-holy water, fresh and steaming with love, bliss, and shakti from the day's pujas. I heard it is a magnificent event, world-altering on the subtle levels. For the first time at the ashram, Gurudev said due to the collective energy of all the participants this year being so high and authentic, the special and much-anticipated *Rishi Homa* would be outside in the amphitheater, allowing everyone to be a part of it.

As I nestled into the amphitheater early to get a good seat, the now five thousand people came ready for the festivities, and the highest blessings from Gurudev. I sat right up front, just to the left of Gurudev's chair, packed in with all the Vedic schoolboys. We joked, laughed and sang for an hour or so, as we waited for Gurudev and the entourage to walk out of the meditation hall, through the amphitheater and onto the stage. Our giggles subsided and the boys and I rested our eyes, basking in a short meditation. What seemed only a few minutes of peaceful bliss was transformed into a charged blast of energy.

With my eyes still closed, I felt the presence of Gurudev enter like many times before, but this was the pinnacle. My body radiated with love, and I opened my eyes to the delight of Gurudev standing at the top of the amphitheater. The resounding experience was a mix of the first time I saw Gurudev walk into the public talk in Irvine, to the mind-blowing, beautiful moment during my first Guru Purnima in Lake Tahoe, when Gurudev performed the Guru Puja—I zapped, crackled, and popped; I was elevated, centered, and rocked.

Within seconds I watched Gurudev walk with one hand in the air, angelically, like Jesus leading his disciples into heaven, like an angel leading a newly departed soul to the next level. Gurudev was as radiant and powerful as I have ever seen him. Behind him walked an Indian man with a stumble-step style, holding the pot of holy water on his head. Exciting and mesmerizing, the entire audience fixed their gaze on him.

What seemed like a half-hour dramatic walk to the stage probably only took a few minutes. Gurudev continued the puja. The water was blessed once more after he took his seat, by being poured over his head, while he went into a deep state of meditation (samadhi). The water trickled into vessels placed around him. If I use the word electrifying too many times here, it is for a good reason and well deserved. The amphitheater was bursting with energy!

Finally, Gurudev came out of meditation and gracefully picked up a pail of this water. The first one was thrown on the little Vedic boys and me—holy smokestacks, Batman! When that cool water touched my body, thrilling waves of shakti rocked me from head to toe, up and down my spine. I was set ablaze, lit up like a Christmas tree on the eve of Jesus's birthday. I could have flown to the heavens right then and there, but I wanted to stick around for the encore.

Gurudev continued picking up these vessels and showered the participants in attendance from the stage. Gurudev then made his way through the crowd, showering all in divine love. An older Indian lady, who I got to know that week, limped over to me. She told me that she didn't get blessed by the water.

Without a blink or a think, I took her gently by the arm, cleared masses of blissed-out folks out of our way to within twenty feet from Gurudev before I yelled, "Gurudev!"

From the look on my face and me holding up the fragile arm of this wonderful lady, he knew exactly what to do. He grabbed one more vessel and splashed the two of us. A double dose of lighting, with a side of bliss.

While Gurudev was soaking people, an older Indian auntie sang two songs. When she finished, Rishi Nityapragya erupted in spiritual rock star fashion. He stood up (this was the first time I saw someone stand and sing a bhajan), took the mic, and busted into his version of "*Jaya Jaya Shiva Shambho*." Rishiji was getting super into it and carrying the whole place along. The joy I felt him sing with was beyond the mountains; actually, it was well beyond the moon.

After he finished, and we had a moment to come down from the highest high, I walked up to him and simply said, "You are the most joyful singer I have ever heard in my life."

He smiled something humungous, hugged me, looked me in the eyes, and said, "You will be too, my dear. You will be too."

It was like he knew everything about me as a friendly father, assuring me what was in my future. I never forgot the intensity of his words, and I have since aspired to sing with the same joy I felt that afternoon. Inspiration, move me brightly.

Rishi Nityapragya's satsangs were extraordinary. Whether in India, Russia, Europe, or the States, Rishiji brought people together from all backgrounds, uniting them with his tremendous love, deep devotion, and explosive shakti.

Over the years, I had the great pleasure of sharing the stage with him in India and the States. At each satsang, during every song, and inside individual notes, my soul was ablaze from the sheer energy that Rishiji created. Like a music magician, he crafted masterpieces from thin air, and recreated ancient chants into aspiring and awesome anthems, effortlessly taking us back to our divine nature.

Personally, some of the most unforgettable music experiences of my life were alongside Rishiji. Night after night in the VM meditation hall at our Bangalore Ashram, with Gurudev twenty feet in front of us, I'd back him up on guitar or simply sing along in joyous wonder, great jubilation, and glorious delight, reaching all-time highs.

One evening before satsang during the Guru Purnima 2008 celebration in Santa Clara, California, Gurudev called Rishiji, Michael Fischman, Von Osselman, and me into his room. My bouncing mind was thinking two things: first, I was in trouble; second, I was getting enlightened. Spoiler alert—neither happened. Gurudev encouraged us to sing simple songs instead of some of the more complicated bhajans in the Art of Living. He was asking us to get back to the basics. This request was right up my alley.

Thirty minutes later, on stage next to Rishiji, the hall erupted in energy, with splashes of absolute bliss. He followed the directions from Gurudev and sang the simple songs so mighty; he was brilliant. I could not get any higher, strumming and singing along. I will cherish all these memories with Rishiji as I continue to celebrate his precious life and the love he shared.

The final day of Navaratri was ending. Just about suppertime, there was an announcement from the stage: "All Indian Art of Living teachers please meet outside the amphitheater." I wondered what was going on. About twenty minutes later, another announcement relayed that dinner would be served in the palm tree field behind the amphitheater, on the other side of the fence. This was an area I'd never seen before, as the gate was always closed. When we entered, there were the Indian teachers, serving us with smiles and joy.

After the Navratri celebrations, Gurudev spoke these words: "The period of the last fifteen days was a divine period. We did all pujas and yagyas. What is puja? Reciprocating what Divinity is doing to us. God makes Sun and Moon go around us, showers flowers, rain and fruits. Imitation of that divine expression is called *puja*. Puja is the most natural way of showing one's gratitude."

With these words, I was more grateful for my first Navratri, one that changed my life and the way I thought and experienced the world forever.

Afternoon stroll with Gurudev at the Bangalore Ashram, October 2001

Teaching music to my friends at Sumeru Mantap
at the Bangalore Ashram, October 2001

CHAPTER FOURTEEN

Strength from India

*Passion is the biggest driving force in your life, but
it should be kept in the right place. Your passion
should go through the filter of your intellect and
wisdom, then it will work miracles for you.*
—Gurudev Sri Sri Ravi Shankar

A few days after the massive celebrations, Matt and I needed a
city break: different food, different atmosphere and more storybook adventures. After going to our favorite restaurant, Pavithra's,
we headed to the barbershop so I could get a haircut. Wherever Matt
and I ventured around town, crowds of locals stared, giggled, and
wondered.

As I was getting my hair cut, Matt surprised me by plopping
down in the chair next to me and blurting out, "Okay, I am ready to
get my dreadlocks chopped off!"

I held my reaction tight inside, as I didn't want to discourage
him or make him change his mind. I was thrilled, but sat there, getting my haircut, and watched the high-level drama begin.

First, they called in another barber, but he looked so perplexed. It was like Sasquatch arriving in downtown Seattle from the
Northwest woods. Two things were going on: one was clearly Matt
and his decision to drop his dreadlocks. Within a minute, a group of
Indian men tried to cram through the doorway while a flock of others stood outside. The barbers screamed and pushed the mad-frenzied pack, looking like a bunch of hungry wild wolves, out the door
as they locked it.

The barber began cutting Matt's dreads off one by one. He finished it, complete with a fresh shave. Now Matt, who minutes ago looked older, dirtier, and of course, much hairier, looked like a teenaged schoolboy. Oh, what a day at the barber.

As we left the barbershop, hordes of men outside swarmed us like we were two top Bollywood stars. Some thought I was Tom Cruise! We fended them off, went for a fresh juice, and came up with a mischievous plan for back at the ashram. Maybe we were both feeling lightheaded from the new cuts. We ventured back and would try to fool everyone into thinking that Matt was a madman from overseas here to cause havoc at the ashram.

Since clothes were dirt cheap, we got Matt new sweatpants, a shirt, and those weird bumblebee-looking dark sunglasses to hide his eyes. On the bus ride back, we not only planned out our pranks but also tucked Matt's shirt in, and pulled up his pants, coming close to a spitting image of irksome Steve Erkel from the American sitcom *Family Matters*. Oh, were we ready to push buttons and make some noise.

As we entered the gates, we first took in that much-needed deep breath of relief and inhaled the ashram's positive-high prana, which is unmistakable in contrast with the polluted and busy city.

We walked up the stairs to the administration building and sent Matt into Sanjay's office to start the ruckus. Sanjay was a very pleasant, soft-spoken, well-mannered young Indian, living at the ashram doing seva. I have no idea why we decided to target him.

I ducked below the window to peek and listen while Matt yelled in the funniest voice ever, "I want to see the saint!" repeatedly, increasing his volume with each statement. He continued ranting about how he'd just arrived from Europe, having traveled all this way just to "see the saint" (Gurudev) who he had heard lived here. He added how he was beaten and thrown off the bus just outside the ashram gates.

It was too much for Sanjay. As he ran off to get someone to help him, we ran too—right to the half-filled amphitheater before satsang. And there they were, Monika and a few of her unsuspecting female Indian friends, sitting in the middle of the venue. I told Matt to stand at the edge of the amphitheater, walking in circles, talking to himself, looking ridiculous—he did a fantastic job.

I ran over to the girls, holding the back of my head, saying, "There's a madman over there, look! He just hit me in the head with a stick and chased after me. Please, I need help."

The girls didn't know what to do, and got really scared, so I broke the news to them with a smile and a laugh. Luckily, they found it funny too and laughed along with me.

We continued for a while, tricking everyone we came across. Finally, we'd both had enough. But as we were about to call it quits, Swami Brahmatej gracefully walked by us and said in his soft voice, "Hello, Jeremy. Hello, Matthew."

We were dumbfounded. How did he know it was Matt? That man is so there, it is inspiring as much as it is perplexing. He was always our favorite person at the ashram, and for me, he still is. Matt and I continue to share bouts of laughter and wide smiles when retelling that tale from time to time.

That same week, Gurudev invited around twenty international devotees to an inauguration of a dental college in Bangalore. The group included people who had stayed after Navratri and our YLTP team.

We stopped in an old Shiva Temple of minimal square footage, low ceilings, and a resounding energy about it. Dean, a veteran teacher from the United States, was with us, all six-foot-five of him. I joked, saying he was the tallest man in Bangalore. His height was a challenge in the temple, and we helped him duck down as we walked and circled one of the Hindu deities. Afterward, Gurudev honored Dean, his wife Shirley, and Bill (as revered teachers) with festive flower garlands. The rest of us received smaller flowers and fruit. I felt honored and holy being in this sacred temple with Gurudev.

Our next stop was the new dental college, where Gurudev was invited to do a special puja to inaugurate the institution. Leaving the bus, we met Gurudev and a few devotees at the beginning of the short road leading to the college. People dressed in colorful wraps lined the side of the road in breathtaking spectacle, throwing flowers on Gurudev and us, smiling like they'd touched the sky and were warmed by the sun.

Halfway down the road was a stunning and colorful decorated elephant, majestic and gallant. Gurudev stood in front of it, and I nearly burst into joyful tears when the elephant bowed down to him. Next, the elephant touched Gurudev on both shoulders with its trunk, one at a time, and then on top of his head—as if the elephant was blessing him. The reverence he gave to Gurudev was mesmerizing.

A man helped Gurudev sit on top of the gorgeous, graceful elephant and it carried him down the road. For some reason, Gurudev was giving me a lot of attention while riding the elephant, saying, "Do you want to come up here for a ride?"

Shocked, I managed to utter, "Yes, please, Gurudev."

He said it once more before the ride ended, but we had to move on to the inauguration inside the college, so I didn't get to ride. I quickly forgot about it with so much going on.

We moved into a hall with a concert floor, a stage with props for the Vedic ceremony, like the ones we had during Navratri, and a couple hundred people from the college on hand to enjoy the festivities. Our group of around twenty internationals was escorted to an area across from the stage where we could see the action perfectly. The older folks were seated in chairs, while the rest of us sat in front of them on the hard, cold concrete floor, covered by only a thin mat.

Initially, I didn't think about having to sit on the floor, but then all hell broke loose. Within five minutes, my legs started to become numb unlike anything I had ever experienced before. It moved up my body, with excruciating pain. I started to panic inside for the first time since my heart palpitations before taking the Art of Living course, though I was still.

Gurudev's eyes were closed, deep in meditation, and my mind took off at hyper speed. *Oh, no, what can I do?* I knew if I tried to get up, I'd fall and cause a scene in front of all the people enjoying a most striking ceremony.

I whispered to Matt, sitting next to me, that something had happened to my legs, and described the intense pain and that I couldn't move. He told me to relax and stretch out if I could as he dropped into blissful meditation, not understanding the crisis I was going through.

I felt helpless. Closing my eyes, I began to scream silently inside like I hadn't since my sleepless nights of suffering with asthma as a child. I didn't make one single movement; I was frozen in time. I prayed intensely like I had never prayed before. I prayed to Gurudev with every cell of my body to help me out of this hell.

Within a minute, I opened my eyes to see Suresh, a devotee, carrying a chair over his head and over the people seated on the ground. Was I dreaming? Could he possibly be bringing the chair to me? The closer he came, the more a wave of enormous love filled and flooded my whole body. He quietly walked up to me and carefully placed the chair down. I told him I couldn't move my body and asked him for help. I don't know how that skinny slip of a boy lifted this extra-large boy, but he did. As blood flowed back into my legs, I asked, "How did you know I needed a chair?"

"Gurudev told me to bring it to you." His soft voice soothed what was left of the fiery pain, as he walked back to his spot across the room. But how did Gurudev tell him anything with his eyes closed and so deeply absorbed in meditation?

With the excruciating pain vanquished, I dove deep into meditation and enjoyed the benefits of the puja. After a magnificent meal served on bamboo leaves, we headed toward the bus.

As I walked out of the college, my head still in the clouds of joyous wonder and bliss, I looked ahead and saw Gurudev feeding that same majestic elephant. Suddenly, I heard several people call out, "Jeremy, Gurudev is calling you over to him." As if this afternoon could get any more out-of-this-world awesome.

I approached Gurudev, and he told me to stand in front of the elephant. Up close, the gray weathered skin looked soft, creviced. A gentle energy filled the large, dark eyes. I was in awe. Lo and behold, the elephant slowly lifted its trunk and with a gentle touch gave me the exact same blessings he had given Gurudev, touching my shoulders one by one and then my head. I was intoxicated in mammalian divinity. With an impish smile, Gurudev handed me some bananas to feed the elephant, another blessing.

As I walked away, frozen in the moment, I asked myself why Gurudev picked me, out of all the people, to come to the elephant. I remembered how he'd called me to ride the elephant, but I didn't get the chance, pressed for time with the start of the inauguration. Gurudev Sri Sri Ravi Shankar takes sweet care of his humble devotees in magnificent ways. Sometimes they are firsthand accounts, sometimes they come as sweet treats, as if given by an unseen hand.

Gurudev says prayer can only happen in two instances. Firstly, when you are very grateful. Secondly, when you are helpless.

That night at satsang someone asked, "Gurudev, we hear stories from devotees around the world who say you helped them, even saved their lives in times of danger. How do you know when your devotees are in trouble and pain?"

Gurudev smiled. "How do you know if someone pulls one of the hairs on your head?"

Wow, that was all I needed to hear. I welcomed the stream of sweet tears of gratitude.

The next day, I saw Suresh walking in the ashram. I stopped him and said, "Thanks so much for bringing me that chair. I was paralyzed in such burning pain; it was one of the worst experiences of my life—you saved me." His eyes crinkled from his smile. I had to ask, "How did Gurudev tell you to bring me the chair if he was in meditation?"

He replied in a humbled voice and manner, "It's times like these that remind me that our Gurudev knows everything."

How many times can a man cry in twenty-four hours? How many times would I cry that season? I sat beneath a palm tree and closed my eyes, and as tears rolled down my face, I wiped my cheek with the back of my hand, yet they continued to fall. I felt nothing but oneness and gratitude for having Gurudev in my life. I knew from that point onward, no matter how much trouble, pain, or hell I was in, Gurudev would know and come to my rescue. This event, and subsequent faith, have propelled me on this path for the past twenty-five years, with each miracle I experience of his. *Jai Guru Dev.*

Our YLTP team was back in the field visiting more slums, villages, and schools. The disheveled, crowded housing was depressing until the children and people poured onto the street. Each time I brought my guitar, and we had satsang with the highly enthusiastic youth and other members of each community. Some days I led two or three satsangs a day, and my voice paid the price.

I had been singing wild and loud for the past three years, but I'd never lost my voice as much as I did during this trip. Before arriving at a place, I wouldn't have any voice—or very little at best. But when I picked up my guitar, closed my eyes in a quick prayer to Gurudev, on the first words my voice was back near a hundred percent, reaching many people's ears. As soon as the music ended, so did my voice, back to strained croaks and throat pain.

This was my repeated experience at the many places we visited. Maybe because of the polluted air in Bangalore, maybe from singing so much, or that I talked too much. Whatever it was, I understood it to be a karma I had to go through and remembered what Gurudev had said about suffering aliments at the ashram.

After returning to America, I experienced the complementary opposite of all that pain I had gone through, as I sang much more, leading satsangs and concerts. Stretching my vocal cords seemed a natural exercise, going from five or ten minutes a day to singing for hours blending with children and others. And my leadership in singing and quantity of performances would grow with each season.

Becoming a full Art of Living teacher back then meant going through two intense programs. The first was a two-week teacher training course, or TTC One, the second aptly named TTC Two.

One day Gurudev walked around the circular Sumeru Mantap after his interview with one of India's leading magazines, *India Today*. What a treat it was to hang out with Gurudev and enjoy satsang in the courtyard with only two or three hundred people! Compared to the hundreds of thousands his satsangs attract in India these days, those were extremely intimate times.

That memorable afternoon, Matt and I asked him if we could take the upcoming TTC One, starting at the ashram a few weeks later, on November 1. Like he had oh-so-many times before when I asked to do something, he replied in all innocence, "We'll see." It was right up there with a parent's "Maybe."

For obvious reasons, Matt and I really wanted to dedicate ourselves deeper on this path, ultimately becoming full Art of Living teachers. By now, all I wanted to do was travel, teach, and advance on this spiritual path—oh, and did I mention play music?

Imagine, here I was on Halloween night (no, it's not celebrated there, the only reason I knew the date was that TTC was starting the next day). Gurudev surprised us with a visit to Sumeru after satsang and danced with around fifty of us. It was the anniversary of a divine event, where Krishna danced with all his *gopis* (adoring devotees) under the full moon, and when the night ended all reported how they felt like Krishna danced only with them alone. That was my experience that very night. The festival is called *Rasleela*; it takes place on *Sharad Poornima* (full moon of the winter month).

Afterward, walking alongside Gurudev on his way back to his kutir, blissed out and grateful, he suddenly turned to me and said, "What are you doing up? You should be in bed, you will start TTC One tomorrow!"

I couldn't breathe, think or act, I felt frozen on the heels of time. As I defrosted, I gave Gurudev a goodnight hug and said, "Thank you!" My words rang with the valor of a warrior telling the king he won't let him down; that he'd do whatever it took to be in his service—and as Gurudev says, "Walk like a king and be a perfect servant."

I started TTC One seven hours later at the refreshing hour of 5:00 a.m., practicing *Padma Sadhana* (Gurudev's gifted yoga practice to his devotees) with two hundred others. This group was mostly Indian with a few internationals in the old meditation hall, but back then, it was *the* meditation hall. A very strong devotee of Gurudev's, Vinod Menon, was our TTC One teacher.

Vinod was very firm and strict to the point of physical discipline—if anyone was late to the hall for a session, their whole group had to carry the tardy member, lying flat, outside, around the meditation hall a few times. He called it "Horizontal." I was the leader of my group, and luckily, we only had to do it once. No, they didn't have to carry me! Most groups looked like they enjoyed it, and it wasn't painful for the tardy member, just awkward.

It was clear to me that Vinod was ocean-deep in Gurudev's knowledge, with a loving innocence reminiscent of Gurudev's, like the other well-regarded teachers I had met over the past two months. Vinod was one of the first devotees to live at the ashram, back in the early nineties. His stories were unparalleled, full of life, humor, and devotion. It didn't take long for Vinod to take a liking to me, expressing how much he enjoyed having me in the course, and asking for feedback involving the comfort of the other international members.

Like the Youth Leadership Training Program two months before, TTC One was an intensive boot camp for the heart and soul. Seva played an enormous role, as we cleaned the ashram, cut veggies, made *chapattis* (Indian flatbread) before dinner, and picked up and took away garbage around the ashram.

"Who would like to come up on stage and give an introductory talk on the Art of Living course?"

Without raising a hand, I quietly walked onto the stage. "Hi, my name is Jeremy. I am from America and have some very important news to share with you. If you're stressed out and not smiling, you're definitely not cool."

A flood of laughter reached the stage in record time, and I arose in my element, at home in front of an audience, no longer seven years old holding a hairbrush for a mic. I poured my personal stories of asthma, heart problems, and insomnia into my first ever intro talk. A flamboyant, heavy-set motor mouth older lady from Mumbai stood up. This lady was intense, always outspoken, and no one really understood why she was in the course.

"Why do you charge for your breathing course? My organization teaches yoga for free, and they give out free drinks."

"Well, that's nice to hear," I said, smiling. With a sweet voice, I continued, "Actually, we give out *gulab jamuns* (a tasty Indian dessert made from flour, milk, and syrup) in our courses!" Roars of laughter filled the audience and were heard all the way to the front of the ashram. She quickly sat down, and we didn't hear much from her the rest of the course.

Matt has always said I have a humor *siddhi* (perfection), which Gurudev must have granted me. Yes, I love to joke, laugh, and enjoy authentic and appropriate (most of the time) humor. That doesn't mean mine is always appropriate, and I've naively insulted people, but for sure my sense of humor has improved by leaps and bounds on this path over the years.

On the last day of the course, a pleasant surprise was announced. Gurudev was on the cover of *India Today*, the Indian equivalent to *TIME* in America, from his earlier interview. I happily helped hand out copies of the magazine around the ashram that day.

TTC One ended on the evening of *Diwali*, the festival of lights.

About Diwali, Gurudev says, "Every human being has some good qualities. Every lamp that you light is symbolic of this. By lighting the lamp of wisdom in you, you light up latent values, and by acquiring knowledge, you awaken all the facets of your being. When they are lit and awakened, it is Deepawali. Don't be satisfied with lighting just one lamp; light a thousand, for you need to light many lights to dispel the darkness of ignorance."

With this knowledge, my heart and mind were set on teaching thousands of people the Art of Living, all around the world. My journey had already begun.

"Gurudev is calling all the internationals to his kutir." I loved it when these messages rang through the ashram. Since I'd been talking to friends, I was late and last to arrive at his kutir. Upon entering the room, Gurudev smiled at me, with that sparkle in his eyes, as if an unspoken congratulations for completing TTC One. He invited me to sit down amidst the twenty or so foreigners already seated. I curled up close by.

A pause of silence filled the room. "Jeremy, would you like to go to Arunachal Pradesh with Ivan and Sarah and help start a Sri Sri Ravi Shankar Vidya Mandir school?"

"Yes, Gurudev, I would love that."

"Okay, please see Mayank tonight about your train ticket. You can leave tomorrow." The evening continued and ended in a blissful blur.

The next morning, I saw Vinod and stopped him to say, "Thank you for everything; I've had the time of my life the past two weeks."

"Yes, Jeremy, it was a pleasure having you on the course. Last night Gurudev was asking me how you were on the TTC."

"Wow, really? What did you tell him?" I asked in wide wonder.

"I told him you were very strong on the course, and that while others were asking questions, you were the only one who had solutions. Gurudev told me that your story reminded him of me, when I was young on this path years ago."

Surprised and overjoyed to hear of this praise and conversation with Gurudev, as if I were not high enough already, I floated around the ashram for the rest of the day, until it was time to go to the train station.

CHAPTER FIFTEEN

On a Northbound Train

*Do not depend on argument. Miracles
and mystery are beyond argument. Love,
Enlightenment and Joy are miracles in Life.*
—Gurudev Sri Sri Ravi Shankar

*A*ll aboard! That evening, Ivan and Sarah, a pleasant British couple who attended TTC One with me, along with other devotees, boarded the train for Guwahati, Assam. Kashi, our yoga teacher
on TTC One, an intelligent, ever-smiling ashramite, was on the train
with us for the first night. Once the train was moving, he asked me
to pull out my guitar. Within minutes, we had the whole train singing with us! What a great thrill, being in community with people we
didn't even know. Our energies were so high from the course and the
ashram, they spread over everyone around us.

The ride was a life-changing experience for me. The third-class
sleeper train had us packed together during the day, and at night we
bunked on these fold-down beds, stacked three high, six altogether
in a barely large enough cabin. With plenty of time to pass, my trusty
yellow cassette player always eased my soul. Sting's *Fields of Gold* was
a soul-saver. I absolutely loved all his songs, especially the ones on
this tape I'd purchased in Bangalore. If stranded on a deserted island,
this is one of the five albums I would take.

The conditions were appalling at times, with sick, mutilated,
and dirty beggars coming onto our train at every stop along the journey, insistent for coins and acknowledgment. The train was infused

with humans on the edge of despair within seconds of coming to a halt at any of the stations.

Gurudev told me not to eat the train food (or any outside food), not that I would have. So I lived on a banana and cookie diet. India has great packaged cookies, or "biscuits," as they call them.

No warning came about another aspect that would try the patience of a saint: tea totters. These were men who terrorized the train cars, seemingly without end, with a few hours break during sleeping hours. "Chai, chai, coffee, chai!" rang out in annoying, high-pitched voices, like fingernails on a chalkboard. Ouch, my ears hurt just thinking about them.

One night, when I'd just fallen asleep, about 5:30 a.m., one of them pulled my foot as I lay motionless on the top bunk, using my guitar as a pillow. I woke up to that terrible sound and with swift reflexes, kicked him in the chest. He left me alone after that.

It was purely a reaction, not meant to be hostile, just a little Taylor coming out at being rudely awakened. Maybe I wouldn't have kicked him had I been a coffee drinker like my parents. I am glad I'm not. I'll take the kicking karma over what Gurudev refers to as "coffee karma" any day—that feeling when one does not have coffee during the day.

Our group was greeted at the train station by shining devotees, happy to honor us with garlands around our necks. Guwahati turned out to be a nonstop, run all over town affair, from this house to that hotel for lunch, to this house to meet another family, to another house for satsang. At each stop were remarkably loving Indian aunties, who brought varieties of food, even if we were not there for lunch or dinner. I was soon full and sick of food, but I couldn't say no to these caring aunties who were so happy to have us in their homes.

I found I was witnessing Gurudev's words regarding these generous people. "Indians will borrow off a neighbor just to feed a stranger." Imagine what they do when they did *not* have to borrow food. When the last auntie came to me with a plate full of sweets, my belly was very full, so I graciously took a few and snuck them in my pocket.

After a couple days we obtained our papers to travel to the most northeastern state in India, Arunachal Pradesh. Enduring a twelve-hour, overnight bus ride to Itanagar, I felt every miserable bump on that winding, run-down road. I was having uncomfortable stomach pain and nausea. Having "Delhi belly" from eating so much over the past two days, I felt like a character in an episode of *The Twilight Zone*.

Just as I dozed off, around 4:30 a.m., screaming police officers stormed onto the bus and abrasively threw Ivan, Sarah, Ashish, our guide from Guwahati, and myself off the bus and onto the cold, dark street.

I clearly heard Vinod's voice in my head saying, "Accept people and situations as they are!" And that is what I have done, countless times before, and thousands of times thereafter. If I could take one lesson Gurudev has taught me, acceptance would be it. It's the difference between nineteen-year-old Jeremy—who would have yelled back at the police, and then probably gotten into a fight and thrown into a foreign jail—and twenty-five-year-old me, who looked these guys in the eyes, took a deep breath, connecting to my source, saw the stress and tension upon these men like snow atop Mount Everest, and then moved along. I saved my mind and smile for the hundred workers I gave an impromptu concert to on the street as they walked to work. What fools did in anger brought joy to dozens more. Ah, where would I be without this self-knowledge? Shh, don't tell me; I don't want to know.

After a few hours, we were free to cross the border and head for the Art of Living center in Itanagar. We would not be allowed to leave the house for two days, however, until Gurudev settled things with the authorities. We thought our papers were in order, but it looked like something had been missed.

We were greeted by Sanjitha, a female teacher from Gujarat, who not only taught me introductory Gujarati, which I still use daily around the world, but also taught me tremendous insights and details about Indian culture while grooming me as a future teacher. We made a fun pair. She loved my music and we thoroughly rocked at satsangs. Still to this day, she jokes and mimics my style of singing in Sanskrit. I am sure she is not alone, to some I must sound like a broken billy goat due to my style and voice.

On the first morning we were allowed to go outside the center, I journeyed up to the roof and played my guitar, just as I used to on top of the water tank at the Bangalore Ashram. Right across the street was a school and when all the students saw me, they started running toward me. As I sat at the edge of the roof a thick swarm of kids ran up the stairs, rushing toward me like a wild pack of bulls. For a split second, I thought they were going to throw me off the roof. Yet as innocent as innocence could be, these kids merely wanted a closer glimpse of possibly the first white person they'd ever seen. This wasn't Bangalore, Mumbai, or Calcutta, not even Guwahati, Assam. This was a restricted state for security reasons, to protect the culture of the native people living there from outside influence.

My whole being was flooded with joy seeing the love and sparkle in these children's eyes, reminding me of my nephew, David, and why I'd chosen to be in my early childhood education program back in Atlanta. I sang them songs, and they went back to school for the day with music in their hearts.

The next morning, Sanjitha told me, "Go across the street and teach people the Breath Water Sound course."

Without hesitation, I ventured out at 7:30 a.m., looking around for a space to teach the course. The best spot, incredibly, was the top floor of a half-built structure. A construction site, there were boards with nails sticking out and rocks littered the floor with nothing stopping someone from falling three floors down. As I walked around the top shell of that building, I set a *sankalpa* (divine intention), saying, "There will be twenty-five people in the course at 8:00 a.m."

Of course, in India, 8:00 a.m. turned into 9:00 a.m., but lo and behold, as I ran a final count of people seconds before starting, there were no more or less than twenty-five. *Jai Guru Dev*!

I went on to teach many courses like these, in the strangest of places, always looking at them with positive energy. Assisting Sanjitha on her Art of Living courses at the center, and leading satsangs at night, it was a glorious time and one that ended all too soon. I was to fly back to the United States just before Christmas, so after a month at the center, I had to get back to Bangalore.

Reversing the Mad Hatter ride, I fared much better. Back on that wild overnight bus ride to Guwahati, this time I was not sick. I stayed a few days with the Sharma family, leading satsangs and eating well.

As soon as I boarded the Bangalore Express, my three-day train ride back home to the ashram, a little girl said, "Sir, aren't you sad?"

I smiled and answered, "No, why would I be?"

"Because you don't have any friends."

I felt like a beacon of joy and energy when I said, "I have the whole world inside my heart." I thought to myself, *You'll see.*

An hour into the journey, I pulled out my guitar. Satsang anyone? I soon had the train singing again. What an extraordinary time in my life. After three eventful days of satsang, cookies, bananas, and the perpetual, "Chai, chai, coffee, chai," I was back home at the Bangalore Ashram for a week of bliss with Gurudev, plus an intimate group of around one hundred people. Little did I know back then that I would refer to these as "the good old days" twenty-five years later.

My goals this week were to relax and enjoy the beauty and serenity of the ashram, spend as much time with Gurudev as possible, and sing in front of him at least once during satsang. Until now, I hadn't had the opportunity to sing a bhajan in front of him, only a thirty-second made up song I wrote as part of a skit on the last day of TTC One. My intention was so strong for this to happen.

The next day, around a hundred people assembled to meet Gurudev in one of the open-air meditation halls. This is known as *darshan,* meaning vision. He usually meets visitors to the ashram at this time when he is there, depending on his hectic schedule. I was there with my guitar, and a lady had already begun singing. She couldn't be heard, and the song's energy was going nowhere fast. When her song ended, my friend Pranav urged me to start singing a bhajan.

I sang the song I learned in the back of that ambulance on an early September morning, on our way to teach in the slums. "*Narayana Hari Om,*" an Art of Living standard, written beautifully by Divya Prabha. As the song took off, I felt an enormous energy rush into the hall, following a cool breeze from outside. I knew Gurudev was on his way inside. I turned my head, with a look of, "Oh my God, I am so nervous!"

Pranav said, "Just keep singing!"

With a slight turn of my head, I witnessed one of the most divine and beautiful moments of my life. Gurudev was dancing and spinning down the sloped path, floating into the hall. I was in heaven.

Seeing Gurudev dancing and grooving to the song I was leading was everything I could ever ask for, the culmination of a sensational season of joy, music, service, wonder, and more.

The song continued for another ten minutes, as he walked around meeting and blessing everyone. After that, I put my guitar down, and hurried to the end of the line. As I looked into his radiant eyes, wide smile, and resplendent soul, I said with the utmost child-like joy, "Gurudev, this is better than Disneyland!" though I've never been to The Happiest Place on Earth.

As he always does with my humorous comments, he smiled with a boatload of joy and giggled with me as my heart soared. I held out my treasured guitar pick in the palm of my right hand saying, "Gurudev, can you please bless my guitar pick?"

Without hesitation and with the energy of a major league baseball player swinging the bat, coupled with a child's innocence, he pulled his hand back and smacked my hand, hitting and blessing my pick, as I stood there electrocuted from the shakti my guru had just bestowed upon me... again.

That night, Gurudev had a satsang in the city, and I asked if I could come with him. For whatever reason, he said with a look of assurance, "No, no, you stay here and sing in satsang tonight."

I was blown away with his instructions and began preparing; restringing my guitar, going over songs, eating early, and arriving first to the meditation hall to set up. That night I sang three songs, and it was immensely powerful, staggeringly beautiful, and all because of the Master's intention. These were easily some of the most powerful bhajans I had ever led. To me it was Gurudev's initiation for me as an Art of Living satsang singer, and a special glimpse of what was to come. Very soon, this style of music would be a huge part of my world, and also special for many people around the world.

The morning of my last day arrived; I would be flying back home that evening for the holidays. What a spiritually enlightened ride. This was something to write home about... or, better yet, write a nonfiction book about.

My friend Steve from California was also leaving that evening, so we both went to hang out in Gurudev's kutir for a while. We agreed to take each other's photo with Gurudev one last time. Steve was adamant about me getting a clean shot and *not* placing my finger in front of the lens and blurring the picture. All day Steve asked me to take his picture in the kutir with Gurudev and must have told me a dozen times not to place my finger in front of the lens. So, he took mine that evening, too, and when I got it developed back home in America a few days later… all I could see was Steve's finger! I did not think he did it on purpose, though.

An hour later, I waited for Gurudev's car to arrive at the gate. I knew this would be the last time I'd see him for at least a couple of months. Vinod's small four-door car approached with Gurudev sitting in the passenger seat.

Nothing needed to be said; now it was time I bid my Master one last goodbye. With a soft voice I said, "Thank you, Gurudev, for all you have done for me. I love you. Please come to Atlanta to meet my family soon."

He smiled and handed me an orange. With the wink of his eyes, he rolled up the window and Vinod drove away.

The shakti from the bright-colored fruit given to me was startling. I floated behind the guard's hut to the right of the gate, plopped down, closed my eyes, and tears of a thousand percent sweet devotion, grateful gratitude, longing love, and the realization of how blessed I was to be with Gurudev this lifetime fell gently. For at least the hundredth time that glorious season, I felt like the most blessed boy on this planet—or any planet for that matter. My path was taking flight. And if the Art of Living was solely about being grateful for everything in life (which it can easily be broken down to), then I, in that moment of tearful joy, was indeed, living the art.

Walking with Gurudev at the Bangalore Ashram, December 2001

Singing songs on the train in India, December 2001

*Gurudev and me in the Old Meditation Hall at
the Bangalore Ashram, December 2001*

*Leading Satsang in the Old Meditation Hall at
the Bangalore Ashram, December 2001*

Steve's finger on the camera lens while capturing the photo of Gurudev and me in Shakti Kutir, December 2001

CHAPTER SIXTEEN

Homeward Bound

There is no dearth of miracles, it is there in abundance.
Only you have to have the confidence and the faith.
—Gurudev Sri Sri Ravi Shankar

*F*lying home to the United States was both exciting and, I'll
admit, scary. As a twenty-five-year-old American college student, I just had the most life-changing experience imaginable.
Coming home was going to be, what? Better, maybe stranger,
possibly harder, who knew? I was ready for anything and everything, though, as Gurudev teaches, "Living all possibilities in life."
Gurudev, this "both feet on the ground" spiritual path, and India
had made me solid, inside and out, from head to heart. This was my
real homeward journey.

I (perhaps selfishly) wanted to stay in India, traveling, teaching,
learning, sharing, and playing music, but it was time to return home.
I was determined to share my heart, feelings, and experiences with
my parents, who truly had little information about Gurudev and the
Art of Living. They knew (Mom more than Dad) how I practiced
yoga, deep breathing and meditation every day. They knew I was part
of an international group (though probably still believed it a cult),
and they tolerated my several pictures of a peculiar looking Indian
man, decked out with a beard and sporting his traditional whites.

However, having their son in India for a whole semester with
this man at his center, reading through various letters and emails of
my accounts, service, group meditations, travel, love, and grace—I'm
sure they suspected I was coming home with ideas and fresh perspec-

220

tives, or maybe they hoped I would say nothing of this supposed non-Christian movement. To them, the course held no resemblance to Jesus, his teachings, or the Bible.

Or did it? Love God (the Divine)—check; love others—double check; be childlike—triple check.

The fact was, Gurudev taught all of this and abundantly more, in his universal and secular teaching, opening us to the beauty in diversity, and giving a deeper understanding of ourselves, our roots, and now, my family.

"Spirit loves diversity!" Gurudev often shared, reminding us how this creation is so vast and diverse. The differences create the beauty in this world, the colors, creeds—heck, even deliciously different cookies make the world dance and sing.

This is but a fraction of what I learned from Gurudev Sri Sri Ravi Shankar as I celebrated my fifth year with him as my spiritual master. I realized during these terrific past months I was no longer an aimless clown, but a dynamic and free individual with lots of room for growth.

After the humbling season in India, complete with firsthand knowledge of poverty and the indelible strength of these people, I knew there was much more yet to learn—more opportunity for my heart and soul to grow. To me, this was it, learning, sharing, smiling, and becoming childlike and never complacent.

I arrived home on December 23, 2001, as a historic year in the United States was on the edge of completion. From the beginning it foretold a time of unrest, first as George W. Bush slid into the Oval Office against the popular vote, to a horrific morning in early September, where the commander-in-chief, his administration, and our glorious nation, born on freedom and brotherly love, were torn and tested beyond compare.

My beloved country not only suffered its most devastating blow, but also came together, united, indivisible, in unimaginable strength. The whole world saw our dark, painful bruises, yet marveled at how we stood strong, together, in the toughest adversity, and moved on like Viking warriors in our daily lives.

This indescribable tragedy didn't sink in while I was in India, my immediate world cloaked in the reality of learning and teaching others. The bombarding opportunities of countless hours of media reports didn't exist like it did for my fellow countrymen. When I arrived home, all that changed.

I primed myself with the strength and serenity of practicing Sudarshan Kriya in my bedroom and fueled my body by devouring a plateful of Mom's homemade pasta before sitting on the couch bombarded, suffocated, with year-end reflection images, news stories, and reruns, mainly depicting the attack on the World Trade Towers.

I had never felt like that before and pray I never do again: Stunned in frozen silence, hot tears of rage trickling down my cheeks as the flickering videos unfolded, revealing the aftermath and destruction. My mind and soul traveled through compassion and grief, doubt of the goodness in this world, and finally dispassion in accepting and letting it go. I soon retreated to my pillow to contemplate reality.

What son doesn't come home from his first international trip with treasures for his parents? I bought Mom and Dad very nice pictures of Jesus for Christmas, which continue to hang on the walls of our Georgia home to this day. Like my parents, I was initially surprised at finding many pictures of Christ over there, but after living in India's rich diversity of harmony, that faded.

Holiday traditions run strong in my Italian-American family. Dad cooked scrumptious seafood and Mom made her mouth-watering lasagna every year on Christmas Eve. I was vegetarian, with no meat, fish, or eggs, though I did eat dairy. While Dad prepared his famous clams casino, I casually struck up a conversation. I'd recently read about St. Thomas (Doubting Thomas) in one of Gurudev's books, and how he'd lived in India. Innocently, I asked my dad how the man got the title "doubting."

My question sparked a wildfire blaze. Not the angry fire of my childhood, "Turn off that music!" This was an unknown intensity, the heat of passion. Dad became animated, hands and arms commanding, retelling me stories of Doubting Thomas. I listened attentively and Mom looked on in surprise. This private session of passionate preaching/teaching lasted quite some time, and I felt a shift in the relationship between us.

Later, Dad went back into his room and Mom remarked, "Wow, what got into the old man? He was so excited talking with you. I have never seen him like that before."

I just smiled; by now, nothing surprised me.

That night, our Christmas feast was shared with family, including my cousin, Joy, now teaching elementary school down the road. Interesting how the familial pull kept many in the same area. I was the maverick.

I didn't have the courage to follow through on my plan to tell everyone about the Art of Living and how I truly felt about Gurudev and being on this spiritual path. Like many things in life, it is easy to slip back into comfort, some may say, comfortably numb. I did, however, plan a road trip back home to Taylor with Joy the day after Christmas.

I stayed with my childhood friend Stan, who had since taken the Art of Living course. We ate vegetarian food, discussed knowledge from both ancient texts and Gurudev's contemporary lectures, practiced our breathing and meditation together and, of course, shared stories about long ago.

My first day back at Kennesaw State University after India, I looked forward to meeting new people, hanging out, and enjoying university life.

Wrong!

In India, there were hundreds and thousands of people on the street, many wanting to talk with you, happy to see you, and children so excited when I was near. Well, you're not in India anymore, Dorothy, I mean Jeremy.

Walking around campus, smiling and being me on a brisk winter Georgia day, I said hello to handfuls of strangers passing by, or those hanging out. Not one, including a group of stuck-up Indian Americans, gave a rat's tail about talking to me, and most totally ignored me. I never felt so unloved. A drenching, cold bucket of culture shock took my breath and confidence away. If I'd rolled over dead on the sidewalk, no one would have turned a head.

Like my first day back at school only a year before, I retreated to my car to lick my wounds. A strange sadness weighed me down as I cranked up the Grateful Dead and ate my veggie and cheese sandwich. Breathing deep and acknowledging the moment, I forgot about the coldness around me and restored my strength.

Time for something totally inviting, surprisingly awesome, and life-supporting—my first time attending an activity of Art of Living in Atlanta! I called Mona Shah-Joshi, one of the main teachers there and someone I knew from Lake Tahoe, and I was on my way.

After the refreshing Kriya, Mona and her wonderful husband, Abhay, gave me a warm introduction to the group. The weekly follow-ups were held in a meeting room at a midscale hotel north of downtown. Soon, Mona let me start facilitating the Kriya for the group and afterward leading satsang!

I felt an enormous amount of joy and energy, picking up where I left off in India, leading the weekly breathing. The music in Atlanta was most fulfilling and perfect practice for what I would be doing for many years to come.

I had three or four songs I sang each week: "*Ganesha Sharanam*," "*Jaya Guru Deva Guru*," "*Om Namah Shivaya*," and "*Om Namo Bhagavate Vausudeva*." I led the twenty-plus participants back from their post Kriya rest period, and would start singing, inviting them to sing the response back and forth, repeatedly. This instant community aspect of the bhajans is called *kirtan*, and it's a popular buzzword in the ever-growing, trendy yoga world.

Satsang is the coming together of like minds, or "the coming together in the truth." This spiritual celebration has three aspects: singing (which I coined "singing yoga"), knowledge, and meditation.

I took to this form of yoga like a young bird takes to flight and song, and it is one that made me a popular name in Art of Living circles around the country over the next year.

Mona, a great leader, guided me, helped me along, and gave me firm feedback when needed, always with a shining smile. I hung out assisting her on courses at Georgia Tech and at our temporary Art of Living center. Around that time, Mona and Abhay had a Sudarshan Kriya follow-up and a satsang at their apartment. As before, she asked me to lead a couple songs after the Kriya. To make sure no one left after the breathing yoga, I placed my chair in front of the door so no one could leave! Some people came only for the breathing; not everyone liked the singing part.

The other two Art of Living teachers were another married couple, Alice and John Holiday, a Black couple who lived in a cool section of Atlanta, with a hip new-age home, which was a place I loved visiting for Kriya, satsangs, and more. John and Alice were older and had been with Gurudev longer. I viewed them as parental figures, while Mona and Abhay were like my big brother and sister.

Sometime in February the most exciting possible news came— Gurudev was coming to Atlanta at the end of April! Once again, my prayers had been answered, the miracle manifested, my personal invitation to Gurudev was accepted in the grandest way. My family was finally going to meet Gurudev Sri Sri Ravi Shankar. After my five and a half years of involvement in the organization and having a spiritual master, they would now have the opportunity to experience something I had been praying, dreaming, and hoping for. I was stoked.

After a quick peek at the dates of Gurudev's visit, I noticed they fell during the last few days before my final exams. If life had a soundtrack, the violins of stress and tension would play, signaling the foreboding of what was ahead. But I only smiled, knowing how busy I'd be helping organize his visit and being with him every day. I didn't give it much thought, but I knew that studying and taking at least the first couple of finals while he was here would be a real challenge.

Academics never came easy to me, yet it seemed different now. Maybe it was because I was older, but I knew and believed it was from the enormous power and benefits from practicing Sudarshan Kriya every day without fail. And of course, the grace of my guru, who always seemed to take care of me, even in the simplest of situations.

School was no different than your everyday occurrences. A last-minute deadline needed to be met—bam, done! A presentation on something I was not up to speed on, again, with ease, no problem. By practicing yoga, Sudarshan Kriya, and meditation daily, engaging in selfless service, listening to Gurudev's knowledge talks, and reading his books, my mind was opened like a portal for the universe to help answer my needs.

I found after spending more time with him that sometimes I felt his presence more when he was not there, as opposed to him being just feet or inches away from me. There's nothing like being around him physically: His presence speaks volumes, enlivens the souls of all around him, brings grown men to tears of joy, and evokes warm feelings of love and gratitude. Many people have these experiences around Gurudev.

Attention college students—a note from an experienced graduate: If you skip the midterm of your economics class to go to San Diego a few days before spring break, you are going to have to deal with substantial consequences. And there I was, on a plane back to San Diego for relaxation, the Southern California sun, and hanging out with the Art of Living group.

Back at Kennesaw State University in March, I was up against the ropes to make the grade in economics. On top of that, I was doing poorly in my statistics class. Math never made much sense to me, unless it was simple and useful, and nothing in this math class was either. I found it a waste of my time, taking a mandatory class for the education program, but one that bore no resemblance to me teaching four, five, six, or even ten-year-olds. Life went on and so did my D averages in both math and economics.

Plans quickly jelled for Gurudev's highly anticipated visit as part of his spring tour of America. We were fortunate, as Gurudev visited America twice, sometime three times a year. Gurudev would give a public talk at the Georgia Institute of Technology (Georgia Tech), one of the nation's top research universities. This is where my family would hear him speak and finally meet him. I could not have been more excited… and nervous.

Gurudev would stay at Alice and John Holiday's home, and we were all busy in preparations for his visit. Being around the Atlanta group for only three months, I saw the same crowd at all our events, yet people came out of the woodwork to help organize Gurudev's visit. This was as interesting as it was funny, but still welcomed and appreciated on many levels. I have seen this happen in other cities over the years—it's just the way it is and a great reason to get people in seva.

Bill Herman called with exciting news of the next Youth Leadership Training Program. My calendar continued to fill with exciting venues. A two-week intensive training open to youth from all over would be held in Brownsville, Texas. (Go ahead, look it up on Google Maps, I had no idea where it was either.) Brownsville is the southernmost city in Texas, consisting of an over ninety-three percent Hispanic population.

After the two-week training, there would be the option of a six-week fieldwork in Belize, Mexico, or Canada. Without a blink, I chose Belize, probably because it sounded like a cool place. I didn't know too much about it beforehand. Thoughts of fundraising began.

The day arrived, the place buzzed, and Alice's house was transformed into an ashram. With Gurudev staying there, it would resemble Grand Central Station for a few days. Like good neighbors, John and Alice knocked on doors and told their street mates they would be hosting a renowned international guest from India and a lot of visitors to their home. They promised that they would do their best to keep people from parking in front of their homes and being loud.

Carrying in potted plants, scrubbing floors, and decorating Gurudev's bedroom, I was in seva full force and loving it. Only one problem, though—Mom, close your ears, I mean eyes—I wasn't studying for my final exams. Mom thought I was glued to a chair in the university library during these long hours of setting up for Gurudev's visit. Gurudev would also have prioritized studying for me over seva.

We saddled up as the sun began to head toward the horizon and headed to the airport to welcome Gurudev to Atlanta. Standing there waiting for Gurudev to come up that most familiar escalator I know oh-so-well, I saw some familiar people in the Art of Living who were traveling with him. Then, just as a brilliant full moon dawns over the ocean at night, Gurudev appeared at the top of the escalator, and I was the first one to greet him with a hug.

"Welcome to Atlanta! Thank you for accepting my invitation to come and meet my family, Gurudev."

He smiled, grabbed me by the arm, and we strolled out of the airport, in front of in-awe devotees while many civilians looked on in wonder. Walking out of the airport with Gurudev, I felt like King of the World walking on a street of gold. My mind on hold, I was floating along with my guru. This was sweetly reminiscent of walking around the ashram in Bangalore with him.

"How is college and music going for you?"

"Really great, Gurudev—everything is wonderful. Thank you." My academic issues didn't seem important to me then.

The walk of a lifetime ended a few minutes later, as John Holiday waited with his car door open for Gurudev to get in. There was an empty seat in the back. I looked at Gurudev for the okay, and he nodded his head in a yes. As I folded my arms and legs to sit down, it hit me that I came with a female devotee, and she had said she would wait for me in the car outside. I got out of the seat and told Gurudev another devotee was waiting for me. He smiled as I said, "I'll see you at Alice's house."

I turned around, walked down the path of cars, and there was my friend, waiting. I'd just experienced the keenness of awareness Gurudev had taught me by example over the years. Respecting the commitment and feelings of another person is important, yet I'd just passed up the luxury of riding next to Gurudev. Would your mind function if a rock star invited you in the ride of a lifetime? This awareness was also the main lesson my TTC One teacher, Vinod Menon, had hammered into us months before in India.

Arriving at Alice's around ten minutes after Gurudev, I was told he was resting in his room. The place was ablaze with life and the energy was fantastic, electric. When Gurudev is in a home or a building, the energy is unmistakable.

I met Gurudev later and spoke with him about my final exams, only three days away, and how I wasn't prepared for them.

He put his hand on my shoulder, saying in a concerned way, "You better go and study for them."

I smiled and nodded, though I knew I wouldn't be doing much studying. I also told him my family would meet him at the public talk.

The next day was a one-day course at a hotel for people who'd completed the Art of Living course and a bunch of us left Alice's to arrange and ready the room. Leaving around midnight, I was naturally hungry from missing dinner with all the excitement going on. I made a quick right into the late night drive-through of Taco Bell. I got some veggie burritos, ate them while driving, and arrived home forty minutes later.

Bright and early the next morning, the one-day course began. It included people from mainly East Coast states. Later, Gurudev left with a handful of people to give a talk at a church.

When they came back, news was Gurudev had given a passionate sermon and the place had gone nuts. How had I missed that one? Staying back to do seva at the course was enough to hold me from giving myself a swift kick in the pants.

I later watched the video, and sure enough, Gurudev and the place rocked. One of the unique traits of Gurudev is how he can remarkably (and naturally) mirror anyone or a crowd; blend in to reach a person or group. At that church, he was a gospel preacher, talking about human values, universal love, and service. His message was well received, and another happy audience was blessed by the master.

When Gurudev returned, he led us through a beautifully powerful and time-vanishing meditation. Next, we had a typical, fun, question-and-answer session. During one question about the relationship between diet and yoga/meditation, Gurudev looked directly at me and Abhay, sitting right next to me, and with his wide smile and joking nature said, "Just as long as you eat the right kinds of food at the right time. We have people here who go to Taco Bell at midnight on their way home. This is not a healthy habit."

Laughter filled the room as I was stunned, almost shocked, thinking, *How in the world did he know I stopped at Taco Bell last night?* I turned to Abhay and said, "Wow, he caught me—I was at Taco Bell around midnight."

Abhay said with great energy, "I stopped there on the way home, too!"

My perception was spot-on, he'd called both of us out. Gurudev knows everything in the world, and especially about his adored devotees.

That night there was a public satsang in the hall. I was thrilled to sing for Gurudev again, this time more formal than the first time in India. I had told one of the teachers and one of the main musicians I knew from over the years, Von Osselman, earlier that day how I wanted to sing at least one song at the satsang that night.

He said, "Sounds great."

I couldn't wait. Sitting on a cushion with the other musicians, including Von, a mainstay at all satsangs, I looked up at Gurudev a mere fifteen feet away. It was my turn to sing, and I went for one of Divya Prabha's popular songs that I knew well.

After the first verse, something strange happened. Von, sitting a few people in front of me, kept looking back at me with the weirdest face, like I was singing reminiscent of a haunted wolf howling at the moon or something even stranger. Maybe I wasn't a harmonious joy to listen to back then, but I wasn't bad. It was my perception that Von wanted me to finish the song in a hurry.

I closed my eyes for the rest of the song, which was not more than four minutes, a modest length for these call and response songs.

After the satsang I confronted Von with, "Dude, what were those looks for, man?! This was my first time playing for Gurudev in a satsang like this, and this is my city!" I must have sounded like that Indian boy smoking behind the bus screaming, "This is my Bangalore!" I was about as smooth as a couple of strips of sandpaper dealing with Von. I was foolish to act the way I did.

He came back with one of his know-it-all and holier-than-thou answers. "Gurudev only likes certain people to sing at public satsangs."

"I am not buying that one, Von."

Then we parted ways. He left and I stayed with a few others to clean up the hall.

The sound technician handed me something I'd never seen before, but it looked like a girl's hair barrette or clip, and he asked what he should do with it. I tossed it in the garbage can, not giving it a second thought. We didn't have a lost and found for hair clips.

Back at Alice's that night I saw Von and began to burn. I did my best to apply Gurudev's knowledge of acceptance, but it wasn't easy. Hanging out with Gurudev, though, melted all that drama. My mind eased around him, and the thoughts went away. It was late and Gurudev told me to go home and study for my finals. I did go shortly after but went right to bed. I had an early morning at the university, the day before finals began, and then would rush downtown to help get the stage ready at Georgia Tech for the public talk.

Mom and my sister Michele had both agreed to come hear Gurudev speak. While asking Mom one night if Dad was going, she replied, "He has to come!" I was pleasantly taken aback at her enthusiasm.

A few days before the talk, Dad was in the living room with Mom; it was now or never. I mustered up the nerve and handed him one of the postcard-size flyers for the public talk. I simply said, "Here, Dad, my teacher is coming from India to give a talk at Georgia Tech."

As he swiped the card from me, he said in a stern voice, "Who's this?"

I replied, "This is my teacher from India, Gurudev Sri Sri Ravi Shankar."

Without any response, he laid the flyer on the end table and walked back to his room. That was one strange interaction with Dad, though I wasn't expecting much.

Hmm... interesting, I thought.

Mom assured me he was going with her, Michele, and David, my two-year-old nephew. Even with Mom's reassuring care, I felt more nervous than ever about my family attending the talk. Luckily, the nerves didn't consume me, with all that was going on with Gurudev's visit and my finals. My life was like a fairytale, and I was having a magical time. Soon, I would get to see what was on the other side of that cascading waterfall below the rainbow.

CHAPTER SEVENTEEN

Family Ties and a Sweet Surprise

When longing is there, then prayers and poems will
come, and a lot of miracles can happen. Enjoy that.
—Gurudev Sri Sri Ravi Shankar

The highly anticipated day arrived where my family would meet Gurudev. I woke up early, did my breathing practice and meditation, and went up to the university for my last day before finals. Did I remember anything the professors said? No. My mind was totally occupied by that evening's event.

Then I headed straight to Alice and John's to see Gurudev before heading off to the venue to help set it up for the talk. I called Mom and Michele to make sure they were all set, and they were. I changed my clothes in the restroom at Georgia Tech and I was ready for anything. I can't ever remember being that excited and nervous. My family at my guru's public talk in downtown Atlanta! Life could not possibly get better than this.

"Nice picture, huh?" I said to a beautiful Indian girl, pointing to the picture of me on the cover of the new YLTP flyer for our summer programs. They were lined up on a table in the Divine Shop area (books and CDs) outside the venue of the night's public talk.

"Yes," she said, in a very pleasant voice, and then, "oh my God, that's you!" Her enthusiasm was spontaneous. "You must be Jeremy; I have heard so much about you from Mona! And now I meet you here."

"Ah, Mona, she is so sweet—I hope she said good things." Extending my hand, I said, "Hi, my name is Jeremy; what's yours?"

"My name is Aarna. I took the Art of Living course with Mona in February."

"Wow, you have a beautiful smile," I said with all the Georgia charm I could muster.

"You have a nice smile, too."

And that was it, love at first sight. Did you think you'd get through this many pages without a beautiful girl involved?

We talked while doing seva and setting up the Divine Shop. I liked her and wanted to get to know more about her. That seva with her totally took my mind off the nervous energy of my family coming there. A true blessing, right?

Aarna was a nineteen-year-old, American-born Indian girl. Short with dark hair, eyes of beauty, and a signature smile that shined something beautiful with each grin, she was super-enthusiastic. That's what struck me first, such comments as, "That's awesome, Jeremy!" This shook me from inside and made me fall for her faster than an eagle swoops from the sky. She was a hip American girl, loved music, had favorite bands, was well traveled, and spoke four languages.

"Four languages! Aarna, are you serious? Is there even a word for that?"

"Jeremy, what do you call it when someone speaks three languages?" she replied.

"Um, trilingual?"

"Yes!" she said, smiling. "Okay, how about two languages?"

"I know, that's bilingual."

"Correct! Okay, last one, what is it called when someone speaks only one language?"

"Monolingual?" I said with a few feet of doubt.

"Nah, you're wrong. The correct answer is… American!"

We both nearly fell over in laughter. We parted ways before the event and agreed to meet outside afterward. I was stoked!

Just as I left the Divine Shop, stepping outside, I saw Gurudev pull up in a car. Sweet. I opened the door for him and proceeded to walk with him into the venue. I gave a good chuckle when he asked me if this was my university, Georgia Tech being one of *the* premier technical universities in the world. He smiled as I told him where my university was located.

I reminded him one last time that my parents were coming and that I was very nervous. He stopped just before the entrance, looked me in the eyes and said, "They will enjoy it; give your worries to me. Have a great time with your family tonight. *Jai Guru Dev.*"

The words were spoken in his sweetest and most loving voice. It's times like these when he is a mix between my spiritual master and father figure. I followed his directions, let it go, and walked in with him.

Shortly after, Von rushed up to me in a feverish panic saying, "Jeremy, did you see my capo? I must have lost it last night at the satsang."

"No, Von. What does it look like?"

"It is a small clip," he held his fingers apart, "around this size."

I said no, shaking my head, and we both walked away in different directions. It was clear enough Von needed this capo thing to play the songs he'd lead before and after Gurudev's talk. Just then it hit like a runaway train—that little girl hair-clip-looking thing the sound technician had asked about after the satsang.

And I threw it away. I only smiled and shrugged.

I spotted my family and went to sit with them. This was wild. I could not believe they were sitting next to me, about to listen to the man who had inspired me and changed my world forever. I was grateful, excited and happy. Sitting alongside my dad, mom, sister and nephew, I glanced over at them and said to myself, "This is it."

As Gurudev was about to lead the meditation, I took my nephew David outside in the commons area to play with the other little kids. When the meditation was over, we headed back in, and things got interesting. Some intellectual-brain-mess of a man started challenging Gurudev, stating how the best creativity has come from depression and anger.

Gurudev was making a point that, "Silence is the mother of all creativity. By being stress free and centered, creativity flows naturally."

There's usually one of these know-it-all men in every crowd, and I think I've seen them all. Gurudev, being the patient king he is, heard the man out and gave a few more lines to support his point.

But to no avail—the guy continued, and the crowd was becoming agitated.

What happened next is so etched in my mind I can reenact it in my sleep. Gurudev took a stick and cracked this guy upon his book-stacked intellect (metaphorically speaking). I have seen Gurudev get firm like this in various cases, but not often. Gurudev spoke a strong, case-closing sentence, followed by, "Are you getting this point?"

My little nephew yelled, and I mean loud, "Yeah!"

The whole place erupted in laughter. I am sure the guy felt like someone getting hit in the head with a ninety-mile-an-hour foul ball at a baseball stadium. Gurudev was smiling, the place was convulsed in laughter, and the whole attention of the audience, at that moment, was on my family. Out of the mouths of babes, high-fives all around.

Children are much more in tune with the world and their surroundings than adults; they have a sixth sense and know more than most give them credit for. This was one of the governing reasons I was in the education program at Kennesaw State University, studying to become a kindergarten teacher. But still it begs me to wonder how David knew what was going on and what was being said as a two-and-a-half-year-old boy. How did he know just when to hit the punch line and knock that irritating guy out? I believe Gurudev used little David as an extension of his humor wings to silence that guy, but regardless of what I believe, it was real and awesome.

The talk ended, and I knew where I was going, taking my family by the hand, right to the bottom of the stage to meet Gurudev Sri Sri Ravi Shankar. Dad asked where we were going. I said, "I'd like to introduce you to Gurudev."

"Oh, we can?" he asked in excitement.

I said, "Follow me."

In what goes down as one of the greatest moments of my life, Gurudev made his way down the stairs where my family and I were waiting.

"Gurudev, this is my family." I could have floated away right there from happiness. All I had wanted was for them to meet my guru. My sincere desire was fulfilled.

He greeted them with a smile and the surprises began.

First up was Mom. She hugged Gurudev, and holding back tears said, "Thank you for taking Jeremy to India; he knows so much about the country now. He talks to all the Indians whenever we are shopping."

Did I tell you she's the president of my fan club?

Gurudev replied, "He's a good boy and a great singer."

Ah, my heart was bouncing down and up and round and round by now.

Next up, my dear old dad. The once cynical preacher from Taylor now was in front of one of the most respected humanitarians in the world. With hands in the prayer position, he greeted Gurudev with an overwhelmingly surprising, "Hi, Sri Sri, we enjoyed your talk. My son, Jeremy, loves you—he has your pictures all over the house."

Oh my God, without a moment to react to that remark and the whole beautiful, life-changing scene going on, Gurudev greeted my sister and her son, David—the star of the show.

I just sat back and took it all in.

"Thank you," I said to Gurudev with the gratitude of a million oceans of love inside my heart. I could have written a song about it, but it wouldn't have done it justice. Plus, the night wasn't over just yet.

As Gurudev headed to the door, we did the same. The super man was surrounded by hundreds of people near the door, and I remember my dad trying to get out of the venue quickly. We left while Gurudev was still inside—I was content. My requested miracle was graciously granted. Bidding my family goodbye, Dad was already his usual five or seven steps in the lead, headed to the car. Michele and Mom thanked me for a wonderful night and followed Dad. I just stood there in utter bliss.

The next moment I looked to the door and saw Gurudev walking out. Surprisingly, there were not many people with him, and he was heading right for me. I looked at Mom and Michele, calling them back, and was surprised to see both running back toward me, Michele with David in her arms. Within half a minute they were lined up with me as Gurudev headed straight for us. Dad was on his way back, too.

"What should I say to him, Jeremy?" Michele asked in a breathless, sincere tone.

"Ask him to bless David," I replied.

Gurudev walked right up to us and greeted Mom and Dad, who'd just arrived, once again.

"Sri Sri, can you bless my son?" Michele said in a most humble manner.

Gurudev put his hand on David's head and responded sweetly, "He's already blessed." Wow, what special blessings for my family. We said our goodbyes once again, this time with even larger smiles.

When I invited Gurudev to Atlanta, back in December at the Bangalore Ashram to meet my family, I could never have imagined how much attention he would give them. Let's call this the greatest night of my life when my family, minus my brother, Jeff, got to meet my guru, and I met a smart, hip, and beautiful girl.

What did I do to deserve this? I thought. Well, one thing's for sure, I didn't question it for long.

After I walked Gurudev to the car and bid him a genuine thank you and goodbye, I headed back to the front of the venue, looking for Aarna. See, this shows how sane I am, or how stoked I was on her. I'd just had this miraculous experience, and still remembered to make good on my word and meet Aarna after the talk. I could have continued to spin around, dizzy with gratitude, floating upon the stars, abounded by blessings and love.

Score. She was right there waiting for me. I told her with a gleam of excitement in my eyes of what had taken place between Gurudev and my family. She shared my excitement, and we drove to Alice's house to hang out with Gurudev.

Gurudev sat in the living room surrounded by a bunch of devotees, watching an old Hindi film. I introduced Aarna to Gurudev. He gave his greetings and a blessing to her, with a look in his eyes that seemed to say, "Hmm, do you like this girl, Jeremy?" Another icing-on-the-cake moment of this incredible night.

After a while, Gurudev turned and looked at me, telling me in a fatherly and loving way, "You better go home and study for your final exams tomorrow."

I replied, "Okay, Gurudev, I will go now."

Leaving was the hardest thing in the world to do, though, being in Gurudev's divine company, chatting and laughing, with this pretty

Indian girl next to me. This was like some far-out dream, taking into consideration what had happened with my family earlier.

"Jeremy, you really need to get home, you have final exams tomorrow!" And that was the last time he needed to say it.

Aarna and I left without hesitation, but I didn't go home. We went to my car two blocks away and talked and listened to music for another hour. It was well after midnight before we said goodnight. So much for studying! I grabbed a few hours of sleep, did my breathing and meditation, and called Alice while eating breakfast.

"Hello, Alice? Is Gurudev still there? Can I come and meet him before my final exams?"

"Let me ask him."

As soon as I heard a yes, I was headed toward the highway.

When I arrived at Alice's house Gurudev's door was shut—a meeting with some other teachers. Another dude, Kamlesh, waited outside the room. I explained my hurry to meet Gurudev, as my finals were starting in about an hour and school was a good drive away.

He said, "You need to get in there," and banged on the door. I would never have done that. Who knew there was another young guy in the organization crazier than me? But it worked! Gurudev came to the door and invited me in as he excused the other teachers.

"Gurudev, I am going to take my first two final exams now." My smiling, open face disguised the lack of studying. I'd completely missed cracking the books, despite his directions.

"Come here, I have something for you," he replied, taking what looked like a candy bar from his silver puja tray.

"Take this with you." He placed a fancy Belgian chocolate bar in my open hand.

"Thank you," I said. Tears of joy rolled down my face as an electric charge from the bar beamed through my body. I gave Gurudev one last hug, then stole a precious moment to show him some pictures from my India trip. He gave his full attention and bid me a final farewell.

I floated into my car and headed up to the university. Halfway up the highway it started to rain, reminding me of the tail end of the monsoons in India. I drove as fast as I dared to make my first exam in time, thoughts of Gurudev on my mind. Was I dreaming again, or was this indeed the sweetest life possible?

I slipped in the lecture hall, dripping wet, just as the economics final exam was being handed out. I had a D in this class from skipping the midterm to fly out to San Diego. I knew I needed a good grade to get me up to the B that I was hoping for. I also knew I had not studied for this rigorous exam. My thoughts were like an episode of *Monty Python's Flying Circus*. I need, I should have, I know… Studying had never made my to-do list.

A quick look over the multipage exam sent an ill feeling into my stomach, and my head felt heavy. I was becoming frustrated, not knowing the material.

Suddenly, I remembered Gurudev's chocolate bar. With relief, I took it out of my backpack and placed it on top of the exam. Closing my eyes, I felt the immense presence of Gurudev inside me. I proceeded with the test. I can't explain the change in feeling, atmosphere, and most importantly, how easily I completed the exam. I finished with the first group of kids turning theirs in. I left with a miraculous feeling that I did well.

Next was the final exam of my most dreaded class, possibly, of all time—statistics. Math— Yuck! With a capital Y. Math has always haunted me, and this course was the perpetual and ultimate body slam to my ego, mind, and well-being. One that kept knocking me down, no matter how hard I worked, how many sessions of tutoring I went for, and no matter how hard I prayed the class got cancelled and we all got A's. Obviously, that wish never manifested. I sat down and was handed the exam by the professor who'd haunted me the whole semester.

I peeked inside its jarring pages, touting math problems that made my teeth shiver. This thing was a beast. After wrestling with one problem for twenty minutes, frustrated, tired, and ready to give up, I remembered the magic chocolate bar—yes! I took the bar out and placed it right on the exam, closed my eyes, and took a deep breath.

To my surprise, when I opened my eyes, the exam was completed—no, silly goose, I'm just joking. What actually happened was, I opened my eyes, looked at the chocolate bar, and was blown away by this cool breeze through the door. Like a holy ocean of eminent saints showering their blessings by the breeze, I soaked in energy, and smiled in bliss.

I put my pencil to the paper and kicked some serious math tail. I have never in my life been that comfortable and coherent while tackling math problems. One after another, the problems worked themselves out. I could not doubt this miracle by Gurudev; I knew he was taking the test for me once again, and I enjoyed being his instrument.

I proudly handed in my test and walked out of the classroom. I reached into my bag, grabbed the gifted chocolate bar in awe, smiled with a tear in the corner of my eye, then opened and ate it with full gratitude and reverence for being on this path with Gurudev. All I could mutter from my cracking voice was a humble, *"Jai Guru Dev!"*

My plans that night, seriously, were to study for my next three exams. Besides which, the chocolate bar was gone. Yet I couldn't help wanting to talk to my father open-heartedly about last night's public talk and meeting with Gurudev (or Sri Sri, as they call him).

I was meditating in my bedroom when our dogs barked their six o'clock alarm symphony, letting us know Dad was home from work. I couldn't help overhearing him talking to Mom about Gurudev—I was dumbfounded. After Dad retreated to his room, I went into my study room, hitting the books for the next day's exams. Yes, now I was finally ready to study.

Shortly, Michele called with the most sincere and grateful message of, "Jeremy, thank you so much for last night; I had a great time. And I don't know what it was, but for the whole day I felt so good. It was so wonderful, thank you."

As I listened to my older sister I saw, from the corner of my eye, Dad come into the dining room. He saw I was on the phone and did something he's never done before, sat down on one of the dining room chairs and waited for me to finish. One half of my mind was finishing the call with my sister, the other half was trembling in nerves about talking to my dad, perhaps for the first time with an open heart about my spiritual master and path of yoga. This space was getting hot.

I hung up the phone, though I didn't want that conversation to end. Turning to me, he said, "Jeremy, how were your final exams today?"

"Great, Dad. I think I did really well."

"Jeremy, I had a great time last night at the talk and meeting Sri Sri. Thank you for taking us to meet him!" His voice was loud, sincere, and surprisingly happy.

My mind went blank at his words and the good will behind them. Any chance of a deep discussion went out the window; I hadn't expected such positive remarks from the get-go.

"My favorite quote was, 'Religion is the banana peel and spirituality is the banana.' Ha, I love that one; I am going to use it when I preach on the Ham Radio!"

"Yes, that is a great line. I love it, too." My voice sounded awkward. I couldn't believe this was happening.

"Thanks again, Jeremy, I had a great time."

Dad walked back into his room. I sat at my desk, asking myself what the heck had just happened. Was the last twenty-four hours indeed my real life, or had I been dreaming the past twenty-five years?

I looked at Gurudev's resplendent picture on the right corner of my desk, smiled, and closed my eyes, slipping into meditation. When I finished, I went into the living room and talked to my mother about last night and her enjoyment in meeting Gurudev. I couldn't have been a happier boy and would have bet my guitar that I was, indeed, the happiest boy on earth. Heck, I am the happiest boy on earth right this minute, writing this extraordinary story of mine. I am happy. Actually, I am happiness.

No, I wasn't avoiding studying. The need to share the experience with my parents overrode the finals prep.

Two days later I took my last exams. I had no Gurudev-blessed chocolate bar, but I was more prepared. Plus, I had tons of residual confidence from my first two exams. Finished, I walked down a hallway of offices when I heard my name called. I took a step back and, inside the doorway, saw my economics professor behind his desk. I had no idea his office was in this building. What's more, I had no idea he knew my name, as our class was huge, and I hadn't talked to him much during the semester.

"Please come in, have a seat." Uh-oh, flashbacks of a guilty conscience culled from my troublesome childhood filled my mind.

"Let me be the first to congratulate you on scoring one of the highest grades in my class on the final exam. Great job, you must have really prepared for this. With the A on this, it moved your grade up to a B for the semester."

As his mouth moved, all I could think about was Gurudev and the chocolate bar. What a beautiful miracle he had blessed me with.

"Wow, that is wonderful news, Professor. Yes, I studied all week long." *Did I remember to cross my fingers?* With a big grin, I said, "Thanks for a fantastic class. I am very happy with my final grade."

After a firm handshake, I walked out of the office on cloud seventeen. Going from a D to a B with one exam? This was awesome. And if my math was correct, statistically impossible. I was as grateful as ever. *Jai Guru Dev!*

In the next breath I wondered how I fared on my math exam. I'd had a low D all the way. It would take another near-perfect exam to get me out of the deep hole. Walking up to my math class, I saw the grades posted on the window. Closing my eyes, I took a deep breath. Scrolling down the list to find my student ID number, there it was—those screaming, red hot, blazing neon numbers on a white page—ninety! I have never scored even close to an A on a math test, never mind this caliber of one. My glorious guru blessed me, taking my exams for me, helping me come clean with an acceptable C in math for the semester. I'd take it.

When final grades were posted online, I could have done cartwheels in front of the computer. My GPA was a welcomed 3.35— three A's, a B and a C—thanks to the grace and love of Gurudev.

I talked to Aarna all the time on the phone, and we met a few times, becoming close. Everything about her was mind-blowing, refreshing, and different from any girl I had ever met. We shared a common taste for music, food, and culture, as well as spirituality, and talked about saving the world together.

I started writing poems for her, and a few songs, including the first one called "You Turn," which was featured on my first all-English album *Back to Taylor Town,* released on my mother's birthday, May 24, 2011. For the record, that's Bob Dylan's birthday, too.

I enjoyed every moment of those six weeks from the night we met till the day I left for Texas to begin YLTP on June 15. Perhaps the greatest part of our budding relationship was it was grounded in self-knowledge. We talked for hours about Gurudev's knowledge, and after ancient lines of wisdom, we'd sit silently for a while, communicating in silence, just as Gurudev has spoken about: "Head to head communication is talking. Heart to heart communication is singing. And soul to soul communication is silence." This is what we were experiencing.

Of course, we also gossiped, laughed, joked, and shared a tear here and there—it wasn't all wishy-washy and airy-fairy stuff.

I had to raise $2,000 to go on the eight-week YLTP that summer. My confidence rocked after fundraising $4,000 the summer before for India. I knew this was going to happen. My mind was totally in the fundraising frame once again. First, I drafted a letter to devotees who I knew would be interested in helping me. I made calls and sent emails. Once again, people responded in waves, and I was grateful for their support. Many people stated how they could not attend these type programs and do seva and enjoyed sponsoring someone like me. They loved hearing about the adventures afterward. It's a place I am now in my life, with a job and many responsibilities in the community, plus various creative projects.

One morning during meditation, I had an awesome idea. Over the past sixteen years, my finest ideas have sprung from this intense process. The deeper I got, the more the ideas seem to flow.

Coming home from India, I weighed much less, and Mom made sure to get every pound I'd lost back on. I wanted to get in shape for the program in Texas and Belize, a small Central American country. My brilliant idea was to go to LA Fitness, the local corporate gym, and ask for a free month's membership, to get in shape to go on a humanitarian college program. I grabbed one of the flyers for the program with me on the front cover, holding the little smiling Indian boy on my shoulders.

I talked to the gym manager, showing him the flyer. Before I could finish, he interrupted in his best Southern drawl, "Son, you can work out here for however long you want, whenever you want. You are doing fantastic work in this world. We need more people like you. Praise the Lord!"

With that blessing, I proceeded to his office where he gave me a VIP membership card with no expiration date or questions asked. I was simply entranced, walking out of the gym with a huge sense of gratitude for my guru. I worked out at the gym as much as I could. It helped being sweet for Aarna, too. I wanted to look my best. Life was flying in sonic speed come June 2002.

Aarna saw me off at the airport, and the next time I would see her was when she picked me up at the same airport two months later. It was a bittersweet moment.

There were twenty of us from around the country, as diverse and awesome as they come in Brownsville, Texas—yee-haw! Matt and I were the comedy; Amol the younger brother; Sam the odd comic know-it-all; Jason and Mark the older brothers; Enoch, the uncle; Radhika, Gabriella, Damien, Sati, Dimple, and Hedda the happy sisters; and Bill was the leader of us all—the train conductor. Could it be anyone else?

Bill made it clear from the start he would not tolerate any of our shenanigans like in India. We promised but felt sure we'd come up with new ones. All of us lived under the same roof in a small Texas home. Who said everything is big in Texas?

The daily sessions were brilliant, and the morning and afternoon sadhana powerful and fun, plus full of laughter, of course. The meals were excellent, thanks to Dimple from Austin and Bill's master hand in the kitchen. We worked together, learned together, the boys took military-style showers one after another, we fought together, sang together, and above all, laughed often and loud while we grew spiritually during those two weeks in Brownsville.

I led a good deal of songs each night in satsang, beginning to find my voice, which was a powerful mix of volume, rock and roll, and sincere devotion wrapped inside my heart, flowing through my tunes, with everyone following along in harmony.

I admit I am not my most respectable self around Matt. Our past lives must have been rowdy, vaudeville or burlesque, who knows?

At one point, Bill stopped teaching, stating, "I'm feeling stuck. I can't go any further without clearing something up with these boys over here."

Matt and I were using some vulgar slang words, having our usual off-the-wall, goofy, good times. As always, the weight fell mostly on me and I found myself in the center of a circle with my eyes closed, listening to praise, one-by-one, from the course participants walking slowly around me. This was meant to lift my spirits in a time of dejection. It worked.

This process was initiated by Enoch, a heavyset Black man in his forties, a college professor by trade. In response to Matt and my weak excuse of, "These words don't have any meaning, we made them up," Enoch replied, "In my experience working with young adults, there are no words that don't have meaning."

We were busted. Later, Bill said he was ready to put me on the next bus to Atlanta that night. Thank goodness he didn't. Matt and I toned it down after that fiasco and the course continued without a hitch.

Each night, I talked to Aarna on the phone, sometimes until two or three in the morning, and mind you, I needed to be up at five-thirty. I only needed two or three hours of sleep, thank goodness. I felt airborne between the course and falling in love with this sweetheart—or was I rising? Funny what distance will do for a relationship, how does that old adage go? Absence makes the heart grow fonder.

One of the highlights in Brownsville was going to a Catholic convent where Bill, Mark, and Jason were teaching an Art of Living course. At the end of each night, I led a couple of songs, and the first night were traditional gospel songs.

On the last night Bill asked me to sing some Sanskrit bhajans. Before I started, he came up and whispered, "Play the new one you just learned, '*Jaya Jaya Shiva Shambho.*'" He also added, "But tone it down a little tonight; don't get too crazy."

I smiled and nodded.

But a few minutes into the powerful song, the energy in the room rose. The group was a mix of twenty of our own YLTP members and around twenty of the new course participants, mainly Mexican Americans. Without any encouragement from me they erupted in energy and devotion. The song took off; all I was doing was steering the vehicle. This started a three-year love affair between me and this song.

When we got home Bill opened one of his standard cans of whoop-ass on me, yelling, "Didn't I tell you to tone it down in satsang tonight? What the hell were you doing going crazy like that? You need to follow my directions and be more sensitive with new course participants like this!"

I didn't speak a word of rebuttal, not even a smirk. As Bill walked away, as angry at me as ever, Matt turned to me and said, "You should have said, 'Hey Bill—I am satsang!'"

My frown vanished, and the two of us almost fell over laughing. I truly felt I was wrongly accused. The course participants took the song to that high level as I was only along for the ride. Bill obviously saw it differently.

Lying in bed, I thought of Gurudev's golden words on blame: "If someone blames you for something you did not do, and you don't react to them, they actually take your bad karma away from you. See this as a blessing; they actually are blessing you in disguise. But, if you react back by yelling at them, the opposite holds true, you take on their negative karma."

I held my tongue and did not defend myself.

The two weeks came to a wonderful ending, and we welcomed the new teachers with a gala celebration. Six of us would now head down to Belize to live and teach in a Mayan Indian village, the others would go to Matamoros, Mexico, just over the border from Brownsville. Matt and few others would go do service work in

Montreal, Canada. Bill, Gabriella, Robyn, Sati, Sam, and I made up the Belize crew, ready to travel for an unknown adventure.

Back at Krishna and Purnima's welcoming home in Houston to rest for a night before catching our respective flights in the morning, I called Aarna. The conversation turned me tickled pink and purple, tie-dyed, when she told me the story of telling her best female friend about how she felt about me.

"And what did you tell her?" I asked innocently.

"I told her I am crazy about you!"

My body quickly blasted through a carnival of emotions, temperatures, and a calliope of sounds, and smells of sweet cotton candy pounded my mind. My heart bounced back and forth, pressing for release from my chest. I couldn't believe what she had just said, and it sounded as good as "Jeremy, you are my Superman."

What was great news for me also felt a bit bitter since I would be away for another six weeks in Belize. I knew distance would only make our connection stronger as the past two weeks in Texas had, but patience was not one of my top virtues.

When I hung up the phone, I dashed out of the house, the heat of the Texas night enveloping me, and soon I was jumping up and down like a wild man, fist pumping into the night sky. I finally had the girl of my poems and songs—the queen of my dreams. Wow, what a lucky boy, what a fortunate life!

CHAPTER EIGHTEEN

I'm Gonna Let It Shine

Any miracle can happen anytime.
—Gurudev Sri Sri Ravi Shankar

L anding in Belize, I was beyond excited looking out the plane window. Whom would I meet, what kind of food would I experience? Zaccai Free, another smiling volunteer with the Art of Living who'd set up this service adventure, welcomed us. Zaccai was a tall, skinny Black dude, sporting nappy dreadlocked hair. I felt déjà vu, reminiscent of when I met Matt on my first YLTP adventure in India.

Zaccai came off as a simple man with minimal needs and old clothes, and he carried a handmade shoulder bag where he kept a pen and a pad for writing, along with other essentials. We connected easily. Being a couple years older than I, Zaccai filled the role of an older brother figure from the get-go.

After a quick sleepover at a modest hotel, we headed away from Belize City to the village in San Pedro, Columbia, where we stayed with a wonderful Mayan Indian couple and their seven children! This humble, happy family embraced us into their unassuming lifestyle. Six newcomers, ready for anything, joyful souls with our minds set on seva and celebration.

Living on the Columbia River opened new experiences, such as washing our clothes in the river water along with the locals. The children bathed there, and we all swam, splashed, and had tons of fun in the water on hot days—yes, that meant every day. After frequent heavy rains, the river rose high and mighty, its fast and dangerously flowing stream ready to take a life in no time, but it was part of the adventurous ride.

In the house, our group slept on the concrete floor just feet away from a large pile of cornhusks. Very communal, neck to neck, males and females, listening to each other snore, and me singing in my sleep. It rained a lot during the night while we slept, coming in through the open windows. I learned a damp, chilly lesson when sleeping by the window on the first night. The host family slept upstairs.

One morning I wrapped my towel around me and headed for the outside shower. Did I tell you the only toilet was an outhouse? For some reason, I looked behind me and on my bum was a big, black, heart-stopping, straight out of a low budget horror movie— tarantula! Ahh...!

Instinctively, I knocked it off and ran to the other side of the room. My brain just emitted exclamation points along with several R-rated expletives, while adrenaline coursed through my veins. Who didn't grow up with nightmares of huge spiders? The kids enjoyed chasing and crushing the villain with a rock. My thoughts swirled in a constant loop about its family hanging around somewhere patiently waiting for revenge on whoever killed their parent, brother or sister. Get me out of here!

Our schedule kept us busy. Group sadhana was at 6:00 a.m., the usual yoga, Sudarshan Kriya, and meditation. It concluded with Bill leading the ancient and melodious Guru Puja. Our main purpose was to learn from these wonderful people; teach the Breath Water Sound course; celebrate life with satsang, dance, and play; and be available for whoever needed our help.

During our YLTP the year before in India, Bill had the idea to take this program to the Americas. The Art of Living had free courses for prisoners and individuals with life-threatening diseases, but this was the first program of its kind. Zaccai was our only connection in Belize; there had not been any programs here before.

I went for a run every day after the morning program, in the hot, baking sun with my shirt off. I had my shirt off most of that summer. The mix of morning yoga, with aerobic transportation like running, walking, swimming, plus eating well, saw me in top shape. Ready for this, girls… I was super tan and looking good, too. The combo platter of music, teaching, and being super healthy came with constant thoughts of Aarna on my mind.

We taught at different places during the day, and I will never forget my first course with around ten ladies from the village. One brought her infant who sat upon her lap. We invited the participants to close their eyes and began the meditation. I peeked to see the state of the course goers and could not help smiling when I saw the lady breast-feeding while meditating. We teach in unique situations. I loved it. Where else could I experience such fascinating life moments? Surely not in Georgia.

Each night during satsang, the kids in the house and community came around to sing, play, and have a good time. Some nights we had improvised skits to go along with the seva aspect of the Breath Water Sound courses. These were a blast. I played music while others acted out crazy characters in street skits.

The most memorable were based on conflict resolution. How can I forget Junior in his tight-fist stance, yelling loudly, on the verge of physical attack? Just then Javier, complete with a soft smile and ease, asked Junior if he would like to learn a breathing technique to help him calm down. Junior agreed, Javier taught him on the spot, and the conflict was resolved peacefully with breathing yoga and smiles. Perfect.

Our room had a nice sized radio/tape/CD player. One of the highlights was playing "Eyes of the World" by the Grateful Dead with everyone dancing along like happy hippies. All I had to push was the play button.

On a routine walk up the river, looking for food to buy from farmers, I was humbled to see how simply people lived, how little they seemed to need. I'd seen this across the spectrum in India before and now here in Belize.

There were two main dishes: one was beans and rice, and the other rice and beans. Yes, it sounds funny, but there is a distinction. Rice and beans sit on a plate, usually separated. Beans and rice is stewed beans poured over a bed of rice. See, I told you, different, poles apart.

One of the main condiments in Belize was the famous habanero hot sauce. Oh, boy—could I go for a splash or two of that right now. I put this on nearly everything and loved the intense spice. I brought a bunch of bottles home in my suitcase, and Dad loved it, too.

Junior, the youngest boy in the family where we stayed, was yelling, "*Jippy Jappa, Jippy Jappa!*" with excited power, pointing to a plant. My ears rang at his high decibels, but my mind wildly raced with the creative potential of these words. Zaccai told us the plant had many uses. It could be chewed raw, cooked as a vegetable, or its most common and productive use, the Mayans used it to weave baskets and knickknacks.

Without hesitation, I started putting notes to the words, singing a most novel song, "Jippy Jappa, Junior Jippy Jappa!" The kids erupted in laughter and started singing along. One by one, I changed the name in the song, and had everyone sing back to me in call and response fashion. I had a huge hit on my hands—a name-game song.

This song proved to be an anthem that summer, one I would later invite thousands of people to sing along with me over the radio, and for sure, one of the more popular songs I have written. It's simple, catchy, and fun. Even after twenty years, during Art of Living Satsangs and in schools where I lead music, "Jippy Jappa" still generates smiles and laughter. While it has not been recorded for my past five albums, I believe it would be a perfect fit for my sixth.

Belize was a creative high for me even with my main muse, Aarna, back home in Georgia. It was one of those lovely early mornings after sadhana; I was walking around the front yard when a force of sound hit me like a Kansas tornado. I began to sing with powerful, longing thoughts of Aarna. "You keep smiling, I'll be rocking, the stars out on the night. You catch a wave that flies you far, but it comes rushing back my way…" This line manifested into a beautiful song called "Wherever You Are." I knew I was onto something special with her in my heart.

Communication-wise, I had limited access to the Internet and international phone calls. Upstairs in the house was an old computer with one of those now-ancient 3.5 inch floppy disks—smile if you remember them. I kept a daily journal to send to Aarna. As it turned out, she was doing the same back home—but in a more creative way. She had made me a website, posting daily entries and pictures.

Though so far from each other, it felt like we were becoming closer each day. My expectations about us as a couple soared through the roof, though Gurudev teaches how expectations do indeed lead to reduced joy. Sometimes, like now, it was most difficult to use knowledge for the betterment of my mind and heart. Come on, who wouldn't have been super-stoked? This was an extraordinary girl. As much as I talked of knowledge, music, and life, I also talked about Aarna—she became a household name that summer.

We travelled to Barranco on the Caribbean Sea where Zaccai once lived on a farm. Like other places I'd visited in India, it could have been easily mistaken for a productive fly farm; enormous flies and mosquitoes were everywhere. We taught the locals several courses, held satsangs, and invited everyone to a vegetarian potluck. During the magnificent full moon in July under a canopy of a black, diamond-studded sky, we gathered in the backyard, mere steps from the warm, dazzling Caribbean Sea, and celebrated Guru Purnima.

After our work was done, we enjoyed a brief, relaxing vacation on the islands of Key Caulker and San Pedro. Some believe Madonna sang about the latter island in her hit song "La Isla Bonita". Hanging out on the beach allowed for interaction with locals, teaching a couple of courses and enjoying a few satsangs where a favorite picture from Belize shows me playing guitar, singing with eyes closed, Zaccai clapping with his eyes the same and a local business owner delving into the music.

"Jeremy, you are good at a lot of different things, but one of your greatest skills is getting under Billy's skin." These golden prophetic words coming from Emily, Bill's wife, who had joined us for the last few weeks, held oh-so-true. Emily had heard Bill's perspective of our unrestrained relationship over the years. And there in the beauty of Central America, another big fight erupted with Bill.

"Jeremy, make sure you're back to help cook dinner tonight, it's your turn to get everything ready," yelled Bill from the sea, as I walked to the Internet café to chat with Aarna.

I kept walking, without looking, slightly raising my arm in the air, which Bill took as a miscommunication of, "Yeah right, Bill. I am on vacation—you cut the veggies," instead of my acknowledgment wave of, "Heard and understood."

I arrived at the house around ten minutes late, and Bill was indeed in the kitchen, chopping veggies, ready to explode. I know ten minutes can feel like eternity to someone like Bill, but I've never missed or flaked on a chance for seva. I'm human and not always on time.

He started tearing into me. I leaned back against the counter, smiling, waiting my turn to bust him with the truth. Bill yelled about me not respecting my commitment, and I shouted back that I had every intention of holding up my end of the deal. The yells went back and forth, building tension into pointed laughter, and then, happily thereafter.

Our most intense fight of the trip was played out in front of his wife and eight-year-old daughter, Tika. I was not proud of my participation. It was her birthday dinner we were cooking. After the air cleared and the fires settled, we celebrated Tika's birthday with Guru Puja.

Our last fourteen days in Central America were at Orange Walk, up north near the Mexican border. We stayed with a large family on the top floor of the home, including their cool and useful rooftop. My last two weeks held more opportunities to teach, share, and learn.

As the days dwindled, I sidetracked some time to set up a quick trip back to Tahoe, and of course, a return to Atlanta to rise in love with Aarna.

Adam, an old friend from Mission Beach, had moved to Lake Tahoe with his family and had been inviting me to come up and record a music album in his home studio for the past year. More confident with my music and having an archive of what I thought were solid songs, I really wanted this opportunity to happen.

Robyn (one of the ladies in our group) and I were teaching a three-day Breath Water Sound course for a youth group in the city that started on Friday. The first two days, we hopped on the ancient, creaky bus that cruised through our village. On the third day, Robyn and I walked down to where the bus usually picked us up and noticed how much quieter it seemed. Waiting, we thought the bus must be running late. After twenty minutes, though, we realized it was Sunday, and there would be no bus!

In the first moments of helplessness, I closed my eyes and prayed to Gurudev for another miracle to get us to the course on time. Within minutes, I heard a vehicle in the distance. As it pulled closer, I saw it was an older truck. Open to all possibilities, I smiled and got the driver's attention.

"Wow are we happy to see you," I beamed. "Can we have a ride to the city, please?"

"Sure, hop in!" The driver was an older man who looked like he was in his seventies. "What are you two doing out here so early in the morning?"

"Well, sir, we are volunteer teachers going to the third and final day of our course called Breath Water Sound. We didn't realize today was Sunday and there wouldn't be bus service. I started to worry and prayed to my teacher for a miracle—and here you are!"

The man's eyes twinkled as he turned his head to look at me for a second. "That is quite a story, and I have one of my own to tell you." He stared out the dusty windshield. "This morning I got a strong feeling to get in my old truck and go into the city. You see, when I was your age, I used to drive my truck into the city to the market every Sunday morning just around this time. It's been at least twenty years since I stopped my tradition of weekly trips. But today, for some strange reason, I got a strong feeling to hop in my truck and go into town. Seeing you two standing there and hearing how you really needed help makes me so happy. This was a real miracle; please, tell me about your teacher."

"Well sir, to start, his name is Gurudev Sri Sri Ravi Shankar, and he often reminds us, 'Wherever there is faith, miracles do happen.'"

Once again, Gurudev waved his happiness wand, and I was transformed into a young child with a tear trickling down my face in deep gratitude for his love. For at least the thousandth time (maybe more) on this path, I was reminded how I am never alone and always protected by the unseen hand.

We arrived at our course on time. This was a marvelous morning in Belize and a great day to be alive—and I mean, really alive.

Days later, Zaccai set up two interviews for us at radio stations in Orange Walk. At the first one Bill, Zaccai, Sati (a college student from Apple Valley), Gabriella (an IAHV Prison Program instructor from Pittsburg), and I talked with the disc jockey about our courses going on in the city. I played a few songs and joked that Gabriella was a backup singer for Madonna—I think they bought it. It was a great warmup to the second one, which rocked.

The disk jockey of Sugar City Radio Station was a musician in a popular Reggae band there. After introductions, I jammed a few songs from my upcoming album.

Catching me off guard, the man asked if I could play a ballad. I froze, my mind blanked. Then I closed my eyes and played a sweet, powerful bhajan by Divya Prabha, "*Kali Durga Namo Namah.*"

The others in our group immediately sang along in grand satsang fashion, lifting the energy in the room tenfold. I'd played the song before, but this was unique, the melody serene, golden and uplifting. I wanted to reach the thousands of listeners and hit them in the heart. As the song ended, my fingers stopped against the guitar strings, I took a couple of deep breaths, then, with a smile, opened my eyes.

The DJ leaned toward his microphone and said, "Wow, that was very powerful. The energy inside the studio has changed. I can feel something wonderful but can't really explain it."

I felt Gurudev's strong presence like he was strumming the guitar for me. When the DJ asked what other kind of call-and-response songs I had up my sleeve, I responded with my signature song of the summer, a song I'd learned in Brownsville on our first day of the program, the traditional "*Jaya Jaya Shiva Shambho.*"

For years, my close Art of Living friends mocked the way I sang the second line, "*Maha Deva Shambho*" with my own rock twist—one that would later be out of tune on my album *Sound in Silence*, because of how hard I sang the phrase. But now I invited the listeners at home to sing along in the response. Though I couldn't hear anything beyond our seva crew and the DJ, I felt the immense power of people singing at home. I followed this with the popular "Jippy Jappa," again inviting the good folks at home to sing along, as I used the names of our team members and the Reggae rockin' DJ to guide the song. It was a blast and a half.

To close our hour-long session in the studio, the DJ asked if I had any rap songs.

What? I took a deep breath and sang this in rap fashion, "Jai Jairam kickin' it strong, on and on, Sugar City Radio puttin' it down for the Orange Walk Town—word!"

Whoa, where did the rap come from? Jairam was my charming nickname in the Art of Living, stemming from Indians who pronounced my name in their cool accents as Jai Ram E. I used Jairam as my band name for my new album and concert tours, as well as the name of my first music website.

What a spectacular morning in Belize! Walking out of the studio, I noticed all kinds of people hanging outside their homes, who had listened to the show. How could I forget the big guy sitting at a table, drumming on the flat surface singing his funky hip-hop version of "Jippy Jappa!" Others yelled, "*Shambho!*" like I had on my rendition of the tune. I felt on top of the world, being cheered from locals as we made our way down the road. I recorded that session with my portable tape deck and still hold the tape as one of my most valuable possessions.

The next morning, however, I was totally out of it, feeling tired and moody. To Bill's displeasure, I skipped group sadhana on the roof. I took myself on a long walk, did sadhana outside, and returned later that morning.

Bill confronted me about skipping our morning routine and I yelled, "Sadhana schmadna—satsang is my sadhana!" with a few other choice words thrown in. My blood began to boil red hot, and I could not control my emotions.

Full of arrogance, anger, and low *prana* (life-force energy), I exploded the negative chaos inside me onto Bill, prompting one last fight of the season. This time, as I would soon admit in an apology to him and the group, it was my fault.

Bill brought up a great point, reflecting how I was like a typical rock star soaring yesterday on top of the world, then in a form of depression this morning. He told how hard famous performers have it, on stage in front of adoring thousands, then alone, isolated in hotel rooms afterward. I was hung over from the radio studio experience and too immature, mentally, emotionally, and spiritually to handle the morning after.

This was a soul-searching moment for me, the kid who dreamed about being a rock star throughout his childhood. Jim Morrison, Michael Jackson, Mick Jagger, Eddie Vedder, you name it, I wanted to be them. But now that I'd tasted a piece of that fame, I knew it came with consequences. Fame was indeed an "empty bowl," as Gurudev often told us, and Bill now reminded me of this.

Another humbling experience under my belt and an essential one, it would be a great foundation for my music journey over the next year and beyond.

The Belize adventure came to an end. Over the two months, I'd grown in many ways, made lasting, meaningful connections with outstanding people, witnessed miracles, and, now in the best shape of my life, was headed back home to a girl I was head-over-heels about.

Let the learning begin, again.

Aarna greeted me at the airport with a hug and small gifts. Our two-month long-distance relationship was about to manifest physically. No more dreaming, no more singing to the sky and longing (though all those emotions were priceless). Here she stood, as beautiful as a summer sunset slipping under the velvet sea.

To help fund my trip to India, I'd sold my Taylor 510 CE acoustic guitar. I'd dreamed, wished, and hoped since then to get a Taylor 710 CE. I played one while in San Diego and fell in love—I knew this was my guitar. Now I faced heading into a recording studio without my fantasy guitar? It wasn't because my pockets were bare either.

In Belize on a call to my mother, she said I got a letter from the university. I asked her to open it, and to our delight, I was awarded a scholarship of $2,100 for my 3.35 GPA, thanks to Gurudev's magic chocolate bar (and my occasional studying).

I knew what I was spending the money on—no, not tuition fees or books—I would get my dream guitar! I immediately had Aarna call a couple Atlanta guitar stores for me to see if they had the guitar. All said no, and to order meant a down payment, plus it would be weeks before it would come in. Bummer.

One thing you should know about me: If the guitar had been on the wall, I wouldn't have bought it. Superstition, maybe? I have a thing about playing these "bad karma guitars," as I like to call them. These demo models hang on the shop walls for a long time with everyone and their brother pretending to be Dave Matthews or Eric Clapton on their strings. No thank you, no way.

On a whim during my brief stop home, I met Aarna at Guitar Center and asked the manager if by any chance he had a Taylor 710 CE in stock. He said they'd had one a few months ago, but it sold quickly. Forcing my prejudice about guitars on the wall aside, I played a couple, but none of them had that special feel, nothing even close. Bummed out, I drove Aarna to lunch down the street to soothe my sorrow.

Returning to the Guitar Center parking lot, she said in her loving, encouraging voice, "Do you want to give it one more shot and see if there is one you like?"

I agreed, yet even before entering, I'd lost all hope. As I was playing the best one of the wall bunch in the back room without enthusiasm, I watched the manager walk in the room with a guitar case, and for whatever reason, I *knew* what was inside. Energy escalated around me, and my eyes widened like a child.

The manager said, "Jeremy, you are not going to believe this. While you stepped out, a wrong order got delivered here by mistake." Opening the case, he exclaimed, "Your brand new Taylor 710 CE!"

Watching that case open was equivalent to an ancient miner prying open a treasure chest of gold; it was beyond words and any description. This magical miracle started in May with Gurudev taking my final exams, the unexpected scholarship, and now, my guru gifting me my dream guitar after a summer of being in his service and love. Amen—hallelujah!

I was speechless. On the verge of tears I yelled, "I'll take it; pack it up!"

In all her practical glory, Aarna asked, "Wait, Jeremy, don't you want to play it first to see if you like it?"

"Um, okay." As the manager walked away with a satisfied-sale smile, I closed the door. I played, for the very first time, "Wherever You Are" for Aarna. It was a very special moment. The rock and roll boy home from a road-trip adventure, his new girl inches in front of him with stars in her eyes, playing one of the most loving songs he had ever written.

Wow, is this life real? Please, someone, anyone—pinch me. On the other hand, don't! I am enjoying this too much if it is indeed some far-off daydream.

Helping to build a home in Belize, July 2002

Jamming with the Garifuna Indians in Belize, July 2002

Jamming with Zaccai in Belize, August 2002

David, Michele, and I at home in Atlanta, August 2002

CHAPTER NINETEEN

Sea of Madness and a Concert Tour

Don't take life for granted! Every moment
there is a miracle happening; every moment,
there is grace; and there is something new.
—Gurudev Sri Sri Ravi Shankar

In Lake Tahoe for the third summer in a row, I was excited that Zaccai came up from Houston to join me. We stayed at Bill's house while they were on a family vacation. Hey, the man needed a little space from me! Over the week, I recorded the album at Adam's house with ten of my pop/rock songs, one solo piano song which I wrote for my nephew, David, and two traditional Sanskrit bhajans, including "*Jaya Jaya Shiva Shambho.*"

Set Your Soul Light Ablaze came out on my birthday the following year, and it was a self-published release. I had a few hundred CDs produced. Do I know how to celebrate? For the level of skill I had at the time, both on guitar and singing, I will always consider it a demo album. That being said, one of my best childhood friends, Dave Weisenfluh, still loves it to this day, as does my brother-in-law, Dave, and my mom and dad. All right, it has an intimate fan base. I think I'll crank up a few tunes now and shake up my neighbors a bit by reliving those glory days.

I started my third semester at Kennesaw State University happy to be back with my family, the Art of Living group, and of course, spending time with Aarna—all hours of the day and night. Both of us in college, we'd meet downtown for food, hang out somewhere cool, and end up at her house or mine. The romance continued for a solid month.

We both knew somewhere inside it wouldn't work because of her traditional Indian parents. But like two young kids resembling Romeo and Juliet, we ignored the warning signs and continued to rise in love, and I mean really rise, as things escalated two parts fast and one third furious. In early October we had "that conversation" about stopping before it got too serious.

I applied Gurudev's knowledge about letting go, being dispassionate the best I could on my broken heart. It helped and I was grateful, but being young with a delicate heart, this hurt, a lot. The breakup brought out rough sides in both of us: fear, anger, and confusion. It was raw, painful.

I dug deep and did what I knew best, pouring my heart out on paper and with guitar strings. I'd never had a reason to write songs like that before, and though it was a tough point in my life, I appreciated the creativity just the same.

After a long, stressful night on the phone with Aarna, I totally ignored the alarm, not interested in going to school that day. Drifting in and out of sleep, a powerful melodic song haunted me, coming from somewhere deep. One side of me wanted to jump out of bed and write it down, but the hurting side wanted to sink into unconsciousness.

My mother watched my two-year-old nephew, David, while my sister was at work. For some odd reason that morning he kept coming into my room and waking me up. "Uncle Jeremy, wake up, wake up."

"No, David, please, I want to sleep. I am not feeling well." I'd fall back to sleep with shreds of this song echoing in my head.

David barged back in and woke me up again. This toddler scenario went on for an hour until I jumped out of bed, grabbed my Taylor guitar and wrote what became "Outside In" (later featured on *Dancing Opposites*). By far the saddest song I had ever written, the lyrics include, "Hung on this sea of madness, I've been rapping out-side your door." And, "Love, I can't understand why you won't let me through your door." When I recorded the track ten years later, there was a bittersweet smile on my face.

I'd always been single—for the most part—with one eye, some-times two, open for that special someone. Aarna was not only a very special someone, but she also shone in a way that kept me singing all the time for her. My creativity hasn't seen a season as full as the one with her. I miss rising in love with someone, but not the heartache. Even as I write this, I am still single and sometimes find myself asking, "What if?"

I stayed busy with my studies, working the afterschool program at an elementary school near my university, and substitute teaching whenever possible. Being active in Art of Living satsangs and courses as a volunteer was my best-loved activity and it gave me tremendous satisfaction and gratitude, as it does to this day.

I finished the semester pulling round-the-clock all-nighters with an uneven match of studying for finals and making a scrapbook for Aarna. This was my first both-feet-in-the-water relationship; I needed closure. I was emotionally, electrically charged, working all hours of the night cutting and pasting pictures, letters, even some flowers I had picked—Aarna loved flowers.

By the last day of finals, the commemorative book was com-plete. As nervous as I was excited to hand it to her, we met near her home just before the Christmas break. Aarna and I talked about the year, and I presented her the scrapbook.

Holding back tears, she nervously said, "This is so beautiful, you should keep it."

I smiled and said, "No, it's for you, for everything you've given me."

A long hug and an extended golden moment looking into each other's eyes would mark the last time we'd see each other until the wonderful invention of Skype.

Another Occhipinti family Christmas approached. Again, we wouldn't be all together. The wind-waving palm trees never looked more welcoming as I landed in San Diego. I needed a break back on the tranquil, soothing Pacific Ocean after the eventful year.

Christmas morning dawned bright and sunshiny. I did one of my favorite things in the world. I called Gurudev. I couldn't think of a better Christmas present to myself. He was at the German Ashram, and I got right through.

"Gurudev, it's Jeremy in San Diego. Merry Christmas!"

"Ah, Jeremy…" he replied in his uniquely innocent and charismatic voice. "Merry Christmas! How are you doing there in California?"

"I am doing really well and had another successful semester of college."

"Are you coming to the ashram for the inauguration of the new meditation hall next month?"

"I wish, Gurudev. I have classes during that time—should I skip them and come anyway?" I held my breath as I looked for permission to break the rules.

"No, no, you stay there and study, you can come back to the ashram when you finish your studies. Have you played some concerts at the colleges?"

"One at my university; it was great everyone sang along with me."

"You should do more concerts at the different colleges and universities in America. That would be good. Talk with Mark, he can help you."

"Yes, Gurudev. I could sing some English songs, some Beatles, Bob Marley, and then introduce bhajans, too."

"Yes, whatever you think is good. After singing you can lead a meditation for them so they can have a nice experience. Music is food for the emotions; knowledge is food for the intellect; meditation is the food for the soul."

"Gurudev, which meditation should I lead?"

"The Ram Meditation."

"And what should I call the concert?"

"Hmm… Sound in Silence. Yes, that sounds nice."

"Gurudev, this is exciting! Thank you so much, and Merry Christmas!"

And his words, *"Jai Guru Dev..."* faded in the same way all my phone conversations with him do. He kind of floats away on the phone, subtle, leaving me absorbed in stillness and gratitude.

I'd just been given the greatest Christmas gift of all-time. I needed an extra moment of silence as his gift sank into my consciousness. I felt my heart pound slowly as adrenaline soared through me. My very own national concert tour, Sound in Silence. I was blessed. As I lay down that night, I was trying to absorb a dream come true wrapped in a Christmas blessing.

Back in Atlanta, I exploded with the news of my concert tour and my music album. My face couldn't stop smiling. Hanging out with my brother was a warm and exciting start to the new year, and I appreciated his support of my music.

One night, while at a Leftover Salmon concert in downtown Atlanta, I asked Jeff to think of the ultimate song to sing/play on my upcoming concert tour. Throughout the show, we toyed with a handful of tunes, but none hit the mark.

Then, in the middle of a huge jam by the band, the lyrics hit me. They were from the song, "Quinn the Eskimo," the Bob Dylan folk fairytale song, a heartfelt favorite I'd been singing with various kindergarten and elementary school students for the past two years. Always an instant hit, it combined the best of all music worlds: an enormously awesome chorus where everyone could sing along, cool rhythm, and three fun verses for me to rap. The vision of me inviting thousands of college kids to sing along was as rock solid as the Pocono Mountains.

After calling Mark Ball, the Art of Living college program director, and telling him about my Christmas conversation with Gurudev, the Sound in Silence College and University Tour got underway on the fast track.

The first show was on Chinese New Year at the cool University of Texas at Austin. After helping create posters and cards to plaster around the campus, I headed for Texas.

Mona, the Art of Living teacher, was my designated transportation to the airport that early Thursday morning, so my dad drove me to her home on his way to work.

Inside the dark car traveling through the Atlanta winter morning, my father and I shared an indescribable, sincere conversation about taking my music on tour to Texas and beyond. It was a moment I'll keep forever in my heart.

I said to him, "Dad, you have inspired me to write, travel, and share my music with many people. I always remember helping you load your equipment into a church or hospital. You performed for all types of audiences with great self-confidence and excitement. That inspiration has remained with me."

He replied, "Jeremy, I did what I could do with music, but it only reached so far. You have the potential to carry the family name far and wide with your music. Take it around the world. Good luck in Austin and have fun."

Holding back tears, I exited the warmth of the car and my dad's good wishes at the gated community, grabbed both of my acoustic guitars and an Adidas sports bag, and bid him goodbye.

As I took my first steps, it started to rain, not Georgia heavy, but a steady fall. With a guitar in each hand, and duffle bag over my right shoulder like a warrior marching into battle, a thought came over me like a Midwest whirlwind in late July. *I could walk to Texas to start the tour. This is my dream coming true—to share my music with millions of people around the world.*

And so began my journey to Texas, igniting my biggest dream. I am very grateful to Dhiraj Dembla, a grad student there at the time, who, with his team, organized this first concert with full enthusiasm. They booked the Grand Ballroom and promoted the show around campus and town with posters and various announcements.

Staying at a devotee's house, I played a few songs that night at the local satsang and told stories from my experiences with Gurudev. Saturday morning, I called Gurudev for blessings before the show. He was at the Canadian Ashram, very busy meeting hundreds of people, leading guided meditations. He was so sweet on the telephone.

Gurudev said, "Hmm, you have a big show tonight at the university?"

"Yes, Gurudev, I am very excited to get the students to sing—can I please have your blessing for a great show?"

"You are always blessed—have fun. *Jai Guru Dev…*"

A living room full of devotees smiled behind me and said, "We love you, Gurudev!" at the end of the call. The show was on.

Though more devotees than college students attended, the show was broadcast on the Internet. This was the earliest I'd heard of a webcast of Art of Living functions, which are commonplace now from wherever Gurudev may be. I made tons of mistakes that night, but like any good artist, I learned from them. By the end of the concert, everyone was singing and smiling.

Here's how most of my tour stops rolled: Fly out of Atlanta on Wednesday or Thursday after classes and then get picked up at the airport by several smiling devotees. Attend the local satsang, play music, and tell stories. Or go directly to the university/college, hop on stage, and perform. Friday night was another concert or satsang, followed by homemade vegetarian Indian food. Saturday, get ready for another show. Sunday was spent visiting families or sometimes even a Hindu temple to play a song or two. I'd fly home Sunday, arriving late at night or early Monday morning, often just in time for my first class.

Keep in mind I was a third-year junior in a challenging education program. How the heck did I leave on Wednesday or Thursday and return on Sunday or Monday, all those weeks, performing in cities around the country?

That is the grace of the master. That is Gurudev giving his divine blessing and me having full faith every step of the way. Did I ever have doubts? Yes, for sure, and stage fright or nerves before stepping out. My mind wandered into the negative zone like anyone else's, but with thoughts of Gurudev, as soon as people started singing "Quinn the Eskimo" with me, all that mental garbage melted like dewdrops in the sun.

Gurudev says, "A master or a guru does not remove the doubt, but he creates more doubt. The more you burn in the fire of doubt, the more strong you come out to be."

This was not only my dream tour, but also the *sankalpa* (divine intention) of my guru. I wanted to get the word out about the goodness of Art of Living and reach as many people as possible during the tour. University students who organized the concerts wrote posts before and after the shows, and I'd post my experiences, too. The goal of the concert tour was to give students an experience of singing and meditation, plus introduce them to the teachings of Gurudev Sri Sri Ravi Shankar.

I stopped at nothing to ensure publicity and encouragement for the largest possible number of college students. I believe in self-promotion. I had an ego, now growing to the size of a Hollywood mansion, as a result of often being on a national stage. I believe self-promotion is the art of spreading great ideas, concepts, and a bigger vision.

The ego loves this type of recognition. Can't you hear my 2003 ego singing, "I am a great musician in the Art of Living, I have shows set up for me, I am flown around the country like a superstar, and, yes, I am good looking and funny, too." *Nice lyrics, Ego—now go back to bed.*

The reality was, I became humbler with each stop, each song, each guided meditation, each story during the experience. I felt the presence of Gurudev while learning more about myself.

Some of the families who supported me were ones who helped sponsor my last two Youth Leadership Training Programs to India and Belize.

On one of my flights, I read an interesting quote by Gurudev that really hit home: "When you have a guru, you cannot be arrogant. Your guru gives you confidence and also brings humility in you. The weakness in humility and the arrogance in confidence are removed. You are left with confidence and humility!" Beautiful.

My list of tour cities grew, and now I was off to the Boston area for four shows. By serendipity, Matt was going to teach a Breath Water Sound course in the same area at the same time.

A sweet snowfall and chilly temperatures greeted me Wednesday night at the University of New Hampshire show. I'd missed this soft, chilled serenity from my youth. I opted not to sing through the PA system, but instead sat on the edge of the stage and sang with the fifty or so students. Not a standing-room-only crowd, but I created a more intimate feeling. This turned out to be a risk well taken.

After the show, one boy came up to me with tears in his eyes, holding his girlfriend's hand, saying, "Thank you so much, Jeremy. I really enjoyed the Sanskrit chanting; it is so powerful. Something was really moving inside of me. And the meditation was just what I needed. I have been going through a rough period in my life, and now this pain in me has lifted."

With tears in my eyes, I gave him a hug and smiled in gratitude. Once again, I was reminded of why I was on this tour: It wasn't about me, it was about the spiritual experience of college students.

As I went to bed, I prayed to Gurudev, as I am sure Radhika Prabu, who organized the show, did, about playing the next day at my high noon show at Boston College in an outdoor arena. Northeast weather in April is like spinning a wheel of fortune, you never know what you'll get.

I woke up to water dripping.

"Oh, no," I said, thinking it was rain. But, to my delight, it was an icicle melting outside the window. The warm, brilliant sun was on the rise in a crystal blue sky. It was going to be a beautiful April day in New England.

I hopped on a bus to Boston with my guitars in tow. Being outside in the bright spring sunlight, on the makeshift stage on the greens of the bustling campus, singing fulfilling songs, inviting others to sing along, was very cool.

The next day I was scheduled to sing a noon show in the student center at the prestigious University of Massachusetts at Amherst. Ari and Jameelah, full-time volunteers with the Art of Living College Team, lived on campus and set up the show. But when we arrived in the small, reserved classroom, it was empty except for Tom Brennan, reporter for the university newspaper.

A quick decision was made to have an acoustic show right smack dab in the middle of the busiest spot on campus. Within minutes I had set up my two acoustic guitars and played a few songs by Bob Marley, Stephen Stills, and some of my originals. People gathered around and I introduced "*Jaya Jaya Shiva Shambho*." Lyric sheets were handed out so people could sing along.

"The singing from both the performer and the audience gave the Campus Center concourse a church-like atmosphere," was reported by Mr. Brennan in his awesome review of the show a few days later. "By the end of the concert, the energy had changed from quiet and reserved to upbeat and lively. Occhipinti bobbed and gyrated with the music while the crowd clapped and sang, and more and more people stopped to see what was going on."

Obviously, this was not the place for a silent meditation, but the community formed from the singing was more than enough joy for me, and most of the concerts usually included guided meditations.

As Matt and I took the train back to Boston together, it started to rain. I had the feeling that Gurudev was waving his wand in another experience to make us grow. Then sure enough, Julia Tang, the devotee who had organized a concert at Harvard for that Sunday, not only forgot about the time change, but she also got lost on the way to the concert.

As a result, we burst through the door an hour late but miraculously about twenty students remained. One woman had led a meditation for the group and was giving a talk on the Art of Living programs as I walked into the classroom, rich with history and people waiting for the musical event. I immediately sat down, pulling out my Taylor 710 CE acoustic guitar and apologized for being late.

After introductions, I burst into the song I started every show with on that tour and beyond, "What Deaner Was Talking About," by one of my favorite bands, Ween. This song, bearing no resemblance to a happy, loving song or a sing-along, was the song I warmed up with. It was a no brainer to play; I could sing it in my sleep.

Looking back, this was a father/son, monkey see/monkey do connection. Opening with a simple, routine song was what my dad used to do with "Battle Hymn of the Republic" at every one of his shows I attended as a child. The apple doesn't fall too far...

I needed to give this gracious crowd a memorable experience as their patience and commitment touched me. I introduced the Bob Dylan tune, getting everyone singing and a community formed. After the song, I added, "Any amount of people singing together forms an instant community, a unity, and that unity is yoga."

Before the meditation, I shared Gurudev's knowledge, "The purpose of words is to create silence."

The group singing, coupled with the Ram Meditation, was the heart of the Sound in Silence concert tour. The New England trip ended with an informal lunch show at MIT. On the flight back to Atlanta the next day, I wrote a song called "Boston" from my great experience there.

"Boston don't delay, paint your smile on the world. And it stokes me just to say... Boston!"

I really needed to "buckle down," as my mom often says, and get ready for finals.

A call came from a female student at the University of New Orleans, a volunteer with the Art of Living, who left a message with my mother about wanting me to come out for a show that weekend. My mother told her that I couldn't because I was busy with final exams. That was good advice from Mom, but I didn't heed the call.

I phoned the girl and flew out the next Wednesday to play a show on Thursday afternoon, followed by two evening satsangs on Friday and Saturday.

Returning home, I took my finals and melted in gratitude when I saw the results: Bam—Dean's List with a 3.78 GPA, getting only one B out of five classes. That semester, I tumbled through a national college/university music tour. I worked hard while on campus, and Gurudev took care of the rest when I was on tour. This was equal to or even better than the chocolate bar finals. Gurudev's voice echoed in my head, "You do 100% and I will take care 100%."

As soon as the semester finished, I traveled to Santa Cruz, California, a cool, hip town, for my second show at the university that season. The strong Art of Living group there included Matt, Erin (from my first Indian trip), and Sam (from the Belize trip).

While there, Matt and I were on fire, up to no good (or really good), thinking of ways to prank people. No one was safe when the two of us had our heads together. We set up one of our fake email accounts with the name Yogesh Panta for many monstrous pranks during this time.

After Santa Cruz, I headed down to San Diego where I had two shows, one at UC San Diego, the other at a new yoga studio in Pacific Beach, my old stomping ground. Gurudev would arrive in two weeks to teach the Art of Living course and give a public talk.

In San Diego, I continued the online fire Matt and I started by writing a post to the Art of Living's eSatsang digest under Yogesh's name. I felt a strong need to bust Von Osselman, who I was struggling with by way of an internal competition regarding music in the Art of Living. Remember, the older Art of Living teacher, the resident musician at all Gurudev's public talks who planted himself with an iron arm in the front row of all satsangs? On the other hand, he was a devoted teacher of Gurudev's, one of the first teachers in America. But I didn't know his sweet and sincere side yet.

I joked about him and myself in the post, meant to inspire people to journey to San Diego, join the course, and attend Gurudev's public talk. Under my alias I wrote: "Jeremy and Von Osselman are jamming together here on the beach every night. Von is teaching Jeremy the art of leading as many songs as possible at every satsang, and Jeremy is teaching Von how to mellow out and be less feverish." A case of brash youth? Hard to say.

People ate it up, believing it or seeing it as a funny joke. Members of the young generation in the Art of Living were having fun. But Von didn't take it lightly, nor did my post fool him. I mean, who else could write that?

A few days later, I was in Palo Alto for Gurudev's forty-seventh birthday celebration. Matt and I were stoked to be on Bill Herman's cooking team for the week. Suffice it to say, Billy had grown to love and trust us as a dynamic duo by now.

As soon as Von saw me, I felt the wave of negative energy. I don't know what he was thinking or feeling. He tried poking a pointed finger with corny lines like, "Jeremy, the big Art of Living rock star," and, "Little Bob Dylan."

It felt childish to me, but I held back my jokes—he couldn't imagine what was coming his way.

Bill wouldn't arrive until late that night and sent a message for me to check out the kitchen and to do the best that I could do until he arrived. Matt was blown away at how I walked with determined confidence into this mess of a hotel kitchen, nowhere near where it needed to be, to make *sattvic* (high energy/pure) food for hundreds of devotees for the next week. An aura filled my spirit, tapping into past experiences and knowledge with Bill.

I barged in like a warrior, throwing things into place, cleaning this, arranging that. I cleared out the cooler and cleaned it nearly spotless while directing Matt and a few other volunteers. I took responsibility and the power needed was granted to me; this is what Gurudev teaches us. "The more responsibility you take in life, the more power will be granted to you."

Just look at Gurudev, who has taken responsibility for the whole world. Spend any amount of time with him and you will see what I mean; he takes care of the simple needs of each person around him as well as large-scale projects such as planting millions of trees around the world.

That night walking with Matt, my guitar slung over my shoulder, I looked forward to singing at least one song at satsang.

At the door stood good old Von and he said, "There's no satsang tonight, Gurudev wants everyone to relax."

Okay, we bought it. I stashed the guitar, and we continued our walk. The night air of Northern California held a symphony of sounds.

Forty minutes later, we walked into the hall and, wouldn't you know, there was Von on stage leading a bhajan. Von's low, monotone voice sounded like the laxative of singing as I sulked in boredom, a raging fire building inside.

I didn't even figure in the possibility that perhaps Von was right about the initial plan for satsang, and then it had later changed. Nevertheless, I took his treachery to heart with my enlarged ego and readied for battle. My mission was to bring youthful energy to the satsang. One song would have sufficed.

Jason McMillan, our good friend from the YLTP the year before in Texas and the leader of the college team with Mark Ball, came over and nudged me. "Jeremy, you gotta get up there and play—we need to represent the college team." He shared my vision for extra liveliness in satsang.

I resisted for maybe a minute. "Okay, Jason, you get a chair, I'll grab the guitar."

That was all it took to rev up my engine. I pulled out a traditional song, let my fingers fly, and the place rocked. Von didn't look so happy, and I did my best to avoid him for the rest of the evening.

After satsang, Matt and I saw Gurudev. It is always delightful to see him, especially after such a long time, though it was hard to believe it'd been a whole year.

His sweet voice melted my heart. "Ah, Jeremy, I heard you are rocking all the colleges with your music. I read an article on one of your shows, very nice."

"Yes, Gurudev, thanks so much for the blessings, it has been wonderful."

"You should play in the satsangs here. Good, good, good—*Jai Guru Dev.*"

On the last day, a group of us were hanging out with Gurudev in his hotel room. Talking, joking, laughing—the usual happy time around Gurudev. The packed room left Matt and me standing, leaning against the back wall directly in front of Gurudev, maybe fifteen feet away. He talked to Divya Prabha about writing more English mixed with Sanskrit songs.

I immediately absorbed his words as if he said them to me. *I can do this*, my heart agreed.

When he started talking about young musicians playing concerts for the youth around the world, I lit up like a neon sign in the darkest night, certain he was going to mention me and my recent tour. Matt and I smiled at each other.

Gurudev mentioned two names of people I knew back in India, but didn't even look at me, let alone mention my name. I was standing right in front of him. *Am I invisible? Hello?*

My breathing became shallow, my face went scarlet, and my heart fell to the floor.

Matt tried to interject, "How about Jeremy, Gurudev?" but couldn't squeeze the question into Gurudev's conversation.

My internal natural disaster meter felt like the first time I met Gurudev and asked the question about his beads. Explosions detonated in my mind while my ego was thoroughly kicked, pulverized, and knocked down. I found myself in the metaphorical frying pan Gurudev has cooked devotees in, at least once or more. This was common territory for me, through a dish served often by Bill. But tonight felt mortally tortuous due to a devastating combination of my overblown tour ego and him ignoring me.

I'd wager everything dear to me, my musical talent, instruments, and skateboards on the fact he knew what he was doing, and the effects inflicted. It was like nature hurling a bolt of lightning into a dense forest to clear away the old underbrush, so new, stronger life could begin. It was time for me to burn and grow—again.

Gurudev is the master of life lessons. Along with his humor, this is one of his trademarks, a specialty—a master chef in the art of cooking devotees when they need it most. I needed and received it. What was no more than ten minutes of real time in a room filled with my guru, best friend, music mentor, and spiritual family seemed like ongoing anguish in tortoise-slow hours.

I blinked and watched Gurudev graciously stand and head toward the car on his way to a meeting. Reeling from the elevator-drop experience, I couldn't move, let alone jump in anyone's car to go "guru chasing," usually a favorite pastime.

As I let out a shaky breath and pushed myself toward the exit, I spotted Sangeeta Jani, one of the veteran teachers from India. The woman is beautiful, pure love, and the mere sight of her lifted a smile back on my comatose face.

She came over and said, "Jeremy, you are so lucky."

What now, is she going to bust me, too?

I almost missed her first words, "We were in the room with Gurudev, and he was talking so highly about you and your music shows in the colleges. He said, 'Isn't Jeremy so innocent?'"

My fractured mind mended slowly at first, her words bandaging the cracks. Then, like an avalanche, exploded together in a fusion of joy while my heart skipped in pounding beats. Overwhelmed by love and joy, Sangeeta wrapped me in a sweet, healing hug before getting into a car that drove away.

I stumbled somehow to a dark patch behind a bush, sat with my legs crossed on the cool ground, closed my eyes, and soaked in the gratitude showered upon me, how much love and attention Gurudev gives to me, truly to us all. Again, like the first time I met him, I'd never felt lower in my soul only moments before rocking higher than a newly crowned king in his court.

Everything he does for us is for our own growth. This miraculous man is aware of what happens on the other side of the world; you think it was even possible he didn't know what effect he was having on his loving devotee, crazy boy Jeremy, less than fifteen feet in front of him in an intimate room setting? Yet a moment later, sending his delightful teacher with the message of love. This is vintage Gurudev. Dancing opposites once again.

Next on Gurudev's California visit was San Diego! Back home to my humble beginnings in Art of Living.

On the first day in this sun-drenched paradise, Gurudev led some of the sessions in the Art of Living course, an extraordinary event. He spoke of the importance of being like kids and playing jokes on people to make the world a lighter place. I felt like he talked directly to Matt and me.

Exiting the hall at a fast clip afterward, we found Von's penny loafer shoes and hid them behind a bush. Permission from Gurudev to play pranks on people? He is the coolest guru on earth! We watched and snickered from a distance as Von looked for his slip-on shoes.

It was very refreshing to watch Gurudev lead some of the course processes. His course, his way, and everyone was engaged. I have learned so much by just observing him over the years. The same held true when he was leading the course participants on those fine days.

The next day, we heard Gurudev was going to SeaWorld, and, quite naturally, we wanted to join him. Having lived just across Mission Bay from the world-famous tourist attraction all those years, I had never been. When you're young living with minimal needs and wants with the high-definition view of the Pacific Ocean twenty-four/seven, the tourist attraction never made my to-do list.

I drove Matt's car back from lunch in Ocean Beach, knowing the area best. We spotted Gurudev inside a car and knew they were headed to SeaWorld. A couple quick maneuvers, some of them illegal, and I pulled the car right into SeaWorld's parking lot as Gurudev and other adults went through the entrance. We paid and rushed to catch up with Gurudev. Guru chasing at its finest.

Intimate moments like these with him are simply timeless. As the small group strolled down one darkened hall, flanked by huge tanks of exotic, colorful sea creatures, I basked in Gurudev's presence. Turning a corner, I saw a large walrus floating in the water of another tank.

In his childlike, innocent and joking voice, Gurudev pointed at the walrus. "Look, he's even bigger than Jeremy!"

Everyone lost it, laughter in divine fashion.

I quickly replied with a one-liner Matt and I often used, "Gurudev, you're good for that one joke a month!"

The walrus humor and playfulness that followed are prime examples of what a unique, extraordinary and childlike master we have on this path. Gurudev reacted to my joke by pinching my cheek, and we walked the rest of the way arm-in-arm.

Now, why might Gurudev have made that joke about me you ask? To be honest, who knows why the man does anything he does? But, on an intellectual level, I have something, we all do, called genetics. I've always been a big boy, though this doesn't mean I'm complacent and can't stand to drop a few pounds at any given time. I am going on a diet tomorrow, I promise.

What does my physique have to do with being big like a walrus? Somewhere in time, the rumor started that I loved gulab jamuns, a popular, tasty Indian sweet. Indeed, I do love them, especially with vanilla ice cream.

I remember the first concert of the tour in Austin, staying at Dimple and Sanjay's house, and Dimple showed me the gulab jamuns. I ate many that weekend, and when it was time to fly home to Atlanta, she sent me on the plane with a whole container of them.

I was welcomed at many homes that season. The families called each other and asked what types of dishes and sweets I liked. Gulab jamuns topped the list. I made up a joke how I was in the Guinness Book of World Records for eating 10,000 gulab jamuns in 2002. It felt like it at times, I must admit.

On the last night of the San Diego Art of Living course, I wanted to lead a song, but, bad luck, Von was there. Singing would have been meaningful on all levels, but I didn't know how to get past Von's authoritarian tactics.

I spotted Daniel White, a fantastic devotee from Texas who played his own bluesy style of bhajans, working the soundboard—the nerve center for microphones, speakers, and bass and treble controls. I told him my predicament and immediately we hatched a plan. Daniel plugged my guitar in on the sly and set up a microphone near him. I pulled up a chair, ready when he gave me the cue.

"When Von starts the next song, I'll slowly turn him down. You play and I'll turn your guitar and microphone up."

Brilliant. You should have seen the look on Von's face when we pulled that one off. Best ever! Thanks, Daniel, may your soul rest in peace.

In glaring retrospect, it would be a miracle if there weren't everyday human tensions and ambitions within a large organization. People have egos, desires, and shortcomings; spiritual seekers are not devoid of these. Von and I were, in some ways, competing for the same opportunities to receive public recognition at Gurudev's events.

Gurudev says, "Don't expect from others what you expect from me, but respect others like you respect me."

If I had been more established at the time, I could have used the same damaging energy to collaborate with and learn from Von. Instead, I was disturbed by my expectations of someone senior to me and failed to establish reverence. As a child, I sought approval from my parents and friends; in college, the professors; and as an adult, with my spiritual master. I learned life lessons when I needed to understand them.

The last stop of Gurudev's memorable California tour was Anaheim (the home of Disneyland), and Matt and I were ready to sing bhajans and dance with Mickey Mouse and Pluto—okay, I'm kidding.

During his public talk, the first time Matt's parents would see Gurudev, I shared in Matt's excitement from my own experience last year with my own family.

Enjoying our last night with Gurudev, I kept a watch for any opportunity to poke fun in Von's direction. It didn't take long. Taking seats up front before the talk, a volunteer walked around with cards to write questions for Gurudev. I had a great idea and wrote out two questions: "Are the musicians on stage rock stars? Can the tall man sitting on stage, wearing the white sweater and holding the guitar, sing, "We Are the World" by Michael Jackson?" I knew in my heart the second question was funny and Gurudev would read it.

Early in the talk, Gurudev picked up the basket of cards. He answered a few questions, and then picked mine. "Hmm, 'Are the musicians on stage rock stars?'" Laughter bubbled around the room as Gurudev tipped his hat to Divya Prabha (my main influence with bhajans) and Phillip Frazier (flute player/composer/extra awesome dude), saying, "Yes, some of these musicians compose their own songs and play around the world."

And then he read the encore. Gurudev's childlike laughter set the place on fire in rich, loud responding laughter from the audience. Von burned on stage for all to see. Score! Matt and Jeremy five, Von two.

Walking out behind Gurudev after the talk, I heard snippets from Von asking, "Okay, guys, who wrote it? Was it you, Jeff? Shirley, was it you? I know it was one of you." Matt and I smiled, stifling our laughter. We didn't have good poker faces.

Later, at a devotee's home, Matt broke down and told Von it was me.

I was at Denny's eating seasoned fries and a chocolate milkshake with Divya Prabha and friends. The ego war with Von catapulted into full swing.

I hitched a bus back to Lake Tahoe to finish recording my album with Adam before flying back to Atlanta for summer classes. As soon as I got home, I posted a descriptive account on eSatsang titled *Gurudev's California Sweep*. I told the above story, adding insult to injury by giving Von a funny nickname.

One email from a veteran Art of Living teacher chastised me that this was not the forum for such a joke—yet other emails flooded in from devotees around the world about how funny that was.

Though I stopped messing with Von, he continually consumed my mind. At Keystone College I'd learned the living reality, "What you hate is what you become." I touched on this earlier in the book but let me refresh your memory. I hated Von and these ill feelings engorged my mind. Envy and jealousy make a powerful combo of negative chaos. I found myself coveting his habit of wanting to lead the songs in various satsangs I attended. This miserable harbor of ill will and wanting continued to shadow me for the rest of the year.

Celebrating Gurudev's forty-seventh birthday in Palo Alto, CA, May 13, 2003

CHAPTER TWENTY

Georgia, Mexico, and China… Oh, Boy!

God gives us miracles every day in our life but there
are times we don't see it. Become aware of it and
see the abundance. Miracles are in abundance.
—Gurudev Sri Sri Ravi Shankar

Being a late June baby, I never thought I'd sit in a classroom on my birthday, but this year there I was with the usual twenty-some females rolling through three—count 'em, three—classes. By taking additional summer courses I'd be on pace to graduate the following spring.

When I told my favorite professor about sitting behind a desk on my birthday, she suggested I bring in my guitar and sing for the class that day. Never one to turn down a performance, I got myself comfortable in front of my classmates.

Some girls cried while I sang "Monika," the song I wrote while in India, gee, almost two years ago. Since I typically close my eyes when I sing, I think I hit their heartstrings.

The performance made going to school on my birthday worth it. Music is intoxicating; I beamed during the rest of my classes. It also helped knowing I'd be flying to Scranton the next day to attend my cousin Jeff's wedding. Of course, I was taking my best girl to the event, Mom.

Driving home from school, I stopped at my favorite pizza place down the highway from my university—Baby Tommy's Taste of New

York—to surprise Mom with pizza. Celebrating with mouthwatering flavors not only sounded great but came with no messy clean-up for the super woman who gave birth to me on this day long ago.

I balanced the fragrant boxes with one hand while opening our front door with the other. The usual crush of dogs met me in the entry.

"Mom?" I called out over the chorus of barking. Silence echoed back at me. This seemed odd because I'd seen her car parked outside. "Mom?"

I walked into the empty kitchen, setting the boxes down, and glanced at the clock. It was after four o'clock, and I knew my nephew would be gone. A flicker of doubt brushed the back of my neck as a thousand questions raced through my mind.

I grabbed the phone and stabbed my sister's phone number by rote. Michele's words sent me into shock. Mom had been rushed to the hospital for heart trouble. I needed to be there, now.

I don't remember hanging up the phone but had enough sense to stash the pizzas up high, thwarting any chance of my dog Coal or the other furry cohorts gorging out on Baby Tommy's pizza.

Flashbacks of my own past manic heart pain and stress flickered like an ancient silent movie in the back of my mind. Shreds of chest-crushing memories tried to surface as I barreled down three unseen streets to the hospital.

A nurse led me down a stark, fluorescent-lighted hallway to my mother's room. As I entered, I was T-boned with emotions like a tractor-trailer bulldozing, crushing the mini car that was my heart. Tears blinded the few steps it took to reach the side of her bed.

Mom laid there, hooked up to IVs, speechless, with tears in her eyes. Her hands lifted from the blankets, expressing her grief in silence.

Stunned with numbness, the only thing I could do was be with her. Dad arrived from work shortly afterward, and she was surrounded by family in the hospital room.

Those family genetics had kicked in and taken no prisoners. Mom had felt uncontrollable heart palpitations, and when she couldn't handle the increasing pain and dizziness, she called my sister to take her to the emergency room at the hospital.

I can't imagine how serious this bout must have been. Mom would normally suck up an attack, not telling anyone, waiting stoically until the palpitations passed. I learned from the best how to shield the horrific, debilitating bouts from friends, family, and the rest of the world. I'd grown up with these attacks until cooling them down to elimination with Sudarshan Kriya and meditation.

Mom had to stay at the hospital overnight and wouldn't hear of us, her boys, skipping a meal. Dad and I trudged home, heated up the pizza, and shared some much-needed bonding. The light of our world would be all right and home soon.

On the table sat a package from Adam in Lake Tahoe. The timing was exquisitely perfect, the yin and yang of a long day. It was the master copy of my first album, in my hands on my birthday.

I turned and looked at the familiar, worn face of my dad, our eyes red-rimmed from Mom's attack yet twinkling in sync at the realization of holding a copy of my first album. My dad grabbed the CD, cranked it up on his system down the hall in his room, and we listened to the entire album over a tray of eggplant parmesan pizza.

I found myself aware of the invisible seatbelt of life, always keeping my arms and legs inside the car that night. I was listening to my music with Dad, fleshing out the lyrics of each song for him, chomping pizza, without my precious mom. For one brief, chilling instance I realized this is what it would be like if, God forbid, anything ever happened to her.

Although Mom was in the hospital on my twenty-seventh birthday, Dad and I shared a very special party with music and pizza, becoming closer by the song and the slice.

Once again, Gurudev's knowledge of dispassion and complimentary opposites helped me deal with the peaks and valleys thrown at me. Where would I be without the appropriate wisdom that Gurudev reminds me of at the right time? "Life sometimes seems very complicated. There is pleasure and pain, happiness and suffering, generosity and greed, and passion and dispassion. When our life is full of such opposing values, our mind sometimes becomes unable to handle these complications and just breaks down. It is then that you need wisdom to guide you through troubled times. Guru is that wisdom."

The next morning, I stopped at the hospital on my way to the airport, leaving Mom a poem I wrote for her with a photo of Gurudev and me taken on his birthday the month before.

One day later, Mom was ready to go home, happy and healthier. She was glad to be back to her regular lifestyle, taking care of the dogs and home. We were delighted, too. Though she was home and doing better, her health made travel inadvisable, and I flew off without her for my cousin Jeff's wedding.

A few of us headed down that ever-familiar Pennsylvania Turnpike into Philadelphia the next day to see the latest incarnation of the Grateful Dead, appropriately called "the Dead." My usual tour buddies Stan and Dave held out for the next night's show near Buffalo, New York, and I would drive up with them.

For this show, I went with two other childhood buddies, two cats still struggling with substance abuse troubles. Silly me, I thought it would be cool for old time's sake. I mean, how messed up could the boys be?

We rented a new truck for the ride, and within minutes, bags of heroin were being passed between the two superstars. I quickly became the designated driver as things cartwheeled out of control. One sat in the front seat, snorting lines of heroin, wired off his ass, while my closest childhood friend duplicated everything in the back with the repulsive addition of puking his burnt-out brains and most of his battered soul into a large black plastic trash bag.

From the front seat addict came slurred yelling toward the back, "Take it easy, we're not even at the show yet. Seriously, I've never seen anyone snort that much that quickly—you could die, dude!"

I applied every inch of Art of Living course knowledge points, keeping my mind half-sane, and the $30,000 rental truck on the road.

Let's make a pie chart and call it Jeremy. One side of me wanted to throw the two idiots out of the moving truck, splattering bodies on the asphalt. Another slice wanted to throw teeth-jarring punches and knock some sense into them. Still, another side wished to teach, to reach these boys through the caustic web of drugs. Less than forty-eight hours ago, I'd seen my mom in a hospital bed. Would tonight go down as another wrenchingly close one in an emergency room?

None of these things happened—they partied, and I drove, insulated by jamming to the music from the CD player. Seeing my close friend in his darkest hour through my limited vision in the rearview mirror was shocking and appalling and kept me in hell for many moments. I had never seen anyone like that before, never mind my childhood friend.

I have to say the concert was barely okay, in large part due to the crowd I was with. After the show, we ended up crashing at a house of one of my old classmates. The broken promise by both guys to drive me back home prevented me from going to New York with Dave and Stan.

I bit my lip and over-accepted the situation, if that's remotely possible. I took a fifty-dollar bath with my unused ticket, missing a great show in upstate New York with two of my best friends from Taylor.

Aren't I lucky not to be there? blinked like a broken neon sign in my mind, creating a sadness that stayed with me, and it was hard not to look at it without a sour taste in my mouth. As dispassionate as I was becoming on this spiritual path, it still hurt to see my best friend so messed up. I had to move on.

Unfortunately, he would pass away from a heroin overdose fifteen years later. The other cleaned up his life, met a spectacular woman, and started a family.

Dear ones, please reach out to me if you struggle with addiction. You are not alone. Too many of my childhood friends lost their long-standing battles with drugs and alcohol—resulting in death. I grew up with these friends, staying out all night, sleeping over each other's homes, sharing goals, dreams, and more. Seeing their livelihoods and talents being swept away by addiction broke my heart. If you need someone to talk to on the phone or share your feelings in writing, please know I am available. If I cannot help, I can indeed point you in the right direction.

Gurudev has shared his wisdom on addiction: "Find a bigger vision—like serving one's society, one's country. You have your entire life ahead of you, don't ruin your life with drugs. You can become a good actor, politician, businessman, and even a good social worker.

Drugs will make your body weak, and you will not be able to enjoy family life, which gets badly affected. Everyone connected with you—relatives, friends—will be so sad and upset.

Spirituality has a big role to play in dealing with such a situation. Meditations, breathing techniques, pranayama, and satsang have helped millions around the world to overcome addiction over substances and alcohol.

Many people have shared that they feel the same high after doing Sudarshan Kriya that they used to feel after taking drugs, but without their damaging consequences. Scientists say that psychoactive drugs are addictive because they cause a surge in dopamine, a neurotransmitter associated with happiness and contentment. Research has shown that meditation increases dopamine levels naturally by an average of sixty-five percent. A session of group singing or satsang also leaves one exhilarated and energized for many hours. These practices build strength in the mind so that one doesn't feel the need to rely on external substances to feel an inner high."

I finished my summer classes with flying colors, three up, three A's, earning my first 4.0 and the prestigious President's List honor. This would be the first of three-consecutive-semesters with high honors. My soul wrestled with the emotional concept of old friends struggling at the bottom dregs of life while I was at the top of my class.

During an open month between semesters, I filled in the blank dates by performing my Sound in Silence concerts. With the buzz of last spring's tour still ringing, shows practically lined themselves up. First gig, Madison, Wisconsin, a place I knew little about.

My Art of Living friend, Reshma, taking a master's program at the Frank Lloyd Wright School of Architecture, set up my programs. The first performance was at a kid's camp, a favorite audience type of school-age children. "Jippy Jappa" was a hit.

My next concert was at an old-fashioned restaurant/souvenir shop. The locals were huge Bob Dylan fans, so I fit right in. I strummed my guitar and sang on the porch for a small crowd and passersby. Like everywhere else, the casual audience enjoyed singing "Quinn the Eskimo."

At high noon on Saturday, Reshma and I strolled through the farmers market, promoting and selling my new CD. We also handed out flyers for my satsang at the local yoga studio that night. Set up in a spot near the flow of shoppers, I employed a great marketing idea by having potential buyers of my album choose a song from the back cover, and I'd play it, like an impromptu concert. If they chose one of the two Sanskrit bhajans, I invited them to the yoga studio that night.

After the market, we walked down the main street and into a New Age shop to hand out flyers. When Reshma told the flamboyant storeowner that I was the one leading the satsang, or *kirtan*, as it is widely known in the yoga community, he went off. This dude ecstatically ran around the sidewalk yelling, "The chanter's here; he's in my store and he is playing at the yoga studio tonight!" This guy was a sight to see.

That colorful cat was first to arrive. He settled himself in the front row, singing like an exotic bird who landed south before the harsh winter. My first yoga studio gig was a success, and I enjoyed the atmosphere as well as the people of Madison.

In July, another online Art of Living buddy from Seattle called Vinay, a cool kid from India who worked for Microsoft, sent me an invitation. The super seva team in Seattle set up a series of shows, and we hustled throughout the Puget Sound area.

In a month, Gurudev was coming to speak at the University of Washington, called "U-Dub" by the locals, which made my concerts timelier and more inspirational. I played at the mall, the Space Needle, dashed south to Olympia to play at Sylvester Park, and then back to Seattle for a studio interview on CNN talk radio.

While in Seattle, a good friend from my Lake Tahoe days, Beth Krambule, invited me down to Portland to help promote Gurudev's talk in the Rose City the following month.

The trip to Portland was more special, as my brother had been living there for around two years with my old band mate, Matt, the original Matt. Ivan, a close friend from Mission Beach, had moved there, too. This was a sweet homecoming for me during the tour to hang with my brother and San Diego friends.

I took the train from Seattle to Portland and was blown away by the natural beauty outside the windows. Thick forests against the brilliant sky broke away now and again for open fields... and of course, there was the twenty-two-year-old Mormon girl from Olympia I befriended. How many pages was that before a girl popped up, anybody counting? In life there are human connections and then there are Human Connections. Ours was the latter. What's the difference? Who cares—it was as authentic as it was awesome.

Nicole was a sweet, beautiful, and open-minded college girl. She was a student at BYU, a Mormon university in Utah, rich in tradition. We talked during the entire ride, with a song or two from me.

Earlier in the book, I wrote about how when I travel, I find people who are open-minded to talk about ancient universal Self-knowledge and there I was—a boy with a smile, and often a song. A half hour into our talk, she told me she needed to take the Art of Living course and later did so in Seattle.

Nicole and I talked almost daily by phone and online after that. I wrote a song for her, one not recorded yet, called "No Clouds." Here's the second verse:

Sweet, sweet Nicole, catch my drift from a bird's eye
All that shines is the love in your bright eyes
Slide on down, a tree 'til you're inside
There you are, there I am—here we are now...

You can imagine how hard it was to leave the Northwest with Gurudev arriving in a few short weeks, but I couldn't complain after the time I'd spent with him in May. But, as millions of his students around the world will agree, we can never get enough of his laughter and love. Go and meet him, you'll see why.

I set up my brother Jeff and some of our friends to go and see Gurudev's talk in Portland. My brother didn't follow through on his commitment—he opted to party instead. I was initially crushed, then let it go. Jeff was the only member of my family left to meet

Gurudev and was not making it easy for me to accomplish a big dream of mine. All I wanted was for him to see Gurudev.

Jeff is his own person, always has been and probably always will be. Brotherly love, gotta love it.

At the end of August, it was time to start my second-to-last semester of college. I felt like a racehorse at the gate. As a group of future teachers, we had our classes in a makeshift classroom of portable trailers, at an elementary school near my home.

Once again came the daily, "Good morning, ladies and Jeremy!" I loved it! Who am I kidding? The classes, along with student teaching, combined their ingredients into the toughest semester of my life.

My student teaching was in a kindergarten classroom, teaching lessons, leading songs and being the do-it-all slave for the older classroom teacher. Copy this, staple that, cut this, paste that—I ran circles like a robot around the school with her various errands.

I still managed to sneak away for a few concerts such as Raleigh, North Carolina, for the second-to-last stops of the 2003 Sound in Silence college tour in America.

At North Carolina State University, I was honored to play in the same theatre as Dave Matthews during one of his solo tours. A fantastic show. They played my album before I came out; everything clicked from the sound system, the venue, and the crowd. For this tour, I was using a PowerPoint display of lyrics behind me. There was pin-drop silence during the Ram Meditation. I can't explain the exhilarating fun on the tour while still making tons of mistakes. That's how one learns, and that's how it worked with the master force of Gurudev's intention leading all the way.

Next up was Dallas. Being a huge Cowboys football fan, this stop held extra excitement, and it was right off the plane, straight to the University of Texas. A diverse crowd met me, and we rocked for a good part of the night.

Narin Shankar, an enthusiastic organizer, set up a bunch of shows, including one at a restaurant. I played at another yoga studio, sharpening my Sanskrit bhajan style. I felt and heard myself become smoother with a varying range of vocals to match the satsang's energy, taking the participants along with me.

Bhajans were my bread and butter; there was much more feeling with them. I was becoming more aware how everyone melted into each song in their own unique way, and being the train engineer, I needed to be with this type of song.

I found myself slowly moving away from being a bit abrasive with the chants, the loud guy. I found a couple volumes (one louder and two lower), two or three more keys, and a few different chords to accentuate. This began a new time of writing my own material... sitting at home in Atlanta on my bed, or on tour.

Kennesaw State University's international teaching program was just getting started. The program for university seniors to teach over in China for their last semester was a no-brainer for me. My friend Daniel Hodge, another student in the elementary education program, had also signed on for the program.

I was stoked to finish my last semester teaching in China. Daniel and I would head out in early February 2004 with no looking back.

Before the adrenaline of China had calmed in my system, the next Youth Leadership Training Program was set for Mexico City during the upcoming holidays, and Matt and I jumped right in.

Planning to teach the Breath Water Sound course to orphans and others, both in Mexico and China, I needed funding. I returned to what had worked for the past two-and-a-half years, calling on the kind, sincere people I knew once again—my Art of Living family who helped send me to India and Belize, plus some great people I'd met on the music tour this year. I smiled and tied up the phone line.

This was humbling, asking not just for myself but for the seva of others. I put together a package, including an openhearted letter about both programs and two color photos including a beautiful picture of Gurudev that Bill Herman gave me, and a second from the YLTP program in Bangalore, with children surrounding me, one on my shoulder.

Everyone loved the packets. Checks started coming in, and again, Mom couldn't believe it. She said I was shameless and couldn't understand where I got the nerve to ask other people for money. But eventually she accepted it and made a joke saying, "Maybe I should do a fundraiser for some new clothes." I love my mom.

Before I could catch my breath from the semester of stress and success, I met Matt in Houston to fly into Mexico City together.

I could easily write another book on miracles all about flying around the world over the past twenty-one years. Matt and I had seats about a plane apart, but naturally, we wanted to sit next to each other. I asked the flight attendant if we could switch seats as the one next to me was empty, but she said no, the flight was full.

Sitting in my customary aisle seat, I briefly (and selfishly) prayed, *I hope an opportunity presents itself for Matt and me to sit together.*

The cabin door shut and locked. In the next moment the attendant came and said, "Okay, you can go get your friend now, this is the only empty seat on the flight. Enjoy."

I smiled, silently thanked Gurudev, and then grabbed Matt.

A never-ending sprawling array of homes, buildings, cars, and people, millions of people, below us caused some serious wide wonder in my mind. We arrived in the world's fourth-largest city with bulging backpacks, trekking around busy streets after midnight. We found the hostel we were going to stay at was closed for the night and hit a hotel across the street.

In a memorable line retold nearly every time we're together, Matt wanted to open the curtains to wake up early by sunlight. I firmly fought against it. "Dude, no way. I haven't slept in for like six months!"

Flashbacks of another small room, another time where the contestants were Matt and Bill sound familiar? We both fell over laughing on our beds. Sleeping in was worth its weight in gold that Saturday morning in Mexico.

We arrived a week before the Youth Leadership Training Program to set up seminars, workshops, and maybe some musical gigs in local colleges, as well. Unfortunately, doors didn't open easily. It was hard without connections, plus there was a language barrier. Ultimately, we played a Christmas music show at our hostel.

As our team arrived, things picked up. I felt more useful with a stronger sense of why I was there.

During a typical day, we visited group homes for teens, playing music, singing, and teaching the simple, powerful breathing techniques and meditation.

Like everywhere I taught, the experiences of the participants were awesome. The look in their eyes, a peaceful stance in their bodies, it's like bringing a basket of freshness to the tired. The teenagers came cloaked in garments of curiosity, distrust, and distance. With music and meditation, the negative wraps fell to the ground. It is easily the most rewarding service in the world.

I spent Christmas there with several other participants. Christmas dinner for me was a pizza at Domino's (shh, don't tell my mom) and then a few of us hitched a twelve-hour bus ride to Playa Zicatela, the Mexican Pipeline in Puerto Escondido, a top surfing spot, just above Acapulco.

The beach was heaven on earth and the Mexican culture was lovely, a holiday gift wrapped in brilliant hues of sun, sea, and sand. Buses filled with families arrived at the beach, and the holiday party began.

Not only did I fall in love with the beach, the food, and the surfing, but also with a beautiful Mexican princess who worked at the bank. As I sang in "Back to Taylor Town," "...*señorita mi amor*, a priceless beauty, but I want more." Call it the story of my life. I'm blown away by the natural beauty of a lovely girl, but either I must leave the area soon or I'm just too damn picky.

Gurudev says, "When you are filled with joy, when you have blossomed in love, only then can you appreciate beauty." I get this point.

After the holiday, the YLTP resumed in a nice-sized home, led once again by Bill Herman. All was well, until... I was to pay Bill for my participation in the course, room, and board—no biggie. But for some technical reason, I could not withdraw money from my account. Cue the dark background music, heavy on the bass.

The next day, we were to practice Sudarshan Kriya in a group; this is the extended version and needs to be facilitated by a teacher. I was genuinely looking forward to practicing after our morning yoga session.

As I settled into a comfortable chair, in that ever-familiar glow of gratitude for this practice and gift from Gurudev, Bill whispered in my ear, "You are not welcome to participate in this morning's Sudarshan Kriya until you pay for this course. Please wait outside."

I opened my eyes, stunned. He was serious.

Holding back the immediate tsunami of destructive emotions, I left and went into another room. I picked up Matt's iPod and slapped the headphones on. The first song played was Krishna Das's "*Baba Hanuman*," a new experience for me. My consciousness rose with the enormous emotions of just getting thrown out of the Sudarshan Kriya session by Bill.

I've had out-of-body experiences in the past while listening to music with headphones, times where the energy in my body swirled, where my mind was at ease, and my heart burst with love, pure emotion, like soaring straight to heaven on a crystal seahorse whose only passion was to fly me to the Divine. This was one of those experiences.

After the song ended, I removed the headphones and began the home practice of Sudarshan Kriya. Dramatically powerful, cool yet sweet, the meditation was as good as it gets on the spiritual path. Here again, were the dancing opposites—Bill kicked me out, setting me on fire. The musical occurrence led to an authentically soul-light-set-ablaze session of deep breathing and meditation.

I love you, Billy. Thank you for the cherished experience.

I could hear Gurudev saying with his signature smile, "Be with the opposites—dance with them."

After this surprise experience, I headed off to the ATM, got the cash to pay Bill, and all was cool on the home front.

With each new dawn we taught disadvantaged youth. These were not prep school kids, but young souls having known despair and abandonment. Though it felt phenomenal being a part of an instant transformation in a lot of the youth, there was more than the techniques going on here. Though I knew what Gurudev was up to on this planet during this lifetime, at the same time it remained a wonderful mystery. It was hard to leave Mexico, but I knew another world of endless opportunities awaited me in East Asia and beyond.

As I was leaving, Bill handed me a hand-crafted card that read, "It gets easier each time." I felt the same exact way about him, too. Our relationship was growing stronger.

After a quick "Mom, Dad, I'm home. See ya later, I love you," in Atlanta, I boogied down both coasts of the United States for concerts and more. I had planned to dig a hole straight down to China to save on airfare, but the hardware store ran out of shovels.

I faced a jam-packed calendar that would make a rock star shake their head. A wonderful family invited me to Princeton, New Jersey, to help me with my fundraiser. I arrived on a record-setting night— perhaps the coldest night in some hundred years.

After a nice satsang where a lot of kind folks helped me out, I headed over the bridge for a satsang in Philadelphia. To my delighted surprise, one of my best childhood friends from Taylor, Dave Weisenfluh, drove down the Pennsylvania Turnpike in a snowstorm to attend. It was a special night on a variety of emotional levels.

I often called Gurudev at the Bangalore Ashram over the last few months to talk about his plans for me in China during my upcoming international student teaching program. I was headed to the Far East as an ambassador of goodwill in search of paths and doors to bring Gurudev's vision of a stress free, violence free society. At the end of the call he'd said, "I don't know what we can and cannot do there, you go and let me know. Please email me once a week and keep me updated on your programs there."

I was most honored when my first Art of Living teachers, Bill and Lucinda Robertson, invited me to their beautiful home in San Diego to lead a satsang. This blew my mind as I flipped back to my younger self entering their home, a peaceful haven, so long ago.

Travel becoming my middle name, I raced back up to San Francisco and got my visa for China. While walking down Geary St., I started singing a simple, fun song called "China." That was pretty much all the lyrics, "China, doo doo doo doo…" I sang this new tune—which ranks right up with the Belize-written "Jippy Jappa" for the most simplistic and catchy tunes I have ever penned—out loud with enthusiasm for my trip. It was a big hit during lunchtime in Chinatown that day; you know I shared it proud and loud.

A week before leaving for China, Von Osselman sent a message for me to give him a ring. Von was very interested in my upcoming trip to China, talking to me about his travels around the world with the Art of Living and sharing valuable advice with me.

During this conversation, our past ego/mind wrestling matches washed away. I accepted Von as he was, the simple, childlike Von, one with a huge heart and a world of devotion for Gurudev. I was instantly freed from taking on his negative karma every time I had ill thoughts about him playing music in the Foundation. I felt incredibly lighter. Sure, Von had his shortcomings, just as I did, and pretty much just like everyone else on this earth. But I realized that our friction was only caused by our similarities. We loved to share our songs in satsang and get the people engaged, we both loved Gurudev dearly and devoted our lives to his work; at the same time, we both traveled for seva, taught, and were very good people inside.

I looked back on how arrogant and harsh I was while dealing with Von over the past few years, and I also realized that I was missing out on the best Von had to offer me, as a mentor on this path and as a friend. I was ready to finally get to know Von, as well as to grow more in myself.

The San Francisco Bay Area family of devotees has always been special to me. Their energy and tenacity are practically addicting. They are a tightknit group of enthusiastic volunteers.

They opened their hearts and put together a fundraiser. After a satsang, which was my fourteenth in seventeen days of performing, they presented me with the final funds needed for my trip. At the time my gratitude knew no bounds and even now, as I write these words, the feeling holds strong.

I met Daniel Hodge at the airport. We boarded a full flight with our seats separated by a vacant middle seat. Bam, it became the only empty seat on the entire plane, just as before.

Flying into Shanghai felt like Mexico City, an erector set of engineering marvel with tons of offices, homes, cars, and people packed solid in a limited space with concrete and asphalt.

I had contacted Leon, an Art of Living volunteer in Shanghai, and he arranged transportation from the airport and put us up in two spare rooms near his office. Score! I was in China as a student teacher through my university and a volunteer with the Art of Living. This was a great initial experience in both roles.

One of the greatest things of being in the Art of Living is the one-world family connection—I can go pretty much anywhere in the world and be well taken care of. Daniel was both impressed and grateful, as there is nothing like finding yourself in China with the help and support of a local.

Shanghai was a city of colorful chaos and modern madness, hordes of people, Starbucks everywhere, cars bumper to bumper, and a cool vibe in the trendy parts of town.

The adventure continued to Nanjing, the historic capital of Jiangsu province with an urban population of over seven million, where we would be living and teaching for the next three months. Nanjing was the slower-paced cousin of Shanghai, smaller and less modern than its Pacific Rim Tiger counterpart.

We were promised kindergarten teaching jobs, a grade level Daniel and I both enjoyed and had student-teaching experience with. But like many plans that season, things fell through the floor into a dank, dark basement. The education officials we were working with plopped us at Ying Tian College, a second-year institution. During the twenty-minute drive from downtown I heard the Godfather theme play in the background of my mind. My balloon of teaching young, fresh faces deflated the further we traveled.

Daniel was not happy, and he had every right not to be—he'd just left his home and family to teach little kids in China. Instead, he was at a dusty, architecturally boring English college in Nanjing.

Like almost everything thrown at me over the past seven years, I quickly accepted that my classroom of little ones had transformed into not-much-taller young adults. It took Daniel a bit longer, but he eased into the new role. This was our final semester of college, and we were going to make the best of it.

Among the locals, well, I was like an American rock legend with my guitar slung over my shoulder and big smile. Daniel was the movie star with his Hollywood good looks, cigarettes, and jokes.

Instant college professors of English were we; this was as far out as it could get. We slept in heavily guarded neighboring dorm rooms at night and by day taught classes to shy, curious, and broken-English-speaking nineteen- and twenty-year-olds.

With no heaters at the college except in our dorm rooms, everyone wore jackets to class. On the first day it was so cold, I took them out into the hallway and taught them yoga—this warmed them up and set the tone for the type of education they would receive. We have budget cuts in the States, but this was harsh.

My Taylor 710 CE acoustic guitar was a mainstay in the classrooms, and we sang all the time. Some of the Sanskrit bhajans I had written recently were big hits: "*Govinda Gopala*" and "*Shiva Shiva Shiva Shambho*." My quizzes were lyrics, my warmups a teaching style of relaxed mantras. Music opened their minds to learning. And that's how it rolled. I showed up daily to each class, guitar and lesson plan in hand, ready to rock and shake up these timid young college kids. I had a lively group of students in my class, and we experienced a lot of laughs, songs, drama, and sometimes even tears.

My heartfelt plans (think of the quote, "If you want to make God laugh, just make a plan") to teach the Breath Water Sound course also fell through that ever-opening, metaphorical Chinese floor.

I called Gurudev in Singapore. He wanted to know how things were going, and when I told him the Breath Water Sound course was hard to get started, he told me, "Forget about everything else, just get all the students singing. And see if they could take a little bit of silence after some of the songs. This would be good."

Yes, Master!

For years, Gurudev has said, "See the past as destiny and the future as free will—and then plan from the present moment and be one hundred percent." He says how foolish humans are, seeing the past as free will and getting hung up in anger, hate, and frustration about things that are over. A level of laziness sets in when humans see the future as destiny, as if they have no say in it. The knowledge is, "Learn from the past, and plan for the future from the present moment." If you add up the time you waste on things that are over and on things not yet here—you can't call it living; as a matter of fact, it's only existing.

I believe most humans just exist, from what I have seen around the world. Eating, working, sleeping, worried about the future, angry about the past, not accepting others, being a slave to their own emotions, being controlled by what others think, not doing something they want to do in life because of fear of what others will think. I call this lifestyle by only one name (little ones, please cover your eyes and ears): Hell.

Now, where was I? Oh, yes—China. Music paved its way for me like trucks used to clear snow on Lincoln Street back in the '80s. I played at the college every Thursday night and outside at Nanjing Normal University on Sunday afternoons. I was also invited to play many shows at local universities, cafes, and other venues. There was a lot of singing and knowledge sessions going on all around the city. The Sound in Silence tour continued.

I created impromptu concerts where I plopped down on a street bench downtown and hundreds of spectators gathered around as fast as sharks on a few pirates thrown overboard. All were quickly broken up by the local authorities, trained in paranoia and following the strict communist Chinese law of "no organizing in public." Hell, with almost one-and-a-half billion people there, I'd be afraid of them assembling, too.

"Hello, Gurudev, it's Jeremy."

"Are you still in China?"

"Yes, I have another month here. Gurudev, what should I do after China? I will graduate in May with my teaching degree."

"Come to the ashram and take TTC Two in May; then you can be a full Art of Living teacher."

"Wow, another dream come true; see you there, Gurudev, and thanks a million for everything!"

The last unit I taught was based on universal human values. This is where things started to gel. I took the universal self-knowledge I'd obtained through Gurudev's teachings over the years and presented it in my own wildly unique way. My level of passion, creativity, humor, and risk-taking shone these last two weeks.

First, I had the students come up with a master list of human values: happiness, joy, creativity, compassion, gratitude, sense of belonging, and the willingness to help others. During each class, energy exploded in personal sharing, hearts opening, and laughter. The conclusion made itself known: If we want more of any (or all) of these values to shine in our lives, we must be more of that value.

Friendliness—get off the couch and shake someone's hand with a smile. Creativity—scribble on the walls. Happiness—wake up and see how blessed we are (double that for gratitude). And the willingness to help others—ask, "How can I be useful to people around me, today and always?" Joy... well, we are nothing but pure joy. Be good to yourself by doing yoga, breathing, meditation, singing, and helping others. You'll see this energy shining like the morning sun bouncing off the moon's fading light on any given summer day.

I popped up with a couple of awesome activities dealing with creativity, friendliness, and service. China has its concepts, like most countries, of what is acceptable or not. It didn't take long before I knowingly led my students to the "not acceptable" side of the street. I inspired my Chinese college students to go crazy in creativity, drawing wild pictures on the concrete floor with colored chalk, a definite no-no. I'm so bad, I'm good. At first, they were timid, but once they warmed up to the idea it was like a pride of caged lions unleashed on a dance floor hearing Serengeti lion music for the first time. This was awesome!

During the sharing sessions afterward, the students told how free and creative they felt, and that they never thought they could draw before. They said how good it felt to do something out of their comfort zones—activities often looked down upon by adults.

Next, we talked about service. I shared my stories from far-flung villages and slum districts in India, Belize, and Mexico City. I asked them to brainstorm ideas of how to help people around campus. First, the students went to the gardeners and gave them cookies with a smile and a greeting. The stunned workers were most grateful for the gestures.

Next, as we talked about friendliness, the students went in groups of three to the gate and talked to the security guards. This was mind-blowing! No one ever talks to them; they just simply stand there and do their job. The blossoming students discovered many interesting things about the guards. The last few groups sang "You Are My Sunshine" to them. This was huge, as everyone was happy and grateful. Human values—pretty simple, eh?

Once, during these lessons, I flew off the handle. Can you believe that? Me? I threw a textbook across the room, into the garbage can (Jordan, for three—he scores!), and tossed all the Chinese currency I had in my pocket up in the air, as if I'd just won the lottery and was now part of some new China dynasty.

Can you imagine the faces of those kids? Better yet, imagine the face of the observing female professor who told the dean of the school who later called me into his office and enlightened me on how disrespectful those actions were. Whoops, not my first international calamity of cultures.

Why did I do those things within the same minute of my life? I shoot from the hip, I teach with passion, I live enthusiasm (and art), and when I see the need to shake my students up a little bit, I do it… no matter what it takes.

My ninth grade language arts teacher, Mr. Joyce, during a lesson, jumped up and down on a student desk, stomping a little piece of chalk to bits and pieces. I forget the moral of that craziness, but I do remember I loved his over-the-top dramatics, and talked about it for a long time… and now am writing about it in my soon-to-be published memoir.

I wanted to get across to my students how true education is not found in any textbook. There are millions of students who live by the book, and subsequently, in life situations, die by the book, i.e., the textbook in the trash can. There is much more to this world and learning than what is found on pages of a textbook.

And in terms of learning a second language—for these students, English—they must come out of their isolated shells and speak with each other, even strangers. Especially strangers. I sang my mantra: "True education is doing something brand new—totally different than what we are used to doing." And, "If you want to learn something new, you have to do something different."

As for the money part, the point I demonstrated in my style was that happiness is not in money or material things, but inside, like a fountain of joy screaming from inside each of us to dive headfirst.

I apologized for disrespecting anyone at the college that day or that season. I have my own way of teaching, and it has worked well so far. My motto: "Teach happiness with happiness." Ditto that for love, compassion, joy, creativity, and enthusiasm.

Imagine a sunny spring morning in May, local flowers in bloom, the sun already warm, and a pleasant breeze blowing through the open window at 8:00 a.m., adding to my happiness. Having just finished my morning practice, I tuned into my favorite Internet radio station for some additional morning pleasure: rock and roll.

As I tucked in my dress shirt and slid on my shoes, the music rose to meet my ears—and then rocked my soul. That old favorite rang out: "Pink Houses," the John Mellencamp anthem! I cranked it up about as loud as it would go. Rockin' around my room, from wall to wall, and some bouncing up and down, the song flooded my heart with a tsunami of memories and a longing for home. I am sure at least one hundred Chinese folks heard the music from my open window—and heard me singing along, loud and proud.

When Daniel came for our routine walk to our classes, he said, "Damn, you were rockin' out this morning!"

I smiled the essence of what classic rock music gave me; I smiled something bright. Please read or listen to the lyrics of the chorus of that tune—then read the title of this book.

*Playing a concert at Nanjing Forestry University
in Nanjing, China, April 2004*

CHAPTER TWENTY-ONE

A College Graduate in India

When you are in the space of service and
surrender, there is no dearth of miracles.
—Gurudev Sri Sri Ravi Shankar

When the Chinese trip came to an end, both Daniel and I earned our B.S. in Early Childhood Education, with a miniature minor in Chinese Culture and College Professorship—just kidding.

Flying into Bangalore, I couldn't help thinking of my first trip there, almost three years ago. This time, I knew for the most part what to expect. I was more centered and happier, plus a college graduate—with honors.

I was blown away with the new meditation hall, named after Gurudev's late mother, Vishalakshi Mantap, or "VM" for short. During construction back in late 2001, I took daily walks with Gurudev up to the top. Looking out at the beautiful land, I heard him point and say, "One day this ashram will stretch as far as the eye can see." I could only imagine his vision on that cool December day.

More people were living at the ashram, but not nearly as many as today. Nonetheless, I got to know everyone quickly. It is easy when you are on stage leading a song in the VM where everyone sees you and you don't have to introduce yourself one at a time.

It is easy to be popular here, in their culture they are innocent and adore musicians, even at the ashram. How humbled I felt to hear praises after singing as my ego dissolved more and more with each growing level of love. I could feel it inside my heart.

"Come on, Jeremy, let's go meet Gurudev!" said Vikram, leading the way to the bottom of Gurudev's kutir. Seconds later, there was the miraculous man. It had been a year since I'd last seen him, and my level of longing for him was high. He came down the last step and gazed into my eyes with a look of lightning, blinked two or three times, then took me by the arm and asked me how I was.

I'd never had a look from him like this before; it felt powerful yet confusing at the same time.

What was that? I thought to myself, watching Gurudev get into his car.

Swami Brahmatej said, "Wow, Jeremy, he sure gave you a powerful look. Lucky you."

Whatever it was, absorbing every concern in my heart, it felt real and wonderful. Darshan can be powerful from one's spiritual master—and that day it was given to me.

Two of my favorite things to do while at the ashram are to hang out with the happy kids in the village nearby and to cross the street to our free tribal school. Hundreds of children from many villages around the ashram attend the school, the first generations in their families to be educated. From worldwide donations from kind and caring devotees and programs, like "Dollar a Day" and "Gift a Smile," these children receive transportation, meals, books, supplies, uniforms, and a quality values-based education.

It's inspiring to see their development over the years, their high test scores for the region, and their endless and bright smiles. Whether sitting in the classroom, playing outside with the children, or having a fundraising concert to sponsor a child's education, it brings an indelible satisfaction knowing I am a part of this education endeavor.

Gurudev spirited off to yet another country for his forty-eighth birthday celebration to plant seeds of love and peace. We enjoyed our own planting party at the ashram by planting trees, making a beautiful, jungle-esque, plant-filled campus even more scenic.

After the fun-filled day, I went back to my room and grabbed my acoustic guitar. My thoughts swirled about my best friend back home and his substance abuse problems, not to mention being in and out of jail like a bouncing ball out of bounds at a playground. Unfortunately, I was hearing a lot of bad news about him at the time.

I wrote "Silent Waves" in one straight shot, over eight minutes of heart-pouring love in song and strum. My creation was for him and anyone who could use the knowledge in their lives:

> *On paths divided many ways, you often lose your grace*
> *Come down beyond these silly games, come back to who you are*
> *Enthusiasm, peace and joy—let it shine right through the haze*
> *And paint your picture of this world, until you call it home...*
> *Govinda, Gopala—Radhe Govinda*

My friend heard the song exactly seven years after the tune was written in a most untimely manner. His appreciation of the sentiment was humbling. He also received another song on a future album, that story and more to come. Now back to our regularly scheduled second adventure in India.

May 27th arrived with lots of anticipated glory. Though Gurudev was not there, around five hundred enthusiastic prospective Art of Living teachers came to their spiritual home away from home, place of rest and battery recharging, the Bangalore Ashram where Teacher Training Courses (TTC) parts one and two began. Fifteen rocking days straight, filled with endless echoes of laughter, tons of pranks, late-night and sometimes all-night ventures around the campus, and of course the main benefit of these brilliant courses—rocket-powered spiritual growth.

When I was on TTC One, we set the attendance record with two hundred participants packing the old meditation hall. My TTC Two had an intimate, cozy, and awesome forty-five participants.

The course was taught by a most humble, centered, smiling soul named Swami Brahmatej. Swamiji was the same teacher who had initiated me as an Art of Living teacher almost three years before, a sincere brother/father figure whom I am still proud to call a near and dear friend.

The course was nonstop craziness. The group of guys from Gujarat were insane enough alone, throw in an ex-model/premier flight attendant from the ritzy side of Mumbai, plus me at the height of manic madness, and you have one off-the-wall group. Pushing each other's buttons, laughing and crying together, making each other stronger by the session, and at the end of the day, a most humble and grateful bunch.

"Help—I am dying of laughter!" My face, stomach, and various body parts ached. The ground even screamed from us rolling on it.

What did we do for fifteen magnificent days on TTC Two? It would be outrageous to describe—you'll have to take it to find out. Currently, the Art of Living Teacher Training Program is a comprehensive, intensively awesome fifteen-day merriment of artful living.

One of the best parts of the course for me was its nostalgic location. The spirit-filled Narayana Hall is a snowball's throw away from Gurudev's kutir. With the going rate of global warmth climate craziness, there might be snow at the ashram by 2032—who knows? This was the venue I had my first Youth Leadership Training Program in.

Gurudev came back from the United States in June. The poignant roar of the ardent crowd in the VM when he walked onto the stage that first night was pure emotional adrenaline, decibels beyond loud, a rage of glory. I could have been cryogenically frozen that moment, right next to Walt Disney, without a breath of regret for the life I had lived to this point. Our gallant-souled giant was back home.

On the second-to-last night of the course, we were nestled together in the basement room of the VM listening to Swamiji's inspiring stories of love and service, as close to each other as a group of children huddled around a flat-screen color television enjoying the surprises of an exceptional movie.

Shortly after midnight, Swamiji pulled out a piece of paper and read the names of the new Art of Living teachers, along with the courses they would be able to teach. Forty-five of us sat in anticipation to learn if we would indeed be one of them with a grand but brief explosion of glee for each person whose name was called.

An hour later, on June 10, 2004, forty out of forty-five course participants became brand new Art of Living teachers, fully equipped with skills, strength, knowledge, and above all, Gurudev's grace behind our good actions. Forty teachers would now set out on their journey, sharing and teaching this precious knowledge, helping others to grow, and most importantly, growing themselves.

I was most grateful to be named one. I was now a volunteer Art of Living teacher and could teach adults the Art of Living course and its cornerstone, Sudarshan Kriya.

Hours later, before noon, the new teachers were welcomed inside Gurudev's kutir, where he personally handed each of us the Art of Living course manual and the sacred Sudarshan Kriya cassette tape.

Honestly, at the moment I kneeled before him in my brand new-white kurta pajama, gifted to me by another course participant hours earlier, I felt this was the most gratifying, humbling experience of my life. As he touched the tape to his forehead and placed it into my two open hands with nothing but unconditional love, I knew how blessed I was in this lifetime. I knew I was chosen to share the most precious knowledge on earth. I knew my life's purpose and was reminded of how magnificent Gurudev is.

When Swamiji's eyes met mine, his smile was reminiscent of the brightest San Diego sun. He handed me a tissue to catch my tears. His love and compassion made the tears flow more. If those few minutes seemed like a lifetime in bliss, then walking outside of the kutir and down the stone stairs to a humongous, beyond-proud supportive cheers of hundreds of TTC One participants and countless others, easily felt like months of magic.

The moment reminded me of when I was seventeen and how far I'd come on this path. The explosion of excitement running out onto the football field the Saturday after Thanksgiving 1993 as my name was announced by "The Voice of the Vikings" was probably near what I felt as I walked down those stairs among the cheers and applause. I was hit with hugs as I walked through the gate. That is truly living at a hundred percent. Tears, emotions, sharing moments of golden glory are not only what I call living in the present moment, but also what I mean when I sing, write, and scream… "Living the Art!"

I taught my first Art of Living course days later in Narayana Hall with another new teacher, a good buddy of mine from South India, Swami Virupaksha.

"Okay, Universe, keep bestowing these blessings upon my life, I can handle all you can give me," I said to myself.

My first course was not only at the ashram, in Narayana Hall only feet below Gurudev's kutir, but attended by thirty-plus dynamically awesome students from Bangalore.

There's an old tradition in India where students or youngsters will touch the right foot of their teachers or elders as a sign of respect. At the completion of the course, the participants lined up to touch our feet. This expression felt inspirational, different than in the past when innocent villagers came up after a Breath Water Sound course—these were middle-class professionals, husbands, wives, moms, and dads.

I must admit a momentary flash of ego crept up saying, "Wow, I am a big time teacher now." But my heart said, "I am so fortunate to be a teacher of this knowledge, to walk with Gurudev Sri Sri Ravi Shankar on this path of knowledge and joy in this lifetime."

In the back of my mind percolated the idea of making a new music album. Not always in conscious thoughts, but in dreams and awakenings off and on. So imagine when one day, Bhanu, Gurudev's sister, so sweet, sincere, and beautiful said, "Jeremy, you sing so nice in satsang—you should record a CD for the youth."

My surprise at her words kicked open the door of my desires. After we talked a while about the idea, I knew there was only one person to ask.

On a morning in June, I received a divine feeling to walk out of group sadhana early, toward the end of my meditation. I found Gurudev walking alone outside the VM. As simple as a young child joining his father for a walk in the park, I fell into step with Gurudev, side by side, a most memorable and beautiful morning walk. Our conversations are light, sometimes serious, infused with jokes and laughter, always meaningful and diverse.

That morning we walked for ten minutes across the campus. On the last path of our journey, leading to his kutir, I inhaled slowly and asked, "Gurudev, Bhanu and I talked about the possibility of me recording a music album for the youth. May I have your blessings for this, please?"

With a smile and a powerful high-five, Gurudev replied, "Absolutely, I think this is a great idea. Just talk to Prasana, and he will take care of it."

I gave him a quick hug, and he walked on with several devotees who had formed around us by then.

As I watched him walk down the brick path, something universally strong and powerful came over me. These were emotions too intense for me to handle, as if my mortal being were squeezed in a vice grip. I ducked into one of the open-air halls, grateful it was empty, plopped down, and slid back into meditation. The immeasurable gratitude I felt was joyfully overflowing in continuous waves. This was not only a sweet moment in my already fairytale life, but I felt lifetimes of garbage melting away: impressions, concepts, fear, and pain. I couldn't have walked faster to Prasana's office that morning to make an appointment.

In July I took a train ride to Mumbai. Then I came down with a terrible upper-respiratory infection on the way back to Bangalore. Loud, jarring coughs, my lungs were filled tight with bone-deep pains in my chest. The discomfort reminded me of my childhood breathing issues. Back at the ashram, I did not get better over time.

One night after satsang, Gurudev stood outside, meeting a small group of us. I went up to him without speaking a single word, pointed to my aching, ill chest and a pleading look on my face that screamed, "I'm sick—please help me!"

Gurudev hit me in the chest three times. The first was light, then harder with the following two—I was hit with an explosion of love. I took a deep breath and smiled. In that same instant, my lungs started to open. I felt some relief and thanked Gurudev. That night, I slept peacefully without pain and coughing. When I woke up the next morning, there was a significant difference. By the following day, the infection was gone—the healing hands of grace and love.

I met with Prasana, a big guy with a big personality, like a bull with the potential for powerful reactions who sometimes smiled. I'd seen him yell before, as Bill did when he was in charge. As the head of the publication department, he had lots of responsibilities. He was also very kind.

Initially, Prasana wanted to make two albums, I had built up quite a bit of material writing English parts to my Sanskrit tunes all summer.

Recording the songs in a South Indian film music studio with professional musicians, in just a day or two was my real concern. How would I make these songs come alive on the album? My last recording experience with Adam in Lake Tahoe had shattered my confidence. I realized that a product is only as strong as its weakest link. In my mind, that link was me, with my limited guitar skills and often-strained voice.

Prasana had faith. My then-level of talent and resume had preceded me. He heard me at satsang and heard stories about my music adventures over the past two years. His interest probably had something to do with the fact that any album I put out as the white American named Jeremy would, indeed, sell countrywide. That was not an ego-singing statement, it was true, as I had a tremendous support group there. I did not know of any other foreign singers around at that time.

Vikram Hazra had told me, "Don't even think about the album a week before you record it. Go plant some trees around the ashram."

I did my best to follow his words of wisdom as he was one of the best musicians in the Art of Living with several of his own albums in the Divine Shop. Everyone loves Vikram.

Prasana and I headed to the studio in his car on one of the last days in July, getting to know each other and sharing some laughs.

When I got to the studio, the guitar was off tune, probably from lack of use, and for some strange reason one of the strings had a buzzing sound.

Meeting the professional Indian musicians was uncomfortable at first, suffice it to say they were as scared of me as I was of them.

We decided to record my original song, "*Om Namah Shivaya*," a cool and easy tune to play… and that's when chaos began. I couldn't hear anything through my headphones, and the room seemed stale and musty. The musicians waited for me to start, set to play live, which was the way we recorded the album, minus the lead and backup vocals.

I started to freak out. "Damn, this is too much. I'm packing it up and going back to the peaceful ashram." I was stressed out of my element. My mind ping-ponged between issues and guilt. I was anything other than ready to record an album in India.

Just then, Prasana walked into the middle recording room I was in and said, "Jeremy, Gurudev just called, and he wanted to give you a message: 'Just relax, have fun, and let go, just like you are in satsang.'"

Sure enough (and after years, these occurrences no longer surprise me), lightness arrived, filling the room, and things started to click, gel, and come together. The session was underway.

We recorded three songs before I was invited into the mixing room to listen to the tracks. Dancing in the control room with a smile, I was surprised to hear how full one of my songs sounded. The guy on the drum pad was rather enthusiastic, not totally a good thing, as it sounded a bit like a cheesy soda commercial after a while, but I loved watching him jam.

The musicians seemed to enjoy this session, different from what they were accustomed to. They arrived an hour late, took an hour-and-a-half lunch, and left right on time. Oh, India.

One-and-a-half days at Silver Studios in Bangalore, and my new album was complete—well, almost.

On my last day at the ashram, Gurudev invited me into the car driving him from his kutir to the VM. This invitation had me jumping with joy. He sat in the passenger seat, and I was in the back. No one else was in the car besides the driver, and we talked the whole time.

"So, Jeremy, what are your plans now that you are done with college?"

"Gurudev, I am leaving to go back home tomorrow. What should I do back in America?"

"What do you want to do?"

"Well," I poured out the overflowing dreams for my future, "I would like to be a full-time Art of Living teacher in university towns, staying a month at a time, blending with the students, playing concerts, and teaching courses. I'll start with Princeton, staying with a family, then Boston and join Radhika Prabu and her team, and hit the West Coast in the winter. What do you think?"

"Yes, this is a great idea. Just talk to Jeff when you get back and he can help you. What about your college loans, how much do you owe now?"

"Probably over $30,000."

"Oh, how are you going to pay that?"

"Well, I can pay the minimum for some time, then once I get a job, I can pay more, but I really want to be full-time now and do seva. May I, Gurudev?"

"Yes. Good, good, good..."

And so my second trip to India came to an end. Like the first, I experienced mountains of growth, glory, blessings, miracles, music, friends, love, belonging, and Indian madness, too. I love India.

I had no idea when I would return. All I could concentrate on was being a full-time Art of Living teacher, going around to various colleges, spreading this knowledge to the youth of the world, and making music. I felt like there was so much in front of me. The sky was a trampoline—the universe was the limit.

CHAPTER TWENTY-TWO

Back to America

The more content you are, I tell you, miracles will
be abundant in your life. How many of you have
experienced miracles in your life? If someone is not
experiencing miracles, don't worry, it will happen
to you too. This is the beauty of this path; there
is an abundance of everything. Be on the path
and bring this fragrance to many more people.
—Gurudev Sri Sri Ravi Shankar

I had thought my return in 2001 to Atlanta from India in the dead of winter traumatized my brain with culture shock. Walking through the San Francisco airport in August 2004, after half a year in China and India, not only shocked my brain but also reminded me of the stark contrast between Asia and America.

Teenage girls passed me, clothed in cut-outs and too tight, too short, neon outfits. I thought I was at a chest convention. And then the college-looking ones... they reeked of estrogen in high volumes. My heart raced, my skin was warm with signs of blushing, I was quite embarrassed, taken aback by what I was seeing in the form of females—could I have forgotten what it was like to live in the United States? One quick reflection reminded me of just how innocent, conservative, and shy Asian women could be. Call me crazy, but I was missing that natural beauty now.

I was back, and it was indeed time for me to adjust.

I needed a headquarters in the area to get my grounding and complete the paperwork to be a full-time Art of Living teacher.

Sandeep Sharma, a kind, cool professional from India and his wife generously offered to let me stay in their apartment in Fremont.

As good as it feels to write at this moment in my life, imagine how phenomenally cool it was to say, "Yes, Gurudev has blessed me to become a full-time traveling Art of Living teacher now." Oh, the ego was dancing a marathon, my head swelled with glee and hot air when I spoke of this. I was now (in the hollows of my own mind) *extra* special in the organization, and in the eyes and heart of my guru.

Sandeep was a superstar—and still is. He was vital in helping me to purchase my first cell phone (yes, I felt like one of the last people I knew to get one), taking me out to eat and to shop, and more. Clearly, I was building this beast of my now post-college life up.

I got in contact with the treasurer of the Art of Living in America, Jeff Houk, who Gurudev had told me to contact about the details of becoming a full-time teacher. The ease of processing paperwork, filling out forms, and getting reimbursements for course-related expenses seemed natural. I was stoked, excited about this new role ahead.

My wild mind dreamt of being on renowned college campuses, almost feeling like a student again. I thought of the hundreds of kids I'd meet daily and the introductory talks on the Art of Living course for college-age folks.

The schedule of classes would be matched with a calendar full of concerts I'd give on campus greens, student centers, auditoriums, coffee shops, and even those smoky East Coast bars. I'd bounce across the country and stay for at least a month at a time in various locations. Once again, I thought Gurudev had blessed me with the coolest service project in the States.

"It sounds like a Pepsi commercial." My friend, Ryan Villasenor, echoed my thoughts after hearing a few songs off the demo of my new album, *Sound in Silence*, at his home in San Francisco.

He referred to those electronic drum pads widely used in Indian films and commercials. Yes, the drummer in the studio had a field day, but it sounded like far off fluff. Not the quality I was hoping for.

Ryan, an awesome flamenco guitarist and recording engineer, played gigs around the Bay Area and had recorded some of the Art of Living musicians I looked up to, mainly Divya Prabha and Daniel White. He suggested we get the master tracks from Bangalore and record live drums over it.

I was all for it. I got the okay from Prasana at the ashram and received the music soon after.

Two months later, on a pleasant Cupertino Saturday afternoon, one of Ryan's talented friends laid down the drum tracks for most of the songs in one take. I sat on the couch and watched the music unfold. I had a lot of faith that this could be a great album. I sent the drum tracks back to Prasana and let it go.

Gurudev's schedule had him in Los Angeles the first week I returned to the States. And even after all the precious time with him in India, I longed to see him. That longing is always there. On the eve of seeing him, something special starts burning in your heart. If you'd won the opportunity to meet your hero, your dream fantasy of spending time with someone you look up to, the delightful tenseness you'd feel inside would be similar.

A satsang that night for everyone who had taken the Art of Living course was being held downtown. Before the satsang we were at Verna's, a devotee's home. Gurudev often visited her Los Angeles home, and we'd shared intimate times with him in her living room and backyard looking over the canyon.

Jeff Houk told me, with a sense of excitement, that he would talk to Gurudev about his plans for me being full-time this season. Colors seemed more vivid, voices more in harmony around me.

When Jeff came out of the room, his face was stoic. He pulled me aside, and I knew something was wrong.

"Jeremy, Gurudev does not remember telling you to become a full-time teacher."

I'd heard Jeff speak, but the words didn't make sense. A few icebergs floated down from the Arctic into the L.A. area that night and were pressed against my body—I was frozen in time. Taking a jagged breath to melt myself out of the ice, I defensively responded, "What? That's absurd! Is this some kind of joke, Jeff?"

"Jeremy, please relax. I am sure there must be some confusion. Tell me the details of the conversation you had with Gurudev, and where you were."

I couldn't believe I had to give this information as if I'd made up the story. I couldn't believe that my guru, my master, who knew all things always, and about me, too, was not recalling this wonderful conversation we had had just over a week ago in India.

Calming myself with some deep breaths, I said, "I was in the car with him on a ride from his kutir to the VM at the Bangalore Ashram. He asked me what I wanted to do now, and I told him that I wanted to be a full-time Art of Living teacher, going to various college towns, spending at least a month in each area." The words gushed quickly and breathlessly.

"Okay, Jeremy, let me go and speak with him again."

As soon as Jeff slipped away, Matt came over and asked me what was going on. He'd seen the conversation with Jeff. I told him, and he couldn't believe it, either. I waited the wait of ages where each second felt like a monstrous click of a grandfather clock. What felt like an endless eternity was about ten minutes.

"Jeremy," Jeff called me to a corner of the room, "I talked with Gurudev, and he does remember the car ride and conversation, but he would like you to get a job for a while, pay your college loans, and then after some time, you can talk with him again about being full-time."

Oh... my... God! My friends, those icebergs melted into fiery hot pitchforks of doom, poking, stabbing me, setting myself ablaze in burning fashion.

"What do you mean, 'Get a job for a while'? Is this some practical joke?!" I couldn't comprehend why the future had been yanked from me. I was bereft, lost, stranded in the endless present with no directions.

"Jeremy, I know how you are feeling now. Please see this from a bigger perspective." His words were not getting through. "I have seen

317

Gurudev change his mind with many people over the years, and it is always for the best of the devotee. He will be out shortly; you can talk to him."

I'd been thrown back in the metaphorical frying pan of Gurudev Sri Sri Ravi Shankar—in the master's creative kitchen. I was burning to a crisp in the hot oil of disappointment and confusion. I was feverish and wanted to talk to Gurudev.

The twenty-minute wait before he emerged from his room was like counting seconds on an asthma-induced sleepless childhood night. Could this be happening? Matt came over to console me, but I was beyond empathy. No knowledge point seemed applicable. My breathing was wild and shallow as my mind leaped violently, performing perpetual jumping jacks.

And here comes the master of masters, the king of cool, the miracle maker and the one who had me screaming inside, shaken and stirred. Gurudev walked outside to the backyard, and we followed him. As he walked continually back and forth, from one end of the yard to the next in a gentle rhythm, I moved next to him and pleaded my case like a spoiled kid asking for his special toy.

"Gurudev, what do you mean that you want me to get a job now? You gave me the blessings just last week to be a full-time teacher."

"Hmm…" sounded his vintage-innocent reply. "No, no, it's okay, just go and get a job for a while, pay your college loans, then we can talk again after some time."

His words burned on my skin like a pail of ice water. "But, Gurudev, the school year has already started. How can I get a kindergarten teaching job anywhere now?"

"No, no, you can get a job."

"Gurudev, my sister is a teacher, she has been working for the past two weeks. There will not be any teaching positions open now. What am I going to do, where will I live?" I felt devastated, perched on the edge of a dark bottomless hole.

"Don't worry, just get a job, it will all be fine."

Just then Dvorah, the comic and bigger-than-life "Shut-up" guru chimed in, "Oh, a kindergarten teacher; Jeremy you will be fantastic with those little kiddos."

I felt barricaded in a windowless room of stifling heat with thick walls closing in, even though I stood outside. I couldn't appreciate or thank her for the sweet comment. And Gurudev merely shuffled away into a car, and everyone followed him to the satsang.

Of the countless satsangs I'd attended, this one was like no other, as I sat in the corner of the hall, burning in disappointment. My ego hysterically screaming, my mind wandered into nothingness, my heart felt heavy, and I couldn't move.

Matt came over from time to time with feeble attempts to break through my funk, but nothing worked.

Gurudev taught us from day one, "Expectations reduce the joy in life." Well, this expectation had totally depleted the joy from me. He was right, he always is. No matter how much I knew and was living the knowledge, living the art, I could not accept this situation. Could I even call myself an Art of Living teacher? I was angry with Gurudev.

This nearly two-hour satsang was an eternity, and I was overwhelmed with the vacuum of a future with no direction. I'd been shoved out of a fast-moving train in the middle of a black, fog-drenched nowhere.

Finally, after I prayed again and again, going through all the mental madness one could sum up inside a human brain, Gurudev began exiting the stage.

Remember Natalie Wood as a child in *Miracle on 34th Street*, toward the end of the movie, where she sat dejected, staring out the car window, saying, "I believe, I believe"? I understood her words much more clearly now.

Gurudev headed to the exit door, meeting and blessing people along the way. I knew what I had to do. I busted out the door early and waited at the elevator for him.

Inside the elevator, with only two or three devotees, I sounded one last wail of pity to my master, "Gurudev, what am I going to do? I had my heart set on being a full-time volunteer!"

In all his brilliant glory, he pinched my cheek while patting me on the back, like a mother comforting, blessing her adored baby. This amount of love was unbearable. The blistering anger I'd felt for the past three hours melted away like dewdrops in the sun, like hate in the light of love. I was coming back to life.

As the elevator came to a stop and we got out, there with smiling faces stood the San Diego devotees: Kinjal and his sister Mrunmayi, Tom, Ashish, Savitha, and a few others.

Gurudev looked right into my eyes and said with all the love of the universe, "Just pick a city, find a job, and know that I am always with you."

With the frenzied excitement of a child granted permission to go to Disneyland, I exclaimed, "I'll move back to San Diego!"

The San Diego group in front of me exploded in a roar of celebration and warm welcome. My heart rejoiced at the sweet moment—me, my guru, my spiritual family, and another fantastic example of a lesson in awesome opposites orchestrated by Gurudev. These grueling three hours felt like the ones I had experienced the first time I met Gurudev in nearby Irvine, seven-and-a-half years before, rocketing from the depths of human despair to the peak of acceptance and brilliant view of the universe.

And once again, Gurudev's words rang true, "A master or a guru does not remove the doubt, but he creates more doubt. The more you burn in the fire of doubt, the more strong you come out to be." *Jai Guru Dev!*

My first week back in San Diego, I found myself on Bobby's door-step. I gave a quick staccato knock. The original Pennsylvania duo was back in action. Bobby had never moved from the beach, minus stints at our ashrams in Canada and Bangalore. Cliché warning: Bobby would give me the shirt off his back... if only it would fit.

I was dead broke, and Bobby took me in. You know the depth of friendship when doors open without questions. I slept on his couch.

Bobby was just the person I needed to hang with during this transitional period. We knew each other well, and there was never anything to hide. The man cooked for me, hooked me up with food from the vegan restaurant he was running, and lent me his car to get to job interviews.

Acting quickly and praying harder, it was do-or-die time on the coast of California—just like those magnificent October days in 1996. Either land a job and an apartment or move back home with Mom and Dad, and I swore this was not an option as a college graduate with a teaching degree. With never any room for doubt, I kept my head down and focused on job searching.

While in India, I'd missed the special announcement of one of my favorite bands, Ween, coming to San Diego to play a show. And not any old show, this was at Cane's Bar & Grill, steps from the sand on Mission Beach—right next to the roller coaster. This was walking distance from both of my past beach apartments. I could find this venue blindfolded. And here I was at the end of September, both jobless and broke as a joke. Even if I had the forty dollars for the show, it was long sold out in a venue that squeezed in seven hundred people.

On the day of the concert, I showed up outside the joint around 4:00 p.m. I didn't have a plan, but I knew I needed to see this band once again at this point in my life. I had to be inside.

I simply walked in the front door, behind one of the workers, sat down as the band ran through a sound check, and acted like I was with the band. That lasted ten solid minutes until I was thrown out by one of the band's crew. Sneaking in—out of the question. My dreams were shattered.

After a refreshing walk on the beach, I returned to the venue and saw the early line of concertgoers, each with happy smiles, tickets in hand. I did the Grateful Dead thing, walking along the line with the index finger of my right hand raised, asking, "Anyone have an extra ticket?" Even if they did, I had no cash.

It's known as a *Miracle* to be gifted a concert ticket in a Grateful Dead (and now, any jam band) parking lot. Goes along with the GD tune, "I Need a Miracle." I didn't receive a miracle ticket from anyone in line that day.

Time ticked on; the show would be starting soon. I closed my eyes, prayed as I always do, but this time for a kind-of-selfish item—a concert ticket. After the soul-searching moments of silence in prayer,

321

I took a deep breath, exhaled, and walked to the ticket counter. With these words and a smile, I looked straight into the eyes of the woman working behind the counter: "Hello, I am absolutely broke, and I need to see Ween tonight. Do you have an extra ticket for tonight's show, please?"

With a returned smile, she picked up one solitary ticket, and without any questions, she handed it to me saying, "Enjoy the show."

I said, "Thank you, and God bless you."

I walked into the show, right to the very front of the stage, with the widest smile and a humongous amount of gratitude for the music *Miracle* I had just received. When the lights went down, I rocked out hardcore in the front row for three straight hours. Ween was on fire that night—and so was I.

Then the masterful words of Gurudev rang true again, "Don't be surprised if miracles happen, be surprised if they don't!"

Given that it was September with schools already in session, plus my only being certified to teach in Georgia, getting a full-time teaching job was not looking good. I interviewed for a lot of positions, most of which I was overqualified for, like afterschool programs and pre-school gigs. Keeping the faith, praying hard, and hitting the pavement, I interviewed for a job as a campus supervisor at a middle school, around a half hour from La Jolla, where Bobby lived.

The interview included the school principal, two vice principals, five other candidates, and me. This was serious interview stuff. I'd never experienced a panel interview.

Not wearing contact lenses at the time due to expenses, I went to the interview with my old pair of glasses, which were noticeably cracked. At the last minute, I put them in my pocket. Now I was nearly blind! What an idiot I was.

They had a list of questions asked in round-robin style. A job interview is never relaxing, but amp this up a million megawatts: being judged among eight others. I was desperate for employment. I used the breathing techniques while the others eloquently answered around me. I felt not at my best, until the last question, where they asked me about the root cause of teenage violence in school.

Thank you, Gurudev, I thought as I felt his grace in the room, the wind of love pounding against my heart.

With skill, I gave what could have been an introductory talk on the Art of Living's program for teens, the Youth Empowerment Seminar, or "YES! For Schools." Like many times before when sharing this precious knowledge, my words came out light and poignant. This is the best part about having a guru—accessing this awesome pool of energy and letting it flow through you like crashing waves of crystal blue water down heavenly Hawaiian falls when you need it.

From the looks on the administrators' faces and their avid attention, I knew I had them. I walked out confidently, putting my glasses back on with a smile. I began to sing the Johnny Nash song, "I Can See Clearly Now."

The next day, driving up to San Francisco for the weekend with Matt, I got the call on my cell phone with the job offer. I happily accepted.

An outdoors, sun-drenched, Southern California middle school campus: it was a cool job with teens and a good share of trouble. My job included supervising students outside before school, at lunch, and after school; supervising the in-school suspension program; and I would also be called on to substitute teach in various classrooms. I really enjoyed my first job out of college, a rewarding chance to engage with students, but there was still a craving for my own classroom.

I got to know the students quickly. A lot of the boys were younger brothers of high school gang members bordering two sides: San Diego and L.A. They were not allowed to wear anything that mentioned either city by name or sports logos. I connected with these teens instantly, and they opened up, talking and sharing with me—but sometimes that wasn't so good.

The worst part about the job was wearing the yellow shirt with "Security" on the back. Oh, the kids had a field day with that one, and I laughed along with them. But I felt I was babysitting sometimes, not teaching.

The money was not great at the middle school. I needed a second job, and quickly. I answered an ad for a nanny position... yes, I was again a "manny" in San Diego. The job was afterschool care of a two-year-old Chinese boy, and it was tons of fun. After a few weeks, their neighbors asked if they could have their same-age boy join in, like two puppies keeping each other company. I agreed. Though not great money, it added up and kept me afloat.

After two months of hard work, sacrifice, kind people helping me out, and diligence, I was back on my feet in the United States. It's my belief that a guru puts his students through these types of situations to watch how they apply the knowledge they have been given, and most of all, to see them shine on the other side of it. I think my eyes sparkled with that shine by December.

In Gurudev's own words, "Many problems have come, many problems have been solved, and each problem has enriched life in some way, has brought up some strength in you."

I got my California teaching credential in November and started looking for jobs around the state, some in the San Francisco Bay Area. I found the perfect gig—a six-month kindergarten teaching job, just across the highway from Fremont, where Sandeep and many other Art of Living friends lived. I flew up for the interview at the beginning of December and I left feeling confident.

Savitha, my friend and fellow musician in San Diego, asked me to drive with her cross-county to relocate near her boyfriend in Boston for Christmas. Road trip! I readily agreed and a week before Christmas we were on the great American highways, driving from sunny Southern California, smack-dab into the middle of winter. I planned to fly from Boston to Atlanta to spend Christmas with my family. After the holiday, I would fly back to San Diego.

During the first hours of the trip, I received a phone call from the principal at the school I'd interviewed at.

"Jeremy, we were very impressed during your interview and would like you to join our school in January."

Sweet! What a blessing, my first real teaching job out of college!

Twice now in three months I had gotten a call for a job while on a road trip. Each one was an unbelievable "get outta here" moment—it makes me want to drive across the States right now. I don't need a job, but maybe my dream girl will call and propose to me!

The soundtrack of the trip included Nelson's "On the Road Again," the Grateful Dead anthem "Truckin,'" and "America" by Simon and Garfunkel.

I volunteered to do most of the driving on the trip. Our itinerary took us to various friends' homes for shelter, even with Bill and his family in Chicago, and, of course, Taylor town. Delayed because of snowstorms in Ohio, I made it home to Atlanta for Christmas night. My family was disappointed at the minimal time together, but at least I made it home and was glad I did. This would be my last holiday visit for a few years.

My adventurous and momentous year began and ended in California. I graduated with honors from Kennesaw State University. I became a certified teacher and an Art of Living teacher while learning, sharing, and making music in three diverse countries. My excitement to return to northern California to teach school and Art of Living was another dream come true. With a prayer of gratitude, I went to sleep and dreamed of endless possibilities for the upcoming year.

CHAPTER TWENTY-THREE

Sittin' on the Dock of the Bay

Reason and faith are completely opposite, yet they are an integral part of life. Reason is reeling in the known. Faith is moving in the unknown. Reason is repetition. Faith is exploration. Reason is routine. Faith is adventure. While reasoning keeps you sane and grounded, miracles cannot happen without faith. Faith takes you beyond limitations.
—Gurudev Sri Sri Ravi Shankar

The first week of January 2005 was a whirlwind. I resigned from my job at the middle school and weaseled my way out of my studio apartment with no time for a thirty-day notice. As a result, the landlord kept the deposit.

I packed my car, kissed San Diego goodbye, and set out on I-5 North, straight to Fremont. I was invited to stay with Neha, a kind Art of Living teacher, wife, and super mommy.

The Bay Area is uniquely different. People who live in California know there are distinct venues between southern and northern areas of the state in the energy, climate, people, music, traffic... well, actually, the traffic is the same.

Arriving in Fremont, I couldn't help but smile and sense positive energy around me, looking back at the past season's ups and downs and now this shining gold prize on the other side. Did Gurudev know all along? Was this his plan, his granted wish and blessing to me? I easily think so.

I was ready to make this new life as special as can be. First teaching job, new city, new home, and tons of Art of Living seva and activities ahead of me. I could be as full-time as I wanted to be with service, as long as I showed up to work each day. Life…

My new job in the Bay Area was teaching five-year-olds. I loved the job and living the dream of having my own classroom. It was a class full of bubbling personalities, singing, dancing, laughing, books, playing jokes, and more. It set the tone for a healthy and positive classroom environment.

With a little charm and a desire to make a difference, I was able to persuade a small music store in Berkeley to donate some musical instruments. Things were moving now.

After two weeks, I hadn't found my own place. Rentals are expensive in the area and, like always, I'm picky. Praying extra hard one day, I did my daily search on Craigslist, a great venue for apartment hunting. I found a lady looking to sublet her place for the last six months of her lease while she moved into a new townhome.

Being cautious of an all-American male in his twenties, she asked if I drank and partied. I explained that I did not drink, do drugs, or smoke, as I was into yoga, deep breathing, and meditation.

As had happened many times over the years, she became excited and interested. I told her I was a student of Gurudev Sri Sri Ravi Shankar and was one of his Art of Living teachers. She told me she'd taken the Art of Living course a few years ago and loved the breathing technique, Sudarshan Kriya! She granted me the place right then and there.

The almost brand new, third-floor, one-bedroom apartment was in a perfect location. It sat across the street from the BART train station in Fremont, and get this, was in the same complex where the local satsang is held each Thursday night. *Jai Guru Dev*! Could you imagine? After those shabby and expensive places, I'd checked out over the past two weeks, waiting for the payoff, I got it. And to top it all off, she gave it to me $500 cheaper than the going rate.

Being with Gurudev, I don't rate these happenings as "big miracles" or "small miracles," I simply call them miracles.

Gurudev always tells us to do our work, have faith and all will be provided, adding, "Faith is realizing that you always get what you need. Faith is giving the Divine a chance to act."

I started teaching the Art of Living course with Neha in Fremont and another great Art of Living teacher, Kalpana, who lived in Berkeley. I taught the course at San Jose State University—and for the first time ever, I taught alone. I also facilitated two or three Sudarshan Kriya follow-up sessions a week. I enjoyed meeting all the diverse people who came to practice the powerful breathing technique.

My spare hours were filled with friends and hanging out. I took the epic and winding ride down Highway 17 to Santa Cruz to play music with my friend Adam and visit other Art of Living friends there. I also drove out to Sacramento State University to play shows.

To add extra dark chocolate icing to an already scrumptious Spring 2005 cake, Gurudev was coming to the Bay Area for a public talk and a one-day meditation course at the beginning of May. Life was good.

Back in China, I never thought my life back home in the States would be this satisfying and fulfilling. Life's little surprises make you smile, and one's guru can make it that much sweeter with rocking style.

"Jeremy, are you playing a concert in San Jose next week?"

"Yes, Dad, how did you know that?"

"Aunt Mary just called and said she saw your name on a poster at her senior citizen meeting."

Wow, what a trip. That's right, I had a relative here in the Bay Area, and I got connected to her via a poster for an Art of Living concert I played with Ryan. Dad had been telling me to get in touch with her for the past three months. I can't make these things up. I called Aunt Mary and we talked, catching up on our lives. She agreed to come to my concert, a concert for peace that included a wide range of talented musicians.

While on stage, I changed the words on the spot to the Beatles tune "Let It Be," singing the line, "Aunt Mary comes to me, shining like an angel, let it be…" she even looked the part. It was a sweet, storybook moment.

The Art of Living organized a tsunami walk to benefit the victims of the recent natural disasters in Southeast Asia. We worked together with the community, creating a nice event at the park in Fremont.

I volunteered to play and had the perfect idea: invite my kindergarten students to sing with me. After the 5K walk, my students joined me on stage and rocked our classroom standards: "The Mighty Quinn," "I Believe I Can Fly," "This Little Light of Mine," and a few others. The joyous sounds of young children singing can't help but put smiles on faces. That, for many reasons, was a cherished day.

I talked to my close childhood friend, Dave Weisenfluh, a lot that season. He was going through a hard time back home in Taylor; living at home, not able to find a steady job, and flirting, or maybe going steady with, the party scene there. He needed a change. I invited him to come live with me and take the Art of Living course I was going to teach at the beginning of May at the UC Santa Cruz, just to get away from the mess he was swimming in. He thought about it and agreed to come at the end of April.

Dave was blown away at the life I had created. It was a bit awkward when I told him there was no alcohol, drugs, or meat allowed in the apartment. I guess I hadn't explained much to him. "How about tuna fish?"

I made a scrunched face as if I'd just stubbed my toe at the pool. "Sorry, Dave, no."

He accepted my lifestyle with all due respect, and I thanked him for that.

During the ride down to Santa Cruz, I surprised him by cranking up "Estimated Prophet" by the Grateful Dead as we approached the Pacific Ocean, with its fitting lyrics about the brilliant California coast. His eyes lit in wide wonder when we approached the glistening waters of the Pacific. That magnificent moment is cemented inside my heart's walls.

The Art of Living course was exceptionally sweet. It was at UC Santa Cruz where I'd played several times, and it is cool, unique, and marvelous. It makes the title "Hippie School" seem distinguished, with its fine forest surroundings.

With Gurudev coming to the Bay Area the week after, there was nothing like teaching his course and inviting all the participants to his public talk in San Francisco and a one-day course in Palo Alto. The course went off without a hitch, its powerful energy and messages alike. People had fantastic experiences. Dave noted the phenomenal sense of belonging he felt with the university students in only six days. And this could rightfully be the best part of all our courses—one love.

"Jeremy, we would like you to sing on stage at Gurudev's public talk in San Francisco?"

My inner self screamed silently, *Wait a minute, Jani. Can you repeat that so I can record it and dance to it all night long when I get home?*

What came out of my mouth? "Yes, it would be my great pleasure."

Another one of my biggest dreams was coming true—to play on stage at Gurudev's event. Two years ago, I harbored jealousy for Von, who was always up there playing music. I realized that my wish had manifested by healing my relationship with him. Once again, I felt free from that self-torment I put myself through.

I got together with Jason Ranjit Parmar, the professional drummer who'd laid down the drum tracks on my *Sound in Silence* album. We practiced one time up in Marin County a couple of days before the event.

I took three days off work, shined up my Taylor guitar, and was as nervous as a baby bird about to jump out of the nest for the first time. My stomach was in knots, and Dave said it was, indeed, nerves.

What a crew in my car that day, driving around San Francisco: myself, Matt from Irvine (and of India fame), Bobby from San Diego, Dave; three boys from the Triboro area of Scranton on board. Anything was possible.

This would be Dave's first time at an event like this, and, more importantly, his first time seeing Gurudev. Matt and Bobby (seasoned vets) would take care of him while I was on stage. On stage with Gurudev... those words felt incredible, a sweet dream coming true with my best friends in the audience to share the experience.

Two hours before the show, Jani, one of the main volunteers, told me Gurudev would like Von to lead the music tonight. I was frozen, shocked, with a strange look on my face. Where was the hidden camera? Had I not learned about the ruse of expectations?

Doing my best to accept the situation, I kindly told Jani that we needed a youthful energy in this special place tonight. He agreed to go back and talk to Gurudev and Von.

Like the ego-smashing episode in Los Angles in August, I couldn't believe this was happening again. I admit there was a great deal of ego in playing tonight, as all musicians have to an extent. Was I burning inside? Yes, I was.

Gurudev didn't make me burn for long this time, though, sending Jani back with the okay for me to play.

Jason and I created the music as folks shuffled into the hall. Some friends joined us as backup singers on stage. After an opening number, I broke out something different and played my humble rendition of the Bob Marley song "Three Little Birds," a fitting song for the crowd. People sang along. After a tune or two, I blasted into my original, "*Hari Hari Om*," a popular song in our groups. Out of the song, I slid into another Marley tune "One Love—People Get Ready," or at least the chorus—in fine satsang fashion.

Just then the energy in the room shifted; people suddenly rose to their feet, looking with wide eyes to the back of the packed hall. Emerging from the doors was Gurudev in his definitive whites and graceful stroll.

Jason, the drummer, said quietly, "Keep it steady."

When Gurudev was feet away from the stage, I transitioned back into "*Hari Hari Om*," and the place was ablaze. Gurudev took his seat then looked over at me singing. My mind flashed through images of a little boy in my backyard in Taylor. His smile told me he was proud of me and trusted me at the music helm in front of two thousand people, most to hear this extraordinary man for the first time.

While Gurudev walked in from one side, Von had walked in from the other. He sat with a friend in the front row. For a brief instant our eyes locked as the intense energy of the room surrounded us. I saw sincere blessings in his smile. This was big. Being on stage was his territory, and he probably wanted to be up there. His smile, though, was comforting.

I played on. After another song or two, Gurudev opened his eyes out of meditation, smiled, tapped the microphone, and addressed the crowd, answering questions from the basket.

Sitting there in front of the crowd, my legs went numb, but I couldn't move. I had to stick it out. A half hour later, Gurudev asked us to close our eyes for a guided meditation. I joyfully and silently stretched my legs while meditating. It was a sweet, deep meditation. The place was still, needle-drop stillness, with passionate energy. I crossed my legs into the sitting position just before he asked us to open our eyes.

A little more talking, joking, and knowledge, and then Gurudev looked over at me with a smile and said, "Should we sing another song?"

Yes! I fired into Divya Prabha's song "*Radhe, Radhe,*" an Art of Living standard. This powerful piece was one I could really sing and rock to. Gurudev sang along and moved with the upbeat music a bit before he walked off the stage to greet and bless the crowd.

There is an immeasurable amount of joy and celebration with that song wherever it was sung. Magical and heightened, the hundreds who chose not to run after Gurudev sang in ecstasy—we were jamming on the good vibes of a great night with our master. I was grateful to be a part of it all.

After I came off the stage, Von met me with a smile and a hearty, "Great job, Jeremy, you played well tonight." That comment, after all I had been through mentally and emotionally with him, was extra special. Thanks, Von.

Dave pushed his way through the tough crowd to shake Gurudev's hand. I was pleased to hear he had met him. He enjoyed the whole event.

After a few more memorable days with Gurudev in Palo Alto, life went back to normal (whatever that means). Finishing the last month of the school year, I was interviewing for various teaching positions for the Fall. Because Dave didn't find the job he was looking for, he headed home to Pennsylvania.

My heart jumped for joy upon hearing that Gurudev would be having a public talk at Emory University in Atlanta. For an extra dose of delight, it would be on Mom's birthday! I quickly made some calls and got two tickets for Mom and Dad. They were excited to go, and I was thrilled for them, yet I still wished I could be there. I asked one of the local devotes to take care of them, and they got to sit in the front, too. Wow, their second time meeting Gurudev!

I recently interviewed both Mom and Dad about both occasions. Dad shares, "After the talk, I worked my way through the crowd and finally shook his hand and said, 'Sri Sri, I am Jeremy's father, and this is my wife Rose, today is her birthday.' He said, 'Happy Birthday to your wonderful wife.' Then he said, 'Jeremy is a great man!' He then thanked us for coming to the talk. From the two times that I met him, I found that he is a very charismatic person, a good communicator, and a humble man."

In Mom's words, "I loved him; he was very soft-spoken and relaxed. He spoke about love and the importance of world peace. I could have stayed there for hours; it was a happy time for me. I love Sri Sri. Dad was pushing his way through others to see Sri Sri, and then we talked to him for a couple of minutes. Dad started the conversation with, 'Jeremy is our son.' It was a lovely birthday gift for me, plus Sri Sri wished me a happy birthday."

Ryan had chosen to step away from his job at Bank of America and to dedicate the next year as a full-time volunteer teacher with the Art of Living. Only a year ago, that had been my intention. Although one side of me—probably my mother in me—wanted to seal the deal on another kindergarten teaching job for the next school year, the other side—probably my brother in me—wanted to volunteer full-time, travel, teach, play music, and be free to attend a special and unique celebration that was going to take place in February 2006.

The big buzz in the Art of Living was the Silver Jubilee, the foundation's twenty-fifth anniversary and one-world family celebration on a grand scale. Held in Bangalore, India, on February 17–19, 2006, at an airfield—the whole world would be there. Gurudev was estimating two-and-a-half million people from over 150 countries. Would I miss this? Not a fat chance.

I had some great interviews around the Bay Area in late May and early June 2005. I gave them my best, but without any feverishness, knowing deep down inside I wanted to be free from a full-time job. Ultimately, I turned down some very cool gigs and was free to roam, teach, sing, and serve that summer. I was able to defer my student loans until I was working again.

A new program blossomed that spring in the Art of Living in America, inspired by the Indian tradition of *Padyatra*, a pilgrimage on foot, as was happening with Art of Living teachers around India. The program equated to volunteers going to cities that had little or no presence of our courses and service projects.

On a sunny Saturday afternoon in San Jose, Rajshree Patel held an inspiring meeting to get the program going further. Feeling unusually shy, I sat against the wall in the back corner and purposely stayed in the background. I had only seen Rajshree before at the California events.

She started talking about longtime Art of Living teacher and musician, Philip Frazier, saying how some musicians in the foundation have a cool way of talking about our programs with people. And to shock the wits out of me, like a great white shark lunging out of the sea—she called me out. "…and Jeremy, too. Where's Jeremy sitting?"

I was immediately blasted, not with a scary strength, but with a most welcome blast of love and attention. I couldn't believe she was talking about me. For those who know Rajshree, she is powerful, loving, devoted to Gurudev, and a woman with great powers of insight, while reading your mind, face, and gestures. She holds a powerfully cool stature.

She continued to use me as a positive example in the meeting, and the result was something beautiful. I decided I would join Ryan in a summer of service, and this program was going to be it. Rajshree mentioned Portland as the city to work in a dynamic team, and with my history there, I committed in front of the group to be on the team.

Ryan and I traveled to Portland and teamed up with an unlikely match—an older, silly, kind-hearted, crazy, devoted, funny (and did I say crazy?) lady named Sara Fix. I knew Sara, though not well, from the Tahoe days. A fourth member of our team in the Bay area was there to help us with paperwork and whatnot back on the home front.

Our main goal was to present our youth course, the Youth Empowerment Seminar, or "YES! for Schools," to the youth of Portland, mainly disadvantaged youth due to family, social, and economic circumstances. Playing concerts was my side focus, too. I was happy to help in any way I could.

I received word that Gurudev had released my album *Sound in Silence* on June 5, 2005 at the Bangalore Ashram. Quite naturally, I was as nervous as I was excited. I couldn't imagine what these tracks would sound like with the live drums on most of the songs.

I was scared, excited, and curious when one of the devotees from San Jose State University brought me a couple of copies. I was blown away at first, then got into the flaws. Don't we all have an editor on our shoulder?

In Prasana's own golden words to me four months later, "I don't care what other people say—I think it's a very sweet album." Thanks, Prasana.

"*Hari Hari Om*" came out the best, by far and wide.

Ryan and I did our thing, playing all kinds of shows, me on acoustic guitar and singing, him backing me up on acoustic and electric guitars. As a bonus, Ryan played his fantastic flamenco music, to everyone's delight.

Ryan and I shared a room in Sara's home. It was tight quarters, and the seva was full-on. Suffice to say, Ryan and I could have used some time away from each other. We laughed, fought, rocked, busted each other, busted Sara to no end, and overall had a terrific summer in seva working toward our programs in rehab homes for teens.

We took a trip up the I-5 freeway to Seattle for some shows and courses. Ryan and I played an impromptu gig at the Space Needle. A whole camp full of school-aged kids showed up with smiles and the camp counselor asked me what we were doing.

I replied: "We're having a free kids' concert." We had the kiddos singing along and invited some risk-takers on stage to sing the cool songs. My specialty.

After a month on this service program in the Pacific Northwest, it was time for further training… 2,700 miles away.

In the middle of July, both Ryan and I were headed to the Canadian Ashram, which is two hours by bus from Montreal. This would be my first time visiting there, though Ryan had been several times. I was going to attend the YES! For Schools teacher training (to be able to teach our course for teenagers). This would be my fifth two-week teacher-training course, and in attendance would be an all-star lineup of close friends, including Bill Herman, and my close friend from New York, Emily Peck. The best part about the adventure was Gurudev would be there most of the time.

Here's one for the ages: The morning before the day we were to fly to Montreal, I asked one simple question, "Do we need our passports to fly into Canada?"

A few phone calls later, the answer was a resounding, yes! The funny thing was neither Ryan nor I had a clue we needed them, and they were both packed away in a storage space in the Bay Area. Oh, snap!

We looked at each other and said, "Looks like we are not going to Canada tomorrow night."

Sara, being the resilient warrior, wouldn't hear of it. She quickly made a plan, had Ryan call his sister and then called another ten or twelve people in the Bay Area until she found someone willing to help us. The guy got out of work early, took Ryan's sister to the storage space in the blistering San Jose heat, and rummaged through our belongings looking for the passports. We stayed on the phone with them as much as we could—this adventure went on for hours.

All of us prayed hard to Gurudev for them to find the passports. But in the back of my mind, I was stressing on how they'd get them to us in time for the flight the next afternoon. Sara called every local Fed Ex, UPS and DHL office to see who could do an emergency overnight, with the deadline fast approaching. We had a gig that night at a cool coffee shop but wouldn't cancel on principle.

After three hours of digging through our things, the pair were about to give up. I had Ryan start the show, while I walked down the road, praying with half of my mind, and guiding the storage diggers with the other. Before the concert, they had found Ryan's, but mine was still MIA.

A few tunes into the show, the dude on the other end of the phone yelled with a roar of victory and relief, "Jeremy—I found it!"

I closed my eyes, and with a deep breath, said a silent word of thanks, then an explosive vocal one.

They raced to the nearest Fed Ex, barely making the cutoff for overnight. We received both passports on time. *Jai Guru Dev.* Retelling the story was a hit in Montreal and best of all… Gurudev was there.

Back in Portland at the beginning of August, I called Rajshree in Los Angles, requesting her to ask Gurudev if I could be full-time with Ryan. I plied her with how perfect it would be, teaching youth courses and playing music until the Silver Jubilee in February. She supported the idea a hundred percent, as did many others.

However, the next day, she came back with my second turn-down on full-time volunteering in one year, almost to the exact date.

And that was it. Ryan and I packed up the car and drove back to the Bay Area. As the tires spun on I-5, I looked ahead with no volunteering or job waiting for me. I wasn't devastated, though I honestly have to say I felt a glitch in my heart. I had no idea what Gurudev had in store for me. If I did, what fun would that be?

Singing at Gurudev's public talk in San Francisco, CA, May 2005

CHAPTER TWENTY-FOUR

The Land of Thai and India Again

*When both your heart and mind are pure and clear, then
positive energy rises in you. But if your mind is full
of negativity, and if you are stressed out, or if you are
complaining about this and that, and grumbling and
griping, then no miracle is possible. Even regular work
which has to happen does not happen. Simple things
do not happen because energy is low and negative.*
—Gurudev Sri Sri Ravi Shankar

*B*ack in the Bay Area I was homeless, jobless, almost moneyless,
but for sure I was not hopeless or helpless. An attitude of gratitude powered me; gone were any desperate noises inside. During
the twelve hours of travel, I made the decision to obtain a teaching
position overseas. Having taught in Belize, Mexico, India, and China
during my college adventures, this was a no-brainer.

Back at the Montreal Ashram, I had talked with a woman who
was on her way to teach in South Korea. Ideas of international teaching started to play in my mind. Shamus Neary, a cool kid I grew up
with in Taylor, had been in Bangkok for the past several years. We
had kept in touch sparingly during my time in China, and I was
excited to reconnect with him.

Sandeep opened his doors to me once again, and I felt grateful
to stay there. My early morning rituals were followed by a sincere
prayer to Gurudev to help me find a job.

After breakfast I followed the old adage, "Finding a job is a
full-time job." I phoned old college professors, researched overseas

teaching jobs, and had phone interviews from Korea and China, wondering where I would be in a few weeks' time.

Jobs in Korea were plentiful yet felt shady. After twenty-something phone interviews, where I was promised all kinds of benefits, I decided to call Shamus.

"Dude, don't even go to Korea. So many teachers come here to Thailand complaining about their Korean positions. Just come here and get a job."

Shamus gave me a link with around fifteen international schools, and I mailed them all my cover letter and resume. That evening, in the last week of August, while driving on Interstate 880 from a satsang in San Francisco, Sandeep called me.

"Jeremy, I would like you to teach the first Art of Living course at my company tomorrow. I think you will be the perfect fit."

Not implementing Gurudev's knowledge of, "Always have a yes mind at first, if later it does not work out, then that is okay," I replied, "Sandeep, you know I'd love to, but I have so much work to do in finding a job in the next few days. I really can't."

"Jeremy, hold on for a minute; I have another call."

Looking at the scattered taillights in front of me in the dark of night, a beautiful, powerful force hit me in the chest like a bundle of roses falling from the sky. The force was followed by Gurudev's subtle and signature voice—he simply said, "You do my work, and I'll do yours." It was a statement I had heard him say several times.

Frozen in the moment with a smile as wide as the Rio Grande, I was inside a driving gratitude meditation, my mind and ego on hold. When Sandeep came back on the line, before he could say my name, I said, "Yes, Sandeep, I will teach the course!"

"Wow, Jeremy, that was a quick change of mind. I am so happy you will be teaching this course; it means the world to me. What made you change your mind?"

"I'll tell you at home tonight. *Jai Guru Dev.*"

I drove up to San Rafael in Marin Country to meet Sandeep at his work and set up for the six-day course. The first night of the course was powerful, sweet, and fulfilling. A great group of open-minded

corporate workers who were looking for peace, joy, and tools to elimi-
nate stress and tension were in the right place at the right time.

Of all the things I have experienced in life, teaching the Art of
Living courses as a volunteer brings me the highest joy. The transformation in the participants and myself is inspiring and fosters an
abundance of gratitude in me.

On the way to dinner after class, I turned my phone on in the car.
One voicemail waited for me. I was flooded with joy, love, and gratitude, as a bright-light smile shone on my face while listening. Sandeep
realized the nature of the call, and I replayed it for him on speakerphone.

"Hello Jeremy, this is Ron Taylor, Director at Concordian
International School in Bangkok, Thailand. I received your cover letter
and resume today and would like to talk with you about a first-grade
teaching position that just opened at our school. Please give me a call
back at your convenience. I look forward to talking with you soon."

Bouncing for joy in the front seats of the car, Sandeep and I
rocked on Planet High. We walked into an Italian restaurant glowing
like comets. After a quick meal, I sat in his car and returned the call
to the director of the school, to find the grace kept on flowing.

Here's the gist of the call. Mr. Taylor was from the Philadelphia
area and knew my neighboring and rival town, Old Forge, well. He
and his wife drove up often for the world-famous Old Forge-style pizza.
Score! After our Pennsylvania small talk, he asked when I could be there.

"I am teaching an Art of Living course now and can be there in
six days."

"What is the Art of Living?"

I gave an introductory pitch on the Art of Living Foundation for
the deal sealer of my interview. Astounding grace. And that was how I
got my first full-year teaching job and my first international contract job.

While finishing the course at night, the daytime was filled with
saying my goodbyes and packing for Thailand. This was the only reply I
received from all my resumes, which wasn't surprising, since at the time
of my interview, most schools were already in at least their third weeks.

Once again, I was giving away most of my belongings, packing the
rest into one suitcase, one backpack, and of course my guitar case. Flying
to Thailand, I couldn't wipe the smile from my glowing face, thinking

of how blessed I was. I mean, so many miracles have been granted and, quite naturally as humans, we tend to take things for granted.

On that flight, I threw a personal gratitude party, basking in the wonder, goodness, and awe of it all. It's no wonder people think I'm a weirdo for smiling so much—if they only knew about the constant carnival of positive energy going on inside, like a portable celebration that goes everywhere with me.

At the Bangkok airport, I was picked up by the director of the school. The personal service extended to food shopping and dropping me at my new home: a two-bedroom, sixth-floor condo. The condo complex and school were both located at the Thana City Golf Resort and Country Club. Though I'm not a golfer, there is serenity with acres of green around.

Up early from jetlag, I did extra-long sadhana, followed by initiating my neighbors to the fact that the new guy was a music man. I played a couple "Ganesh" bhajans, as it is tradition in India before one starts something new.

Walking into the school and my new classroom, I felt ready for anything. Bring it on. Meeting with my female teacher assistant from the Philippines—what a surprise to have my own assistant—I saw a skyline of little six-year-olds trying to sneak a peek into the window.

As schoolteachers know, it is a challenge stepping into a classroom after the school year's begun. I welcomed twenty students, mainly of Thai/Chinese background into the class, introduced myself, played a few get-to-know-you games, and broke out the guitar for a tune or two.

Concordian is an English and Chinese bilingual immersion school. There were two sections of first grade. The students alternated between two classrooms. On Monday, I had twenty students in my homeroom all day, while the other class of twenty was next door in Chinese. On Tuesday, they switched, and so on.

I told people, "I have double the students and half the time." But I loved it. I was teaching forty students to read, write, sing, dance, add and subtract, laugh more, and other age-appropriate academic and nonacademic goodness. I felt most fortunate to be there.

After the first week, I went to visit my hometown friend, Shamus, his wife, and his baby boy, Sean. He lived on the other side of town, so we did not get to see each other that much. However, it was still great to know a Taylor boy was in the same foreign city as I was.

I was now an IB-PYP teacher, that's short for International Baccalaureate—Primary Years Program. The director of the school asked me and my teaching partner if we could attend the next PYP training just before the school's fall break in October. Guess where it was—Bangalore! I attended the three-day training and spent the rest of the week at the ashram while Gurudev was there. This Thailand adventure was getting cooler by the second.

My first Art of Living album, *Sound in Silence*, had now been out in India for four months. Most of the sales were from devotees. The Indians made a big deal with lots of attention, praise, and here-and-there criticism, too. Although I wasn't satisfied with the recording, I was happy people liked it. But I knew I was capable of much higher quality.

I brought back a useful, creative tradition I had followed in California and Atlanta, usually on weekends where I had more time after sadhana. Before I started yoga, I placed my guitar case by the pillows where I sat for Sudarshan Kriya and meditation. I didn't have to open my eyes to pick up the guitar and start singing/writing bhajans.

From October to December, I reached creative heights, writing most of the English and Sanskrit songs that later were highlighted on my second album, *Simply Satsang*.

I will never forget (actually, there is little I've forgotten this life-time, minus some useless math equations) the fine October morning in 2005, sitting on my bed at the ashram, completing the song "Govinda." I knew this song would become a hit—it rocked and was fun to play. I was getting quite good at rocking three verses, a chorus, and a bridge out. The lyrics, mainly pointing at Gurudev's love and inspiration, as well as this spiritual path, were poignant.

I quickly ran up to see him. With perfect timing, Gurudev stood outside the buildings where he usually meets people. Standing face to face, I sang the vintage first verse:

> *Giving me love by waves of grace*
> *your home is in my heart,*
> *filling me up with holy love.*
> *Endless laughter, (this) child grows,*
> *unto my perfect Self,*
> *a heart so full of love explodes…*
> *Govinda, Hari Hari—Gopal*

Imagine being able to write something so meaningful and, within minutes, singing it to the world-renowned humanitarian and spiritual leader who has changed your life and millions of others around the world. He loved it and asked me to sing the second verse:

> *Living the art, the art it lives,*
> *a nest inside your heart,*
> *for sending smiles out to the world.*
> *Reversing anger in such pain,*
> *right back to who you are,*
> *you feel it shining when you sing, you sing.*
> *Govinda, Hari Hari—Gopal*

"Wonderful song, Jeremy. Keep writing English and Sanskrit songs; this will inspire youth around the world."

"Yes, Gurudev. I have many more songs. Thank you."

Thailand was growing on me, and I prayed I might be growing on a particular Thai girl. Don't roll your eyes, you knew this would happen. I had a huge crush on one of the office girls at school, Mai.

A natural Thai/Chinese beauty, Princess Mai is described in my own words: pale white skin, perfect body, a smile that melted my mind and rumbled my heart, soft-spoken, shy, resplendent eyes, and I think she liked me but was too shy to say.

I wrote a poem for her and showed up early at work to put it on her chair tucked under her desk, with an apple, a fruit I knew she liked. For Christmas, I wrote her a song called, "Heart's Away," recorded it for her on both the guitar and piano and watched as she listened to both songs in my classroom, all smiles and shy.

I had started at the gym, was eating fruit for breakfast, vegetarian Thai food for lunch, and a salad for dinner. Raw food made me look and feel my best. I received my first tailored pants and shirts from my good friends at Emporium Tailors on Sukhumvit Road. I was looking good come December, and everyone's compliments floated around me.

I went on a creative rampage, writing songs, recording them on CD, making Christmas cards, and more for Mai. It's times like these when I am most inspired. I wonder why girls get my best creativity.

In Montreal back in July, I'd asked one of the teachers at the Canadian Ashram a question in a group setting. "Why is it when I have a crush on a girl, I can write a whole album in one night? And when I am not into a particular girl, I sometimes wonder if I can even write another song?"

After tons of laughter and shock from the conservative section, came this answer. "My dear Jeremy… make the Divine your girlfriend, then you will always be inspired and creative." Beautiful knowledge, I know, but it was not helpful to me at this stage in my life.

Mai soon faded into the sunset of my heart; she got a new job in northern Thailand. Though I was sad to see her leave, I wished Mai luck on her new adventure. Another remarkable woman got away. Once again, I grew from a life lesson in letting go; I moved on with grace.

My first season passed quickly, and I found myself back at the Bangalore Ashram for three weeks during the holidays. I would be rooming with another American, Kris Keyes. When I told some of the other foreigners there, they said, "Wait until you meet Kris, you are going to trip out." That's all they would tell me.

Kris was not your typical foreigner at the ashram. He was full of muscles, sported a shaved head and face, tattoos mainly of American cartoon characters that Kris fondly referred to as "American mythology" over most of his body, and he wore shorts and a sleeveless basketball jersey almost daily to show them off. He could easily be mistaken for a WWE wrestler, and he was by the little schoolboys there from Kashmir.

An American rock star in his own right, Kris was the leader of the band Gargantuan Soul prior to coming to the ashram. His goal was to make a big splash with his music here. Every day, Kris sat cross-legged on his bed next to mine in his boxers, writing and singing songs on his mini keyboard.

One main reason I came to the ashram was to record my next album, *Simply Satsang*, but Kris talked me into helping him with his new album. I'm a pushover for rock stars. Kris pushed me, though, to new creative and skill heights on the guitar, as well as songwriting. I added cool Sanskrit hooks to some of his songs. Kris and I worked out and practiced those songs every day. We went into another studio in Bangalore and banged out the demo with the help of two friends from Canada.

Unfortunately, the album was never completed. I would later record one of the songs, a very powerful tune, "Spending My Life with the Master," on my album, *Dancing Opposites*, which rings the honest lyrics:

> *Spending my life with the Master,*
> *it can never be better,*
> *my life before was disaster,*
> *now I'm here with the Master.*

I believe Kris spoke for all of us in the studio that day.

You know I love concerts, but I have never seen one as outrageous as the one I saw firsthand outside the Forum Mall in Bangalore on Christmas Day 2005, where Kris was set to perform. He was taken to a room where he could warm up while I handed out last-minute flyers for the show.

When it was time to get Kris, he was decked out in new neon-green sneakers, a sleeveless vest coat with nothing more than a tank top underneath, a backwards Tupac Shakur–esque bandana on his head, and he was pumped.

As we made it to the ground floor, the mall was packed with shoppers. I felt like Rocky Balboa's manager, leading him to the ring before the big fight.

Kris grabbed a microphone from a vendor on the first floor, screaming, "Yo, what's up Bangalore? My name is Kris Keyes, and I am playing a concert outside…" And cut. Someone turned off the PA system on the unwelcomed announcement. *Damn, this kid is nuts.*

Outside, a crowd awaited him. Kris handed me his bag to put somewhere safe, so I stashed it under the Art of Living table near the stage.

I wasn't gone thirty seconds and then I heard, "Yo, yo, yo, Bangalore, what's up, baby?"

I couldn't spot Kris anywhere. Then I saw he was on top of an auto rickshaw with the cordless microphone, yelling his brains out. Five seconds later, his big frame crashed through the rickshaw canopy, which barely keeps out the rain during the monsoon. Kris stood on the metal bars, and they caved like thin aluminum.

Kris ran toward the stage, mic in hand, looking like a wild beast blazing a trail of madness, with a pack of angry auto rickshaw drivers chasing his tail, wanting to kill him. This is their life, their livelihood, their source of income, and for many, their shelter. And Kris just gave them the biggest American slap-in-the-face one could imagine. Like I told Gurudev the week after, "I was forced to almost be violent." These uncontrolled men were swinging furiously as Kris tried to get on stage. The show was going nowhere fast.

In prime position for fending off these frenetic dashers, I had to swing defensively, throwing punches and smacking a few in retaliation who'd hit me first. Flashbacks of the streets of Taylor as a teen-ager blazed across my mind.

Finally, the drivers backed off when one of the local Art of Living teachers agreed to pay for the needed repairs.

I was Kris' bodyguard on stage and in the limelight. I remember one over-zealous kid who kept trying to touch Kris. Doing my job, I sent him flying a couple of times. I am a peaceful man, but the scene was chaos. This was one of the craziest events of my life. I am certain Kris was the talk of the town.

And despite all his mannerisms, looks, and the way he fools around when with Gurudev and others, Gurudev fully accepts Kris as he is, a testament to the master's compassionate and unconditional love for everyone.

Someone once asked Gurudev, "What is the most challenging thing for you as the founder of the Art of Living?"

"In the Art of Living, we have the whole spectrum of people and personalities. On one end, we have teachers and volunteers who follow all the norms of society and have perfect behavior at all times—they are very kind. On the other end, we have teachers and volunteers who act very crazy, causing all kinds of trouble, pushing buttons, and keeping everyone on their toes."

An outbreak of laughter followed this. And yes, this is true. And one might ask where I fall on that continuum? I am either so far left I am right or floating from one end to the other.

Over the years, I've been fortunate to be in many rooms with Gurudev, and with an audience of fifty or a hundred people, or sometimes as few as two or three. Here's one that stands out for me.

There were a handful of foreigners at the ashram in December before the Silver Jubilee with tons of work to be done before the whole world arrived in two months' time. In this meeting, there were only the foreigners, and this one lady from Europe complained about the conditions and people at the ashram. Essentially, she was getting all her buttons pushed, as we all have, though she was super vocal about it. And then Gurudev changed his tune. I have never heard Gurudev speak so firmly.

"Listen, the whole world is coming here in just two months for a once-in-a-lifetime celebration. We have much work to do, we have to put these little botherations behind us for two months and keep working. There is no other way. Do you know the only difference between all of you and me?"

It seemed like everyone in the room held their breath.

"I can drop this whole thing in the ocean at any given moment—can you?"

His speech was mind-blowing, refreshing, and grand. Gurudev, on fire, blasted her. What a lucky woman, when a master gives you that much attention, in that fashion, it is a mighty blessing. Though I am not sure she saw it that way at the time.

And he is right, as volunteers, we have our own levels of fever-ishness, like with toys in our childhood. Even on the spiritual path, it is like we traded the toys of our youth for courses and events we feel attached to as we organize them. I have not been devoid of this.

When I look back, I see how much I have grown on the level of dispassion. Having the ability to be unattached from events and live lightly, while not being lazy and unproductive. It's a rare and won-derful balance—a happy balance.

Gurudev gives us the funny, effective mantra of, "So what!" He tells us we will be six feet under in a few short years, so what's the use of hankering over little things? Live life from a much larger dimen-sion, live the art of living. Be happy, productive, grateful, and useful to those around you. This, to me, and probably millions of other devotees around the world, is living the art.

When Gurudev says he can drop this whole thing in the ocean, he means it. Gurudev Sri Sri Ravi Shankar is lighter than the finest feather, yet stronger than mountains, oceans, and sounds of glory on earth. He adds, "Your life is infinite. You are as old as these moun-tains, and you will remain forever." The mystic shines.

Singing in the VM at a Bangalore Ashram satsang, December 2005

CHAPTER TWENTY-FIVE

The Silver Jubilee

*I tell you, we should give miracles a chance to happen
in life. Nobody's life is devoid of miracles. Only we
don't believe in them. All the cultures and philosophy
in this world are based on miracles. In fact, they
thrive on miracles. Just remove all the miracles from
the Bible and you will feel as if the Bible does not
exist. Similarly, if you take any scripture in the
world, it is full of miracles. But we think miracles
are a thing of the past and not of the present. I tell
you, it can happen even today, in the present.*
—Gurudev Sri Sri Ravi Shankar

In January, I taught my first Art of Living course in Bangkok, a
class of twenty people from nine different countries. Art of Living
Thailand was set in motion for more goodness to come.

Shi-Yu, from Taiwan, was a teacher at my school and took the
course with her sister. Sudarshan Kriya and the universal and powerful knowledge blew her away. She continued her daily breathing
practice and came every Sunday morning for the follow-up. She
and her sister wanted to attend the Silver Jubilee with our Bangkok
group. We decided she would ask the director for the three days off
from school first. This was about three weeks before the event, and
she was granted the time off.

I was to ask the next week, to spread out the requests. I woke
up extra early, did my daily routine, and prayed to Gurudev like a
bull needing to break out of a steel-caged fence to run free with the

herd. I needed to be in Bangalore. One of the main reasons I took a job overseas was to be closer to India to attend this once in a lifetime event. There was no way I could miss this. Never, not, no, no, no.

Calm and confident, I walked into the director's office and asked for the time off. Without any problem, he agreed. *Jai Guru Dev.*

We assembled an all-star lineup to represent Thailand at the Silver Jubilee. The fifteen included Rohit (a young American devotee who came to visit me from California), Shi-Yu and her sister, and a handful of devoted volunteers.

The Silver Jubilee was pretty much how I imagined it—an open sea with rows of seats, rock-star sized video screens that seemed to go forever, and an enormous stage to top it off. Right in front was an impressive spread of 3,800 southern Indian musicians, making up a brilliant symphony. The first of its kind, they had little, if any, time to rehearse with each other before their performance. They sounded magnificent.

The whole front section was for international attendees, giving us very good seats, yet we still relied on the large video screens to see the action up close. It was great meeting people from around 150 countries worldwide in the essence of the Art of Living—a one-world family.

Matt and I were together once again. At one point, we communicated from maybe fifty feet away, as I called him to come over to my section. Seconds later, he threw a Clif Bar snack to me, and it smacked someone right in the back. Ow! I apologized on behalf of Matt and myself. Luckily, that person was able to practice acceptance. Even separated by fifty feet in a foreign country, we're a boatload of trouble.

When Matt finally made it over to Rohit and me, it marked an important moment in time, when a button-pushing trio was formed, causing mayhem over the next many years, leaving the victims—I mean, targets—with the question, "Who made these three characters Art of Living teachers?"

By March, work was growing in fun and memories. I taught regular Art of Living courses; I was in great shape from walking in the humid climate, working out, and eating well. I bought a skateboard and was skating at the local skateboard park, too. I explored the city on weekends. And met a beautiful girl.

"What book are you reading?" My natural inquisitive personality broke the ice with this cute college-looking Thai girl at the BTS Skytrain station one fine Saturday afternoon in March 2006.

"Oh, hello. It's a science fiction book about aliens I just started reading. My name is Dear, what's yours?"

Dear and I connected. Though I was twenty-nine, she twenty-two, the age difference didn't matter much, at first. We would meet at trendy coffee shops, go out for vegetarian food downtown, or walk around the city taking pictures. We shared tastes in bands like the Beatles, Radiohead, and Pink Floyd. She quickly became vegetarian, loving this new lifestyle change, and of course I took her to the best non-meat joints in town. She took the Art of Living course, and it was a sweet relationship for a while.

After our awesome weekend on the beach at Hua Hin in June, I was finishing my first year at Concordian, about to head to Vietnam on a seva trip. And that's when the relationship started to fall apart or got tiring for me. Maybe, like many people say, I was "too damn picky." Who knows?

One day at my place, Dear was in one room doing college work, I in another. I called her and she wouldn't answer, like she wasn't there. I picked up my guitar, rang out the always-faithful G Major chord, asking, "Where is Dear?" I wrote her a song in moments, two verses and chorus. The second verse stands out for me:

Dear, she lives,
somewhere in my mind,
crazy-painted princess,
turning all my words to rhyme.

In the end, it didn't work. I was single again. I knew single very well. I moved on and was grateful for the memorable times.

Extra! Extra! Read all about it: the one and only Art of Living Silence course on my thirtieth birthday, the exact same day I finished my first full year of teaching. Splendid. Yes, that's how the cards stacked for this guy, as a divine birthday gift from Gurudev on my special day.

Besides being a big day for me, this was a big day for Art of Living Thailand—going strong since my arrival in September. True teamwork through and through, we celebrated with four days of: fun yoga, deep meditation, profound wisdom, homemade vegetarian food, selfless service, and nightly bouncing bhajans in satsang. How sweet life could be… how sweet, indeed.

Vietnam's got Ho Chi Min,
and hoochie-coochie all around,
but that ain't why I'm in town.
String of concerts, songs of joy,
but they don't want love anymore.
I pack my bags onto another flight, another town…

The definitive first verse from the title track on my album *Back To Taylor Town.*

Vietnam was fascinating. I remember being stoked at all the pedal and motorbikes crowded at any given intersection. They were like a pack of wandering animals, piercing and crawling through the traffic, and I never saw an accident. Lots of history in Ho Chi Min City (formerly Saigon), and being an American boy, it might have run a bit deeper than most.

I was there on an Art of Living trip with a course planned, meetings, introductory talks on our programs, and I had a bunch of cool concerts set up at the local university. This was my thing, and I made the best of it. Getting students to sing, talking with them about the wild-bouncing mind and leading them in meditation. It was hard to leave.

Back in Thailand in the August heat, I was excited for the new school year, and especially curious about our new director from the States, Tarek Razik. I'd met him twice on his visits to the school. He seemed cool, but with bosses, one could never tell.

I taught first grade again that year. I met the new teachers in the first week and was charged up for a second school year.

On Friday afternoon, at the end of the teacher orientation/staff development week, I poked my head into the director's office to say bye. "Hey, Tarek, great first week. I look forward to the start of the year on Monday."

"Yes, Jeremy, I do too."

Piercing my ear, a wonderful specimen of familiar music faintly coming through my new boss's laptop speakers. I exclaimed, "Oh my God—you're a Deadhead!"

Looking around his office, he replied, "How did you know that?"

"I can tell you the exact show you're listening to right now."

"Go ahead."

"That's *Eyes of the World* from March 29, 1990, at the Nassau Coliseum."

"Wow, that's impressive. Yes, I am a Deadhead, and I guess you are, too. Come in and have a seat—check this out."

Tarek took out his collection of old ticket stubs and various Grateful Dead collectables. My new boss was a Grateful Dead fan like me. I could not have scripted this any better myself. This was going to be an excellent year.

For whatever karmic reason, satsang wasn't happening in Bangkok. I had my guitar, ready to play at the drop of a hat, but the group was mainly into breathing, with knowledge and yoga thrown in. Deep inside I was longing to sing bhajans with everyone.

One day I woke up with a great idea and called my friend and fellow volunteer, Helen. "Helen, I need your help," I said in desperation. "I need you to help me start satsang here in Bangkok. I need it, we need it, the city, country, and world need it. Please help me; please."

Miraculously, Helen called the next day with the wonderful news that she had met Adrian Cox, an American who owned Yoga Elements in downtown Bangkok, the premier place to practice yoga in town. It turns out he was looking for someone to lead *kirtan* (which refers to the call-and-response fashion of singing bhajans) at his studio. It was perfect and we both had a desire to get this going.

We set things up for the following Friday. It was fabulous to be singing again and with a fantastic group of yoga lovers. I continued for a couple of weeks until Adrian kindly told me my style of kirtan was not what he was looking for at the studio.

I was fine with his decision and transferred the weekly Friday satsang to our Art of Living Center on Soi 12. A lot of the people from the studio joined, plus the Art of Living folks, and we had a fine weekly tradition, one which would last for several years. I will always be grateful to Helen and Adrian for supporting my dream of sweet sing-a-longs in Thailand.

I got word Gurudev would be at the Bangalore Ashram for Christmas and New Year's Eve for the first time in about fifteen years. I couldn't contain my euphoria.

Along with this, I was ecstatic to learn the new Guru Puja course was going to be held during this time. I had an intense desire to attend this course. Hearing Bill sing this divine and ancient song while performing the gratitude ceremony, called *puja*, back in Lake Tahoe in June 2000, had wrapped around my soul. I wanted to learn. Now was *the* opportune time for me; what a Christmas gift!

Gurudev says, "The best puja, the best form of worship, is to be happy, to be grateful."

I was becoming a semi-professional in gratitude by now.

In the late nineties, Gurudev visited Kashmir and was heartbroken with the conditions. The Art of Living brought one hundred and twenty children from Kashmir to the Bangalore Ashram. For sixteen years, Gurudev cared for these boys and transformed them with his love. After their education, they went back to Kashmir and have since settled.

I met these boys in 2004 and began learning from them; I was also one of their teachers. Numerous interactions over the years were remarkable, from youth courses in the Old Ashram to English lessons, singing, and playing games. The joy that these youngsters brought to my life was unmistakable.

Singing with the boys from Kashmir on Christmas was a no-brainer. We practiced a selection of traditional songs, had a few other ashram kids join in, and we were ready to rock for Gurudev and several thousand people in attendance at the outdoor amphitheater.

A group of us spent all day decorating the stage and surrounding area with Christmas lights and decorations. 'Tis the season! After other cultural programs, it was time for the Christmas carolers to shine.

After the first song, Gurudev asked with a smile, "Are you going to sing a song from Thailand?"

I smiled back and busted into "Santa Claus Is Coming to Town." Suddenly, white flakes started falling across the stage. It's snowing on Christmas in Bangalore! Well, almost. Gurudev sprayed us on stage with fake snow via a snow-spraying toy gun.

Could you imagine how awesome this was for the kids and me? Our very own Santa Claus sat ten feet away, center stage, spraying us with fake snow, living love and innocence like a five-year-old. Living the art and teaching us by example how to live it. On a finer level, Gurudev is the child most humans left behind, the one they lost in the ever-so-popular trade of intelligence for innocence.

"I refuse to grow up," Gurudev stated. It hit us where it needed to at that fantastic moment of our lives—right in our hearts.

After the satsang, I wandered inside the meditation hall, sat down, closed my eyes, and with a smile on my face, meditated. During the deep, blissful silence, an excellent idea came to me: to organize a community fundraising event in my hometown, though I didn't yet know what to support. Like all great ideas that have come either while practicing yoga, Sudarshan Kriya, and in this case, meditation, they are on point.

Back in Thailand, I called my old-school Art of Living friend, Justin Fiore—the soul who got me into the Foundation ten years before (talk about being grateful to another human). I knew he could steer me in the right local direction to find a worthy cause.

Justin reminded me about a fourteen-year-old boy from his high school in Old Forge who'd broken his neck and injured his spinal cord in a football game the previous September. Justin is a master with words, and tears welled upon hearing the heartbreaking story of Kiel Eigen. I knew this was the cause. Kiel was paralyzed yet determined to fight the toughest fight of his life, with the goal of someday walking again.

The first thing I did was call Kiel's mother and ask if this was a good idea, and she was thrilled. I called the mayor of Old Forge and notified her of my plans. Kiel's mom put me in touch with Jo Ann Colianni, who worked at the Old Forge Bank and oversaw Kiel's fundraisers. She turned out to be a distant relative of mine through marriage—wow.

I assembled a team of hometown friends to help organize the event: Guy Giannone, Paul Brennan, Dave Weisenfluh, and others. Justin was onboard—though he lived in Indiana—as was Sandeep from Fremont.

Kiel's injury broke down the rival barriers, and the two schools came together on various occasions to raise funds for him. By the end of February, the ball was rolling.

I had experience organizing events, mostly wherever I was living at the time, but this was from 8,600 miles away. When I called someone after midnight Thailand-time on a school night, the person in Scranton took me seriously, well, for the most part. The hardest thing was not being there to lead the charge.

Gurudev throws various kinds of metaphorical curve balls to us devotees during the organization of events and courses. This is one of his mysterious ways of making us stronger.

For the venue, I booked Nay Aug Park in Scranton—a park I visited often as a child—for Sunday, July 8, 2007. I wanted the auspicious 7.7.07, but someone had already booked it. I had set a powerful *sankalpa* (divine intention) for this event to manifest and be successful. Daily prayers to Gurudev were heard loud and clear.

Maybe I should have been more surprised when I saw an email in May that said Gurudev would be having a public event in King of Prussia, Pennsylvania—two hours from Scranton—on the very same day! Having him on Earth during this event was enough to make me smile and be faithful. Having him in the States made me jump for joy. But having him only two hours away at the time of the event blew my mind, raised my soul, and I invited him personally to the event as a special guest. Unfortunately, like always, every moment of his U.S. visit was already booked. But in my heart, Gurudev came to Pennsylvania for Kiel, myself, and the event.

Over the next five months my life was filled with joyous work. It was school, Art of Living courses, and satsangs, working out at the gym, and then late nights on the phone and computer getting things in line for the event.

I often use the word "picky" to answer the multitude of folks who ask why I am still single. But, for this season, I was just too damn busy for a date—and I loved it.

The event looked great on paper: a benefit walk in the morning; a DJ, who was my old college roommate's wife, Nikki Samsell; four bands, including myself with some hometown friends; and Kiel's dad playing classic rock with another friend to kick off the festivities. Activities for kids included the mobile "firehouse," which the Scranton Fire Department brought on site; Heroes of Humanity Awards for community members who were doing wonderful service; a raffle with cool donated prizes; a drama show collaboration by the high school students from Riverside and rival Old Forge—one love; and the park's pool and food stand were a stone's throw away from the event. We were set to rock.

About a month before I flew home, I wrote a song about how my world travels brought me closer to my hometown, Taylor. As I sat down and grabbed my guitar on a busy Friday night in May, a happy riff jumped off the fret board of my Taylor guitar, suggesting the theme, feel, mood, message, verses, and chorus of a song I completed ten minutes later.

"All these adventures gonna lead me—Back to Taylor Town!" I added the affectionate "town," being inspired by the likes of the two music masters, Bob Dylan in his tune, "New York Town" and Mark Knopfler's lyrics in "Sultans of Swing."

The song highlights three of my adventures around the world: Vietnam in July 2006, Mexico in December 2003, and various trips to India. For the record, a line in the second verse may suggest why I was single all those years.

Senorita mi amor,
a priceless beauty,
but I want more.
I set my sights onto
another place, another time.

Loosely translated: picky.

I was pleased with the song and knew it would be like an anthem song for my friends and family back home. This one was for them. Things were in motion, and though it would be a while until the fundraiser, I had done what I could from afar.

My second school year at Concordian in Thailand was brilliant. I had a super connection with my boss and with its foundation in music. My two classes were nothing short of lively, dynamic, humorous, smart, and tons of fun.

Our school did the unthinkable in January, moved into a state-of-the-art campus halfway through the school year. I gained so much experience that year with the help of my boss, my teacher assistant Kathy, and of course the great six-and seven-year-olds who ruled my life. By the middle of June, I was in a dedicated place as an educator. I signed for my third year at the school.

In May, I got an invitation to attend the Guru Puja Two course at the Bangalore Ashram. I couldn't have been happier, until I looked at the dates for the course, which fell on my last couple days of school. I couldn't believe it. I called the ashram, pleading my case to push the course back a few days, to no avail.

The next day I mustered the courage to ask my boss if I could have the last two or three days of school off—as close as we were and as accommodating as he could be at times, he had to decline on principle. I knew that was coming. What kind of closure would that be for a teacher?

So, as I've done countless times over the past ten years, I retreated to what is always heard: prayer. Day after day, I prayed to Gurudev for the course dates to work out in my favor. My satsang group even sent out an intention for me one night after meditation.

One week later, the course had to move forward a few days because of the impressive All-Indian TRM—Teacher Refresher Meet happening just before my birthday. And the Guru Puja Two course now started the day after my thirty-first birthday. What a heart-warming gift from my Guru.

During the Guru Puja One course, I learned the history, meanings, and pronunciations for the ancient gratitude song. After six months of chanting along with a recording of Gurudev's sister, Bhanu Didi, I couldn't wait to come back for the second course and learn how to perform the puja. My desire to do this was strong and, combined with the intention and daily prayer, Gurudev's grace granted me yet another miracle.

I had lost count of them by this stage on the path. Wait, could it be? Yes, I think it is… another one.

For the past ten years I'd desired, longed to be with Gurudev on my birthday. I came close a couple years in Lake Tahoe. This year, on my tenth anniversary being in the Art of Living, I would spend my birthday with Gurudev at the Bangalore Ashram.

The TRM was open by invitation only, for the Art of Living teachers around India. The ashram was closed to visitors during the course. But I asked if I could come two days early before the Guru Puja course, and they sweetly agreed.

At the ashram, I felt a marvelous energy, a natural acceptance to be at the ashram where I did three of my teacher training programs and was among many teachers I knew. Sitting in a few of the sessions, I was blown away at the intense individual energy and powerful force as a collective rocking group. I sat in tears, listening to many of their heartfelt stories of teaching corporate heads and professional athletes, to reaching out to the poorest of the poor in remote villages around the country.

Being among the senior-most teachers, who meant the world to me, like Sangeeta Jani, Vinod Menon, Tanuja Limaye, Rishi Nityapragya, Swami Brahmatej, and Swami Sadyojathah, was beyond words. The course ended on my birthday. I felt electric to be in satsang with Gurudev that night.

Instead of feverishly pushing myself into Gurudev's kutir that day, I hung out with Gurudev's sister, Bhanu, as she floated from one meeting to another on the ground floor of the VM meditation hall. I can't explain how delightful and graceful this woman is.

While she talked, I sat behind the stage at the grand piano. The group asked her to sing and in her melodious voice, she sang "*Krishna Govinda, Govinda Govinda—Govinda Shyam Radhe Krishna.*" A new song to me, and though I'm not the best at figuring out songs by ear, I couldn't put a wrong finger on those ivory keys the moment her soft, soulful voice reached my heart. I was in musical meditation, giving accompaniment to one of my favorite people in the world.

Dressed in my Indian traditional clothes, I grabbed my Taylor guitar and headed out early to satsang that night. Before Gurudev arrived, I sat in the front row, singing songs and strumming along with others.

I had only one desire this night, one simple and selfish at the same time. When Gurudev is at satsang, he calls people to the stage if it is their birthday or anniversary—there's always a celebration around him. As you might imagine, some people take advantage of this and run up when at best their birthday or anniversary may fall that week or month. My lone birthday desire was to be called up before the masses assembled on stage. I'd have settled for after they left the stage; I didn't want my special once-in-ten-years birthday to be in the middle of chaos.

In mid-strum of my guitar, I felt the ever-familiar blast of shakti, the tidal wave of awesomeness when Gurudev entered the hall. As soon as he settled in his seat and looked around, he stunned me beyond belief.

Looking directly at me, he signaled for me to come up. At first, I had doubts he was talking to me. I turned to see if it was for the person behind me. But he looked at me with his vintage smile and called me up.

It was truly me, he'd given me my divine birthday gift, my desire fulfilled with immediacy, another dream-come-true with my guru on this path.

Arriving on the stage, I kneeled and bowed at his feet. He placed a colorful wreath of flowers around my neck and told me to sit next to him. The hall was packed, easily over five thousand people, and I sat there on my special day, perched like a minor king in my blissed and blessed world of love. This was the most significant birthday gift ever, and I hadn't told him of my special day, nor spoken words of my desire. Somehow, he seems to know everything.

The Guru Puja Two course with Bhanu was unutterably poignant. On the last day, when she gave us our silver puja kits and ordained us as Sanskrit pundits, I couldn't have wanted anything more. The chanting and performing of the puja brought a wealth of gratitude for the knowledge on this spiritual path, dating back thousands of years in the holy tradition. I was set to fly home now, experiencing panoramic heights.

Tying up the loose ends over the week back home in Taylor, the first annual Community, Service, and Celebration Day was ready to kick off. Mom, Dad and my oldest nephew, David, drove up from Atlanta. Justin drove in from Indianapolis, and Sandeep beat everyone, flying in from California. The support of these people created enough joy and gratitude to start a love party.

The day was a great success. People came out for the benefit walk, including both the Old Forge and Riverside football teams with no rivalry bouts. Aunt Alice, Aunt Jo Ann, Uncle Ed, cousins, and childhood friends attended.

I played a solo acoustic set in between two bands, and then played with a full band, including a drum set for the first time in my life. There was a lot of music in the park that day.

A couple more hundred people would have been beneficial, but after costs, we raised close to $5,000 for Kiel, and what more could I gratefully ask for? A group of us went to Salerno's Cafe in Old Forge for pizza to celebrate one fantastic event. I was already planning next year's at the dinner table.

My third year teaching at Concordian was as good as ever. I was, however, now a victim of the American-led economic landslide the world was cringing and reeling over at the time. I never thought too much about economic worries, and for sure thought they couldn't affect me.

As it turned out, I was exceptionally wrong. Like other international schoolteachers and workers around Thailand, my salary was linked to the falling fast and furious U.S. dollar. In 2005 it was forty Thai baht to the dollar, a nice paycheck. But now, it was a deteriorating twenty-nine baht to the dollar. I taught first-grade math and knew this was not a good equation.

There was nothing that could be done, and I started flirting with the idea of changing schools. Come December when it was time to sign on the dotted line for another year, I did so with a smile. However, I was clear with my bosses and myself that my fourth year at Concordian would be my final one. Time for me to stretch my wings again.

The year started solid with a powerful Art of Living course. There were notably more healing experiences reported by the participants on this one. Reading the handwritten letters from the course members right now, I remember their sharing—here are a few:

"After practicing Sudarshan Kriya yesterday, I have absolutely no pain in my neck, and I can move it easily. This is the first time I have been free from pain and tension in my neck in five years. Thank you."

"On Thursday afternoon, I did not want to join this course because of the chronic pain in my back. I knew there would be no way for me to sit through six days. After practicing yoga and the breathing for three days, the pain in my back is gone. This is a miracle."

"This morning when I woke up, I was smiling, singing, and felt the best I have in many years. I looked at myself in the mirror and said, 'I am happy right now.'" The author, a twenty-eight-year-old American girl had punched me in the arm and said, "You rock, Jeremy—this course has changed my life."

Interestingly, I'd ignored my own symptoms of pain and harsh digestive aches in the celebration of the students' transformations.

I'd recently had a colonoscopy and was diagnosed with ulcerative colitis, the main symptom being excessive blood-mixed diarrhea, which took a heavy toll on my social and work life.

A week prior, the doctor had prescribed the frantically famous steroid, prednisone. I knew this beast well, as I used to take it when I suffered from asthma, but only as a painful injection. Knowing its harsh side effects, I swallowed it down, hoping for a Western medicine cure for this nasty, life-draining aliment. I understood that this was a serious medical issue and that it was present in my family, specifically in several distant cousins on Dad's side.

My sleep and mind paid the price of the steroid with intense nightmares of a madman with a knife chasing me in the kitchen. I also yelled at the gym in sporadic bursts like I was about to kill someone—this was not me. I stopped taking the pills cold turkey… and all hell broke loose.

I was at school and fading fast. I felt sick and exhausted, wondering if I'd make it to the last night of the Art of Living course. I went home and hit the pillow.

I woke up thirty minutes later and my world had turned upside down. The lingering effects of the drug or withdrawals had spread to my back, I felt paralyzed. I couldn't move, my body frozen with fear, pain, and confusion. I cried and prayed to Gurudev at the same time.

During this most insane moment of my life on my bed, unable to move, crying tears of agony, I wondered how I was going to teach the sixth and final night of the course starting in two hours.

I called my friend, fellow schoolteacher and Art of Living student, Kate, in tears and desperate. I explained I needed help, and she agreed. But before she got there, my body warmed, I wiped away the tears, carefully lifted myself out of bed, got dressed, and stumbled down the street. Kate was at the end of the road, and we hopped in a taxi and headed downtown to finish the course.

Any ailment I'm feeling seems to vanish when I sit down to teach a course or lead a satsang. The energy and grace of the final night floated me along, but when it was over, I was a physical mess, throwing up out the window of the taxi on the way home. My stomach turned into a mashing machine of karmic debt, like a garbage truck mashes and mixes waste. I felt this was the end, I was dying a slow death.

The month of March 2008 was extremely ruthless, my worst since those hellish days of asthma in my youth that I had suffered. My stomach felt like sharp knives stabbing deep inside constantly. My body and soul felt fragile, breakable. I lost twenty-five pounds with my back, butt, and legs hurting around the clock. I missed days of school and stayed home, making countless runs to the bathroom, feeling like I'd pass out each time I looked into the blood-stained toilet.

Looking at my caved, gray face in the mirror slapped me with reality. I finally called Gurudev, and he said, "Be with it and be strong. You are going to be fine. Come and see me in Bali next month."

And that was that, as Gurudev's visit to Bali fell on my spring break. I counted the seconds as a sanction of wellness enveloped me enough to travel. Nine of us, including Kate, and Narin, my student who later became the Foundation's country coordinator in Thailand, traveled to Bali for the Art of Living Silence course.

Seeing Gurudev walk through the doors of the Inna Grand Bali Beach Hotel on Sanur Beach, my smile amplified. I slipped into the elevator with him as he was going up to his room.

It was Gurudev, me, and around four or five executives of the hotel. The manager introduced them in proper and businesslike fashion.

Gurudev is always kindly attentive when meeting people. An instant later, he pointed to me, saying, "This is Jeremy; he is an Art of Living teacher from America, now living in Thailand."

As he gave me that ever-familiar, mischievous smile, I felt elation higher than the tip of Mount Everest. Gurudev lifted me to heaven, which I had missed over the past month.

As we walked into his room and sat down, I told him about my misery.

Lovingly slapping me on the face and pinching my right cheek, he said, "Don't worry, you'll get stronger." And in that instant, love danced inside my soul, and I floated out of his room, dancing on a cloud of bliss. My guru had rejuvenated me once again.

From that moment, I began to start feeling better. During that week, my pain slowly reduced, as did the number of visits to the bathroom. It would take another two months for all the blood to be gone from my stool. Over the next three months, I regained the twenty-five pounds I lost in February and March. *Jai Guru Dev.*

Gurudev's public talk at a beautiful Hindu temple was well attended by everyone from the course, plus several thousand local Balinese. I felt grateful to be on stage with Gurudev's sister, Bhanu, and several close friends.

When it was time, Gurudev gave me that look and I soared into the divine Divya Prabha Art of Living anthem, *"Narayana Hari Om."* With Gurudev and around four thousand people singing along in call and response, I felt as though the expansive ocean of love soaked me thoroughly every moment.

In wonderment at another powerful healing experience, was it seeing Gurudev walking into the hotel, the love and respect he gave me in the elevator, and his hand on my face? Was it the deep meditations, the song at the temple, or maybe the early morning swim with him in the ocean on the last day of the course? What rocked me? Who knows? Who cares to name and label or intellectualize on this path, especially about the vast ocean of grace from Gurudev. Wonder evades the smaller mind.

As he, the guru of joy, always says, "Turn all your questions into wonder—that is enlightenment."

Back in Scranton that June, I found myself playing music under a tent for Mom, Dad, and a bunch of childhood friends at the second annual Community, Service, and Celebration Day. This time, it was held a stone's throw from my childhood home, right behind the high school. This event was remarkable, another dream coming true. From this summer's celebration, a nonprofit Vikings Helping Vikings was formed to help send high school seniors to college. It gave us all the great opportunity to feed the roots of our community—the youth.

Feeling strong, creative, and happy, I was back to myself after two months of recovery from Ulcerative Colitis. Reconnecting with my family and childhood friends was also very healing. I found myself sitting on the same hills I ran up in the hot summer sun as a high school football player. I listened to inspiring stories from friends stationed in Iraq during the war, some who started their dream businesses and others who created beautiful families. For the second year in a row, I learned much about myself by going home and being with loved ones.

The day after the event, I was on a fast flight to Portland, Oregon. Gurudev was giving a public talk, and this time I would take my brother by the hand to meet him. After two weeks of preparations and plastering posters for the visit, Gurudev arrived in Portland. I had the old San Diego crew on board (my brother and old band mates), with tickets in their hands and a traditional Thai shirt on each of their backs. Simply perfect—simply satsang.

The talk was not only fantastic, but Gurudev invited the whole crowd to India. Eagerly anticipating Gurudev coming down the aisle and introducing my brother to him, I couldn't believe this would finally happen.

Jeff got up a few times during the event, probably for a drink of water and a smoke. When I saw him get up one last time at the end, I tried to stop him. An ache drenched my body, why would Jeff bolt away from meeting him?

As Gurudev started making his way down the aisle, my thoughts screamed, *Where is Jeff?!* And instead of introducing my brother to Gurudev on this special night, I introduced my friend Ivan, who had already met Gurudev in California. I couldn't believe my brother had disappeared at the critical time.

I followed Gurudev and hung out in the lobby as he met people. Scanning the area, I spotted my brother there in a corner, and called him over. "Jeff, come here, I'll introduce you to him." But to no avail.

The look on my brother's face and stance of his body started changing as Gurudev got closer to him, on his way to leaving. I couldn't believe my eyes. As I walked by him with Gurudev, I saw something so strange and beautiful. It was like Gurudev put an innocent spell on Jeff; he looked like a little kid again, shy, smiling, with a giggle and gleam in his eyes. I didn't know what to make of it, but I knew something was happening.

As we got to the elevator, Gurudev said, "I see your brother over there." And that was it, I melted away, done for the day, blissed out, confused, loved, happy, bewildered, and grateful; instantaneously.

I didn't ask my brother, but I would pay heavily to know of his experience during that moment. Jeff and I bid each other goodbye moments later. His hug spoke a thousand words, full of love and gratitude. I felt silent, content, and serene letting go.

Twenty minutes later, I was upstairs in Gurudev's meeting room. Half of my mind was on him interacting with a group of devotees. The other half wondered what happened with my brother when it was time to meet Gurudev formally. Hundreds of thoughts bounced off all sides of my mind, trying to make sense of it all.

After many moments consumed by this mind mess, I turned my full attention to Gurudev. Catching the end of one of his jokes, I finally let go and was grateful that my brother was here tonight. My complete wish had come true; my whole family had met Gurudev.

The next morning, I flew to Santa Clara, California, to celebrate Guru Purnima with Gurudev.

*Hanging out with the Vedic schoolboys at the
Bangalore Ashram, December 2006*

*Singing at the Community, Service and Celebration
Day in Scranton, PA, July 2007*

Singing at Gurudev's public event in Bali, Indonesia, April 2008

≈◉ ◎≈

CHAPTER TWENTY-SIX

Another New Beginning

Miracles are in abundance! I think everyone
has had some miracle or the other. We
don't look for it, they just happen.
—Gurudev Sri Sri Ravi Shankar

My last year in Bangkok and at Concordian was another fine one. By January 2009, I had accepted a new position as a kindergarten teacher at a brand-new school on the shores of the Red Sea in Saudi Arabia. KAUST was the king's new city, which featured a world-class science and technology university. I was ready for change, new challenges, and of course the opportunity to pay off my college loan hanging over my head like a cuckoo clock singing each waking hour.

While planning this move with Gurudev, he was in full support. His final words rang in my ears, touched my heart, and will always stay with me. "Just remember, Jeremy, the more money you make, the more seva you need to do." *Yes, sir.*

By some natural law, things started picking up with my music the last season in Bangkok. Satsangs were rocking extra and often. There was a new crew coming every Wednesday to the Art of Living Center to sing along, made up of lively yoga teachers and yogis in the local Bangkok yoga circle. Each satsang was something sweet and new for me. The space lent itself to a lot of in-the-moment creativity and I enjoyed the new wave of excitement.

On spring break that April, I was invited to the Bangalore Ashram to record my new album, *Simply Satsang*, in the studio attached to the publication building. Plus, Gurudev was there the whole week. Life could not be better than this.

As icing to this already super-sweet cake, a full-page interview of me was featured in the April issue of the *Thailand Yoga Journal*. The article introduced a lot of people to the benefits of the Art of Living course and Sudarshan Kriya.

By the beginning of June, I found myself attending going-away parties every other night. Leaving the school was heart-wrenching, as was leaving the Bangkok Art of Living family. Things were good, fulfilling, and steadily pacifying in Thailand, yet I understood it was time to walk away and discover the next heaven that awaited me.

Back in December 1995, I first saw the band Phish live in concert, six months after assembling their double live album, *A Live One*, in the CD warehouse. Since then, I had attended seventy-seven shows from coast to coast.

I saw Phish four times in the summer of 2009: Pittsburg, Pennsylvania; Noblesville, Indiana; and twice in East Troy, Wisconsin. During the last show at Alpine Valley, at set break in the lawn, I got comfortable on the green grass, crossed my legs, straightened my spine, relaxed my hands, closed my eyes, took in a deep breath, and heard, "Are you meditating?"

I could only smile upon opening my eyes, seeing a young concert-goer, full of wonder and happiness. "Yes, I meditate daily," I replied.

"I've been praying every night for the past three months to find someone to teach me how to meditate. Now I see you here."

We talked during the whole set break about the Art of Living, meditation, and the link between the breath and the mind and emotions. I even demonstrated one breathing technique for him among the party-crazed crowd.

My set-break friend went on to the take the Art of Living course at his university in September. We've stayed in touch.

For years, Matt and I talked about how we wanted to reach out to people at concerts and bring them the gifts of yoga, breathing, and meditation as tools to calm their minds. And quite possibly, give them a different experience at these shows.

Matt and I were two of the few sober folks at any given Phish show. There is a table dedicated to people who were sober, many who had overcome addictions. I would visit the table often for stickers and candy. Luckily, for Matt and me, it was much easier letting that part of our lives go than for others.

Gurudev says, "You see, the nature of the mind is to seek happiness and ecstasy and long for the highest form of peace and satisfaction, and as a result one gets into the trap of drugs. People who are addicted to drugs do not exhibit peace, ecstasy, or freedom, but instead become dependent, depressed, and sick. This clearly denotes that drugs are an empty promise and do not deliver."

On June 24th, I turned thirty-three years young. My mind flashed through episodes of toddler Jeremy defying locks to be outside, a youthful dancing machine entertaining the neighbors, and the dark nights of breath-choking asthma and scavenging the streets of Taylor at midnight for relief, until the adventure of San Diego brought a new dawn of brilliant sunshine and happiness into my life.

In July, I spent a wonderful week with Gurudev at the Chicago Hilton, culminating in the auspicious Guru Purnima full-moon celebrations.

After these intense, incredible years of yoga, Sudarshan Kriya, meditation, singing, seva, knowledge, and wisdom, plus the extraordinary delight in being around Gurudev so much as I have, I can honestly say I am one happy boy—creative, caring, and calm. I live the life I created here or anywhere and live the life I love right now, each day. I am living the values Gurudev has shared with me and living the love that is inside my heart and the universe.

Suffice it to say, after all this love, experience, and appreciation, I can easily say, I am indeed living the Art of Living.

EPILOGUE

In Art of Living, we don't believe
in miracles, we rely on them.
—Gurudev Sri Sri Ravi Shankar

Spring break fell in April during 2012, and I found myself back in Bali. How could I ever forget the wonders during that special journey so many eventful years ago?

This time I came back to Bali with a beautiful woman on my arm. I had met Claudia the previous summer, during the memorable 2011 Guru Purnima celebrations at the Canadian Ashram. There must be a beautiful woman at the end of a great story, right?

A lover of yoga and dancing, with natural beauty, grace, and innocence thrown in made for a remarkable woman. Talking, texting, and video chatting since September, our long-distance relationship had grown strong. Flying her to visit me in Bali was not only daring, but a no-brainer. We spent a few days getting to know each other better in the hills of Bali before Gurudev and the Silence course participants arrived at the Inna Grand Bali Beach Hotel.

I received a message from an Indonesian devotee that Gurudev would be having an intimate satsang at a resort on the beach… and to bring my guitar. Marvelous.

Claudia and I showed up at the resort (think seven-star rating) and were treated like royalty as soon as I said, "Hi, this is Claudia, and my name is Jeremy—we're with Gurudev Sri Sri Ravi Shankar."

Being the first to arrive, Claudia and I were mesmerized from our first sights of the backyard and the breathtaking natural scenery. We looked out at the sea and over at the magnificent sheer cliffs. Around forty seats lined in rows had been arranged in the yard. Cloth-draped tables with heated food containers lined the back, and in the front stood a white, wooden gazebo with a chair in the middle for Gurudev.

I placed my guitar case next to the last seat on the right of the front row. As always, I was ready to rock. Together, Claudia and I walked around the yard, taking photos and enjoying nature at its breathtaking best.

Fifteen minutes until the party kickoff. Gurudev, followed by around ten others, walked out of the villa into the backyard.

"Hello, Gurudev! This is Claudia; she's an Art of Living teacher from the Dominican Republic."

"Oh, hello, how are you doing?"

His words were lyrical, but you should have seen the look on his face. Imagine, this is the first time I've ever introduced a woman I was dating to Gurudev. He knew I'd been mostly single, and his look flashed with as much interest as it did surprise. That look is burned into my memory forever. If only we could have sat in the green grass and talked about her for an hour, but there was no time for chit-chatting—yet.

We joined the group and walked around the backyard with Gurudev and the owner of the resort. Others joined us for pictures and laughs. Gurudev was generous enough to pose for pictures with Claudia and me. My Nikon camera clicked at record speed.

The intimate leisure in the yard ended as crowds of people arrived. Time for satsang. With the setting sun painting the sky in softening hues, Gurudev led us in a beautiful meditation. When we opened our eyes, the sun had but seconds left before disappearing for the night. He looked at me and gave me the nod to start the music.

No mics, no amps, and yet my voice and guitar carried as far as where the fish swam in the dark waters. Maybe they danced in the sea that night in celebration with us.

After a few songs, several other musicians took over the singing, and the satsang continued. I slipped out of my seat, walked up onto the stage, kneeled, and talked to Gurudev. Not surprisingly, his first question was, "So tell me about this girl you're with."

My smile stretched and shone beyond imagination. Claudia might have been the first woman I introduced to Gurudev, but the future would hold several other delightful females yet to know.

We continued to talk, joke, and smile about my new relationship, in a father-to-son sort of way. These cherished moments with Gurudev are simply the best. Moments that will glow in splendor and hang on the inner walls of my heart.

After the delicious vegetarian feast, Gurudev invited a small group of us for a walk around the resort with him and the owner. We climbed down steep stairs to the edge of a cliff, where we watched waves crash upon the stones. I was totally blown away when seawater began to splash us, Gurudev included, and we felt like little children once again.

I protected my camera from the water by stuffing it under my shirt every time the waves broke wildly against the rocks. I'm glad my eyes were free and not stuck looking through the camera lens during one of the greatest, most intimate moments with my guru.

In bed that night, listening to the treasures of sound from Balinese critters outside my window, I contemplated reality once again. *Is this life even real? How am I so blessed, blissed out? Am I barely scraping the shores of this Divine Ocean of awesomeness? Or am I deep underneath its warm and cooling waters?*

No need for answers at that moment. I drifted into dreamlike states of consciousness as the cool Bali night air lulled me to sleep and the pillow of grace, where I lay my head, warmed my soul.

This life is of storybook proportions—like a fairytale flanked on the fantastic free-falling mountains of glory. If gratitude were gold, I would now be a rich boy singing 'bout his soul. The mystic shines again, and I am ever grateful.

On Guru Purnima 2009, Gurudev Sri Sri Ravi Shankar gave me his divine blessings to write and share my life story with the world. Initially, his blessings were for this book.

Since completing *Ain't That a Miracle?* in both writing and storyline, my life continued to shine an array of multi-colored rainbows, riding this rollercoaster spiritual path—Gurudev's blessings have since extended graciously forward.

My second book, *Dying to Live*, part two of my life story, begins at Guru Purnima 2009 in Chicago, and concludes in 2020. Thank you for reading part one of my life story; I invite you to dive into part two next.

Jai Guru Dev.

Write encouraging stories and inspire others. Every situation we can turn into positive—we should be determined to do that. If you don't share positivity, you will get into depression. So the way to get out of depression is to write positive stories and encourage others in a positive mode. Can we all do that? Challenges do come, but never let challenges make you negative. If you keep talking positive, you will pull positivity from within you and fill others with positivity and hope. Today people are filled with negativity, and they need your help. If you can't do physical seva, at least you can write nice stories and experiences. Everyone's life is touched with miracles. Miracles have not left any individual untouched; there are plenty in everyone's life—recognize them. And here in the Art of Living, there is an abundance of it. In Art of Living, we rely on miracles. Share your stories with others so their enthusiasm is uplifted.
—Gurudev Sri Sri Ravi Shankar,
Bangalore, India, February 1, 2017

BIBLIOGRAPHY

1. *Holy Bible*, AJ Holman, CSP Super Giant Print
2. *Bhagavad-Gita*, Juan Mascaro, Penguin Classics, 1962
3. *The Upanishads*, Juan Mascaro, Penguin Classics, 1965
4. *Krsna, The Supreme Personality Of Godhead*, His Divine Grace A.C. Bhaktivedanta Swami Prabhupada, 1969
5. *Autobiography of a Yogi*, Paramahansa Yogananda, 1946
6. *Be Here Now*, Baba Ram Dass, 1997
7. *Sri Sri Ravi Shankar: The Way of Grace*, David Lucas Burge & Gary Boucherle, 1996
8. *Celebrating Silence*, Gurudev Sri Sri Ravi Shankar, 2001
9. *An Intimate Note to the Sincere Seeker*, Gurudev Sri Sri Ravi Shankar, 2021
10. *Stumbling Into Infinity: An Ordinary Man in the Sphere of Enlightenment*, Michael Fischman, Morgan James Publishing LLC, 2012
11. *Looking Inward: Meditating to Survive in a Changing World*, Swami Purnachaitanya, Penguin, 2022

ABOUT THE AUTHOR

Jeremy Occhipinti is a passionate educator, creativity coach, singer-songwriter, and the author of the book *Ain't That a Miracle? An Unlikely Journey into Music and Meditation.* He is well-known for his original English and Sanskrit-style songs. He has written and recorded five music albums and has performed his unique concerts in diverse locations, including international schools in Asia, the Middle East, and the US.

Jeremy joyfully celebrates life, spreading his message of human values worldwide through music in yoga studios, churches, temples, schools, restaurants, and coffee shops. Jeremy has been a part of the World Culture Festivals in India and Germany.

He is now on a mission to help others manifest their dreams and live a more balanced, productive, and successful life. Many people have benefitted from his twenty-five years of experience in spirituality, his love for music, and teaching, combined into a robust life-transforming set of spiritual tools.

Jeremy has volunteered with the Art of Living Foundation for over twenty-five years. He enjoys being a kindergarten teacher and creativity coach based in Asia.

If you are intrigued by miracles, interested in service, and want to share your art more efficiently, you can join Jeremy Occhipinti's growing community at jeremyocc.com

Made in the USA
Middletown, DE
12 December 2022

18188754R00219